Greetings,

Please accept this copy of *Family Man:
The Biography of Dr. James Dobson*
as an expression of our tremendous
appreciation for your faithful
support of Focus on the Family.
We hope you'll enjoy an insider's
view of Focus on the Family and our
founder, Dr. James Dobson.
God's richest blessings to you!

*Jim Daly and your friends
at Focus on the Family*

FAMILY MAN

FAMILY MAN

THE BIOGRAPHY OF

DR. JAMES DOBSON

Tyndale House Publishers, Inc., Wheaton, Illinois

DALE BUSS

FOR DEBBIE

ᘛᘐᘐᘒᘒᘚ

Visit Tyndale's exciting Web site at www.tyndale.com

TYNDALE is a registered trademark of Tyndale House Publishers, Inc.

Tyndale's quill logo is a trademark of Tyndale House Publishers, Inc.

Family Man

Designed by Dean H. Renninger

Published in association with the literary agency of Wolgemuth & Associates, Inc.

Library of Congress Cataloging-in-Publication Data

Buss, Dale.
    Family man : the biography of Dr. James Dobson / Dale Buss.
      p. cm.
    Includes bibliographical references and index.
    ISBN-13: 978-0-8423-8191-8 (hc : alk. paper)
    ISBN-10: 0-8423-8191-0 (hc : alk. paper)
    ISBN-13: 978-0-8423-8192-5 (sc : alk. paper)
    ISBN-10: 0-8423-8192-9 (sc : alk. paper)
    1. Dobson, James C., date.   2. Christian biography—United States.   3. Focus on the Family
(Organization)—Biography. I. Title

BR1725.D62B87 2005
269′.2′092—dc22   2005018562

Printed in the United States of America

10   09   08   07   06   05
10   9   8   7   6   5   4   3   2   1

TABLE OF CONTENTS

ACKNOWLEDGMENTS

I am indebted to many people for supporting me and for helping make this book a reality.

Most of all, I'm deeply grateful to Dr. James Dobson for participating, and for his kindness and cooperation throughout a long and winding process, particularly when other demands on his time were greater than ever.

Special thanks to Danae Dobson and Ryan Dobson for contributing hours of stories about their parents and for Danae's willingness to help me out with a myriad of details. Thanks also to Shirley Dobson for sharing so openly.

Paul Hetrick of Focus on the Family was a sturdy pillar on whom I leaned throughout the project. He not only helped me shape my original notion for this book but also shepherded it in its proposal form, advised me along the way, facilitated interviews, and quickly and patiently answered all of my questions, big and small.

Likewise, Robert Wolgemuth has been invaluable as agent, encourager, adviser, editor, and friend. Bobbie Wolgemuth, his wife and colaborer, also has been a godsend.

Many thanks to the fine people at Tyndale House for their enthusiasm for this book, as well as their professionalism and patience in dealing with someone writing his first full-length book. They include Doug Knox, Janis Long Harris, Lisa Jackson and the Team 4 editors, Caleb Sjogren, Sharon Leavitt, and Suzanne Page.

I'm also indebted to Sherry Hoover, Becky Lane, Teri Lempuhl, Bobbie Hill, Lianne Belote, Kathy Dooley, and others—current and former Focus on the Family staff—for their scheduling and research assistance. Don and Barbara Hodel, Jim Daly, Diane Passno, Tom Mason, and Paul Batura also provided invaluable feedback.

Thanks to my wife, Debbie, for her unshakable love and patience, and for the inspiration she gave me to tackle such a project. I'm grateful to my kids, Kaitlyn and Andy: Their arrival led me to Dr. Dobson in the first place, and they've hung in there with me ever since.

Also, thanks for enduring support from David and Shirley Buss, Henry and Helen Tata, Tom and Kathy Hennings, Steve and Jane Shaver, Jeff and Diane Jezierski, Dan and Diane Muller, Randy and June Marcial, Alan and Amy Buss, and Brian and Brenda Buss.

Rick and Janet Salomon, Art and Ginger Shingler, Ed and Joy Bissonnette, Jeannine Jezierski, and Jeannie Jones all lent their assistance to me in important ways or at crucial times.

I also am indebted to editors who welcomed my newspaper and magazine stories about Dr. Dobson over the years, beginning with Tim Ferguson, then of the *Wall Street Journal*; Karl Zinsmeister, of the *American Enterprise;* and Teresa Palagano, of *Folio.* Bob Dutko of WMUZ-FM in Detroit has been a special personal champion since the day he learned of *Family Man.*

Thank you as well to the several dozen people who spent hundreds of hours being interviewed for this book. I wish I could list you and thank you individually!

Dale Buss
July 2005

INTRODUCTION

The challenges in researching and writing this book were to reveal more about a man who is already very self-revelatory, to convey the humanity of someone whose closet disgorges no skeletons, and to put into a broader and even historical context a major actor in a hugely important cultural, social, and political drama that continues to unfold.

Even at this writing, James Dobson's story may be far from complete. Considering how he deliberately raised his profile in 2003 and 2004, in part to rally evangelical voters for the 2004 election, Dobson's legacy may be no more ready for final analysis now than it was the first time I wrote about him more than eighteen years ago.

At that time, I was a new father, hungry for the advice I gleaned from the paperback copy of *Dare to Discipline* that my wife had given me, and benefiting from the homespun encouragement I often heard on Dobson's daily broadcast.

As a journalist, I considered Dobson's story interesting and realized that it had been largely untold in the secular media. I was a reporter for the *Wall Street Journal* at the time, and an editor gave me the go-ahead to write a piece assessing Dobson and his ministry. My story was slotted for the world's foremost daily bulletin board for traditional, albeit not overtly Christian, values: *The Journal*'s editorial page.

So on April 23, 1987, I arrived for an interview with Dobson in his office in Pomona, California. My wife, Debbie, also sneaked in some conversation about our one-year-old daughter. We sat in the studio as Dobson taped two segments of interviews with Pat Williams, a top National Basketball Association executive, and Jill Williams, Pat's wife. The couple shared how they had revived their once-moribund marriage and were now adopting a huge and diverse brood of foreign-born children. (Sadly, Pat and Jill Williams have since divorced.)

Following the interview, my wife and I rode with Dobson in his Buick Century station wagon to a nearby church where the weekly chapel for the Focus on the Family staff was taking place. Shirley Dobson, his wife, was the day's speaker.

I still have the tape of my interview with James Dobson; it provided a synopsis of what he had accomplished and where he was headed at the time. "What we're trying to do is nothing more ambitious than connecting us again with the wisdom of the Judeo-Christian ethic whose transmission was interrupted in this century," he told me. "I have no doubt that there is a great hunger for those principles and those values that have stood the test of time."

If Dobson had retired right then and moved with his beloved Shirley to their condo in the California mountains, his legacy would have been both far-reaching and secure. In fact, at about that same time, a Focus executive vice president, Rolf Zettersten, completed a biography that related much of the story of his boss's life to that point, mostly from Dobson's perspective.

On the other hand, my commentary almost didn't see publication. One major obstacle was Dobson's deep concern that *The Journal* would refuse to use the honorific term *Dr.* in front of his name. The newspaper's policy, no matter who was involved, was not to use *Dr.* unless the subject was a physician. But Dobson rightly pointed out that he was known far and wide as "Dr. Dobson" and that referring to him in any other way might well confuse as many readers as it would enlighten. In the end, *The Journal* stood firm, and Dobson reluctantly stood down.

When my piece ran in October 1987, it introduced Dobson to the elite of American politics, academia, and media who, for the most part, still had no idea that he existed. Little did any of us, even Dobson himself, understand then how dramatically his ministry and influence would grow over the next eighteen years—not only in the Christian milieu but also in many other arenas.

CHAPTER ONE

CAMPAIGN MODE

> *I don't want to sound like a prophet here,*
> *but we saw this coming.*
>
> JAMES DOBSON, ON *Your World*
> *with Neil Cavuto,* FOX NEWS,
> NOVEMBER 12, 2004

For James Dobson, the stakes on November 2, 2004—Election Day—couldn't have been higher. The renowned child psychologist, best-selling author, popular radio host, and founder of Focus on the Family had devoted his entire life to the preservation of the family, and now all he held dear seemed to be hanging in the balance. Although he had rarely before campaigned in a way that could be considered strictly partisan, this election year Dobson had become convinced that he had no choice but to jump into the political fray with both feet. And when he did, he determined to give all he had for the cause.

By the time the 2004 campaign was over, Beltway heavyweights from Tom Daschle to Arlen Specter, media pundits, Democratic operatives, *Focus on the Family* listeners, and Dr. Dobson readers from coast to coast had gained a much better appreciation for who Dobson was and what he could accomplish.

During the 2004 election season, Dobson was already in the midst of a full slate of appearances at campaign rallies around the country when pro-family groups in northwestern Iowa urgently summoned him: We need you to come to Sioux City. In 2003, State Judge Jeffrey Neary had approved a "divorce" for two Sioux City lesbians who were united in a civil ceremony in Vermont. Iowa recognizes neither civil unions nor gay marriages, and traditional-family advocates worried that Neary's action set a back-door precedent for overturning the status quo in their state. He was a married father of three children, served as a Boy Scout leader, and delivered children's sermons at his church, but Neary didn't back down after protests over his decree granting the dissolution. So now, an ad hoc local organization called the Judicial Accountability Center was trying to make Neary pay with his job in a retention vote scheduled for November 2.

Dobson was weary from having crisscrossed the nation for several speeches, and he was due for an important rally in Sioux Falls, South Dakota, the next day. For someone who hoped to influence the election of several U.S. senators, a wayward judge in an obscure precinct of the Great Plains might not have seemed a worthy target. But the invitation to Sioux City for October 2 was red meat because over the previous year, Dobson had invested himself in a relentless effort to get Americans to recognize judicial overreach and its ill effects. So after Dobson agreed to target the bull's-eye on Neary, more than five thousand people gathered for a rally at the Tyson Events Center in Sioux City, where maintenance workers covered the hockey rink with plywood for the affair.

Just as he had in many of Dobson's other appearances during the campaign season, Tony Perkins, president of the Family Research Council, preceded Dobson, exhorting the crowd to go to the polls in November in defense of traditional family values. Then, Sioux City Mayor David Ferris introduced Dobson to the crowd. Federal regulations governing the political activities of charitable organizations restricted any speaker at the event from overtly endorsing particular candidates, but there was nothing to stop Dobson from issuing the criticism he had come to deliver—and he didn't disappoint his hosts.

He started by berating a court system that he described as being led by liberal judges who, seemingly determined to allow same-sex marriages, are creating laws rather than interpreting them. He encouraged the activist and the outraged among his audience to voice their opinions by voting and "maybe find some of these people another line of work. . . . Now judges are telling us they want to redefine the definition of marriage!" he intoned from behind a cherry-wood podium, in a steel-blue suit, his ruddy-blond pate intensely spotlighted against the precisely engineered blackness of the rest of the arena. "We say, 'Not in our lifetime!' I don't mean to be disrespectful," he continued over the cheers, "but you've got one of [those judges] right here—Judge Jeffrey Neary."

But while Dobson's message was similar, the logistics of his presentation in Sioux City were different than at the rest of the rallies he led during the campaign season. All of the others were organized by Family Policy Councils, which are state level-affiliates of Focus—meaning that Dobson could dictate conditions in the arena. He always preferred to keep the house lights up during his addresses, so that he could see, read, and draw from the reactions and energy of the crowds. But wanting to ensure that their celebrity speaker could be clearly seen on the overhead video screens by everyone at the large gathering, the independent organizers of the Iowa affair had insisted on a thoroughly darkened house. Reluctantly, Dobson had gone along.

He shouldn't have. After he finished his speech—pupils still dilated after blinking into the spotlights for a half hour—Dobson turned to his right and began to move at a wide angle, in a direct line to his chair. But he couldn't see the stage, and Dobson had forgotten that the podium was perched on a promontory perpendicular to the dais. There was no guardrail to signal trouble, and the six-foot-two Dobson plummeted off the edge of the six-foot-high stage as if into a pit. On his way down, Dobson reflexively grabbed a potted plant that marked the edge of the platform. His head could have hit the wood-covered concrete or struck the large speaker boxes located below. But instead, at the last moment, Dobson's lower leg caught on the edge of the stage as he was falling—flipping him so that he landed on his side and back rather than his head.

The crowd gasped, and Dobson's wife, Shirley, and daughter, Danae, rushed from their second-row seats to attend to Dobson, as did about two dozen other people from the audience. By the time anyone reached him, Dobson already had pushed himself up to a sitting position, leaning on one of the speakers. Shirley got behind him and cradled his head, and a doctor in the audience reached him seconds later. Blood was pooling beneath him, so the doctor immediately checked for a deep cut on Dobson's head. He quickly realized that it was Dobson's leg that had been gashed in the fall, and it was bleeding profusely. But soon, Dobson was hobbling the distance of about a block to the arena's "green room," where speakers waited before taking the stage. After about a half hour of emergency attention, family members and aides took him to a hospital emergency room a few blocks away, where a doctor used five stitches to close the nasty slice on his leg.

About two hours later, a patched-up Dobson, grateful that his pratfall hadn't been much worse, boarded a private jet borrowed from a Focus supporter and flew to his next rally in Sioux Falls. Later, Tom Minnery, the Focus vice president of public policy who accompanied his boss to Sioux City, reflected on the near catastrophe. "There he was sitting in a pool of blood," mused Minnery. "I don't know a lot of people who ended up giving blood for what happened on Election Day."

◦◦◦◦◦◦

Ultimately, Dobson's sacrifice of blood and sweat, if not tears, paid off. While political mastermind Karl Rove may have been the architect of the reelection of President George W. Bush and of the Republican surge in November 2004, James Dobson could very well be called the construction foreman. Some commentators quickly argued that more than any other single factor, it was Dobson's exhortation of evangelicals and conservative Catholics to flock to the polls and vote their values that informed and motivated their stunning turnout on Election Day. And Dobson wasted little time in serving notice that he would act as a fulcrum for judgment by believers on whether President Bush and Congress were coming through for them during the new terms they had been granted.

Election Day "was a battle not just for the selection of a president," Dobson said on his *Focus on the Family* radio show several days after the November 2004 election. "It was a statement of who we are as a people and what we will be in the future and what our children will value and how they will see right and wrong. All of that was hanging in the balance."

As soon as John F. Kerry finally conceded the presidential vote in the late morning of November 3, Dobson completed an almost perfect box score from the day before. There was Bush's win, of course, in which "moral values" figured more significantly than any other specific motivation, according to exit polls. *New Republic* editor Michael Crowley supposed that "Dobson may have delivered Bush his victories in Ohio and Florida." Bans on same-sex marriage—which Dobson had identified as the single gravest threat to the American family—passed comfortably to overwhelmingly in eleven of eleven states where they were on the ballot.

Shocking the Beltway crowd, South Dakota Senator Tom Daschle fell to evangelical Republican John Thune after Dobson had personally targeted Daschle for obstructing the confirmation of Bush's judicial nominees. Like-thinking Senate candidates in Louisiana, Oklahoma, and North Carolina also rode Dobson's overt support to victories that surprised many handicappers. Though Iowa Judge Neary was retained by voters, his 59 percent of the ballot was significantly below the support he had garnered in 2000. And even beer magnate Pete Coors lost his Senate bid in Colorado, a defeat some attributed to Dobson's clear lack of support.

The only blotch on Dobson's personal scorecard was California's approval to issue a $3-billion state bond to fund embryonic stem-cell research. At the eleventh hour, Dobson had allied with actor and conservative Catholic Mel Gibson to put together a California-only radio broadcast opposing the measure, but they weren't able to stop its passage.

Dobson didn't waste any time, however, before he tried to leverage his winning touch into a boost for what would be his most important post-election issue: gaining the appointment of pro-lifers to the Supreme Court. Just a day after the election, pro-abortion Republican Senator Arlen Specter predicted trouble for any known pro-life nominees, and Dobson and his allies immediately began trying to derail Specter's ascendance to the chairmanship of the Senate Judiciary Committee. Specter survived the challenge, but only after days of backpedaling and making unprecedented promises to Senate conservatives that he would help Bush's nominees—pro-life or otherwise—get approval.

One person who wasn't surprised by Dobson's impact was Charles Colson, the founder of Prison Fellowship and a close confidant. "Clearly, he played a major role in this election," Colson says. "More than anyone else, he mobilized the evangelical base."

ುౖ౧ఞ౧ఞ

It took Dobson about twenty years to reach the point of exercising such unvarnished partisanship and practicing such aggressive politicking. In the eighties, he had veered from writing family-advice books and doing his radio show into fulminating on public policy, but only when he felt that legislators, judges, entertainers, and journalists had begun giving up on and even trespassing on the traditional values he was trying to protect. He served on federal commissions that addressed ills such as pornography and gambling and developed the ability to overwhelm Capitol Hill switchboards with his listeners' plaintive phone calls.

After spending much of the nineties unsuccessfully prodding the GOP to join him in his concerns about eroding social values, Dobson backed away from Republican presidential candidate Robert Dole in 1996, largely because of his mushy views on abortion. In 2000, Dobson welcomed the pro-life and openly Christian George W. Bush but did little to generate votes for him—and by Karl Rove's estimate, about four million evangelicals stayed home, nearly costing Bush his first term.

But four years later, events had transpired that propelled Dobson onto the campaign terrain in an unprecedented way. For one thing, he had more freedom than ever, having recently turned over the day-to-day administration of Focus on the Family to Don Hodel. Dobson was also feeling completely healthy again after battling some serious medical problems over the previous two years. And finally, Dobson had been able to free up more of Focus's resources from Internal Revenue Service rules that restrict political advocacy by not-for-profit institutions.

Nevertheless, his decision to accelerate himself and Focus to the next level of political involvement was a difficult one for Dobson. He was well aware of how previous lunges into the political arena had tarnished the ministries of others, including Jerry Falwell and Pat Robertson. And he well understood his friend Colson's staunch opposition to partisan political involvement for figures like them. "I've always argued," Colson says, "that religious leaders should remain, not above moral issues of course, but above partisan issues so that you don't make the Christian movement hostage to one political party. Either that, or they should step down from their Christian position, as Robertson did when he gave up his ordination" to run for president in 1988.

Dobson widely acknowledged both his own hesitance to take this step and the perils therein. "There are dangers [in becoming too partisan]," Dobson said in a *New York Times* story in May 2004, "and that is why I have never done it before. But the attack and assault on marriage is so distressing that I just feel like I can't remain silent."[1] Yet even as late as a few days before the election, he was still telling the *Times*: "I have been very reluctant to use my influence in the past, because if you marry a politician, you could be a widow in four years."[2]

But in the end, Dobson took the plunge. "His position, as he put it to me," Colson says, "was that you don't live or die by elections, but if ever there were a decisive election involving the future of the family, this was it. I agreed with him on that and didn't try to discourage him, because if he felt the freedom to do it and that it wasn't putting his ministry in jeopardy, then he should do it."

Actually, Dobson sensed no freedom regarding the decision to cross the great divide into partisanship and take Focus with him. Instead, he felt absolutely compelled to do so, coming to believe that this decision was at the same time a logical, necessary, and even divinely inspired culmination of everything he had accomplished and everything else he had strived for over the previous quarter century.

Dobson reached his moment of reckoning in August 2003, after making the keynote speech at a rally outside the Alabama state judicial center in Montgomery. The crowd was protesting a decision by a federal judge to remove from public view a monument there called The Ten Commandments, which had been commissioned by Judge Roy Moore after he was elected the state's chief justice in 2000.

"When I saw what that [federal] judge was trying to do despite the will of the people of Alabama and I participated in that rally, that's where my determination to try to make a difference in the 2004 election originated," says Dobson. "I saw the excitement of the people. I saw how they longed for a voice and how frustrated they were by having their views overridden by leftist judges and by the inability of the Congress to get anything done to protect their values. It was an exhilarating experience.

"While we were still in Montgomery, I said [to aides] that I have tried to remain out of the political arena for twenty-six years, because I didn't want to drag Focus into the mucky-muck of presidential elections and all that that means. I had never endorsed a presidential candidate in my life. But in Montgomery, I said that's got to change. For the first time, I felt an obligation to do what I could through direct involvement in an election. I didn't know what influence I could have, but I was going to use whatever God had given me, because I simply couldn't sit this one out."

Less than a month later, in a banquet hall at The Broadmoor resort in Colorado Springs, Dobson gave the first clear public signal that he had reached such a decision. He had been invited to deliver the keynote address to the Council for National Policy, five years after he had prodded the group with his speech accusing its powerful Republican members of abandoning evangelicals.

Though he was targeting the other side this time, Dobson's speech was just as forceful. He held forth about judicial tyranny much as at

Montgomery, complaining specifically about how Democrats in Congress had filibustered in a politically motivated attempt to prevent the confirmation of several of President Bush's judicial nominees to the federal appellate courts. But toward the end of his speech to the Republican movers and shakers who had gathered from across the country, the de facto host declared something he hadn't said anywhere before.

"If we can't get attention any other way," Dobson said, "I'm prepared to go to South Dakota and see if we can get the attention of at least one [person]."[3] He didn't mention by name Senator Daschle. But it was clear that Dobson was threatening to campaign against Daschle in the senator's own home state of South Dakota. During his last term, Daschle had fought hard against the appointment and confirmation of constructionist, often conservative, judges. The Democratic superstar had done more than anyone else in Washington, for example, to defeat the nomination of Miguel Estrada, who had withdrawn his name as nominee for the U.S. Court of Appeals just a few weeks before the Broadmoor event because he was facing certain defeat. And Dobson wanted to see Daschle removed from office.

The CNP crowd gave Dobson a standing ovation at that point and cut short the conclusion to his speech. "I'd have to take a leave of absence, and it couldn't involve Focus, and I was going to clarify that," he said later. "But in those cases where we might be able to influence this horrible injustice that's occurring." Dobson concluded his speech, "Let's see what we can do. I don't want to do it, but I might."

⁛

By early 2004, Dobson left little room for doubt that he indeed had decided to thrust himself to the forefront of efforts to elect like-thinking Republicans and to defeat frustrating Democrats in November.

In April, he sent mailings, made radio commercials, and stumped for the candidacy of U.S. Representative Patrick Toomey, a conservative in Pennsylvania who tried in a Senate primary that month to defeat Specter, the Republican incumbent. His efforts "weren't quite enough," Dobson notes, because Specter won that election by just 1.6 percent of the vote. The next month, Dobson appeared along with Colson, other national evangelical leaders, and local pastors before more than twenty thousand at a "Mayday for Marriage" rally at Safeco Field in Seattle.

Yet overall, Dobson was increasingly frustrated by the tethers on his ability to speak freely on political issues. These restrictions included not only the tax-favored status of Focus on the Family, which precluded partisanship by its executives, but also new limits imposed by federal campaign finance reform.

"It had gotten to the point where Focus could send out only one or two letters to our constituency advocating a legislative call to action, and our entire budget limitation for the year would be expended," about a quarter-million dollars, says Paul Hetrick, Focus's vice president of media relations. "And this was during a crucial election year, and at a time when the country was being moved further than ever toward a moral and cultural precipice."

Dobson was also growing tired of the timidity on gay marriage and other issues that was being displayed by all too many of his allies on Capitol Hill. So by May, Focus on the Family's board authorized an unprecedented break with the organization's structure of the previous twenty-five years and created Focus Action, which would serve as an overtly political ministry. Focus Action would still be restricted by tax laws from explicitly endorsing specific candidates. And contributions to Focus Action would not be tax-deductible. But neither would the IRS be able to limit Dobson and others when they were speaking out for Focus Action's positions. "All the funds contributed [to Focus Action]," Dobson wrote in a letter to supporters, "go straight to the battle for righteousness."[4] Also, Dobson had decided to become much more proactive in making personal endorsements of candidates as a private citizen, even though he well understood that there would still be a fuzzy line in public perceptions between his personal position and that of Focus.

Not wasting any time, Focus Action placed ads in the home newspapers of many senators opposed to the defense-of-marriage legislation on Capitol Hill. The group also organized get-out-the-vote efforts to thwart these same senators. And it put together voters' guides with information on the scores of judges who would be on state ballots across the country in November. Meanwhile, Focus on the Family initiated a nonpartisan voter-registration drive called iVoteValues.org, a campaign it hoped would register more than one million Americans to vote.

With all this going in the background, in June Dobson took the National Press Club podium in Washington, D.C., for the first time. Dobson prelabeled his speech there as one of the most important he would ever deliver because he was speaking both to media elites and to politicians, and also because the address would be rebroadcast several times on C-SPAN and other national cable-TV networks.

Massachusetts officials had begun issuing "marriage" licenses to homosexual couples in mid-May after the state Supreme Court's six-month waiting period had expired. Beating back gay marriage "is the most important social issue that we will ever face," Dobson told the Press Club audience, which seemed mostly friendly because many Republican aides and other sympathetic Beltway denizens had joined the meeting. "Family is the ground floor. It's the foundation: Western civilization itself seems to hang on this issue. If you undermine [marriage], weaken it, tamper with it, you necessarily threaten the whole superstructure of the family."

Yet, Dobson told the audience, the fight to get Congress to back the Defense of Marriage Act was going poorly at that point, and he was saddened by the difficulty of persuading even some of his usual allies on Capitol Hill to go along. Shortly after this speech, in fact, the U.S. Senate proved unable to muster the sixty votes needed to endorse the amendment.

Indeed, in answer to a written question at the Press Club speech about whether he believed the American culture was "beyond hope," Dobson concluded, "I don't believe it's beyond hope. The pendulum of the culture swings back and forth, going to one extreme, and tends to come back. I'm hopeful and prayerful that it may return. It may take social upheaval to make it happen." But then Dobson seemed to fudge that conclusion with his next bit of soliloquy: "I don't know what's necessary to have people see things differently. As of right now, we're heading in the wrong direction, especially with relation to the family— which is the sum total of everything I believe in my life."

Yet just eight days after the Senate acted, the House of Representatives did pass its own defense-of-marriage legislation. Then in August, the California Supreme Court voided the nearly four thousand same-sex unions that had been created in San Francisco earlier in the year. Voters in Missouri that same month also heartened Dobson and his allies by approving a state constitutional amendment that banned gay marriage. The vote was an overwhelming 72 percent to 28 percent.

While Dobson may not have realized it at the time, the electoral momentum for the autumn was swinging back decisively in favor of the truths and candidates he supported. And it would continue to come their way right through November.

CHAPTER TWO
PATERFAMILIAS

The leader of the band is tired
And his eyes are growing old
But his blood runs through my instrument
And his song is in my soul—
My life has been a poor attempt
To imitate the man
I'm just a living legacy
To the leader of the band

"LEADER OF THE BAND,"
BY DAN FOGELBERG

For someone who would go on to spend a lifetime dispensing meat-and-potatoes advice about childrearing to traditional families, James C. Dobson had a decidedly unusual early life. He was born into a hardscrabble existence as the only child of an itinerant evangelist and actually was left for a year in the care of a great-aunt while his parents traveled several states leading revival meetings. But faith abounded in the Dobson household, and its palpability overwhelmed all circumstances.

For generations, in fact, the identity of Dobson's family had been intertwined with the gospel. Immigrants from England to America during Colonial times, James Dobson's maternal ancestors joined the holiness movement, a revival that began in the eastern United States and spread throughout the region. By the early 1900s, Dobson's maternal great-grandfather, G. W. McCluskey, and his son-in-law, Michael V. Dillingham, had become charter members of the Church of the Nazarene, one of the main holiness denominations. They joined after an episode in which Dobson's grandfather, Michael Dillingham—known in the family as "Little Daddy"—decided to lay his gun down on the altar at a revival meeting he was passing by rather than kill a man with whom he'd just had an argument. One of Dobson's grandmothers became an ordained pastor. And in the first of several profound, revelatory moments that seemed to preordain Dobson's future in ministry, McCluskey also claimed to have received a promise from God in prayer that every family member in the next four generations would serve the Lord.

Dobson's paternal grandfather, North Carolina native Robert Lee Dobson, was born in 1866, the year after the Civil War ended. He became a highly successful businessman as co-owner of the first Coca-Cola bottling plant in Texarkana, Texas, and then in other cities throughout the South.

James Dobson Sr. was born in 1911, the youngest of five boys, including twins named Robert and Lee, with a sister, Elizabeth, to follow. James soon became known for his artistic bent: At the age of three, he declared that he wanted to be a great painter. As a teenager, he struggled with whether to accept what he described as "a call to preach." He eventually decided to forgo the ministry and, instead, enroll in the Art Institute of Pittsburgh. He racked up highest academic honors in college, but after graduating in the midst of the Depression, James quickly became a near-starving artist. He was still struggling vocationally and essentially ignoring—if not rejecting—God in 1934 when he met and married Myrtle Dillingham, a preacher's daughter and a bit of a spiritual rebel who had vowed not to marry a man of the cloth.

At that point in his life, the man who would eventually become known as a prayer warrior hadn't yet reckoned with the power of prayer. His mother had been praying continually that James would eventually come back to the fold. And one night in the fall of 1934, when he was visiting his parents' home, James decided to give in to the pleadings of his spiritually fervent brother, Willis, and attend a revival meeting at their local church. The only seats available by the time they arrived were in the front row. And by the time the service was over, under the convicting eye of the evangelist, James had yielded once again to God—a man finally broken after seven years of rebellion. The whole family cried, and the virtually penniless artist prepared for a life as a virtually penniless preacher. Only a year later, after he had fully committed to the ministry, did he receive a pair of letters—one, a generous job offer that had been extended but mistakenly not mailed by the Art Institute of Pittsburgh a year earlier, and the second an apology for the mistake.

Nazarene theology includes two characteristics in particular that shape the approach of the denomination's clergy, and did so especially in James Dobson's era. The first emphasizes the role of free will and the responsibility of each human soul to respond to and embrace the gift of grace from Jesus Christ. The second is the holiness doctrine—the conviction that by continually forswearing sin after salvation, an individual should strive to model his or her life after Christ.

Like the typical Nazarene pastor, James felt an awesome accountability both for the size and the spiritual condition of his flock. Under his first pastorate, the tiny Nazarene congregation in Sulphur Springs, Texas, grew quickly. He became known as "the man with no leather on the toes of his shoes" because of how much time he spent on his knees in prayer for his flock and his family. At twenty-four years old, he earned a total of just $429 during his first year in the ministry, according to records that his son would find later, and James gave back to the church a remarkable $352 of that.[1] For several years, James served as both a local pastor and a traveling evangelist throughout the Southwest. The common denominator of most of his services was a successful altar call, when at the end of a sermon he summoned individuals who were spiritually moved by his message to leave their seats and come toward the front of the church to declare their faith or recommit themselves to it. "His greatest passion was winning people to Christ," Dobson Jr. says of his father.

The elder Dobson wasn't given to as much overt emoting and Bible thumping as other Nazarene evangelists, but he reached people with his deep sincerity.

"Jim Sr. preached a lot of love and grace" rather than fire and brimstone, recalls H. B. London, a cousin and close friend who was born about eight months after Dobson Jr. London's mother, Lela, was Myrtle Dobson's sister, and the extended clan spent most holidays and vacations together.

"But [my uncle] had huge expectations of himself. If he did preach a message and no one came to the altar that night to accept the Lord, he would take that personally sometimes. He would spend long and agonizing hours in prayer and Bible study some days, almost as a recluse." On such occasions, James Sr. examined what he might have done to inhibit rather than to promote his audience's embrace of Christ.

"My father was sometimes not a very social man," echoes Dobson Jr. "He tended at times to stay within himself, and at times he was given to depression." Indeed, the elder Dobson clearly struggled with self-esteem, a problem that his son later would identify as a key trouble sign for youth. "He would never have been able to write a book," the younger Dobson told *Christianity Today*, "not because he couldn't write it, but because his assessment of himself was so low he couldn't have risked putting an idea out there emotionally, with the possibility of having it rejected."[2]

In that significant way, at least, the next James Dobson would be a very different man from his father.

James Clayton Dobson Jr. was born by cesarean section on April 21, 1936, in Shreveport, Louisiana, where the family had moved. The delivery was so difficult that the doctor advised the couple not to conceive any more children. For Dobson Jr., being an only child was a huge influence on his developing personality. Later, a more traumatic impact was leveled by a desperate decision that his parents made when Dobson Jr. was just out of kindergarten.

The intensely loving relationship between James Sr. and Myrtle Dobson provided a solid backdrop for their son's childhood. In fact, later on, the template of their marriage contributed significantly to Dobson's own ideal model, both for his own life and in the family advice he gave.

"When Myrtle walked into a room, Big Jim [Dobson Sr.] would just light up like a Christmas tree," recalls Marge Smith, a Nazarene pastor's wife whose husband oversaw congregations throughout the Southwest. "I've never seen a couple more devoted to each other."

But his parents' singular focus on each other ended up hurting Dobson Jr. as a young boy. Torn between her desire to support her husband in his increasingly successful but solitary ministry and their son's need for parental attention, Myrtle Dobson chose to spend most of her time on the road with James Sr., leaving six-year-old Jimmy in the care of his maternal great-aunt in Hot Springs, Arkansas. He would spend first grade there.

"[My mom] went everywhere with [my dad] and sang and played the piano. They just needed each other emotionally," Dobson Jr. says of his parents. "So I stayed with my aunt, and my mom and dad hugged me and loved me and told me they'd be coming back every six or eight weeks. And then they drove off one night and I sat in the dark, on the floor, depressed over having been left by parents that I was very close to.

"That year was hard on me," he adds, and some believe that the experience had something to do with Dobson Jr.'s later dedication to the preservation of the traditional home.

Dobson's aunt and uncle did their best, "but I remember when it was Halloween and they never even thought about putting out a pumpkin," he recalls. Not surprisingly, despite his aunt's best efforts to guide him that year, "I became pretty bratty," he remembers, telling the story matter-of-factly. However, very close to the surface lurks the irony of the childhood miscreant becoming the child-raising expert—of the early day-care victim becoming a leading champion of traditional stay-at-home mothers.

"I was kind of a troublemaker in church and in the neighborhood during that time. Teachers were calling my aunt about me," Dobson recalls. "Some kids in the neighborhood felt I was too rough. But for good reason: I had been abandoned. I didn't take my anger out on my parents; I just missed them." Dobson understood that his father was "so dependent on my mother that he didn't believe he could do [his revival tours] without her. But we both needed her."

H. B. London recalls his cousin feeling "puzzled and confused" by the absence of his parents. "Jim was left with older people in a strange community, and probably as a result of that, he also didn't have a lot of friends during that year."

James and Myrtle Dobson's decision to leave their son with relatives while they were on evangelistic tours was somewhat common among Nazarene evangelists of that era, Marge Smith maintains. "The Lord was first; it was drilled into them," she says. And Dobson's extended family did their best to keep little Jimmy on track, emotionally and spiritually, during his parents' long absences. One healthy sign was the empathy that the young boy displayed for the downtrodden. It was 1942, and World War II was raging. "In our neighborhood, there was an Italian boy my age and the rest of the kids called him Dago," Dobson recalls. "I left the comfort of the group to form an alliance with that boy because I felt sorry for him."

Within that year, however, Dobson Sr. saw that his son was becoming more like his great-uncle and great-aunt than his parents, the son recalls. "[Living apart from them] was hard on me. I can look back and see that I apparently had felt abandoned even though I wasn't angry with my parents. Yet I think I would have been as time went on."

In the nick of time, Dobson Jr. believes, "my mom and dad made it up to me." His father bought a house in Bethany, Oklahoma, "and let my mother have me for the next eleven years. He traveled alone, which was very hard for him." The adulation that Dobson Jr. gives to his father's memory today is rooted, in part, in the sacrificial decision made by his dad those many years ago.

Suddenly in the Dobson household, the child-raising dynamic shifted radically—from a lack of parental attention to the doting that is typical for an only child being raised primarily by his mother. One of Myrtle Dobson's best assets in trying to cultivate a normal upbringing for her son was her God-given personality. She was a born entertainer with a tremendous wit—an extrovert and go-getter, a talker and a socialite. "She loved to give dinners and parties and to cook for her family, and she was always involved with her circle of friends," remembers Dobson, who inherited similar gifts from his mother. Marge Smith says, "Every time we'd get a crowd together, she'd tell stories about the funny things that happened in the pastorate. Jim's just like his mom. He wanted to be like his daddy, but his dad was so quiet and just had a grin."

London says that in addition to being lively, Myrtle Dobson and his mother were "persuasive and cunning. They could get us to do anything with a look or a pout." Thus equipped, Myrtle Dobson set out to shape Jimmy with energy and sensitivity, and she created as much freedom for him as she could. It was a task made more difficult by the fact that the evangelist's family continued to move in and out of small communities in Oklahoma and Texas. When her son was feeling particularly lonely after one move, she quietly pressed a twenty-dollar bill into his hand—an extremely generous gesture by the standards of the day, especially in a household that couldn't really afford to part with the money. "Spend it on anything you want," she told him. Dobson never forgot the kindness.[3]

At the same time, Dobson has made famous his mother's talent for discipline, which she directed entirely toward him. In *Dare to Discipline*, for example, he recounts her reasonableness on issues such as tardiness or failure to complete a homework assignment. "But there was one matter on which she was absolutely rigid: She did not tolerate 'sassiness.'" He recounted the times that she disciplined him with a shoe, a belt—even a girdle with metal snaps. "She knew that back talk and 'lip' are the child's most potent weapons of defiance and they must be discouraged."[4]

Dobson Jr. says that he got most of his philosophy of discipline from his mother, "and she got most of that from her parents. At that time, it was handed down from generation to generation. Parents had an intuitive awareness that you disciplined with love, that you balanced those two factors, and if you got them out of balance, you were in trouble. She had such a great understanding of that aspect of child rearing. And she was so committed to me. She would have laid down her life for me in a heartbeat, and I knew it. But because she loved me, she wasn't going to tolerate sassiness and back talk and disobedience."

James Sr.'s extended family pitched in as much as possible when it came to Dobson's upbringing. His uncle Lee Dobson, for example, periodically deposited five dollars in a special bank account for the boy and took such an interest in his nephew that paternal relatives took to calling him "Jimmy Lee."

The family's extensive participation in church activities and integration with the broader Nazarene community, along with its expectations, reinforced Myrtle Dobson's hand in raising her son.

"The church emphasized what you *didn't* do more than what you *did* do," London says. "Growing up, there was no going to movies, no wine, no card playing, no buying or even going to lunch on Sunday—many times not even the taking of a Sunday newspaper or the wearing of a wedding band. Our mothers didn't wear wedding bands because of what the constituency might think about their 'adornment.' We went to church every time the door was open, including Sunday school as well as church in the morning, Sunday night services, and Wednesday nights, as well as the two or three revivals that would roll into town each year."

"It was," as London told *Christianity Today,* "camp meeting all the time."[5]

Yet by the time young Dobson was sixteen, he again began to demonstrate some of the same sorts of rebellious behavior that many years later would cause millions of parents to turn anxiously to his books and radio shows for help. Some of it was a normal manifestation of being an adolescent boy, he says, but Dobson also believes a good portion of it was directly related to his father's absence. "I was taking on my mother for the first time," Dobson says. "I was drifting in the wrong direction. Not very far, but enough. I had an attitude that was sort of, 'Tough, this is what I'm going to do.' My mother never took that from me, and she wasn't going to take it this time."

In a foreshadowing of the decision that Dobson Jr. later would make when his own ministry was keeping him away from home too much, his father shut down a thriving career as the Nazarenes' top evangelist, sold their house in Bethany, and moved his family south to San Benito, Texas, a small town near the Mexican border. "My mother had simply said, 'I need you,'" Dobson says. "My dad had a four-year slate of revival meetings lined up, but he came home and canceled four years of meetings with one stroke. We moved south and he took a church in order to be home with me. He saved me."

⋈⌒⌒⌒⋈

Despite the fact that he had spent most of his boyhood under the constant guiding hand of his mother, Dobson Jr. was more impressed by his father. Even though the evangelist's presence in his son's life was erratic—the exact opposite of what Dobson Jr. would prescribe today—the sweetness of their times together seemed to more than offset the pain of the absences. Jimmy Dobson cherished the several-day stints when Dad would be home between month- or six-week-long evangelistic circuits, and they would spend hours on end together, often building things in the garage. Father taught Son, whom he nicknamed Bo, how to play tennis, and he intensely coached his tall-framed, athletically gifted boy in the nuances of the fast-rising sport. Much of the time, they hunted in the cool of the morning as the chipmunks and songbirds came to life in nearby woods, and Dobson Sr. would reflect on the wonders of creation.

"An intense love and affection was generated on those mornings, setting the tone for a lifetime of fellowship," Dobson Jr. says. "[We had] a closeness and a oneness that made me want to be like that man . . . that made me choose his values as my values, his dreams as my dreams, his God as my God."

So strong was the son's unmitigated admiration for his father that Dobson Jr. perceived some weaknesses in his dad as strengths. Dobson Sr.'s income was modest, and sometimes his generosity overcame his better economic sense. He was known to give away much of his income from a revival meeting to someone who seemed needier than he. Dobson Jr. recalls more than once the family praying for God to follow up with an extraordinary provision in such cases. On one occasion, Dobson Jr. believes, God came through memorably: A $1,200 dividend check from Coca-Cola stock showed up in the mail the next day. "Those dividends are what really kept us from being in need," Dobson says. A relatively small inheritance that Dobson Sr. received after his father's death in 1935 helped sustain them as well.

"We were able to eat better than some of my friends and able to take vacations and things, but I had less than anybody else on the block had," Dobson Jr. recalls. "My friends' fathers all were businessmen, and they had bigger houses and nicer things. But I never perceived myself as deprived in any way."

As Dobson grew older, he and his father discussed important books and great ideas; as a result of these interactions, Dobson became more aware of his father's spiritual sensitivity and mental acuity. The elder Dobson read widely in the areas of medicine, biochemistry, astronomy, sociology, and music, among others. At his father's funeral, Dobson Jr. told those in attendance that his father had left a book beside his big chair, opened to a description of the molecular structure of DNA. Next to the book was his father's own handwritten list of the twenty essential amino acids in humans and how they are genetically coded, which he called "God's four letter words." "My father was probably deeper than I am, spiritually and maybe intellectually," Dobson said.

Though the elder Dobson chose preaching as a career, he never abandoned his gift for art. In fact, even as an evangelist, his talent for drawing and painting helped define him vocationally. He developed the unique ability of drawing huge pictures on white sketch paper to illustrate the sermon points he was making or the song someone was singing; then he might give away the drawing to the person who'd brought the most people with him to church that night. Dobson Sr. later was a professor of art at Point Loma Nazarene University in San Diego, and in semiretirement he became a professor of art and history at Mid-America Nazarene University in Olathe, Kansas.

Even though Dobson did not inherit his father's aptitude for art, he was influenced by Dobson Sr.'s ability to lock onto a topic, an idea, or even a skill to be mastered and engage it tenaciously. London says that "Uncle Jimmy would be obsessive about something, like learning to play tennis, or he'd want to learn about astronomy or earthquakes or whatever it was, and he deflected that into Jim's personality as well. His expectations of Jim were pretty strong."

In an early demonstration of Dobson's own affinity for intellectual synthesis, he took notes on much of what his father had to say about life and the Lord. In fact, by the time Dobson was a budding author, his father's vast and varied experience and intellectual breadth paid off in another way: Dobson Sr. was a primary early reader and sometime editor of his son's professional-journal articles, research papers, and initial books. "Few people realize," the son also said at his father's funeral, "that most of my writings are actually an expression of his views and teachings."

"He also had a certain vulnerability to him that had a great impact on me," Dobson says. "I could hear him preach sermons that I'd heard him preach before, but I'd still sit there and cry. I just had a very tender feeling toward him."

Dobson Sr. suffered a heart attack in September 1977. The doctor who reached Dobson Jr. told him that his father might not live through the night. Dobson and Shirley quickly cut short a speaking engagement at the Texas Pediatric Society in San Antonio and boarded a plane for Kansas City. The doctor also told Dobson that his uncle, James McGraw, had died in the same hospital at 10:30 that morning. So it was with much fear and sorrow that the Dobsons landed at the airport that afternoon. But they soon learned that Dobson Sr. had rallied and become stable. In fact, he had become fully cognizant and was eagerly anticipating their visit. Father and son cherished the days after the heart attack, not knowing how much time they would have left. On December 4, seventy-nine days after the first attack, Dobson Sr. had another one, from which he did not recover. He was only sixty-six when he died.

Naturally, Dobson's own heart was heavy when he gave the eulogy at his father's service in Olathe, Kansas, on December 7. He laid bare his feelings about his father, their relationship, and the importance of the two of them being able to share eternity. He closed by noting that "James Dobson was not a perfect man. It would be unfortunate to eulogize him in a way that would embarrass him if he were sitting among us. My father had a generous assortment of flaws, even as you and I. But I loved him, perhaps as much as any son ever loved his dad."

It would be several years before someone else wrote a tribute to a father that would evoke many of the same feelings that Dobson Jr. had for his own dad.

In 1981, balladeer Dan Fogelberg wrote "Leader of the Band" about his own father, and the heartrending song made it to the Billboard Top 10 that year. Like James Dobson Sr., Lawrence Fogelberg had managed to become a largely local hero in his vocation but achieved legendary status in his son's esteem. In Dobson's mind, Dan Fogelberg could have been writing about Dobson Sr., with lines such as "His gentle means of sculpting souls took me years to understand." Dobson Jr. eventually told how the song had touched him, reading the entire lyrics of the tribute on a *Focus on the Family* broadcast and concluding about his father: "He was the leader of our band."

Dobson finally became aware of a vast extra dimension of his father's legacy in 1985. That's when he received a letter from Alene Swann, the sister of his uncle, Jimmy McGraw, who had been with both her brother and Dobson Sr. at the Kansas City hospital in 1977. "She shared something that she hadn't been able to tell me for seven years," Dobson said later, in one of his many recountings of the incident. She said that even before Dobson Sr. had his heart attack, he had been praying day and night for three days for his brother-in-law and was determined that he wasn't going to die. He also was praying for himself, asking the Lord for some more time to serve him and win more people for Christ.

"Toward dawn of that [third] morning, he said the Lord spoke to him," Dobson says. "My father didn't say that often; he didn't throw those words around. When he said the Lord talked to him that morning, you could be sure he'd had a conversation with the Lord."

James Dobson Sr. told Alene that he had heard God say to him, "Son, I have heard your prayer. I know your love for my people and your passion for the gospel of Jesus Christ, and I know you've asked to have more time to reach others for me. And I'm going to grant that request. You're going to reach thousands of people, perhaps millions of people, coast-to-coast and around the world. But it isn't going to be through you or your brother-in-law Jimmy McGraw—it's going to be through your son."

"My uncle died that morning," Dobson says, "and my father had a massive heart attack the next day. He was never able to tell me that story. I didn't know it until 1985, when I was asking, *Lord, how long do you want me to do this? Am I to continue in this responsibility?* The last line of Alene Swann's letter to me was, 'The end is not yet.'

"I saw for the first time that Focus on the Family isn't a product of my creativity or my words or my thoughts or my writings; this is God's answer to my father's prayer, and it explained why every door has sprung open for this ministry from the early days, why we made incredibly wise decisions about this ministry when we didn't even know the issues. It came out of my father's prayer life, his intense relationship with the Lord, and his desire to serve him."

Not hesitating to draw an analogy between his circumstance and that of a biblical father and son, Dobson concludes: "And the Lord has just transferred that one generation down [to me], as he did with Solomon when he allowed him to build the Temple instead of David."

ᏫᏣᏃᏪᏬᏋ

After leaving an indelible mark on her young son's character—and ultimately on his vocational success—Myrtle Dobson also loomed large in Dobson Jr.'s life near the end of her own. In 1980, a few years after her husband's death, Myrtle moved from Kansas to a condominium in Southern California to be near her son and his family.

But Myrtle Dobson's move hardly constituted a smooth transition. Not surprisingly, she struggled greatly with the loneliness she felt after her husband's death, echoing the aloneness she had lived through when he was a traveling evangelist. Immediately after Dobson Sr.'s death, Marge Smith—who had been widowed herself a few years earlier—felt compelled to stay with Myrtle Dobson many nights when her friend was overcome with grief. "She absolutely couldn't cope with his being gone; they were just so much a part of each other," Smith says.

Once relocated to California, Myrtle Dobson transferred her intense demands for companionship to her son. "She was very disappointed when she [was not] the center of his attention," Smith says. By then, Dobson was busily building up Focus on the Family, "and he just couldn't do it. He'd make a point to eat with her once a week, and he did well to do that."

Eventually, afflicted with Parkinson's disease, Myrtle Dobson retreated physically as well as emotionally, and Dobson had to place her in a nursing home near his house in Arcadia, California. At one point after his mother had lost interest even in eating, doctors inserted a feeding tube into Myrtle while Dobson was out of town. When he returned, Marge Smith recalls, he "couldn't come home and say, 'Take that tube out of my mother.' But she lived on and curled up into a fetal position. He'd stand over her bed and beg the Lord to take her." Myrtle Dobson died in 1988.

Two things are most important to Dobson: ensuring that his family and other loved ones get to heaven, and living the best possible Christian life while on earth. Everything else is secondary to these two goals, and everything else of importance stems from them. For Dobson, the primacy of these two imperatives flows from his relationship with James Dobson Sr. and from his Nazarene roots.

Dozens of times over the years, Dobson has stressed passionately that the worth of one's life and, by extension, one's success in rearing children, can be measured only by the knowledge that family members and loved ones will be together in heaven for eternity.

"How can anything else compete with that?" Dobson asked in one radio broadcast. "How can anything compete with it? Keeping the circle unbroken on the other side: That must be our ultimate objective as mothers and fathers. Nothing even comes close to that in significance. In terms of making money or leaving an empire to our children or all the other things that people huff and puff to try to gain with the years they invest—nothing is of any significance compared with bringing our children up in the fear and the admonition of the Lord. That has to be where our value system starts."

Dobson has made this point so often with his own offspring, Danae and Ryan, that the latter began calling it the "be there" talk—"be there!" with their father on the other side of eternity. As an adult, Danae finally bought her father a plaque that he still keeps in his office. Its theme is, "Be There!" and its message from the kids is, "We get it."

However, some Christians dispute the importance of this goal, citing the biblical admonition against loving family members more than you love Christ (Matthew 10:37). Dobson acknowledges the caveat but contends that it actually underscores the urgency of helping those you love, love God.

"And why wouldn't we be together [in heaven]?" he asks. In 1 Thessalonians 4:16-17, he notes, the Bible says that Christians who are still alive when Christ returns to earth will be caught up in the clouds with Christians who already have died. "'And so we will be with the Lord forever,' it says. Who's *we?* I think that Scripture implies being there with loved ones."

The other notion that has shaped much of Dobson's philosophy and life is a bit more complex, and its complications come largely from the particulars of Nazarene theology. Because of its emphasis on individual free will, explains London (himself a former Nazarene pastor), his denomination believes in a "theology of standing" in many ways: "It means you can lose your salvation. You're constantly striving to measure up. [Our] definition of sin is that it's a willful transgression of God's law. And salvation isn't automatic as in the Calvinist viewpoint. As a result, not only is there guilt but also pressure to measure up."

Dobson stresses that salvation is a gift from God and can't be deserved by anyone. "If we could have earned our salvation, we wouldn't have needed a Savior," he says. Nevertheless, Dobson believes that the Christian's part of the "contract" also calls for heartfelt repentance and right living after embracing salvation. This doctrine was strongly developed in the eighteenth century by John Wesley, the British founder of Methodism, and later further shaped by the Nazarenes. "There is a call on our lives to be as clean as possible with the help of Jesus Christ," Dobson says. "We fall short; we sin. But we seek forgiveness for sin, and it's very much a part of our theology that we're obligated to live as holy a life as we can.

"I do believe that someday I'll kneel before the Lord, and I want to hear him say, 'Well done, good and faithful servant!'[6] What I do and how I live is important. In Matthew 7, Jesus said there will be those on [Judgment Day] who confess him but whom he never knew. Why? Because they didn't *do*—D-O—the work of his Father.[7] It's an emphasis on attempting to walk the talk."

Dobson is hesitant to discuss this aspect of his beliefs in public because some people misinterpret this holiness doctrine as an assertion that, with enough effort, a person can live a truly sinless life. Nobody, he affirms, can avoid sinning in the sense of having shortcomings, faults, and other flaws that display our mere humanity. "But from the Wesleyan perspective, sin is a *willful* disobedience or defiance to a *known* law. When you refuse to do what God tells you, you know it and understand it. The apostle Paul writes that we have a conscience within us, so that none of us has an excuse.[8] The concept of sanctification is that God gives humans the ability, through the Holy Spirit, to live without deliberately defying God.

"Just look at Hebrews 10:26," which promises God's vengeance on those who insist on sinning after learning the truth of the gospel, Dobson says. "That's interpreted very differently by my Calvinist friends. But I don't believe you can disobey God deliberately, do all kinds of heinous things, and then just go sweeping into [God's] kingdom.

"The characterization that is made by people who don't understand it is that Wesleyans think they're perfect or that they think you can live without any shortcomings. That's crazy. But I try real hard not to shake my fist in God's face and defy him, and God gives me the encouragement and strength through the Holy Spirit not to violate a known law. And that's very important to me."

It's clear, London says, that "a large part of the pressure that [Dobson] puts on himself to be such a perfectionist and to achieve may come out of this theology, or at least out of the inward pressure that we Nazarenes put on ourselves to be loved and appreciated—to be the best at what we do."

This also helps explain the high expectations that Dobson places on others in work, in relationships, and in life. And if the heresy of fist-shaking at God sounds familiar to his fans, that's because Wesleyan theology also, as Dobson puts it, "influences my approach to child rearing. I've talked about having a three-year-old son, and if you tell him to go open the door and he misunderstands your command and he closes it instead, he'll never be aware that he's done the opposite of what you just asked him to do," Dobson explains. "But when he stomps his foot and says, 'I won't do it,' that's when he's most likely to face the consequences."

This worldview has influenced "nearly everything about me," Dobson says. "My teaching all comes out of my theology."

Understanding the roots of Dobson's worldview, it's also easy to see his Nazarene views reflected in the bedrock beliefs that motivate which social and cultural issues he chooses to emphasize. This is one reason why, for example, he is so willing to oppose gambling and gaming interests even though, for American society as a whole, betting no longer equates even vaguely with sin. He believes it is an acknowledged evil whose continued indulgence he can't ignore. He has been greatly influenced by the mail and phone calls that come to Focus on the Family, often from spouses of those addicted to gambling. Because he views gambling as a social sin, he feels compelled to fight it for the sake of those affected by it. Dobson applies this screen even more harshly to abortion, a more broadly acknowledged sin whose commission by millions of people each year grieves him deeply.

But Dobson pushes no one harder than himself, always conscious that his ministry isn't his own but God's. Within his determination, there's the constant glimmer of acknowledgment that he has accomplished what he has only because of his father's prayer.

"Sometimes it makes people uncomfortable because he's so fully committed," says his college classmate and longtime friend Wil Spaite. "His sense of ambition has always been there. But more important than that is the sense that he's being divinely guided."

CHAPTER THREE

STRIVER

His ego strength is phenomenal.

ARCH HART, CHRISTIAN PSYCHOLOGIST
AND FRIEND OF JAMES DOBSON

From the moment he sprang forth from the Rio Grande Valley into the wider world, it was clear to many that James Dobson was going to be really good at something. His early friends and associates noticed right away that he was equipped with all the tools to start and run a successful ministry—or grocery store or hospital department or car wash or church. One admirer noted that "everyone seemed to listen to what he had to say and to go to him for advice." Another friend from those days, Sandee Foster, says that she "knew during that period that [Dobson] would amount to something. It just showed. He had it, and you couldn't miss it."

Indeed, when he arrived at Pasadena College in the fall of 1954, Dobson sported many attributes that presaged success in campus life: high intelligence; quick wit; a certain charisma; and blond, crew-cut good looks. Long and wiry, he was also well coordinated and an exceptional overall athlete. Although he had dabbled in other high school sports, competing as a high hurdler on the track team, for example, Dobson's passion was tennis. He practiced up to six days a week, eleven months a year throughout high school so that he would be good enough to play on a collegiate tennis team. Once he shook off the dust of those small-town Texas courts, he had no doubts that he would succeed at tennis in Southern California. And by the time he was done with Pasadena College tennis, Dobson had served as team captain.

In addition to tennis, Dobson found that college offered a whole new world of opportunities. "College was an extremely happy time of my life," he says. "I loved everything about it. I liked to learn and develop. I loved my professors. I had a ball in the dorm with my guy friends. I was also very excited about the girls. Those four years represented a time of considerable growth and maturation for me because I came out of a little Texas town, and my world was pretty narrow. Everything began to open up for me. It was a time when everything seemed to come together."

But Dobson's many advantages couldn't paper over some aspects of his upbringing, and friends say that, like many great achievers, he was at least partly motivated by a desire to have a better material life than he had enjoyed growing up. His parents had to scrimp and save to make sure that he could attend a Nazarene school.

"It was one of the great objectives of my dad's life to have me go," Dobson says. "And his mother told him that, of all the cousins, she was worried about me most [economically]." Dobson also pitched in to help pay for college with a succession of summer jobs, including working as a recreation-department coach, doing construction work, and even toiling on the assembly line at a Lincoln-Mercury plant in Los Angeles, where he put front bumpers on cars and hoisted an eighteen-pound air gun over his head.

Still, Dobson seemed to have a sense that whatever he put his hand to would prosper. "Jim's parents and grandparents really conveyed to him a sense of destiny, that he would be used of God to touch the world in a special way," says Wil Spaite, a fellow tennis player and Dobson's confidant at Pasadena College. But while clearly a big man on campus from the early going, Dobson still had to decide how that golden touch would be administered.

⚜

Coming from a family where a calling to ministry was nearly a birthright, Dobson didn't take what might have seemed the obvious path: entering into formal ministry training. Nazarene doctrine is very strict in that pastoral candidates must be certain that they've heard a call from God. His dad had felt this call as a seventeen-year-old, but Dobson never sensed any such holy prompting. And his parents didn't pressure him to testify that he had.

Meanwhile, Dobson's cousin, H. B. London, didn't think he had received a call into the ministry either. He wanted to major in business.

The two of them had grown up together, cousins and best friends, and began rooming together at Pasadena College. But as close as they were—and partly because each of them had been an only child—it wasn't a surprise that they began to act like quibbling siblings. "[Jim] would clean half the room, and I would clean half the room. If he swept his half first, he'd just leave the stuff on the floor right in the middle of the room and step right over it until I could get to it," London recalls. "Neither one of us was going to do more than his part."

Soon, however, London encountered some real struggles at Pasadena and began to buck the school's authority. His father, a Nazarene pastor in Missouri, had been dismissed after having been accused of an affair. The news left his son feeling rebellious and lonely. Pasadena College asked London to leave the school when he was a sophomore. He returned as a junior only after agreeing to give up baseball, track, choir, and other activities. Born of the same hardy stock as his cousin, and in many ways similarly gifted, London rallied from that point, marrying his college sweetheart, Beverley Haile, at the age of twenty. She was nineteen. Under her influence, he decided that he'd heard the family call to the ministry after all, finished college and seminary, and headed to his first church in Whittier, California, at the age of twenty-three.

Dobson saw the trauma that his uncle's moral failing had caused his beloved cousin and the entire extended family. As with many of his other life experiences, he diligently applied that lesson later on. And time after time as his ministry developed and grew, Dobson remembered the importance of avoiding a personal misstep that might embarrass not only himself but also the Kingdom of Christ.

ᴗᴄᴇᴀᴄᴠᴄᴊ

Four men influenced Dobson at critical junctures while he was in college, providing him with the same type of strong male mentorship he received from his father. Each had a Ph.D.— the same honorific that later would become an integral part of Dobson's persona and career success.

Dr. Eddie Harwood was an English professor who immediately recognized Dobson's potential as a writer and pushed him hard to excel; Dobson took four classes from Professor Harwood. Dobson credits Harwood not only with teaching him how to handle the rigors of writing a serious work but also with passing on the demanding editorial technique that Dobson uses when evaluating the work of others. They remained friends until Harwood's death in 2004.

Dr. Clyde Narramore, a pioneer in Christian psychology, offered to spend an afternoon with any promising student who wanted to enter the field of mental health. In a two-hour visit, he impressed upon Dobson, among other things, the worthiness of behavioral studies as a godly pursuit and the importance of postponing the commitment of marriage until after his career was established.

Dr. Ken Hopkins, who had graduated from Pasadena three years before Dobson and had just earned his Ph.D. from the University of Southern California, was instrumental in Dobson's decision to enroll at USC graduate school instead of attending the University of Texas. (Dobson's entry to USC kept him within the orbit of Shirley Deere, the eventual Mrs. Dobson, at a crucial time in their relationship.) Hopkins became Dobson's major professor in graduate school.

But the man with a Ph.D. who had the most impact on Dobson clearly was Dr. Paul Culbertson, who became his major professor in undergraduate school and mentor for years to come. It was during a freshman-year class with Culbertson that Dobson quickly opened his mind to the study of psychology and to the possibility of lashing it to his Christian worldview. Culbertson was the one to introduce to him the formula for a biblically based study of psychology that later became Dobson's hallmark. It was Professor Culbertson who helped Dobson shape the powerful concepts that would serve as the core of his future ministry and was Culbertson who began equipping his protégé with the philosophical tools to promote those ideas with confidence.

"[Culbertson] was a brilliant man," says Wil Spaite, who also became a psychology major and shared most of his classes in that field with Dobson. Culbertson actually had been invited to teach at the much larger and more prestigious University of California–Berkeley up the coast near San Francisco, and he possessed a great understanding of Sigmund Freud, Abraham Maslow, and the other secular masters of the still-young field of psychology. But Culbertson was drawn to Pasadena, Spaite recalls, "because as a Christian, he wanted to be able to educate Christians. He was a rare combination of a brilliant mind and a heart for God. He often would say that he still wasn't totally sure whether he was to be a psychologist or a theologian. In a way, he was saying, 'Whatever you do, do it as a minister, not necessarily as a clergyman.'" Clearly, Dobson was absorbing Culbertson's every teaching.

Culbertson's devotionals at the beginning of class sometimes would go halfway through the session, Spaite recalls. "It wasn't because he was in opposition to psychology or neglecting it, but because he had a deep, profound relationship with God. He would teach in his devotionals that God desired persons to be made whole—and that psychology was a means to bring about healing even though God was the ultimate source of it. I can still remember him talking about how Christ regarded the infinite worth of every person. [Culbertson] had a sense of destiny about himself and his students."

Shirley Deere was a part of Dobson's destiny almost from the first time she saw him walking across campus in his tennis shorts in the spring of 1957. "Hi, Legs!" she blurted out in greeting.[1] He was a twenty-year-old junior; she was a native Oklahoman and a nineteen-year-old sophomore education major from Gardena, California. The former high school cheerleader was a brown-haired beauty with a radiant smile. She already had developed a reputation as "a bit of a Bluebeard" at Pasadena, as Dobson recounts: "She had dumped some of the nicest guys on campus." The two didn't establish a personal connection until summer, when each was living in the dormitories on a lightly attended campus. For their first date, Dobson took Shirley to a Sunday evening church service and then, afterward, to dinner at a fine Italian restaurant in Hollywood. They dated throughout his senior year, and as they began to spend more time together, Dobson really turned on the charm, one time sending her a love note rolled up in the neck of a Coke bottle.

Humor, as well as displays of affection, became early threads in the fabric of their relationship. On one of their first dates, for example, at a Long Beach, California, amusement park called The Pike, Dobson insisted that they ride a rickety old roller coaster—over his date's staunch objections. Sure enough, she screamed the whole way, and shortly after walking off the ride, Shirley apparently fainted. "It scared me to death," Dobson remembers. "All these people were gathered around, and I was bent over her. I'm patting her face and talking to her and trying to bring her around. And then I saw this little smile—she had faked the whole thing! She had played a joke on me because I'd forced her to ride that thing."

Shirley saw beyond Dobson's charisma and found she liked what else was there. "I saw that he was an unusual young man, and I had dated several different young men by then," she says. "I won't say that's what attracted me right away, but I came to see that he was unusual in his depth of character, his focus on what he wanted to do in life, where he wanted to go. And I saw that he was a leader."

As they went steady over the next couple of years, the two made an impressive sight on campus. Sandee Foster, who later would become a family friend, was attending the Nazarene high school adjacent to the college at the time, and she remembers slipping into the receiving line in 1959 when Shirley Deere was crowned senior homecoming queen. "We were hoping to pass for college kids and shake hands with the queen we had seen glide gracefully about the campus," Foster says. "Jim was right beside her, shaking hands too. It was like he was letting other guys know that he was with her, and she was with him."

But the couple's path to that happy occasion and beyond was hardly as smooth as their victory stroll that evening. For one thing, they had to deal with the psychological impact of Shirley's troubled childhood, which had included an alcoholic father, her parents' divorce, and a mother, Alma Deere, who struggled financially until she began her second marriage to Joe Kubishta in 1951. When Shirley Deere tearfully told her new boyfriend about her past, his reaction was to succor her rather than reject her. They talked for more than an hour, and he reassured her that rather than being put off by her revelation, he had gained a greater appreciation for the strength she had demonstrated to make it through such hardship.[2] Yet Dobson instinctively understood that the experience had scarred Shirley deeply. And later, when their relationship had grown serious, it was he who brought it up again. "I want you to know that I am hereby pledging myself to your happiness as compensation for the years you lost at home," he told her. "That will be one of my major objectives as your husband."[3]

Dobson would say later that his future wife's vulnerability on this issue helped him fall more deeply in love with her, because she obviously had learned to rely on God from her earliest days. "She lived in very dire circumstances, but then she heard that the Lord was preparing a mansion for her, and she learned to pray and depend on him," he says. "And so from the beginning she has been a godly example to her children, her friends, her church, and me."

Another, more unsettling, strand of their relationship was the perpetual cat-and-mouse game they played as each one tried to figure out how serious they should be and whether the other partner in the relationship felt the same way. Dobson later concluded that this strong dynamic must have developed as he and Shirley realized that they had finally met their match. What ensued was essentially a power struggle, and it intensified as each began to look at the other as a potential mate. Years later, Dobson would use their pas de deux as the main inspiration for his book *Love Must Be Tough.*

This dating equivocation surfaced almost immediately. Dobson says that he "held the relationship very lightly" at first, given that he was a "big man on campus" and Shirley was "a lowly sophomore." But by the end of their first summer of dating, Shirley told him that she wanted to resume dating a boyfriend from the previous spring. Dobson later recalled his response as a crucial early moment in their relationship. "I said that was a good idea, because there were some girls I wanted to date too," he says. "She said that she wanted to go with him and me too. And I said, 'No, go with him.' I set her free at that moment. If I'd said, 'You can't do that to me; maybe I love you!' the relationship would have been over, stone-cold dead—I know Shirley. But I was confident enough to do that. She never dated him again. She stayed with me."[4]

The pattern would recur, most dramatically after Dobson's graduation as an undergraduate from Pasadena in May 1958. He had decided to enter graduate school and wanted to avoid facing a two-year military draft. So when his number came up, Dobson rushed to join the National Guard and serve a six-month commitment, with reserve duty that would continue for five years afterward. Encamped several hundred miles north at Fort Ord, California, Dobson continued his intense relationship with Shirley long-distance. But their separation began to take a toll, and at the end of his Christmas leave, Dobson confronted Shirley with a shocking intention: He wasn't planning to marry her. He was going to graduate school at the University of Texas once he finished his active duty, and he believed that she should be free to enjoy her senior year at Pasadena unburdened by any obligations to him.[5]

Now it was Shirley's turn to practice tough love, and she stoically accepted what her boyfriend had said (though she now says she later retired to her dorm room and cried for hours). On his long drive back to Fort Ord, Dobson quickly decided that he had made a mistake, so he called her the next day to take everything back. The cat-and-mouse game was on again, as Dobson enrolled in graduate school at USC instead of going back to Texas.

Shirley Deere became not only homecoming queen but also senior class president and most eligible bachelorette on campus. But Dobson finally drew an end to the uncertainties by determining that he wasn't going to be a beggar in this relationship. One evening he pulled over the 1949 Mercury convertible he called Ol' Red and gave his beloved a moonlit speech. He was going somewhere in life, he told her, and he wanted her to come along. If she didn't, he would move on.[6] Shirley opted in, and their relationship was forever defined.

However, Professor Narramore had warned him about getting married too early. "He had said that I was going to need my Ph.D. if I was going to do this right," Dobson says, "and if you're going to get it, you'd better not get married too quickly. You'll have children and they'll be sick all night and you'll spend three hundred dollars on medical bills and the pressure will be too great on you and you'll drop out." But by waiting until the summer after Shirley's graduation and until he had completed a year of his master's degree work, Dobson believed that they had heeded his mentor's advice as much as was practicable.

Yet before they could consecrate their love, the couple came close to self-extinction. After picking up a used 1957 Ford that Dobson had bought to replace the deteriorating Ol' Red, Dobson leaned over to kiss his bride-to-be—just as two cars in front of him abruptly stopped. No one was injured in the resulting three-car collision, but the front end of his new car was demolished. And the couple was so embarrassed that they didn't reveal the true cause of his role in the accident until the publication of a 1989 hagiography about him.[7]

James Dobson and Shirley Deere were married on August 27, 1960, with James Dobson Sr. presiding. Many agreed that, with her charm and industriousness, the bride reminded them very much of Myrtle Dobson. Shirley wore only a simple silver band, because although Dobson had saved one hundred dollars to buy his bride something nicer, he had used the money to pay the insurance deductible for his accident instead. A year later, after cashing in some savings bonds, Dobson bought Shirley a new ring.

They moved into what Dobson calls a "stuffy, L-shaped" apartment where they spent the next few years. Shirley landed a job teaching second grade, and her husband taught a sixth-grade class for a year, followed by two years as a teacher of seventh and eighth grade science and math, in order to meet the educational psychology requirements of his graduate program.

Like most young couples, they scraped by financially in the early years as they worked toward their still-forming dreams. For the first five weeks of their marriage, the Dobsons had only one hundred dollars between them, and hot dogs and beans became their favorite meal. That first Christmas they had planned to drive the several thousand miles to Oklahoma to be with James Sr. and Myrtle Dobson, but they were forced to cancel the trip when Dobson discovered he had made a sixty-dollar error in the checkbook.

Dobson had obtained a $750 federal loan for graduate school, which he immediately began paying back at the rate of ten dollars a quarter. "I forgot a payment once, and I realized it two months later," he says. "I called USC and apologized and said I was really embarrassed. And they said, 'Are you kidding? You're just about the only one who's paying it back'!"

Despite Dobson's steep tuition bills for his Ph.D. program, the couple managed to hoard $2,200 for the down payment on their first house, a bungalow in Arcadia, California, just west of Pasadena, where they moved in 1964. Quickly, they experienced some of the surprises of owning a first home. "I dug up all the grass and buried it in a ten-foot hole, which later sank and looked like two graves in the front yard," Dobson recalls. "And while spreading the dirt to make a new lawn, I accidentally 'planted' eight million ash seeds from our tree and discovered two weeks later that we had a forest growing between our house and the street."[8]

More important, the Dobsons added a room to their house for a nursery and filled it with furniture for their first child, baby Danae; they would adopt James Ryan four years later.

During the midsixties, Dobson learned firsthand about the crushing financial pressures that often face young parents—a problem that would only accelerate for Americans as his own ministry to families took off in later years.

When Danae was two and a half years old, for example, Shirley decided to begin teaching again, this time as a two-day-a-week substitute, to provide additional income. They enrolled Danae in a small nursery school near their home. But one day when Dobson was about to drop her off, the little child clung to his arms and begged him not to go; she was terrified. Familiar as he was with a young child's sense of abandonment from his own experience as a six-year-old, Dobson decided then and there that he and his wife had made the wrong decision and that he would do everything necessary so that Shirley could stay at home with their daughter.[9]

Such traumas also were a big part of the reason that Shirley was dead set against her husband's consideration of attending medical school in 1965 and 1966, as he was winding up his Ph.D. program with a 3.91 grade point average. She simply didn't want to endure another long period of time and financial pressures. Whenever her husband bandied about the idea, in fact, she would go outside to rake leaves to vent her anxieties.[10] Soon, Dobson was invited to join the faculty of Childrens Hospital Los Angeles, and three years later, he also became an associate clinical professor of pediatrics at the USC School of Medicine.

From the beginning, Dobson says, his wife recognized his role as family captain, but she also understood that her role, while different, was just as vital. "She taught me a lot about being a husband," Dobson says. "First, she believed in me before I believed in me. I was a student; I hadn't done anything remarkable, and she'd say things during that first year or two such as 'I'm so excited about what God's going to do with your life' and 'I'm so pleased to be part of your team' and 'There's not much that you couldn't do.' It gave me the confidence to compete and succeed. A good woman can make a man, and a wrong woman can destroy a man."

∽∽∽∽

Content that his own family life was developing satisfactorily, Dobson began to focus on his professional ambitions. In his seventeen years at Childrens Hospital and fourteen years at USC, Dobson's biggest accomplishment was directing a massive clinical study for dietary treatment of children with phenylketonuria (PKU), a genetic disorder that causes progressive mental retardation. Dobson oversaw a $5 million study that involved fifteen medical centers throughout the United States, hundreds of personnel, and frequent travel to stay connected with it all. His scientific articles were published in the *New England Journal of Medicine*, *Pediatrics*, and the *Journal of Pediatrics*, and the textbook he ended up writing about the disease was recommended by the Menninger Clinic. It was called *The Mentally Retarded Child and His Family*; Dobson wrote five chapters of it and was coeditor.[11] "If you can have only one book on your shelf about mental retardation, this should be it," the clinic once said. Afterward, Dobson testified before Congress about PKU and was instrumental in obtaining federal government testing of Native American children and those of other ethnic groups who are especially susceptible to it.

Dobson, however, isn't the type to settle perpetually into any kind of a comfortable niche or be satisfied only by predictable and limited progress down a well-trodden professional path. He was always probing for how to reach that next level of achievement or influence—how to leapfrog the inertia of complacency into a new arena of challenge and potential. And those opportunities weren't apparent to him on the clinical career track. But fortunately, Dobson's dual position at USC School of Medicine and Childrens Hospital required his presence only four days a week, and month by month, Dobson took growing advantage of that fifth day to fashion his own separate career in counseling, speaking, and writing.

"In the [USC] School of Medicine, if you're not an M.D., you're an allied-health professional, and [Jim] was chafing under that label because he thought it conferred second-class citizenship," says Mike Williamson, a friend who hired Dobson at Childrens Hospital. "[Jim would] go to the [administrators] and ask, 'What's here for me? Where's my future with Childrens Hospital and the university?' He loved the university and wanted to advance as fast as he possibly could there, but he was drawn into counseling and relating to people through more than just research."

Friends had gotten early clues that Dobson might someday address the plight of the family. At about the midpoint of his college career, Dobson had driven with Wil and Polly Spaite to a tennis match at the University of California–Riverside, and Polly remembers discussing the future for their young son, David. "Rather out of the blue, [Jim] said, 'What are we going to do for the family?' " she says. Dobson's thought was expressed in a somewhat remote, academic way, Wil Spaite says, but it was a foreshadowing nonetheless.

Dobson reports that his doctoral program gradually had exposed to him more and more facets of the eroding jewel of the American nuclear family. In addition to his fulfilling his requirement as a teacher, Dobson served briefly as a high school counselor, a school psychologist, and a school district administrator of psychological and nursing services. In all these positions he dealt with stressed and troubled families all day long. And upon his appointment to the staff of Childrens Hospital in 1966, Dobson began to see some of the seamiest aspects of the deterioration of family life.

"With the patients he was working with and the parents he was working with, he was seeing the results of divorce," says Bill Maier, who served a practicum at Childrens Hospital about a quarter-century after

Dobson's time there and who later became a vice president and psychologist-in-residence at Focus on the Family. "So while the kid he saw might have had a medical or physiological problem, there also was more family dysfunction, and that added to the problem. It was a relatively new phenomenon, but he also was seeing the increasing impact of single-parent families, and lots of the kids who were served at the hospital were below the poverty line. He was really seeing what might lie ahead for the family in America."

And while the knowledge Dobson downloaded as a psychologist was expanding, so also were the wit and wisdom that he uploaded to live audiences. Dobson, in fact, began to master the art of public speaking in 1964, when he was still three years from his degree completion. He said that he wanted to learn how to think and speak in a public mode, because psychologists were expected to do that. But in addition to being one who always had warmed to the spotlight, he was running a large medical research program where the emphasis was on organizational competency, rather than public communications.

Dobson was confident that he could draw on the family gift for verbal communication. So he began to accept just about any speaking invitation he could garner, including from churches and PTAs, where he would talk about aspects of child psychology that had an immediate, practical impact. Dobson also began to teach an adult Sunday school class on the family at First Church of the Nazarene in Pasadena. Within two years, the class grew from a couple of dozen parents to more than two hundred at a time. He sometimes used the class as a focus group and a research corollary. Often over the twelve years that he led or cotaught it, Dobson had parents fill out surveys about their child-rearing experiences, a tool that he would broaden and implement to great effect for research for books later on. He also tried out ideas and anecdotes on the friendly crowd as he tested and refined his communications skills.

"We cut our parenting eyeteeth on [Jim], continually lamenting to him and asking for advice every time our young children entered a new phase," says Sandee Foster, the old friend who also attended the same Nazarene church. "And sometimes people would raise their hand and say something dumb, but he'd always handle it with such finesse. Or people would say iffy things, and I would ask myself, *I wonder how he'll get out of this.* But he always did. He worked through the situation with that person and in front of the class."

By the time "Dr." Dobson graduated from the University of Southern California on April 3, 1967, a confluence was developing between his personal gifts, concerns, and ambitions, and the vagaries of a deteriorating culture. "It took me ninety-three months to finish my doctoral program, and after I sailed through my final orals—which are always a big challenge—on the way home I prayed a prayer and even wrote it down later," Dobson recalls. "Essentially, I said to the Lord, 'You've got people who are very willing to serve you, but they're not qualified. And people who are very qualified who aren't willing to serve. I now have a measure of qualifications, and I'm deeply willing. Please use me.' That kind of became a prayer for my life."

Dobson sent up his prayer almost exactly a year after *Time* magazine ran its cover story, 'Is God Dead?' and the now-famous question became a set piece for his professional coming of age. "The sexual revolution had come along and contradicted the idea of moral purity and lifelong commitment," Dobson says. "Children were considered an inconvenience, and abortion had made a mockery of procreation. All those things assaulted family life. I was watching everything I cared about being mocked and vilified, and it gave me this passion to do something to protect and preserve it. It came right out of that revolutionary period in American history."

Soon enough, the entire country would see what James Dobson intended to do about it.

CHAPTER FOUR

DARING TO
DISCIPLINE

Roses are red,
Violets are blue.
When I was a kid,
I got spanked 'cause of you.

POEM WRITTEN TO JAMES DOBSON
BY A COLLEGE STUDENT, 1997

T
he late sixties in America created a problem begging for many
different solutions. It seemed that the relationship between kids
and adults in general, and between children and their parents
specifically, was one area where breakdowns had become endemic.
And yet even James Dobson—a highly skilled communicator and a
man not afraid to speak his mind—wasn't sure what he should do
about it. In fact, it hadn't even occurred to Dobson to write a book to
showcase his thoughts.

Dobson's success as a speaker was increasingly eclipsing the professional rewards of his work at Childrens Hospital and at USC School of
Medicine. And at that point, the medium was as important to Dobson as
the message, because he was learning how to become a professional
communicator. While he was beating the drum in defense of the traditional family from the beginning, Dobson experimented with a number
of different specific messages, depending on the audience and the occasion. He noticed that child rearing was always a popular topic—not
only how to handle kids but also how parents could teach their children
responsibility in a world that seemed to be spiraling downward fast.

One Sunday afternoon in 1970, Dobson believes God brought the
next step literally to his front door. The social chairman of their church

fellowship called the Dobsons and asked them if they would entertain a couple who was new to First Nazarene. No one knew much about this couple, but the Dobsons enjoyed hosting Francis "Doc" and Joyce Heatherly when they showed up that evening. What Dobson discovered was that Doc Heatherly had just retired as director of marketing for Zondervan, one of the nation's largest Christian publishing companies. And to Heatherly, it was the most obvious thing in the world that this bright, articulate, passionate Christian psychologist and speaker ought to write a book about what he thought on the subject of discipline. The next day, after being tipped off by Heatherly, representatives from Zondervan, Tyndale House, and Word publishers called Dobson at the hospital.

Dobson immediately took to the idea of writing a book, and the publishers took to him. "I was impressed that he'd done a lot of research and spoken to PTAs and church groups about his theories," says Wendell Hawley, who had just become a marketing executive for Tyndale. The publisher, based in Wheaton, Illinois, a western suburb of Chicago amid one of the major pockets of evangelicalism in the Midwest, would establish itself in the seventies with the publication of *The Living Bible,* which became the most popular paraphrase of the Scriptures.

"This wasn't someone who'd just gotten his Ph.D. and decided to write a book about discipline. And we knew that it would resonate at least with conservative Christians who'd always believed that discipline should be part of the home environment," says Hawley, who had returned from Army service in Vietnam shortly before he first met with Dobson. "[At the time] I had three young children myself," he continues. "Our family was going to welcome such a message because everything was in turmoil. When we arrived in Wheaton in 1969, even there, there were [American] flags flying upside down by the Wheaton College campus."

Zondervan and Tyndale House each offered Dobson a contract, the latter padded with an advance of five thousand dollars. Word didn't enter the derby, Dobson recalls, because the company already published the books of another family-advice expert named Charlie Shedd. Dobson couldn't decide which publisher to favor, but Heatherly recommended Tyndale House because of the marketing expertise of an executive named Bob Hawkins. That was the tiebreaker for Dobson. A mere six months later, after a feverish writing effort, *Dare to Discipline* was published by Tyndale House. Dobson requested 250 copies of his freshly printed treatise to send to friends and colleagues. He autographed them all, and then he and Shirley carefully packaged each one of them, addressed the envelopes, stamped them, and wrote fourth-class instructions on the labels. Then they knelt beside the pile of books and laid their hands on the packages as they prayed. They dedicated the work to the cause of Christ, loaded them into the back of their red Volkswagen Beetle, and took them to the post office.[1]

It was the last time Dobson would have to do that sort of thing himself.

✺✺✺✺✺

Dobson understood from the reaction to his speeches that *Dare to Discipline* would tap into a subject with a lot of sizzle. Three significant factors made for a highly favorable climate when *Dare to Discipline* hit the bookstores in 1970.

The sixties, of course, had brought the Vietnam War, an end to school prayer, the rise of drug addiction, rampant sexual experimentation, the civil rights movement, campus bombings and shootings, race riots, the beginnings of the decline of mainline Christianity, the assassinations of the Kennedy brothers and Martin Luther King Jr.—a dramatic change of tableau in America from the relatively calm fifties.

Dobson burrowed into the underlying causes and beneath much of the mayhem found what he thought was the key contributor: "a sudden disintegration of moral and ethical principles, such as has never occurred in the history of humankind." As he wrote, "All at once, there were no definite values. There were no standards. No absolutes. No rules. No traditional beliefs on which to lean. Nor could anyone over thirty even be trusted. And some bright-eyed theologians chose that moment of confusion to announce the death of God. It was a distressing time to be young—to be groping aimlessly in search of personal identity and a place in the sun."[2]

A second major factor in the nation's receptiveness to Dobson's message was that the popularity of his predecessor as America's most trusted adviser, Dr. Benjamin Spock, had begun to wane. Back in 1938 Spock had been discovered by a Doubleday editor who was searching for a psychoanalytically oriented pediatrician to write a book. The Yale-educated pediatrician had been attracted by Freudian ideas and had begun to develop a psychological approach to child rearing in his New York City practice, making him a perfect candidate.[3] After five years, Spock finally produced *Baby and Child Care*. And when returning GIs and their wives began the baby boom in 1946, his timing could not have been better: The book sold spectacularly, the first wave of what became a burgeoning market for child-care advice in the fifties.[4]

Interestingly, while later on Spock would come to be regarded as the father of the permissive-parenting philosophy, that wasn't really his purpose, as Dobson points out. Spock was only suggesting that the fate of children couldn't any longer be entrusted to God or to mere custom but that adults had to pay more heed to the mysteries of children's growth and to their own needs as individuals.[5] But the practical result of that repeatedly reinforced suggestion was to untether new parents from the reliable, though rather formulaic, tactics that their own parents had used. In many cases, this simply paralyzed Spock's readers rather than equipped them with new parenting tools. By the sixties, the cry had arisen that children had been "Spocked when they should have been spanked."[6]

Also by then, Spock—who had become an A-list celebrity across the world—began slipping out of the realm of legitimacy because of his outside activities. Under the spell of socialism, he began to make strange—and estranging—assertions. For example, Spock suggested that the Soviet Union's "strong sense of purpose" was to be admired, in part because of how it resulted in a stable and effective system for raising children.[7] By 1967, when he officially retired from his career as a child-care adviser at the age of sixty-four, Spock was spouting antiwar messages in the media and eventually became a full-blown activist. "I guess I've said all I can about babies," he said. "From now on I will try to talk to youth about their problems."[8] In December 1967, Spock was arrested for civil disobedience during a demonstration at an Army induction center in New York City, and in January 1968, Spock and the rest of the "Boston Five" (including the Reverend William Sloane Coffin Jr.) were arrested on charges of aiding and abetting draft resisters.[9]

But in making the transition from therapist to moralist, Spock's moral authority vanished because his vast constituency of millions of parents didn't want to come with him. And as tensions between America's youth and its adult "establishment" worsened during the close of the sixties, it became very easy for parents, pundits, and even sympathizers to wonder whether Spock's ideas actually were to blame for much of the mess. In March 1968, Christopher Jencks, a Harvard sociologist, wrote an article for the *New York Times Magazine* titled, "Is It All

Dr. Spock's Fault?"[10] *Newsweek* weighed in six months later with a five-page spread, wondering, "Is Dr. Spock to Blame?"[11]

The third major reason that Dobson's timing was perfect was tied to the first two but still distinct. Partly due to doubts about how Spock's theories were playing out, a decided split was emerging in the American child psychology community between "child-centered" theorists and a new corps of "parent-centered" thinkers.[12] Dobson became the first credible member of the parent-centered group to lay out a convincing case for a retreat from the child-centered wanderings of the previous quarter century.

And he made the case with gusto.

There really was no mistaking Dobson's clarion call to parents, educators, policy makers, and the culture as a whole. He wanted parents to reverse much of the child-rearing advice they'd been given since World War II—all of which, he believed, had come home to roost in the turbulence of the sixties. His was still a rather lonely voice at that point, but because his prose was so piercing and his view so clear, Dobson was heard. He wasn't sure what the American public's response would be, but some close associates sensed that *Dare to Discipline* was the right book, by the right man, appearing at just the right time in the nation's social and cultural history. For example, Mike Williamson, Dobson's colleague at Childrens Hospital, predicted in 1971 that *Dare to Discipline* would become an immediate best seller and move two million copies. Indeed, the book became such a phenomenon, and so quickly that already by 1972 it was one of fifty books selected to be specially rebound and placed in the White House library.[13] But Williamson had underestimated: Today, the book and Dobson's 1992 update, *The New Dare to Discipline*, have sold more than three million copies—and counting.

Yet even Dobson agrees that *Dare to Discipline* was far from a literary tour de force. Those who haven't read it might deduce that *Dare to Discipline* systematically walks the reader through the psychologist's carefully developed philosophy of child rearing from infancy through the teenage years. But it's far from such a linear tome. Instead, it's nearly equal parts parenting guide, political manifesto, mass-culture analysis, and handbook on the illicit drug counterculture. The book is actually a somewhat loosely packaged collection of essays and snippets of advice whose subjects are mainly united by being Dobson's passions in those days.

"It wasn't a how-to; it was about what was happening to the culture," Dobson says. "I tried to show the linkage between the trends in the culture and how people were living their lives, and the instability of the family. It's really a social statement that coincided with my professional life."

The book opens with a sharp summation of the legacy of Spock. "Children thrive best in an atmosphere of genuine love, undergirded by reasonable, consistent discipline," Dobson wrote in the introduction. "In a day of widespread drug usage, immorality, civil disobedience, vandalism, and violence, we must not depend on hope and luck to fashion the critical attitudes we value in our children. That unstructured technique was applied during the childhood of the generation that is now in college, and the outcome has been quite discouraging. Permissiveness has not just been a failure; it's been a disaster!"[14]

It moves through instructions on teaching respect and responsibility to children, lays out what Dobson calls "the miracle tools" for shaping kids' behavior *before* it has to be remedied, and harshly criticizes the increasing lack of discipline in schools. The book also engages in an entertaining riff about how hippies, who seemed to be having a good time in the carefree sixties, would become common bums if they didn't change their life philosophy. The book sounds an early warning about sex education and the endless battles to come between Christians and secularists in this arena.

Another chapter discusses the destructiveness of drug abuse and offers a primer to parents on warning signs. *Dare to Discipline* ends with a practical list of tips for mothers to help them get through the minefield of modern child rearing, including a section that discusses faith or scriptural principles at length.

Dobson kept the overtly spiritual content of the book to a minimum, trying to find the widest possible audience. But in the end, his source of inspiration was clear to all.

In *Dare to Discipline*, Dobson also sounded some themes that jumped out at secular critics then and have offended sensitive sophisticates ever since. To a large degree, they also have since defined Dobson to mainstream culture, for better or worse. One of Dobson's suggestions for gaining control without nagging children, a suggestion he learned from his mother, was for the parent to cause minor pain when necessary, something he says could "provide excellent motivation for the child." A handy way of inflicting this pain without causing marks or injuries, Dobson went on, is to compress the trapezius muscle that lies at the base of the neck. "When firmly squeezed," he wrote, "it sends little messengers to the brain, saying, 'This hurts; avoid recurrence at all costs.'"

Actually, the move is reminiscent of a technique used by the character Mr. Spock on the TV show *Star Trek* to render assailants unconscious. And sure enough, Dobson recounted how he personally had employed this method in a real-life incident of heroism that couldn't have been scripted any better. An elderly drugstore owner was surrounded at the entrance to his store by four young hoodlums who had knocked bottles and cans off his shelves, tipped his hat down over his eyes, and were mocking him. When Dobson confronted them, one of them begged Dobson to hit him so that the delinquent could sue him. Instead, he "grasped his shoulder muscles on both sides, squeezing firmly," Dobson wrote matter-of-factly. "He dropped to the ground, holding his neck. One of his friends said, 'I'll bet you're a schoolteacher, aren't you?'" In fact, at the time Dobson was teaching. "All four of them ran. Later that evening I received a call from the police, saying that these four boys had harassed merchants and customers along that block for weeks."[15]

Also in *Dare to Discipline,* Dobson introduced his thoughts about spanking. Dobson warns parents to differentiate clearly between childish acts of irresponsibility (which should be discouraged but not outright punished), and direct challenges to authority (which *must* be punished perhaps with a spanking). He recommends that spankings cause at least brief, real pain and be administered with a neutral object such as a small switch or belt, not with the hand, because the latter should always be seen as "an object of love rather than an instrument of punishment."[16] Dobson adds that it's important to "spank *immediately* after the offense, or not at all" and to go over reasons for the punishment.[17] And most important, after the spanking has been dealt out, the parent must conclude the episode with sweet reunion, in which the parent's love for the child is reaffirmed. Done properly and in control, Dobson argues, the "violence" of spanking should not beget real violence later on by the child.

Today, physical punishment has slid into broad disrepute among child psychologists, the result of a steady decline in their regard for the practice since the Spock era. Some, in fact, have organized movements in an attempt to ban spanking; in November 2004, the House of Commons of the United Kingdom actually voted on such a proposal, although British lawmakers overwhelmingly defeated it. Penelope Leach, a British psychologist of the child-centered camp, cofounded an organization called End Physical Punishment of Children (EPOCH) in 1999.[18] Also that year, Dr. Steve Ambrose, a clinical psychologist and director of research for Children's Institute International, a private Los Angeles–based organization, said, "It's worrisome that spanking remains such a part of the American culture, in view of scientific evidence demonstrating its ill effects. There is a wealth of research data showing that violent parenting produces violent children; so does negligent parenting. We are not saying parents shouldn't discipline their children, but there are more appropriate and effective ways than hitting them."[19]

Such views persist even though the American people have demonstrated their utter determination to ignore this advice. A Children's Institute International poll in 1999, for example, found that 55 percent of parents still believed that "a good, hard spanking" of their children was necessary in some situations, about the same level found in a poll a decade earlier. A recent ABC News poll discovered that about 65 percent of American parents endorsed the use of spanking in some situations, reflecting about the same proportion as in 1990.[20]

When psychologists, media commentators, and others want to criticize Dobson, they often start with his advocacy of spanking, as if his endorsement of any form of corporal punishment provides prima facie evidence that he is some kind of Neanderthal. Yet Dobson's philosophy about spanking is much more constructive and even more humane than his uninformed critics give him credit for; his approach has been consistent ever since he first outlined it in *Dare to Discipline*. In fact, some might argue that achieving the desired effects without engendering bitterness in children is one reason that most American parents still endorse the use of spanking after a generation-long effort by critics to get them to stop.

Having staked out his position on spanking, Dobson elaborated on it frequently after *Dare to Discipline*. And despite the increasing protests of his opponents, he has never backed down.

‌ ‌

Dare to Discipline stoked a passion for writing that Dobson had been nursing his entire life and that would never be extinguished. Actually, he became a "published author" at the age of 19, when *Sports Illustrated* ran a letter to the editor that Dobson had written. Olympic athletes were still required to be amateurs in those days, and Dobson took exception. "I wrote that our American athletes were being penalized by that rule," Dobson recalls. "It wasn't necessarily a great intellectual point, but I wanted to see if I could get something published.

"When it comes to writing, I'm like an artist who sets up his easel and can get lost in it," says Dobson, who often observed his father doing just that with a painting. "I enjoy making words string together in a coherent manner. Most writers these days just throw their stuff down and then expect some [editor] to clean it up for them and make something logical out of it. But I like the art associated with writing—putting in a little more blue here or red there, some yellow there."

And once he moved into writing for a living, Dobson developed his own unique approach to the craft, which addressed the common reader, not fellow professionals, as his primary audience. "A lot of psychologists have come along and written books, but they tend to write them for their peers," says Wendell Hawley, the former Tyndale House executive who first worked with Dobson. "[Jim] writes so that the average person understands what he's saying. That's his secret. Plus, he always uses excellent firsthand illustrations that provide important windows for readers to see things more clearly."

Dobson also set his own publishing agenda in the wake of the success of *Dare to Discipline*. The subjects of most of his books follow the timeline of Dobson's own experiences as a husband, parent, and ministry leader. "One thing I failed in doing early on," says Hawley, who retired in 1995, "was that I'd come to him with some of my own ideas about great books that he could do. It took me awhile to realize that he had ideas of his own and that it was whatever was percolating strongest in his own heart that he'd turn to for his next book."

Dobson's second book, *Hide or Seek,* published in 1974, criticizes America's skin-deep value system and provides parents with comprehensive strategies for handling challenges to their children's self-esteem. Dobson's first book about spousal relationships, *What Wives Wish Their Husbands Knew about Women,* came out in 1975. In 1978, two new Dobson titles debuted, *Preparing for Adolescence* and *The Strong-Willed Child,* just as Danae was becoming a teenager. In many ways, the model for the strong-willed child was Dobson's daughter. Dobson wrote the book for parents who struggle with what he calls "the assertive toddler, the self-propelled youngster," especially when that child is contrasted with siblings who are what Dobson terms "compliant."

By the mideighties, Dobson turned mainly to the challenges that were coming upon middle-aged readers, many of whom had been following his advice for more than a decade. For example, *Love Must Be Tough,* published in 1983, dealt a somewhat controversial prescription for avoiding rupture in relationships, especially marriages. Just as the Dobsons had each occasionally backed off from each other while courting in college, Dobson advised the person who most desired to salvage the relationship to relax his or her grip a bit in order to create the best chance for restoration. "The central idea of that book is radical," says Joey Paul, a Christian publishing executive and Dobson associate in those days. "People would ask, 'What do you mean by suggesting that a woman step out of that situation with tough love?' And he said, 'I think it's biblical, or at least not antibiblical, and as a psychologist I know it works.'"

In 1990, shortly after Dobson had plunged into a defense of traditional values in the political realm, he coauthored *Children at Risk* with Gary Bauer. His scope broadened in 1993, with his first and only largely theological work, *When God Doesn't Make Sense.* Dobson's most recent book, *Bringing Up Boys* (2001), and the planned *Bringing Up Girls,* give him a platform to lay out his thinking about how important it is for parents to take disparate approaches to raising each gender, and to rally readers to a new appreciation of the inborn differences between boys and girls, differences that the feminist and homosexual movements have tried so hard to erase. He even found time to coauthor with Shirley two devotionals, *Night Light* and *Night Light for Parents,* as well as another book, *In the Arms of God,* in 1997.

Confirming that Dobson's appeal to the reading public remains strong, *Bringing Up Boys* got off to the fastest sales start of any of his books, with 1.2 million copies sold within its first two years on the market, facilitated in 2003 by the release of a companion video series starring Dobson.

As his ministry and other demands on his time have grown, Dobson also has refined how he actually goes about writing a book. For many years, he persisted in handwriting entire manuscripts on legal pads, with a No. 2 pencil, in his relatively small and sometimes nearly indecipherable script. Dobson then would tape the individual sheets together, end to end, in one huge scroll that stretched dozens of feet. Dobson literally cut sections out and threw them away or taped them in elsewhere, and sliced open the scroll for new additions. Then secretaries transcribed the scroll into a manuscript.

Well aware of the quirkiness of his approach, Dobson had some fun with it on an early book by taping all the sheets in sequence around his office in Arcadia one night so that in the morning Dee Otte, his secretary, could begin transcribing his writings.

Otte recalls, "I came in early to do it and I got very frustrated right away because I couldn't find the beginning of the book so I could start typing. He had done it on purpose. When he came in, he asked right away if I'd finishing typing it and pretended just for a moment to be upset that I hadn't."

Dobson finally yielded to modern technology and began using a computer to write in 1989, when he bought his son a Macintosh Powerbook 100 to take to college with him. He purchased a Powerbook 100 for himself as well.

In the eighties the Dobsons began leaving home for several weeks nearly every summer so that he could ensure uninterrupted hours for his writing. For these quasi-sabbaticals, Dobson has ended up in friends' homes in Palm Springs and on the shore of Lake Michigan. More typically he holes up in an apartment in London or another location in Great Britain with his wife and sometimes his kids. He loves English sightseeing during his breaks, and Dobson's relative anonymity there removes most distractions of celebrity that he encounters in the United States.

Nevertheless, as early as 1992, when Dobson was writing *When God Doesn't Make Sense,* his fame caught up with him even on his escape to Great Britain. Attending a church service one Sunday morning in Edinburgh, Wendell Hawley and his wife, Nancy, were surprised to see Dobson being mobbed in the back of the church after the service.

"They had seen his film series over there and recognized him," Wendell Hawley recalls. "He hadn't expected that. It was wearying for him to be recognized even over there. But he was gracious to everyone."

The Hawleys were visiting because Dobson had asked them to fly over and advise him on writing a particularly difficult portion of *When God Doesn't Make Sense.* Dobson was still struggling with his own feelings about the 1987 death of four of his friends, including Focus board member Hugo Schoellkopf, in a small-plane crash. These men and Dobson all had been together one night at a Focus retreat in Elk Canyon, Montana. The next morning en route to Dallas, the small plane carrying them plummeted into a remote canyon.

"I loved those men like brothers, and I was staggered by the loss," Dobson wrote in *When God Doesn't Make Sense*. Asked by family members to speak at their funeral, Dobson wrote that he was at a loss to explain why God would have let their untimely deaths occur. "But I did say that God had not lost control of their lives, and that he wanted us to trust him when nothing made sense."[21]

Nancy Hawley recalls that Shirley made dinner for the four of them one evening "and then we spent time on our knees praying. As we were praying, we could hear the fax machine ticking away in the background, with messages coming in from all over the world, including the White House. Yet here he was prioritizing the fact that God had called him to write this book."

CHAPTER FIVE

PACKING THE HOUSE

*If he was going to speak to a group,
he felt that he owed it to that group
to "work out" in advance.*

PEB JACKSON, AN EARLY EXECUTIVE
OF FOCUS ON THE FAMILY, ON DOBSON
PREPARING FOR LIVE SEMINARS

James Dobson was a professional success right out of the chute, but in the early seventies, he could hardly imagine he would one day receive faxes from the White House. While career options for him were burgeoning, Dobson and his wife were happily building the kind of traditional family that was prescribed by his books and that still held sway on television sitcoms.

Shirley miscarried a baby a few years after Danae was born, and doctors told her that she wouldn't be able to bear more children. Wanting to round out their family, the couple adopted James Ryan—on the very same red-letter day that the initial copies of *Dare to Discipline* came out. "Both," Dobson says, "turned my world upside down."

Shirley was very content with that era's common role of stay-at-home mother and was a staunch supporter of her husband's career ambitions. "Being a full-time mom was a role that I loved right from the beginning," she says.

The Dobsons never were the Cleavers—who was?—but they sure tried to raise their kids as much as possible according to the principles that Dobson simultaneously was making famous. One thing was clear from the start: Neither Danae nor Ryan was "compliant," one of the two ends of the personality spectrum that Dobson had formulated and written about in *The Strong-Willed Child.* Instead, Shirley affirms, "Both, in their own ways, are very strong willed."

"God gave us those kids," Shirley says with a smile, "because if we'd had compliant kids who were easy to raise, we would have thought it's just due to Dr. Dobson's way of discipline." The kids picked on each other—she on him more than Ryan on her, Danae allows, perhaps reflecting the fact that she was more obstinate. But on her own, Shirley would only go so far to firmly admonish her kids; she relied on the author of *Dare to Discipline* to, well, discipline his kids.

Neither child delved into "deep sins that put scars on their lives," their mother says, and she was certain of one reason for that: fervent prayer. "When they were young, I set aside a day a week for fasting and prayer because I knew, being in a family ministry, where Satan would be most likely to attack: our family," Shirley says. Dobson also fasted and prayed one day a week, each Wednesday for more than six years. However, the physical demands of his schedule required so much of him that regularly depriving himself of food took too much out of him, and he stopped the routine fasting.

With four members now in their family, the Dobsons decided to sell their bungalow on Eighth Avenue in lower Arcadia. Ever seeking divine direction in financial affairs, Dobson decided to make a For Sale sign, put it out front, and see if God would produce a buyer. After a month with not even a nibble, he took in the sign for a year, and then put it out again. The second time, the house quickly sold to the first "looker" for $31,000, their asking price. The Dobsons had paid $21,900 for it and had already reduced the mortgage balance substantially, so they stood to make a paper profit of about $16,000 on the sale. Dobson gave $1,600 as a tithe to his church, but he also wondered if he should give the 5 percent realtor's fee.

"The house we were buying cost $50,000," he says. "We needed every dollar we could get to close the deal. I resisted giving the money to the Lord, although I continued to think about it."

Dobson says that God didn't give him a chance to make a bad decision on that issue. "Sure enough, the next Sunday I was telling our Sunday school class about the sale of our house—not even mentioning the dilemma I was pondering," Dobson says, "and someone in the class, a friend of mine, piped up and said, 'Don't you think that since God sold your house for you, you ought to give him what would have been your real estate fee?' That settled the issue."

Between the remaining equity from their first house and some proceeds from book sales, the Dobsons were able to trade up to a larger home farther north in Arcadia, at 348 Harvard Drive. All the streets in the subdivision were named for famous colleges, and Harvard Drive was particularly tree covered, and the houses were on good-sized lots. The Dobsons and their neighbors had big backyards, and the previous owners of the Dobsons' new home had planted about one hundred rosebushes in the backyard—a significant lure for Shirley. Azaleas clumped in the front. The Dobsons added black shutters and painted their new home a fresh, classic white.

"I liked living in a Williamsburg-style home because I'm a creature of order; I like things to be organized," Shirley says. "I came from a dysfunctional family. We didn't have much when I was growing up. So roots and a home were important to me. When we were able to buy a nice home, I was proud of it, not in the wrong way, but I liked to make things pretty. I'm a flowers and candlelight and crystal kind of woman. I always wanted to have a very warm and loving home." Dobson adds, "It wasn't an expensive house, but it was our dream house." Shirley would have liked to have stayed there for the rest of their lives and have grandkids there.

Yet while the Harvard Drive house was about 2,500 square feet, or twice the size of the Dobsons' first house, the kitchen and den were small. So they planned to add a family room and expand the kitchen immediately. But the quick addition turned into a nearly three-year nightmare. "We didn't have enough money to do it all at once and hire a construction crew and just get it done," Shirley recalls. "But we had a friend who was a teacher and very good at construction, and he would come and work on Fridays after school and all day Saturdays and then go home and to work for another week. For a long time, we actually had to do the dishes in the bathtub. It was very frustrating, and very frequently on Saturday nights I would just stand there and cry. There was just debris everywhere, and Ryan was two at the time and getting into nails and sawdust."

Yet after the room was finished, it became the highly useful gathering place that the Dobsons had intended, says Danae, who was seven years old when the family moved into the house. "My mom could be cooking while other people were watching TV in the den, and we could be together," she says. "We would have devotions in that room as a family on Saturday mornings, have breakfast, and just kneel down by the kitchen chairs and pray."

The neighborhood did have its quirks, principal among them the fact that all of the houses on the Dobsons' row backed up to the outer grounds of Santa Anita Park, one of the nation's most venerable horse tracks. On the weekends during the three track seasons each year, as the Dobsons sat in their backyard, they could hear the race announcer and the crowds. Another effect of the raceway was the heavy traffic between the Dobsons' and the main road out of the subdivision. "You had to be able to drive a wedge into traffic in order to get through," says Danae, "and Dad would often force his way through, and Mom would say, 'Jim, you're going to get hit,' and he'd say, 'As long as they see me [coming], it won't be a problem.'"

Often, the Dobsons' destination was Pasadena's First Church of the Nazarene, where they made many lifelong friends and extended relationships with other couples they had gotten to know while attending nearby Pasadena College. Often, the Dobsons invited families out for Sunday lunch at Beadles Cafeteria, just a short distance from the church.

Other friends emerged from the business district around Dobson's office and their neighborhood in Arcadia, which they considered rather a tight-knit community even though it was just one of the many booming suburbs of Los Angeles.

The Dobsons enjoyed their circle of friends and were quick to play practical jokes with both new acquaintances and old friends. John Waltrip, who owned a music store across the street from Dobson's office in Arcadia, says the two men "encouraged each other in our new ventures." One day, Dobson's sense of humor emerged when he encouraged John's wife, Flo, to try out one of the new exercise machines in the family room of the Dobsons' home on Harvard Drive. What Flo Waltrip didn't realize until it was too late was that he had put shaving cream on the seat. She returned the favor by creaming the doorknob to the Dobsons' bedroom.

During Christmas vacation one year, Dobson and his friend Jim Davis, both relative beginners at skiing, spent the day at California's Heavenly Valley, where they skied down a very difficult slope called Gun Barrel. Davis was in the lead, and as he approached the bottom of the hill, he saw a ski patrol member furiously trying to wave him and others to a stop: The sun had created a major hazard in that area by melting snow into a pool of water about fifty feet across and about a foot deep.

Fortunately for Davis, he heeded the warning in time. But Dobson didn't notice a thing. He casually whizzed by the stationary Davis—and slammed into that vast pool of ice-cold water at full speed. "He water-skied for a second and then did the splits and fell face forward," Davis remembers, chuckling. But Dobson, perhaps embarrassed a bit at his spectacular pratfall, would get the last laugh. "Unbeknownst to us," Davis says, "he took a huge breath and just lay there in the water; he was absolutely submerged. After about ten or twelve seconds, the ski patrol guy kicked off his skis and ran into this lake, and I was right behind him. We were about to turn [Dobson] over in the water—and he got up and said, 'Gotcha!'"

Naturally, this prankster characteristic made Dobson's friends want to get him back sometimes. For instance, one day the Dobsons were at the beach with USC colleague Mike Williamson and his wife, another couple, and the Dobsons' dog, Siggie (named after Sigmund Freud). When the women noticed that the canned dog food they'd brought was in the shape of meatballs, they fixed Dobson a "meatball" sandwich. "He bit into it and even did a double take and said, 'This is good!' even though he was thinking that it was horrible and he was going to die," Williamson recalls. "And he ate a lot of it before the women finally began laughing hysterically and admitted what they had done."

ᴄ◌⌐ᴄ⌐◌ᴄ

Despite happiness on the home front, something began to gnaw at Dobson, as it became clear that James Dobson the orator and writer was begetting James Dobson the workaholic.

By the midseventies, Dobson was struggling for the first time with the extreme challenges of what charitable friends called his tremendous "capacity for work" and what less generous observers identified as workaholism. Once his early books proved popular, of course, writing became a more important and demanding medium for him. Requests to speak came in from across the country. Meanwhile, demands on Dobson at the hospital and at USC School of Medicine grew unabated. In short, he was faced with the potential for three to four full-time jobs. And until he could decide which one or two of those career threads to pull, he just kept weaving them all. In a sense, at that point he was over-committed by design. He fully realized the situation was untenable, but he was still letting things play out.

"I hit the ground running as soon as I got my degree in April 1967, and I never stopped," Dobson says. "The whole world exploded for me, and that's where my family was at greatest risk—I could have lost them right there. It was pretty heady stuff to have just finished school and have everything just waiting for me." Dobson's father realized that his son would always have a tendency to work too hard. So on a plane trip to Hawaii for a vacation with his wife in 1968, James Dobson Sr. took out a pen and spent much of the five-hour trip composing and writing a letter to his son:

> *I'm very happy for your success, which is now coming in like showers. It is important for men, in all vocations, to experience the realization of their dreams. [And] to this point you have been largely untested, but trials are inevitable. If frustration and heartbreak do not come relative to your career, you must mentally prepare for it in some other areas.*

Then the letter shifted to his father's main concern, which echoed the struggle in Dobson Sr.'s own life when he was away from his son most of the time during his decade as a traveling evangelist:

> *We must all pray definitely, pointedly, and continuously for your children. They are growing up in the wickedest section of a world much further gone into moral decline than the world into which you were born. I have observed that one of the greatest delusions is to suppose that children will be devout Christians simply because their parents have been, or that any of them will enter into life in any other way than through the valley of deep travail of prayer and faith. Failure at this point, for you, would make mere success in business a very pale and washed-out affair indeed. But this prayer demands time, time that cannot be given if it is all signed and conscripted and laid on the altar of career ambition.*

In the midseventies, Dobson began to reflect more and more on the convicting message that his father had written him in that letter. He spent several months establishing priorities and some order around his hectic activities. In a devotional routine, he and Shirley knelt in prayer by their bed nearly every night, and during that deliberative season they devoted extra time to praying together about Dobson's career plans.

Soon, Dobson began taking a series of decisive steps to form his burgeoning ministry into a superstructure that would serve him well for the next quarter century, as well as provide some relief from the stresses that were bogging him down at home. First, while continuing to write, he took a one-year sabbatical in 1976 from both the hospital and USC. Then, within the space of two years, he started Focus on the Family, leveraged his popularity into the beginning of a radio career, and dealt decisively with the opportunities that were opening up because of his speaking gift.

In some ways, the last challenge was the most difficult.

⚬⌁⌁⌁⚬

Dobson didn't enter professional life believing that he was a natural public speaker. So, as in every other area where he had established a goal, he worked very hard at becoming a great one.

Gil Moegerle, one of Dobson's earliest associates outside USC, describes him as "a man working harder than any public speaker you know, but not wanting you to know it."

Dobson would first craft a speech over the course of weeks or months at home or in his office, then plan small engagements where he would try out a theme or a particular story or a certain pace at one point in the address. Once home, he'd edit and refine, add and delete content as necessary.

"I worked hard at figuring out how to communicate with people," Dobson remembers. "When I was speaking at PTAs, I know I didn't know how to do that. But I made a study of it, and I accepted every speaking engagement that came along, including once driving five hours to address fifteen parents in a living room in Redondo Beach."

The preacher's kid also certainly had some factors in his environmental, and presumably genetic, background that kicked in when he determined to work at becoming an accomplished speaker. His father had always shied away from emotionalism during his evangelistic messages. Instead, the elder Dobson had drawn crowds with his humility, his prayerfulness, and an integrity that shone through his words. Dobson Jr. also had observed his uncle, the evangelist Holland B. London, engage audiences; his delivery was rapid-fire and heavily emotional, bringing people to the precipice of tears one moment and swinging them to hysterical laughter the next.

One technique that Dobson Jr. borrowed from both his father and his uncle was the use of illustrations every three to four minutes. "He also learned from them how to apply what you're saying to yourself or someone you love," says H. B. London, son of evangelist Holland B. London.

Dobson himself lists another influence on his approach to speaking:

Reverend Reuben Welch, a Pasadena College professor who eventually became chaplain. "You felt it was just you and he in a conversation," Dobson recalls. "To some degree I tried to pattern myself after him. People relate to someone who talks with them rather than one who 'speaks' at them. They can't relate to ministers, for example, who have no eye contact and nothing of themselves revealed."

Dobson also learned from Jesus Christ, who often addressed crowds using parables. "He told stories—why did he do that?" Dobson says. "He could have simply delivered three points out of Isaiah. But he knew that stories communicated with the human heart." Dobson once told Moegerle, "You should always be watching for human stories and keep a record of every poignant one, and then when you speak, tell the stories and ask yourself what concepts they illustrate. Then, you throw in a few concepts. That's how you influence people."

In fact, intriguing stories were so valuable that Dobson developed his own system of cataloging them, beginning way back when he was a college junior. The index consisted of three basic categories of stories—prose, ideas, and humor—in each of two divisions, which Dobson called "what will preach," meaning it was good enough to talk about, and "what will write," meaning the anecdote had enough substance to be included in a book or article.

"I'd be driving down the road and hearing or thinking something would be a good illustration, and I'd grab a piece of paper and write just enough of it down so that I could remember it," Dobson says. Later, he would add a third major category, "what will speak," for his radio show. (And he would have clerical assistants move the entire scrawled and jotted database to a computer, where it's been thoroughly cross-referenced. Now, Dobson or his researchers can pull up an anecdote from his forty-five years of experience with just a key word or two, much like an Internet search engine.)

Dobson also learned from the best secular communicators, especially when it came to the crucial area of humor. For a while in the early eighties, he recorded the monologue delivered each weeknight by Johnny Carson on *The Tonight Show* and then watched it the next morning during his workout; Dobson was trying to pick up pointers from Carson's mastery of pace and timing in his delivery.

He also learned from others' struggles behind the podium. In the late seventies, for example, he heard a speech by the great Christian thinker Francis Schaeffer. The founder of L'Abri Christian communities in Europe had recently published his seminal work, *How Should We Then Live? The Rise and Decline of Western Thought and Culture.* But Dobson noted painfully that the brilliant writer had trouble coming down from his lofty intellectual plane to communicate with a lay audience. "I was enthralled by being there listening to him," Dobson remembers. "But then I looked around, and there were about three or four thousand people there—and everyone was asleep. I felt like someone ought to stand up and say, 'Listen to what this guy is saying!' But he was an intellectual, not one who made things easy for people to understand."

Brewing together all the influences—the family gift of oration, his perfectionism and hard work, the cultural sensibilities of his era, the legacy of his professional education, and his own ideas about what made for appealing rhetoric—produced a style that was uniquely James C. Dobson Jr. from the start, even as he continually refined it. He began with a base of intellect, passion, and sincerity; layered on the masterful harnessing of emotion, anecdote, and humor; and delivered his words in a unique and authentic voice that seemed to be one part sophisticated psychologist, one part aw-shucks Texan, and one part avuncular everyman.

Although Dobson had the academic training and the preparation and the context, he was able to translate that to the average person. Peb Jackson, who later became one of Dobson's key advisers, says that his friend "was able to break down the issues—the biblical and psychological and parenting and cultural issues—and put them in a way that people could understand and relate to. [People would say], 'He knows me, he knows what I'm thinking. He understands me.' How he described events in everyday life for people made them feel he understood them. That's a gift."

Just as important, Dobson improved after each appearance. "I discovered on occasion that I would have an audience in the palm of my hand but that the next time people appeared to be bored," he says. "The material sometimes would be different, but it would always be good stuff. I thought about that, and then it hit me that it's not good enough just to give people good stuff if they're bored. You have to entertain them, reveal a bit of yourself, and have some humor. If you're not willing to do that, your audience becomes a lot like a room full of children—and adults have a shorter attention span than kids do." Dobson could make this comparison legitimately because he had taught both children and adults during the several years he was developing as a speaker.

"You have to grab people in the first two or three minutes, and then every three or four minutes from there on out you have to put something in your speech that's really worth listening to. Most speakers won't pay the price to do that. But you have to realize who you're dealing with and what they need." And, says Dobson, he always remained keenly aware of how his particular rhetorical concoction for that occasion was connecting with the audience, taking notes about where it needed refinement for next time. "I have a barometer in my head when I'm speaking," he says. "It measures not air pressure but surface noise in the audience. When you're not connecting with people, they'll shuffle and cough."

Dobson learned the hard way about a few things. Very soon after his graduation from USC, he was asked to speak to a big Japanese church in Los Angeles. He spent weeks preparing for the address so that he would be as relaxed as possible when he finally stood in front of the congregation. But he got lost on the way and arrived at the church late and out of breath. Even worse, he'd forgotten to find out who his audience was going to be. Having anticipated and readied himself to talk with a crowd of a few hundred adults about discipline, when he finally got to the church and bolted down the aisle to the front, he was shocked to find that he would be speaking to an audience that consisted solely of junior high students. One of Dobson's first experiences with a major extemporaneous speech also became one of his most painful.[1]

He quickly got wise to the importance of audience selection and preparation. Dobson "didn't necessarily want people to go listen to him again if they'd heard him before on the same subject," says Peb Jackson, who was an account executive with a public relations concern that helped promote Dobson's early appearances. "But I never got tired of him; I could listen to him speak on a topic ten times, and it would never get old." One reason that Dobson preferred associates and friends not to attend his addresses again and again was that the very purpose of his intense speech preparation was to be able to grab the audience at opportune moments with a story, a phrase, an appeal that would induce genuine emotion, and he simply didn't want the audience to be peppered with people who had heard him share the same illustrations. For him, that was like telling a joke to someone who had heard it.

This was true pathos, because Dobson came to the conviction early on that his audiences really *needed* to hear his messages. That's why Dobson never strayed into lip-quivering and other histrionics. Yet, he badly wanted to reach his listeners. A smattering of tears in the crowd would tell Dobson that he had achieved his objective of communicating on a gut level with those who had come to see him. *Lord, do it again*, he sometimes prayed before a speech, asking God to touch his audience deeply.[2]

☙❧

Mac McQuiston was well acquainted with teeming crowds of Christians. He had been an advance man for the Billy Graham Evangelistic Association, organizing citywide committees of churches to sponsor and promote the movies produced by Graham's World Wide Pictures unit. But that was nothing compared with what he was about to experience, beginning in 1976 when he took over a marketing firm as the agent for a talent named Dr. James Dobson.

At the time, Dobson was doing he-said/she-said seminars with Joyce Landorf, a family-oriented Christian author and speaker. The agency had paired them up for appearances called Family Forums at churches around the country. He'd talk about strong-willed children and what wives wished their husbands knew about women, and she'd counter with what women needed to know about men. But while the events were popular, they were inefficiently booked: McQuiston noted that, depending on the size of the market, Dobson and Landorf could have 500 people in the crowd—or 2,500. So, taking advantage of his experience with Billy Graham Ministries, McQuiston organized citywide events featuring Dobson and Landorf. The first one, in 1977, drew more than 1,200 attendees to a weekend seminar at a church in Santa Barbara, California.

Soon, Dobson was drawing even bigger crowds on his own—two to three thousand people a weekend. Many had read his books, were attracted by his plainspokenness, or had heard about him through the informal networking among evangelicals. Charging about twelve dollars a ticket for the events, which he called Focus on the Family, Dobson often generated revenues of $24,000 to $36,000 at a time. Dobson felt the money needed to be channeled into worthy causes, so he incorporated his ministry as a not-for-profit organization, also called Focus on the Family, and used it as a platform for donating much of his speaking proceeds to other ministries.

As Dobson's twelve-month sabbatical from USC School of Medicine and Childrens Hospital neared its end, he was faced with a dilemma. When he had applied for the sabbatical, he had committed to
return to his position within a year. But in spite of his pledge, he felt
that God was clearly leading him in a different direction. Dobson made
an appointment to see Dr. George Donnell, physician in chief of
Childrens Hospital and the department of pediatrics for USC School of
Medicine. He was surprised when Dr. Donnell spoke first.

"I know you promised to return to the hospital after a year, but I'm
not going to hold you to that commitment," Donnell said. "I've heard
about the interesting things you are doing and it would be unfair to
force you to return. I have a pediatrician I can put in your position."

Dobson was thrilled with the arrangement, agreeing to fill in
whenever they needed him. This allowed him to maintain his title as
clinical professor of pediatrics and his relationship with USC School of
Medicine and Childrens Hospital, but also freed him up to follow what
he felt was God's leading in his life.

When he left behind his full-time position at the university, he gave
up the familiarity of a field he knew very well, the comforts of being a
valued part of a large and capable staff, and the security of being backed
by two of the most respected institutions in Southern California.

"At that point, I had to decide if I wanted to pitch my tent with psychologists and psychiatrists and climb that ladder in secular circles, or
to try to influence parents and husbands and wives and the general public," he says. "And I specifically chose the latter. I had been in the other
world; I had written a number of articles for professional journals. But
I got less fulfillment out of that world than from feeling that I could
make a difference with people. That's the big change that occurred in
1977 when I left the university and opened Focus on the Family. It represented the choice to move in another direction."

It wasn't as if Dobson was coming in for a hard landing after leaving
behind the two-position, seventeen-year career. Actually, he simply
jettisoned one multipart career for another that he found much more
exciting. And whatever time vacuum he had created momentarily by
going on his own, Dobson quickly filled with more speaking engagements. He addressed crowds for three hours on Friday night and then
all day on Saturday, usually remaining on duty during break times,
meals, and even after speaking sessions so that he could offer bites of
counsel to the attendees who swarmed around him by the dozens.

Then he would fly home to Los Angeles from wherever he'd roamed and often spend a few days recuperating.[3] Naturally, the routine was punishing to his family as well as to McQuiston, who at times was working for Dobson on a nearly full-time basis. Dobson knew the pace was not sustainable. "His family was starting to suffer," remembers Rudy Markmiller, Focus's first big financial contributor. "He was espousing being a good father and husband and yet his schedule and what he felt the Lord wanted him to do took him away and started preventing him from being exactly what he preached."

Peb Jackson recalls that Dobson first started talking to him about his draining schedule on an airplane to Columbus, Georgia, for a Focus seminar. Dobson was in turmoil because he had just left home, and [seven-year-old] Ryan was saying to him in essence, "When are you coming home, Dad?" "Dobson said, 'This is violating everything I believe in. I have to do something about this,' " Jackson recalls. During that time frame he made a decision to stop speaking, even though as a communicator it could have affected his ability to earn a substantial living.

Once again, Dobson's progress had filled his schedule right up to a breaking point. One night in the spring of 1977, as James and Shirley Dobson prayed about a solution, Dobson felt led to a passage in Exodus 18 that he interpreted as speaking directly to him. In the story, Moses was working too hard settling disputes among the Israelites all day, so his father-in-law, Jethro, told Moses that he needed some help. "If you do this and God so commands, you will be able to stand the strain, and all these people will go home satisfied," the end of the passage reads.[4] Dobson didn't know exactly how God would satisfy the thousands of people who were clamoring to hear him speak, but he knew what he had to do.

The demands of serving Dobson's booming ministry had taken up about half of McQuiston's schedule, leaving him little time to focus on other projects. But the agent didn't foresee what was coming when the two had lunch the next day at the Marie Callender's restaurant on Baldwin Avenue in Arcadia, a short distance from Dobson's home and the offices of James Dobson Inc., the legal entity he had set up previously as a base for his independent ventures. Dobson bluntly told McQuiston that he had decided to cancel all but two of his speaking engagements for the entire next year. The stunned McQuiston was speechless. "Mac, *say* something!" Dobson implored.

"I didn't question it because I knew his walk with God, even though [the decision] was painful for me," McQuiston recalls. "He said he'd prayed about it and God had spoken to him and he needed to be with his family more. But he said that God didn't deal with one side of an equation without dealing with the other, meaning that he wasn't going to leave me out. God was going to show me what was to come." Indeed, in the space of another year, McQuiston would join a booming Focus on the Family as its first executive vice president and chief of staff, the first of two long stints with the ministry.

But it still wasn't clear how Dobson would satisfy everyone else.

⟡

An answer was quick in coming. A few weeks later, Dobson told Francis Heatherly about his decision to stop speaking, not sure what the implications would be for his relationship with his second publisher. Heatherly suggested that Word videotape one of Dobson's final seminars and produce a series for churches.

Dobson rejected the idea at first. The cost was one issue: McQuiston figured a budget of $30,000 would cover filming, and another million dollars would be needed to produce and distribute the seven film sets.

"This video project will cost a fortune, and I don't want your blood on my hands," Dobson said, fearing that it would be a flop. But the Word people were adamant, and McQuiston was willing to put his shoulder into the deal even though, at the time, he believed it might help land him in the unemployment line. Dobson hadn't canceled what was to be his next-to-last seminar, planned for early 1978 in San Antonio, where he already had been widely hailed for a speech he delivered a year earlier. McQuiston booked him for the auditorium at Trinity University, which held about three thousand people and whose layout was ideal for filming. "We had a great event chairman and a very good committee, and there was lots of enthusiasm," McQuiston says. Things were coming together. "I knew we would sell out. I thought, 'This is the place.' I told Word that's where we should film it."

Yet when the day came, it didn't seem as if even $30,000 would yield what Word, McQuiston, and Dobson had been hoping for. The lighting and sound were primitive even by the standards of the era. In fact, lighting glitches almost botched the videotaping process entirely, delaying Dobson's entry into the arena by about fifteen minutes. McQuiston recalls, "It was time to begin, and Dr. Dobson said, 'We can't keep these people waiting any longer.' I said, 'We've got to film this,' and ten minutes later he said he was going out anyway. I said, 'Just give us ten more minutes,' which he did. And finally they fixed it." It was a harried Dobson who finally took the stage.

Word used only three cameras, compared with a multiplicity of lenses that would be used to preserve such an event today. The images were recorded on a single video track that was contemporaneously edited by McQuiston, meaning that the seminar got on tape basically like a live event, with limited options for tidying up in the post-production process. "I was going to sit in the truck where they controlled all the cameras, and I'd tell them when to pan the audience because I knew when people were going to laugh or cry—I'd been with him long enough to know just how the audience was going to react," McQuiston says.

Even after what McQuiston and Dobson perceived as a successful event that was well captured on video and after they'd flown to Word's headquarters in Waco, Texas, to observe some editing, Dobson's doubts persisted. "I don't believe people will sit for seven hours and watch one man speaking on a screen," he told a cadre of Word executives who had flown to Arcadia to encourage him across the finish line.[5] Having already invested nearly $100,000 in the venture overall, the publishers harbored their own doubts. But they also saw an opportunity to leverage Dobson's popularity into a whole new medium that they hoped would, in turn, sell many more books. Everyone's fears were based on the simple reality that, indeed, nothing like this had been tried, and there was no guarantee that the typically frugal evangelical-church board would invest a few hundred dollars or devote a series of Sunday night services to one-man presentations on family living displayed on 16-millimeter film.

Nevertheless, McQuiston was convinced immediately that the video series, which had been named Focus on the Family after the seminar title, would do well. "I'd seen how well it had been received live and that it was meeting the needs of the audience."

Soon, aided by some effective marketing by Word, Focus on the Family created a unique phenomenon in Christian communications. Millions of people, the vast majority of whom had never read a word written by James Dobson the author, flocked to churches on a Sunday evening to watch this remarkable character known as James Dobson the orator. Word also created a Betamax version of the tapes that made use of the earliest VCRs. Focus even created a one-hour TV special out of the third film in the Word series, *What Dad Needs to Know about Fathering,* and called it *Where's Dad?* Focus constituents and others sponsored its airing in dozens of local markets across the country, and the special made it to military bases around the world and into a Spanish version. The ministry had to hire more than two hundred people within a three-month period of 1981 just to fulfill the demand for resources and information created by *Where's Dad?*[6]

Within a few years, Focus estimates, more than one hundred million people worldwide had seen the film series.

In the ensuing several years, the multimedia ministry of James Dobson and Focus on the Family grew in every dimension, including the continued strong attendance at churches that were showing the video series. His fast-growing radio program was greatly swelling audiences that previously had been built by word of mouth. In 1982, Dobson wanted to tape an updated video series, so he began hitting the road again to speak on a limited basis. And this time, Shirley Dobson joined the program as well.

As always, Dobson was haunted by the possibility that, even after everything he had accomplished and even after people had clearly demonstrated their eagerness for his prescriptions and stories, God might shut him down. In a sense—then as always—Dobson never was completely removed from the pressures implicit in such responsibilities.

"Almost as if he were going to be entering a track meet and there were stakes, he felt that he needed to work out," Peb Jackson says. "So he practiced.

"We'd decided that the first major event should be in Fort Wayne, Indiana, where there was a bedrock of Focus support," Jackson explains. "Jim was very skeptical about holding a large-scale event, though. He had never spoken to more than three thousand people at a time and could envision himself being in an eight-thousand-seat arena with a dozen lonely souls sitting in one corner, listening to him and Shirley talk. I tried to put on my best face and let him know it would be okay. And it was. We were inundated with reservations and commitments, and subsequently had trouble filling all the requests. It was an exciting time." There was no reason to worry; the arena was sold-out within twenty-four hours of ticket availability.

Indeed, it was clear that God had not shut down Dobson. In fact, fueled by the synergism of a multifaceted ministry and a persona that never wore out its welcome, more people than ever wanted to come and hear James Dobson in the flesh. The twist of adding Shirley to the program, *An Evening with James and Shirley Dobson*, only increased the intrigue, as she discussed the trials of growing up in a home broken by alcoholism and the healing that she found in God. The couple filled or nearly filled not only the Fort Wayne auditorium but also venues with about fifteen thousand people in Seattle, thirteen thousand in Phoenix, nineteen thousand in Denver, and eleven thousand in Boise.

Finally, after the Dobsons had assured themselves during more than two years of on-the-road refinement that they actually had a presentation worth preserving for the ages, Word taped the series *Turn Your Heart Toward Home* in front of more than sixteen thousand people shoehorned into Cincinnati's Riverfront Coliseum in March 1985. And in subsequent years, an estimated forty million people would flow to their churches to see that presentation as well.

CHAPTER SIX

THE VELVET
MICROPHONE

We needed to do thirty minutes a day.
He just had more to say.

JON CAMPBELL,
CHRISTIAN-RADIO EXECUTIVE

James Dobson can't stand Phil Donahue. But the silver-haired liberal talk-show icon could take an ironic form of credit for catapulting Dobson to success.

Donahue, of course, is the Cleveland-born media man who, in the seventies, became the original king of daytime talk television and established a model for Oprah Winfrey. While on a TV station in Dayton, Ohio, Donahue had come up with a revolutionary concept: a talk show for "women who think." Typical daytime fare on local television in those days was light and domestic, featuring a pleasant host, cooking and exercise segments, and the occasional past-his-prime crooner. But Donahue was determined to get more out of his audience, so he talked about substantive subjects ranging from current events to homosexuality to marriages in crisis. He allowed members of the studio audience and even telephone callers to ask questions as well. His first guest, in 1967, was Madalyn Murray O'Hair, the celebrity atheist. The formula worked so well that in 1974 Donahue moved his show to Chicago, called it *Donahue,* and began to syndicate it nationwide.

At the peak of his popularity in early 1978, Donahue was trying to schedule a show on spanking, a reliable topic for generating controversy. He already had lined up a representative from the permissive school that retained the upper hand in academia and the media. Dobson, well-known for *Dare to Discipline* at that point, would make a nice counterweight, the host thought, so one of Donahue's producers contacted Dobson and asked if he would appear on the show.

By that time, Dobson was already fully accustomed to appearing on television. In the late sixties, on a lark, he and Shirley went to a taping of the game show *Let's Make a Deal*. Host Monty Hall sashayed into the studio audience and selected contestants who had dressed in weird costumes to attract his attention. Shirley pasted cloth birds all over herself and wore a sign that said "My husband is for the birds." Hall came to her and Dobson with a chance to win a new Chevrolet Camaro. "We were poor as church mice because I'd been paying school bills and had just finished my Ph.D.," Dobson says. But they got "zonked" in their subsequent effort to make a deal with Hall.

By the early seventies, however, Dobson's TV mien had grown much more professional. He made frequent appearances as a child-rearing expert on talk shows in California, including Regis Philbin's show in Los Angeles. Dobson was asked to talk about raising children on a series of shows that were hosted by ABC's Barbara Walters. Benjamin Spock and Jonas Salk were also included on her panel of high-caliber experts. Just after *Hide or Seek* came out in 1974, Dobson went to New York City to appear on seventeen shows and interviews in two days, including an appearance on the game show *What's My Line?* Increasingly, Dobson was being recognized as a sort of male counterpart to Dr. Joyce Brothers, a well-known psychologist at the time.

Dobson even gained some experience dealing with a difficult host before Donahue came courting. He was becoming a regular on *The Dinah Shore Show*, but that ended, he says, when the famous hostess declined to hold up one of his books in front of the camera, as promised. "She was a prima donna," Dobson says. "I don't quite know whether she thought the same thing about me."

But in 1978 when Donahue wanted him, Dobson was much busier than he had been even a few years earlier. So, pleading the press of other duties—and also fully conscious of Donahue's contrary sentiments on spanking—Dobson declined the invitation to appear on his show. "I knew the program was likely to turn into a 'circus of controversy,'" he says.

But Donahue persisted, calling Dobson in person later that afternoon and trying hard to convince Dobson that he would be evenhanded. Dobson finally relented. For the sake of convenience, Dobson also scheduled another appointment in the Chicago area for the same day.

Dobson flew into Chicago along with a gathering February blizzard and took a cab to Donahue's studio downtown. "Everything Donahue told me proved to be wrong," Dobson recalls. In the first place, after Donahue polled his audience to find out how many of the women in attendance believed in spanking, nearly all of them raised their hands in support, but the host selected two women who opposed spanking to open his show. Then Donahue gave his antispanking guest, also a child psychologist, every minute of the opening segment to state his case against spanking without as much as a nod to Dobson. Aggressive and on the attack, Dobson's opponent scored heart-and-mind points with lines such as "Children are people, and people are not to be hit."[1]

"And I'm still sitting there; I haven't said one word," Dobson remembers. "At about that point I decided I ought to contribute, so I volunteered and began making one of my points—and Phil Donahue cut it off in midillustration and left it hanging. No one knew what I was saying. It was downhill all the way from there. He didn't give me any opportunity to speak. My confidence shook, and it was the worst performance of my life. I had an excuse, but who cared? The whole nation saw me not being able to articulate my point of view. And it bothered me a lot, especially because Phil Donahue hadn't been straight with me."

A crushed Dobson slouched back to his room at the Hyatt Regency Hotel at O'Hare Airport amid the mounting snowfall and subzero temperatures. Standing at the window watching the blizzard—and, as he joked later in a vintage Dobsonian nugget, "trying to decide whether to jump or not"—he asked the Lord why he had allowed him to look so bad on a stage that was so big. The clear though inaudible answer reminded Dobson of the many Christian servants who had sacrificed much more on the altar of their faith: *What makes you think you're always going to come out looking good? And besides that, it's my business. Quit worrying about it.*

And indeed, a few hours later, Dobson drove to nearby Carol Stream, Illinois, and recorded the trial run of what would become the first *Focus on the Family* radio program in the studio of a radio-advertising representative. "That was the beginning of the entire ministry," Dobson says. "What I saw as a disaster, in my frustration, was the beginning of what is going on today."

As his frustration with the personal and professional limitations of live speaking appearances mounted in 1976—and before the videotaping of his seminars offered a partial solution—Dobson began to consider the idea of getting out his message by radio instead. "I felt that the Lord wanted me to do radio," he recalls—and many of his friends agreed. But lacking the funding to get started, Dobson came up with a twist: He would offer publishers the rights to his next book, *The Strong-Willed Child*, in exchange for a grant that he would use as seed capital for a radio program. Dobson figured he needed thirty-five thousand dollars to get going. Though some publishers demonstrated little enthusiasm for the idea, Kenneth Taylor, president of Tyndale House, had learned to trust Dobson's judgment. Besides, his most popular author had stopped asking for advances after *Dare to Discipline*, so this was the least he could do. Taylor took up Dobson on the offer and referred him to Doug Mains, who headed his own radio marketing outfit, the Domain Agency, in Carol Stream. The studio was located in the miniature Bible belt of evangelical residents, publishers, and colleges in north- and west-suburban Chicago.

In 1977, the world of Christian radio was much different than it is today. The whole marketplace remained a quaint backwater, echoing the early days of general radio broadcasting, when just about anything that went out on the airwaves had been considered good enough—because there was nothing else with which to compare it. Christian broadcasting consisted almost entirely of studio-produced tapes of rehashed Sunday morning sermons, which the sponsoring ministries typically would cut up into fifteen- or thirty-minute segments and wrap with a short introduction and conclusion, including an appeal for contributions. Producers paid anywhere from twenty-five to two hundred dollars a day to place these commentaries on mainstream stations, or on the small but growing number of full-format, Christian-owned and operated stations, which inevitably were low-powered, low-budget affairs. At a time when the spread of cable delivery was revolutionizing television, the wizardry of technical special effects was recreating the movie business, and the Top 40 pop sound was sweeping secular radio, Christian radio remained largely an anachronism.

"It was pathetic; it was an embarrassment to the cause of Christ," asserts Moegerle, who eventually became executive producer of Dobson's radio program, a senior vice president of Focus, a primary fund-raiser, and a board member. "It was often unthinking. It lacked production values, because American evangelicals didn't seem to value artistry. When you're more than happy to worship in a converted grocery store, you don't miss the stained glass. You got the same impression from listening to Christian radio then." Moreover, Moegerle feared, the business actually seemed poised for deterioration, because the industry's key players—evangelical broadcasters including Martin DeHaan, John Jess, and J. Vernon McGee—were aging. "No one knew where the next generation was coming from."

Dobson seemed to have the right stuff to do something fresh and different with this medium, so he looked at the chance as "a dream come true," recounts Moegerle, who began handling *Focus* as a client for the Domain Agency after having worked in the radio advertising business for several years. "I'd wanted to try to find some small way, as one person, to help change things in Christian radio, and when I met Jim, I knew almost immediately that my relationship with him would be my opportunity to do that. And sure enough, he shattered the mold, and from the moment he stepped in, his standard was sky-high. He knew communication, how to hold attention, how to appeal to emotion, and how to tell a story."

But *Focus* didn't immediately find a smooth track when it debuted in the form of a fifteen-minute weekend program on March 26, 1977. Mains and Moegerle had done yeoman's work to leverage their reputations in the business to get thirty-four mainstream and Christian stations around the country to take a flyer on Dobson—whom most secular radio executives certainly had never heard of—and his idea for a radio show. Yet the length of the show became an issue from the start: It wasn't long enough for Dobson to say anything substantial and still spare a few seconds to appeal for funds. "Weekly programs were a dying breed," says Christian radio executive Al Sanders. "Because of the way radio was changing, audiences had gone to a daily experience with broadcasting, and weekly programs were losing their appeal."

Dobson agreed, but because he still was wrapping up his commitments to USC School of Medicine and Childrens Hospital, he felt he couldn't spare the time to do any more. Sanders, a Christian radio-marketing pioneer, had an idea. Sanders met Dobson in early 1978 at a Seattle rally led by Charles Swindoll. Dobson was at the rally to promote his last few seminars. Through his Los Angeles–based Ambassador Agency, Sanders represented a fledgling radio show hosted by Swindoll, the pastor of a large evangelical church in Fullerton, California. A talented expository preacher who deftly used humor and anecdotes, Swindoll had become a force in Christian radio by airing tapes of

the dynamic pulpit presentation of his sermons rather than studio per-
formances—a twist that fully unleashed his skills and energy as a
speaker.

When they all returned to California, Dobson met with Sanders at
his Arcadia office. "Dobson was a bit discouraged because he was nearly
out of money from the Tyndale grant, and his show wasn't paying its
way," recalled Jon Campbell, Sanders's son-in-law and associate, who
died in the summer of 2005. "'What do we do?' he said. We suggested
daily radio, and we said he needed to do *thirty* minutes a day, not fifteen. We knew that longer formats build relationships more quickly
and help with long-term positioning. Plus, they weren't that much
more expensive than producing and placing fifteen minutes."

The broadcast also experienced some false starts with what went
out on the airwaves. "As we talked about the on-air sound, we were
convinced that, if two people could have a genuinely animated conversation with each other—with the microphones eavesdropping—that
the radio listener would find that absolutely fascinating," says
Moegerle. "Philosophically, it seemed as if there was a contradiction
there, because you'd think that if someone addressed you head-on and
talked to you, you might feel more interested because it was suppos-
edly direct communication. But we found that people loved to listen to
two or more people who were really going at it."

At first Dobson attempted to create this two-way communication
with a female cohost on the radio broadcast, just as he had in his speaking ministry. Moegerle recruited Flo Schmid, a professional announcer, radio actor, and the mother of five children, for that role in
the early broadcasts. She and Dobson would join Mains at his studio—
including that first day in February 1977—with Schmid asking the
questions and Dobson answering. Sometimes they also recorded in a
studio in Glendale, California, near Dobson's home and office. But
from the start of this new approach, the conversational give-and-take
they were looking for didn't happen. In an effort to improve the dynamics, Moegerle arranged to have Dobson and Schmid sit on the same
side of the table, both looking at him in the control booth; but all that
did was keep them from the visual cues that they got from sitting across
from each other. "Something about the chemistry never came
together," Moegerle says.

The interest in Dobson was so high that Word put together a collection of tapes of that first year of broadcasts and was able to sell sev-

eral thousand copies to churches. But Dobson and Moegerle started to think that the kind of talk they needed on the air was something similar to their lunchtime banter. "Contrary to feeling any intimidation, I loved to talk to him," Moegerle recalls. "I was a father of three kids, and I was in the middle of the types of dilemmas that he tackled in each broadcast. I would just come up right out of my chair, saying, 'You're kidding! That's how you solve that?' There was energy and a real-life give-and-take, and that's what we wanted."

In retrospect, Dobson believed that God was lining up the circumstances like dominoes for *Focus on the Family*'s breakthrough to take place. It was just up to Dobson to topple the first piece.

Once Dobson had finally severed ties with USC School of Medicine and Childrens Hospital in mid-1977, he became impatient for the radio program to progress rapidly, so the growing pains were distressing to him. Then, within a period of little more than two years, he made a series of decisions that turned his prospects completely around.

First, in late 1977, Dobson made Moegerle—who was still working for Mains—his cohost, beginning a highly effective on-air relationship that would continue for nine years. Second, in 1978, he switched his account from Domain to Ambassador, Sanders and Campbell's agency, which was closer to his home in California. That led, within a few years, to Dobson's third significant decision: to approve daily programming, which began in late 1981.

Though Dobson had given up most public speaking, he still felt caught in a personal time vise, so at first he remained adamant about sticking with fifteen-minute segments even though they would be aired daily. For several months, in fact, he taped thirty-minute segments, and then Moegerle and Mike Trout, a radio production engineer who worked for Ambassador and later would join the ministry, edited them into two 15-minute segments, giving radio stations an option. Soon, that wasn't working either.

"There just wasn't enough takeaway value or listener impact from a quarter hour compared with a half hour," Sanders says. "A half-hour program typically can be devoted to setting up a problem in the first fifteen minutes and solving it in the second fifteen minutes." Added Jon Campbell, "We weren't even a year down the road when Jim said that we needed to do thirty minutes a day. He just had more to say."

The relationship with Ambassador also led to the fourth consequential development for Dobson: joining forces with Charles Swindoll, Ambassador's hottest client. Ambassador began packaging Swindoll's *Insight for Living* and Dobson's *Focus on the Family* as an innovative hour's worth of programming, and the fit proved symbiotic. A significant overlap began to develop between Dobson's listeners and Swindoll's, and the two Texans hit it off personally as well. "They were both putting cookies on the lower shelf so that people could relate to Christian radio much more readily and personally," Campbell recalls. "They just took things to another level in terms of being contemporary, relevant, and very gifted communicators. They became a tremendous one-two punch, which not only helped each of their ministries but also gave more credibility to Christian radio generally."

Focus on the Family continued to grow at a meteoric rate. "It became the broadcast that any Christian station wanting to be successful had to have," Sanders says. "As a pivot point in their format, they had to have *Focus on the Family.*"

Yet Dobson hadn't cemented his path until he made a critical fifth decision, which involved refraining from a temptation. By the early eighties, Dobson had become such a bright light in Christian broadcasting that he was being eyed by secular talent scouts as well. One night in 1983 he was a guest for a two-hour block on Larry King's graveyard-shift radio show for Mutual Broadcasting System. Based on that performance, executives from Mutual invited Dobson to try out for his own slot, which would entail hosting a program similar to and adjacent to King's. Mutual even had a sponsor lined up that was willing to take on Dobson: Purex bleach. Mutual's president, Marty Rubenstein, said to Dobson during a meeting in his Washington office, "If you accept this offer, I will make you a very wealthy man."

Dobson tried out on a Sunday night, and he performed well, with many of his *Focus on the Family* fans calling in to lend their support and ask questions. Mutual extended the offer of a permanent slot, but Dobson concluded that it was a siren's call, and he refused the offer. "Christians called in, and that made me uncomfortable because I couldn't answer them in the same spiritual context that I would on my show; it just wasn't appropriate for network radio," Dobson says. "I might have reached a larger audience, but I didn't worry about that. And accepting Mutual's offer would probably have been the end of Focus on the Family."[2]

The net outcome of these five decisions was the creation of a powerful momentum for *Focus on the Family* by the early eighties, as the number of stations carrying Dobson's program grew. By 1982, the program was aired on nearly two hundred stations. Five years later, that number had already climbed to nearly eight hundred. By 2003, it aired on more than two thousand stations across the United States and hundreds more around the world. Foreign affiliates were excerpting, scripting, and then translating the program into French, Russian, and Spanish and broadcasting on hundreds of stations across Europe, the former Soviet Union, and Latin America. Dobson also recorded daily, ninety-second *Commentary* spots that by 2003 were carried by about three hundred general-market radio stations across the country, including major outlets such as WOR in New York City and KNX in Los Angeles. He also recorded similar snippets that were seen on about eighty television stations around the nation. The short radio spots were heard in English in cities worldwide, including Singapore and Johannesburg. Similar concise commentaries were translated into eight languages and aired in several countries, including Argentina, Indonesia, and Slovakia.

"The human family is the same everywhere, and they all respond to that warmth," Dobson says. Yet aggressively expanding his radio audience internationally was an idea that Dobson wouldn't embrace for many years. "When we started the international division of Focus in the early eighties," says Jim Daly, current president and chief executive officer, "[Dobson] was very concerned that his middle-class, American value structure had no relevance overseas, and he didn't want to be perceived as trying to build some kind of global empire. So he just backed out of it. But once he got evidence of the response to *Focus on the Family* radio outside North America, he began to accept that he had something relevant to say to other cultures." And even though Dobson did not have the time to speak much abroad in person, his lack of personal appearances actually worked advantageously in many countries—especially those with non-Western cultures, where humility is highly valued, Daly says.

Eventually, this groundwork would help produce a truly global network for *Focus on the Family*. Today in China, where most of *Focus*'s 220 million listeners abroad live, staffers in Los Angeles are able to sufficiently contextualize about 70 percent of the Dobson commentary scripts. The staff then records them in Mandarin and airs them on huge state-run outlets, including China National Radio and Beijing National Radio. As a result, "Dr. Doo," Dr. Dobson's on-air name in China, is a well-known family expert. "It's still limited access," Daly says, "but at least we've earned the right with the government to speak on a variety of issues there." And as the Chinese have taken to Dobson's radio commentaries, doors have opened to other Focus programs there, such as training in premarital counseling. The broadcast has become a vital part of a millennial push by Christian ministries in China, and some experts believe that push could result in that vast communist nation's becoming a Christian—or at least a Christianized—country within a decade or so.[3]

Focus on the Family hasn't quite reached the international ubiquity of Coke or McDonald's, but the name still pops up in places that surprise Westerners abroad. For example, Ravi Zacharias, an American evangelist and Christian intellectual, told Focus executives in late 2003 that he had been in a shopping mall in Malaysia, a Muslim country, at around nine o'clock one evening when the intercom blasted out a promotion for the *Focus on the Family* commentary on a local station.

"Have you ever listened to that?" he asked a young saleswoman, who said she hadn't. "You should," Zacharias continued. "It will help your family and your life."

৩৩৩৩৩৩

Many observers with varying perspectives have tried to dissect Dobson's radio appeal.

Some cite his unusual ability to multitask. "He's listening to a person and is focused on them during the show, but there's always a portion of his mind that is analyzing the broadcast even then," says Bobbi Valentine, who was executive producer of *Focus on the Family* for most of two decades. Dobson has a computer in front of him and can press a number of keys that instruct producers what to do; occasionally, his coworkers say, he even types commands in complete sentences in the midst of an interview. "He'd have his heart totally involved in the conversation, his heart breaking for someone, but he was still able to tell the producer what he needed," Valentine says. "It sounds like a contradiction, but he has compartments in his mind. Most people can't do both; they lose connection with the guest."

Others stress Dobson's penchant for quality and his attention to detail, including the effectiveness with which he taps the ever-growing catalog of anecdotes he started in 1957. "I'd be amazed how we'd be in the middle of some tapings, and he would have a reservoir of unbelievable memories of things that would be pertinent to what we were doing," says Gary Bender, a network TV sportscaster who filled in as Dobson's cohost for the first half of 2001. "It would seem to come out of nowhere, not be premeditated or preplanned."

Dobson is highly deliberate about word choice, even when taping an interview for a show that he can have edited. "Live radio actually can be easier because it's out there and gone, so in a way you can't be as concerned about choosing your words as carefully," says Bill Maier, who began hosting the ministry's weekend radio magazine in 2002. "But in taping a section, you have to stop and start a lot, and there's a certain skill to that so you don't throw off a guest." John Fuller, Dobson's permanent replacement for Bender as cohost and Focus's vice president for broadcasting, says his boss "doesn't mind looking for a word or grasping or struggling a bit. He comes across as genuine that way."

At the same time, Dobson works hard to make the honing of his delivery come off as unscripted. "He said being natural means you're going to repeat, stumble around, sometimes rephrase things—not be perfect, like reading a script," Gary Bender says. "When he first started, he said he had a terrible time trying to be natural, to be a communicator who didn't sound as if he was reading something. But he got to the point where he understood who he was, that he could do it, and do it in a special way."

Ambassador owner Al Sanders notes, "He's just a perfectionist. When we started working with him, he'd be taking a whole day just to do one program. I said he could probably do eight of them in a day. But I was wrong, and he was right, because that care was what made his program so distinctive." Later on, Sanders says, he tried to get Dobson to take a page from a number of successful radio broadcasters—from Larry King to Howard Stern to Don Imus—who have allowed live cameras into their studios and broadcast the proceedings on cable television. "Again, that wasn't possible because of the desire that he has to achieve and project perfection on his program."

Dobson still devotes considerable time to the craft of communicating, and recently he began transmitting his philosophy to Maier and to other new, complementary voices. When Dobson and Maier were filming a video series on parenting in 2003, for instance, the mentor noticed that Maier, who had spent most of his media career in radio, would seldom break eye contact with the camera. "One thing that you have to do to make yourself more relatable and to be more conversational," Dobson told him, "is to occasionally look down and break eye contact with the camera, just like in conversation."

More than anything, however, Dobson emphasizes the effective generating and channeling of emotion. Trading on it is especially tricky because if he ever had come off as insincere and manipulative of his guests or his audience, Dobson's appeal would be for naught. What he manages to do is optimize the impact of genuine emotions.

"Usually if he's critiquing me," Maier says, "he'll say the content was great, very educational—but where's the pathos, the heart, the emotion? Recently I was doing a show on foster care, and he complimented me on the show. But then he played the tape back and said, 'Right here,' when that woman said such and such, 'you could have said something empathetic like how hard that must have been for her.' He said, 'Make sure you go for the pathos. That's what makes good radio.' That's why his own radio shows have been so compelling, with such memorable interviews."

Ambassador executive Jon Campbell said that Dobson "has a high believability quotient, which begins with his passion. He is genuine; he is sincere; he has a wonderful humility and a servant's heart, yet strength—and that's a unique combination. Those components are just downright powerful." More clinically speaking, he adds, "What *Focus on the Family* did was bring programming that had depth and stability that was fresh to the fullness of the body of Christ, let alone to the culture of the day. Jim taught that biblical principles applied in the high takeaway environment of the culture at large. We'd had lots of wonderful [radio] Bible teachers over the years, but not someone teaching God's precepts so relevantly"—and mostly in the highly relatable context of family and relationships.

Still others isolate Dobson's speaking habits and the instrument of his voice itself as his most valuable assets on the radio. Regular listeners are familiar, for example, with his occasional, folksy tendency to drop the *g's* in words ending in *-ing* or how he throws a slight pause—just the tiniest of hitches—into a phrase in what seems to be a spontaneous bit of hesitation but which is often deliberate.

Some admirers grasp for descriptions of those qualities of Dobson's voice that make it unique, but the exercise is like trying to cage a hummingbird. There's a bit of a provincial tone that bespeaks his origins in the Southwest; an underlying, sonorous tenor; an avuncular, crackling timbre that is reminiscent of the TV actor and pitchman Wilford Brimley; and just a hint of a nasal twang of the sort that made the late Mason Adams, the longtime voice of Smucker's jam commercials, so interesting to listen to. In fact, such is the warmth and distinctiveness of Dobson's voice that one imagines—if he truly ever runs out of other things to do—he could make a great living as a voice-over man for TV commercials.

Strong topics and content obviously have been crucial factors in *Focus on the Family*'s success as well. Somewhere in the more than seven thousand shows that had aired through 2003, *Focus* touched on nearly every aspect of the human drama, family relationships, spiritual life, and the social, cultural, and political backdrop that influences life in America. Nearly every significant leader from across the spectrum of evangelicalism sits to chat with Dobson, as do celebrities ranging from the late Reggie White, the spiritually uncompromising pro football Hall of Famer, to former president George H. W. Bush.

But based on listeners' requests for tapes, the most popular broadcasts feature Dobson interviewing relatively ordinary people dealing with extraordinary circumstances, such as Guy Doud, a compassionate, award-winning Christian teacher whose story first aired in 1988, and Kyle West, who was born with cerebral palsy and told Dobson in a 1999 show about his desire to become a missionary.

Dobson, an early master at integrated marketing, gives plenty of airplay to discussions of his own books, but he doesn't hold the microphone jealously. "Rival" family-oriented authors, including John Trent, Gary Smalley, and Dennis Rainey, are frequent guests, as are many other Christian authors and speakers.

The format almost always involves a guest or two in the studio or an entire panel of people, conversing with Dobson and his cohost. On some occasions, Dobson simply turns over the half hour to play a prerecorded tape of some especially powerful presentation. Dobson doesn't open up the show to phone calls from listeners, partly because the program is broadcasting continuously throughout the day in local markets. And Focus staffers can't recall his ever having simply delivered a half-hour monologue except on tapes of his speeches.

Dobson has always maintained a good deal of flexibility in the schedule, too, especially in the last fifteen years, so that he can turn on what might be called his constituency switch. If the debate over a cultural issue is climaxing in the media or if a new bill or court decision in Washington is changing the cultural landscape or if a TV network or some giant advertiser is pushing the envelope of decency again, Dobson is quick to shuffle his schedule so that he can urge his callers to rain down phone calls on Washington or Procter & Gamble or CBS. Listeners don't seem to resent the element of unpredictability that stems from whatever has inflamed Dobson's passions at the moment; it is one of the reasons so many tune in.

As Dobson's career became a legend, of course, he and his broadcast also benefited increasingly from the simple fact that he was, well, Dr. Dobson. "Being who he is at this point, he can be interviewing a peer and it's not an issue," Maier says. "He can interrupt Charles Colson, if he thinks it adds to the flow of an interview. It's more difficult for me to do that."

Alan Keyes, former Republican presidential and senatorial candidate, says Dobson's strength is in his sincerity. "Eloquence isn't just about words and how you say them," says Keyes. "It's a lot about what you're saying and who you are. Dr. Dobson's great strength is who he is, that people who are listening to him are taking his words to heart, not because he says them with a certain inflection or superficial linguistic elegance. It's because they know this is a man of character and that his words come sincerely from his heart."

CHAPTER SEVEN

DEAL WITH A DEVIL

*Ted [Bundy] was exhausted. He hadn't
slept for several nights. His face was
washed of color, stained of tears. He was
thin, even frail-looking, and he wore two
shirts as if he were already trying to shut
out the chill of death.*

ANN RULE, IN *The Stranger Beside Me*

Despite the success of his books, his radio show, and the ministries of Focus on the Family, James Dobson was facing a crucial professional crossroads as the eighties drew to a close and he turned fifty years old. The titanic forces of federal and state governments, Hollywood, the news media, and other major institutions seemed to be grinding down the American nuclear family and the traditional values he held dear. In response, Dobson had begun weighing in—on *Focus on the Family,* in his monthly newsletter, and through the occasional media interview—on important political, moral, social, and cultural issues that were facing the nation.

At that point, Dobson had managed rather dexterously to do so largely without making himself a lightning rod for critics of "the Christian right." As *U.S. News & World Report* noted in 1989, "Dobson's is not a household name."[1] As much as possible, the fact that he still remained somewhat anonymous in the secular world was a product of his own design. Dobson was trying to alert his constituency about urgent public-policy matters while at the same time preventing himself from becoming too tempting a target. He realized the media might begin attacking if he raised his profile too high, if he seemed too eager for contention, or if he said something that would allow himself to be painted as an extremist. So Dobson disciplined himself to be careful, even as he was forthright in his public comments about most divisive matters. Given how much was at stake, he was determined to be on his guard.

As was his routine since the early days of his ministry, fifty-two-year-old Dobson continued to set aside regular segments of prayer time during his day. He still recalls asking God specifically to protect him from making any sort of misjudgment that might fracture what he had accomplished already or discourage his supporters and damage the cause of Christ.

Then Ted Bundy came along. That January in 1989, across the country from Dobson, the most heinous murderer in American history sat in a tiny cell in Starke Penitentiary in Jacksonville, Florida, doing some praying of his own. After two decades of playing a diabolical game of cat and mouse with police and prosecutors, the forty-two-year-old Seattle native finally confessed to brutally killing at least thirty-eight young women—and he was probably responsible for dozens of other murders as well. As January waned, the death-row celebrity seemed to be trying to settle his accounts on earth and also wrestle with the question of his eternal fate. Yet while he still may have retained influence on his afterlife, Bundy's earthly options were definitely running out. Finally, on January 17, Florida governor Bob Martinez signed the death warrant and scheduled Bundy's execution for the afternoon of January 24.

Before Bundy could breathe his last, he and Dobson would rendezvous for a short, intense, and bizarre season, each searching for a kind of validation in the other—the two men made unlikely but resolute allies by the issue of pornography.

For as Bundy grappled with the roots of his savagery, he said he wanted an outlet he could trust to communicate a message to the world: Violent pornography had helped drag him into depravity, and it could do the same to other susceptible young men. He chose an interview with Dobson for delivering that message. Dobson, meanwhile, had opened himself to the possibility of just such a conversation after his recently completed service on a presidential commission that thoroughly investigated and unequivocally condemned the hard-core porn industry. He believed that an exclusive interview with Bundy could underscore in a dramatic way the vicious toll exacted by smut purveyors who seemed to operate with impunity in this country.

Dobson and Bundy struck a deal: Dobson would interview Bundy about the controversial role of pornography in Bundy's life and crimes. Bundy had a right to hold a general press conference as well as to grant a single interview to the person of his choice in his final days, but he chose to forego answering reporters' questions, speaking only to Dobson.[2] According to the agreement, Dobson was free to do with the tape whatever his conscience and his cause led him to do, provided that all of the money generated would go toward the fight against pornography.

The twenty-nine-minute interview occurred in the late afternoon of January 23, just nineteen hours before Bundy was executed by lethal injection. After his execution, there was a continuing cloud of predictable speculation, not only about the role of pornography in feeding his bloodlust, but also about his true motives for giving Dobson the interview, how many more women Bundy actually might have killed, whether he truly had repented of his almost incomprehensible sins, and whether or not he had come to a saving faith in Jesus Christ.

For Dobson, the agreement with Bundy also created a gamut of high stakes, emotionally charged circumstances, and significant events—the going price for placing himself in a vortex of history. He was pressed on every side by reporters and producers. Dobson received nine hundred requests for interviews in a three-day period. Some members of the media made wild financial offers, even up to $500,000, for an exclusive interview with him about Bundy's final message to the public. Dobson was also assailed mercilessly by critics who charged that he had been duped into facilitating a final, profoundly cynical bit of self-aggrandizing theater by one of the greatest con men who had ever lived. They said that in the psychologist's desire to strike out against violent porn, he had himself been blindsided.

Before the spectacular episode was finished, Dobson demonstrated to his broadest audience a supple sensitivity as an interviewer, a willingness to clash with the secular media, and a determination to follow his convictions to the end. The crucible also highlighted in a completely new way some of Dobson's profound passions: his righteous anger at sin, his compassion for the repentant, and his deep concern for the eternal destination of any human soul—even one of Satan's errand boys.

When the swirl created by the macabre and sensational turn of events finally subsided, Dobson concluded that he indeed had done the right thing. But he would never be the same, and neither would his role on the national stage.

ᘏᘏᘏᘏᘏ

By the mideighties, Dobson had begun to feel limited by the constraints of a ministry that essentially amounted to preaching to the choir. And as the enemies of everything that he held dear became more power-ful—the abortion industry, the homosexual lobby, radical feminists, the mainstream news and entertainment media, and sundry other secu-larists—Dobson was becoming hounded by the conviction that maybe it wasn't enough for him to help shore up the family one household at a time. He wondered if his voice could also have some influence in the arena of politics and policy, where he believed antifamily forces had be-come increasingly entrenched. He already had found jumping-in points, beginning in 1980 when President Jimmy Carter appointed Dobson as one of hundreds of delegates to the White House Confer-ence on the Family and later, to a small task force that summarized their findings. The presidency of Ronald Reagan opened the public-policy door wider when Attorney General Edwin Meese spotlighted the issue of hard-core pornography and established a commission to in-vestigate the industry and its considerable criminal links.

In April 1985, Meese appointed Dobson to an eleven-member commission that would study the effects of pornography on individu-als, the family, and American society at large.

It was a given that the conservative-leaning group would overturn the findings of the first presidential commission on pornography that had been appointed by Lyndon Johnson nearly two decades earlier. Johnson's liberal-dominated panel essentially had concluded that por-nography was beneficial as a marital aid, as a source of information about sex, and even as a form of catharsis for the sexual tension that was increasingly evident in the culture.[3] After lengthy hearings in six U.S. cities, the Reagan commission discovered that under the sheen of such soft-core material as *Playboy* and *Penthouse* magazines—which defined pornography in the minds of most Americans—a pernicious hard-core porn industry had taken root and was thriving rather surreptitiously. A huge market had developed in sex shops and elsewhere for material with, as Dobson put it, "a heavy emphasis on violent homosexual and lesbian activity."[4] These materials included sadomasochism, bestiality, scatological fetishes, and self-mutilation—as well as so-called "snuffer films" in which actors and actresses, both voluntarily and unwittingly, were actually murdered as part of the filming of sex acts.[5]

The commission concluded that about 85 percent of the multibillion-dollar pornography industry was controlled by organized crime, especially the Mafia. And the commissioners provided a road map for mobilizing law enforcement against the industry.

As a student of the human mind, Dobson became especially riveted by another tie between criminal behavior and pornography: the role of the most perverse materials in encouraging serial rape and murder. He was intrigued by a study coauthored by John Douglass, who was at the time the FBI's chief profiler of multiple murderers. The study noted that 80 percent of American serial killers had used pornography at one time or another. "We heard testimony from many [men] who got hooked on hard-core porn through the doorway of soft-core porn and walked through that progressive experience leading to harder and harder, more violent material and eventually coming to a place where they crossed the line from fantasy to reality," Dobson says.[6]

Related to this little-recognized problem, Dobson believed, was a news and entertainment media establishment that turned a blind eye to the ravages of the porn industry. Media executives cited First Amendment concerns for their unwillingness to attack porn publishing, but Dobson believed that the libertine ethic of America's cultural elite was even more to blame. He specifically saw a stonewalling of information about the role of hard-core porn in encouraging killers. "Don't tell me there aren't strange men watching [the most extreme materials] and thinking, *I could do that*. I don't understand why the secular press is so determined not to let that connection be known," Dobson said later. "Suppose it's only one out of every ten thousand men who are susceptible to the blood-sodden excitement provided by hard-core pictures and movies," he said. "That's hundreds of thousands [of men] in the U.S. and Canada."[7]

By the time he had completed his service on the pornography commission in the summer of 1986, Dobson had spent much of the preceding fourteen months analyzing the work of pornography kingpins and adult-movie stars, and he was relieved to ease what had been a very intense focus on the subject matter. It had been "the most difficult and unpleasant responsibility I have undertaken in my adult life," he said later.[8]

What Dobson didn't know was that the pornography monster soon would come back and attempt to consume even more of him.

⁓⊶⊷⊷⊶⁓

By definition, serial rapists and killers are off-the-charts individuals. But Theodore Robert Bundy was a singular creature even among this tiny minority. He grew up in what he later described as a "solid Christian home" with two wonderful parents in the state of Washington. But from the start, bright little Ted lived in a construct of lies. He was born in 1946 in a Vermont home for unwed mothers to Eleanor Louise Cowell, and as her family strove to protect that secret, Ted Cowell was raised to think of his mother as his "older sister" and to refer to his grandparents as his parents. Eleanor Cowell changed the boy's surname to Nelson because it was common, and she moved to live with relatives out West. In 1951, she married a Tacoma cook, Johnnie Culpepper Bundy, who adopted Ted. The confusion of those early years sewed "a lot of hostility" into the psyche of the boy who became known as Ted Bundy—"a lot of power issues," according to John Douglass, the FBI profiler who served as the lead analyst in the cases of Bundy and many other serial killers.

Throughout the sixties and seventies, as Bundy completed high school, graduated from the University of Washington, dropped out of law school, and nurtured a career as a Republican political aide, he was also ruthlessly killing attractive, unsuspecting females one at a time. His modus operandi was to snatch them off the street or date them, secure their affections, and then turn on them. Either way, he ended their lives by brutally assaulting or raping them, or both, then murdering the victims and often disfiguring or dissecting the corpses.

After more than a decade of losing a spectacular game of wits with their brilliant—and often mocking—prey, the police finally caught up with Bundy in February 1978. He had murdered two Chi Omega sorority sisters on the campus of Florida State University in Tallahassee. A few days later in Lake City, halfway between Tallahassee and Jacksonville, he kidnapped and then killed a twelve-year-old girl, Kimberly Leach, who earlier that day had been elected first runner-up to the new Valentine Queen at Lake City Junior High School. Finally, in the early morning of February 15, a patrolman stopped a suspiciously moving orange Volkswagen Beetle. After determining it had been stolen, the officer chased, subdued, and arrested the fleeing driver: Ted Bundy.

Bundy was smart and suave, but he had committed the biggest mistake of his criminal career by getting caught in Florida, where the death penalty was often the punishment of choice. And once he began confessing to and sharing details of his killings a few years later, the clock to execution began running down for Ted Bundy. At that point, Bundy shifted relatively quickly from trying to avoid responsibility for his deeds to attempting to influence how he would be perceived after his death.

He also may have been affected in a strange way by the 1977 Utah execution of Gary Gilmore, who was accused of murdering a motel owner and a gas station attendant. Gilmore's death was the first death by execution in the United States in ten years, and it became the focus of an enormous amount of attention for years afterward, including Norman Mailer's book *The Executioner's Song*.

Ann Rule had gotten to know Bundy by working side by side with him at a telephone crisis hotline for women in Seattle during the sixties, and she later wrote her own book about him. She believed that while he stewed in prison, Bundy became "jealous of all the publicity that [Gary] Gilmore was getting. And I knew that if the day ever came when Ted saw the shadow of the death chamber and knew his time had run out, he would want to go out in a glare of klieg lights and with his last words ringing in everyone's ears."[9]

But Dobson, as well as others who knew Bundy, had a different view, especially John and Marsha Tanner. The state prosecutor from Miami and his wife regularly ministered to inmates in Florida prisons, and they had befriended Bundy in 1986. Over the next two and a half years, the Tanners spent a total of no fewer than six hundred hours with the killer, talking with him, praying with him, building the closest possible thing to a normal friendship with the most celebrated inmate on death row. Like so many others before them, they found Bundy communicative and articulate, and they gradually managed to tap into his introspective tendencies as well. Among other things, they learned about what they came to regard as a sinister trinity that both enabled and intensified Bundy's bloodlust: pornography, alcohol, and possibly demonic possession.

As Bundy began to reckon with his death, John Tanner recalled, he gradually focused on trying to understand the first of the three factors and determined that he wanted the world to do the same thing. Bundy said he was certain that pornography had contributed to his own sick makeup and the commission of his crimes. And as a voracious reader and student of current events, Bundy also had come to believe that society underappreciated the power of pornography to spur on killers like himself. After learning of Dobson's service on the presidential pornography commission, Bundy read the two-thousand-page report and asked Tanner to inquire about the possibility of an audience with Dobson.

"Bundy didn't respect the press, and he was afraid they'd distort his message," Dobson said later. "He'd read my books, knew I was a commission member, [and] had respect for me. And he asked, when that time came, if I would interview him to make sure the message got out." Dobson also later said, "He had read the whole [presidential] report on obscenity. I was in total agreement with his concerns. He wanted to talk to me because he wanted the world to know what had led to his murderous rampages, and to warn parents about it happening to their own boys."

Once Dobson responded positively to Tanner's initial inquiries, Bundy wrote a nine-page letter detailing his recollections and insights on the issue and sent it to Dobson via John Tanner in August 1987. The appeal of Bundy's proposal was hard to miss.

"I'm not sure if you could ever feel honored by a serial killer," says H. B. London, who has remained a close confidant of his cousin. "But in a way [Jim] felt honored that Bundy had developed confidence in him that, if he talked to Jim, at least someone would hear what he had to say in his last days."

Peb Jackson, then one of Dobson's top aides, says that his boss "obviously was concerned about the role of porn in anyone's life, let alone an aberrant [life], and here comes a poster boy for exactly what Jim saw as the extreme end of what could happen if you get hooked on this stuff."

Nevertheless, from the start, the decision about whether to get involved with Bundy was a difficult one. Dobson and his advisers clearly recognized the potential for anything more than a cordial brush-off to become problematic for him and his ministry. The tone of one initial discussion, Jackson says, was, "Do we really want to do this? Do we really want to associate our name with the horrific Ted Bundy in any way? People were saying it was just Bundy's trying to justify why he did all this. Jim's position was, 'Sure, just like anybody probably would. But the facts are that pornography played a big role, and this is something the public needs to hear.'"

So Dobson told Tanner he was willing to strike a deal with Ted Bundy; and when the time came, he would fly to Florida to fulfill it.

৩৩৩৩

All of the parties, including the Tanners, had agreed that it would be a good idea for Dobson and Bundy to get somewhat acquainted before the cameras started rolling. But Dobson had never been enveloped by anything like the tunnel of death he first entered at Starke Penitentiary on the evening of January 22, the night before his formal interview with Bundy. To get to the inner sanctum where Bundy was being held, he and the Tanners had to pass through seven steel gates, each with a checkpoint manually operated by a guard. To get through the metal detector at the third gate, the three had to undergo a procedure that, after September 11, 2001, would become routine even for airline travelers: shedding belts, shoes, tie tacks, and any other metal objects that might trip the detector. Finally, they made their way to a visiting room where they were separated from Bundy by a glass wall with a built-in microphone.

As they started to talk, Dobson said later, it became clear that Bundy was "very agitated and upset. He had been confessing all day, and he was emotionally distraught and exhausted." Other advisers and friends, Tanner explained to his guest, had been urging Bundy to "go to his grave silently," in an attempt to preserve a shred of what dignity he retained. At the same time, Tanner said, Bundy was being interrogated for up to eighteen hours a day during those final weeks, because as his list of confessed crimes grew, authorities pressed even harder for leads and details about other unsolved crimes that could be tied to him.

Dobson and Bundy met and then discussed in person, for the first and last time, their decision to do the interview. Bundy repeated for Dobson the clear profession of Christian faith that the Tanners, by then, had heard so often. "He was about to be executed, and he was scared and upset from having recounted all those horrible murders," Dobson recalled. "He was just going through a very difficult time. But I supported his execution, and I never told him otherwise. And before I left, I said, 'If you don't want to do anything, there will be no hard feelings. What would God have you do?'"

Bundy replied, "Tell the truth."

"Well," Dobson responded, "that settles it, then." He walked up to the glass between him and the prisoner and put a hand up to it, the closest thing he could think of to an affirming handshake, and a haggard Bundy matched the gesture on the other side. Dobson left the Tanners there with their condemned friend.[10]

Bundy had actually changed his mind a few days before Dobson's visit, deciding to conduct a final press conference with a small group of reporters, but then he had another change of heart and canceled the conference. That turn of events underscored yet again the unique access he was giving Dobson. But at that late hour on January 22, after securing a final commitment from the exhausted Bundy, Dobson didn't commit himself to release even so much as a partial transcript of what would be said the next day, much less a videotape of the complete encounter. "We wanted to be confident," Jackson said, "that this was the genuine thing."

And there was another factor: Dobson's own doubts about whether he wanted to carry through with the whole arrangement. These doubts had accompanied him on the plane to Jacksonville from Los Angeles, persisted through his time with Bundy and the Tanners on January 22, and even awakened with him the next morning, the day of the intended interview. "I was in the hotel, and I just didn't want to go do it," he said. "I wasn't feeling adequate for it. To step into that prison and come out with the media all over me, I knew was going to be tough. As I was getting dressed that morning, though, it was as if the Lord said to me, *I sent you here because I knew that you could handle it. That's why I chose you for it: I knew you could do it.* And with that, I just went out and did it."

⁙

The interview was held in a lunchroom at Starke Penitentiary. Wearing a long-sleeved T-shirt under a peach-colored prison work shirt, Bundy was brought in, handcuffed and surrounded by four guards. Dobson was told not to touch him, but he did shake Bundy's hands—both of them because of the handcuffs—briefly. Bundy was clear-eyed and alert. Dobson noted to himself that Bundy appeared "much more confident" than he had the evening before. Bundy was wearing a wedding ring on the fourth finger of his left hand, representing his marriage several years earlier, after he already was in prison.

Then, with one camera on Dobson and another on Bundy, and several prison guards on the perimeter, the actual interview began. In an appropriately sober tone, yet with the relaxed nuance that Dobson's radio guests found so inviting, the psychologist began by asking, "Ted, what is going through your mind right now?" Bundy sighed slowly, then answered: "For the moment, I'm feeling calm, in large part because I'm here with you."

But Dobson wasted little time on niceties and proceeded to get to the meat of the interview, leading Bundy into a several-minute discussion of what Dobson called the "antecedents" and the "roots" of Bundy's murderous behavior. He immediately focused on the role of Bundy's admitted addiction to violent pornography.

"I take full responsibility for whatever I've done and all the things I've done," Bundy said, looking directly at Dobson before closing his eyes and dropping his head. "That's not the issue here. The question and the issue is how this kind of [pornographic] literature contributed and helped mold and shape the kinds of violent behavior [in which I engaged]."

Bundy said that hard-core pornography fueled his actions, "creating a kind of separate entity inside. It's like an addiction. You keep craving something that is harder. And then you reach a jumping-off point." Moral and practical barriers to barbarism, even in his own life, "are assailed by a fantasy life fueled by porn. [Porn] was an indispensable link in the chain," Bundy explained.

Then Dobson shifted into what could be interpreted as a more sympathetic mode. He asked Bundy how he reacted after his first murder. "It was like coming out of some kind of horrible trance or dream," Bundy answered, "to have been possessed by something awful and alien . . . and to wake up and in the eyes of the law and in the eyes of God to be responsible." And while not solely blaming pornography for his depravity, Bundy opined that "pornography can snatch a kid out of any house today" and that slasher movies and other cable TV fare were nurturing future serial killers.

Dobson probed further. "You really feel this deeply, don't you, Ted?" Tears welled up in Bundy's eyes as he asserted that all of the violent men he had known in prison were into pornography.

"What would your life have been like without that influence?" asked Dobson. Again tearing up, Bundy answered, "It wouldn't have involved the kind of violence that I've committed, I'm certain."

Having accomplished the bulk of his mission, Dobson finally edged closer to the soul of Ted Bundy. Dobson asked Bundy to help him understand the desensitization of conscience that had allowed him to kill. He asked Bundy if he felt remorse. Then, in much the same way he asks his radio guests to describe their feelings about a given situation, he asked the killer what he felt after murdering Kimberly Leach. "Where were you, Ted?" Dobson said, the emotional pitch of the interview rising. Bundy responded softly, again appearing to fight back tears: "I can't talk about that."

Awhile later, near the end of Bundy's composed and articulate remarks, he noted without apparent self-pity that "it gets kind of lonely [in my situation]." Then Dobson reminded him that every human eventually faces death. "It is appointed unto man . . . ," he said, citing the first few words of Hebrews 9:27 and assuming that Bundy knew that the verse went on to say that every person dies once, then faces God's judgment.

∞∞∞∞∞

By closing the interview in this manner, Dobson made it clear that he had been partly motivated, as H. B. London says, "[by hoping] to make an impression for the good of the man" and perhaps to encourage Bundy to solidify his commitment to the Lord while there was still time. The Tanners and others had told Dobson that they believed Bundy genuinely had adopted and expressed a sufficient faith in Christ. But Dobson wanted to be sure Bundy fully understood his need for a Savior.

Later, Dobson reprised his conflicted feelings this way: "To those who say that Ted Bundy should burn forever in eternity, I would only say, 'So should I. So should all of us.' None of us deserve eternal life. It's a free gift. You don't have to earn it. And it's not more difficult for God to forgive Ted Bundy than it is for [him to forgive] me. It's simple repentance and believing on the name of Jesus Christ. That's what we teach. Do we believe it?"

Dobson was forever moved by his time with Ted Bundy and felt compassion for the tortured man who had confided in him. "When I said good-bye to him that night," he recalled, "and they took him down the hall with his hands cuffed behind him, and he turned around and said good-bye to me and I knew he was going to his death—as much as [it] was deserved—it's still an emotional experience to be one of the last people to talk to a person who's been condemned to death."

Late that evening, the Supreme Court called Bundy to let him know that his final appeal for staying his execution had been denied. Several hours before his execution, in the early minutes of January 24, the Tanners spent nearly an hour and a half with Bundy, praying and taking Communion. They didn't have the common elements of bread and wine or grape juice, so they improvised, locating some tomato juice and peanuts with the help of prison guards. As they said good-bye, Bundy told them that he was going to "meditate on God's Word and take a nap."[11]

Five hours before he was killed, Bundy called his mother in Tacoma. Her son insisted to her, "a part of me was hidden all the time, but the Ted Bundy you knew also existed." In a house packed with friends trying to ease her through those dark days, Ted's mother said her last words to her son, "You'll always be my precious son. We just want you to know how much we love you and always will."[12] He spent his final hours with his lawyer and a Methodist minister. At 7:02 a.m., he was led into the execution chamber. At 7:16 a.m. on January 24, Ted Bundy was dead.

To Dobson, the scene outside Starke on the afternoon and evening of January 23 evoked images of a lynching or a medieval beheading as protesters, mostly hostile to Bundy, milled and vented.

"I like my Ted well-done," read one placard held aloft outside the prison. "Toast Ted," read another. In all, some two thousand spectators gathered before dawn, noted the *Washington Post*. "They laughed and hooted, and after it was all over, they cheered."[13]

Dobson understood the cathartic effect of Bundy's execution for Floridians and for many Americans —especially the families of Bundy's victims. Yet he was disturbed by the kind of "frivolity" at the scene that reminded him of "a football weekend at an Ivy League school" and, at the same time, by a ghoulishness that he could compare only to a Nazi concentration camp. He said, "It is not funny to take a human life. There is nothing humorous about it. There is nothing that warrants a celebration, even when it must be done. It must be done with dignity." The experience was horrific, even surreal, for Dobson, who said it's "never to be forgotten."

Even more troubling to Dobson was the horde of media people, many of whom were there to wait for him to emerge from his time with Bundy. "There were three hundred reporters and nineteen satellite uplink dishes," Dobson estimated. "People were waiting for any word at all." More satellite-uplink trucks showed up for the Bundy deathwatch, Peb Jackson was told, than for any other news event in Florida history.

This radio "preacher" from California was unknown to nearly all of the secular press, and Dobson had remained frustratingly elusive to them even as he moved center stage in this riveting and historic drama. "People who were upset that he got the [exclusive interview] were saying that Bundy was going to pull the wool over this guy's eyes. I told people, 'Do you understand who this James Dobson is?' They kept calling him 'Reverend,'" Peb Jackson says. "I would ask, 'Do any of you know what PKU is? James Dobson was a research professional even before he was in the field he is in now.' They couldn't handle that. Professional newspeople just couldn't make the leap that this guy wasn't a reverend. They were trying to compartmentalize him."

Nevertheless, Dobson remained their only conduit, not only for the pornography angle on the Bundy story, but also for any sort of last glimpse of the man. "[While Jim] was inside getting the interview, I was outside negotiating with every news service you can imagine," Jackson recalls. "They all wanted an exclusive, and many of them were offering big money, jets to come down to pick up the tapes and maybe a couple of hundred thousand dollars to Focus on the Family for an exclusive of that tape. But we made a decision that we didn't want to go that route or be seen as capitalizing on the effects. So we made the decision to give the tape to everyone at the same time, to no one exclusively. The only provision was that the tape would be aired in its entirety—not edited."

Dobson emerged from the interview confident that releasing a tape of the entire conversation was the right thing to do, believing that Bundy's comments and the manner in which he delivered them would leave little doubt that hard-core pornography had played some significant role in catalyzing his violence.

Yet in the immediate aftermath, Dobson began to realize that wasn't necessarily the message that the world would receive. The epiphany came in his appearance that evening on a local TV station in Jacksonville, where other psychologists ridiculed Dobson's contentions about the role of pornography in Bundy's crimes. Dobson himself had compounded the difficulty of the situation because that appearance was the only interview he gave right away. "Everyone and their dog wanted that final interview [with Bundy], and here Jim comes out of left field to get it," Jackson says. Then, by turning down countless dozens of other media requests for interviews after his time with Bundy, Dobson seemed to fan the press's resentment.

Soon Dobson would experience the mighty wrath of the powerful national media establishment that he had scorned.

Although Dobson had no desire for personal profit, he has never doubted the value of the Bundy interview in the fight against pornography. For one thing, Focus on the Family raised a substantial amount of money to fight pornography from sales of the videotape at twenty-five dollars a copy. Nearly all were sold within a year of Bundy's execution, with donations totaling more than $964,000 for tapes. After Focus deducted $361,000 to cover the costs of production, reproduction, and mailing, the ministry distributed more than $600,000 to several antipornography organizations scattered around the country and one in Great Britain. "These tapes are circulating today in homes, churches, and schools across North America," Dobson wrote in early 1990.[14]

Dobson also remained convinced that the interview furthered the understanding of how the slippery slope of pornography is constructed, with soft-core porn at the top, often leading to hard-core stuff and eventually down to a ghastly bottom that very few people ever see.

H. B. London agreed with his cousin. "I don't doubt that Bundy was psychopathic and a con man to the very end. However, I don't discount some of the things that he said just because he was a con man," London says.

While Dobson never wavered, he did spend part of the next few months openly wrestling with the importance of his encounter with Bundy. "Some of our listeners are tired of hearing about Bundy," he conceded on a May 1989 radio show that featured his interview with the Tanners. "[But] it's extremely important to get a window into the mind of this terrible killer."

Inevitably, the tape received substantial airplay—in snippets on evening news broadcasts and in its entirety on Maury Povich's talk show and other venues. In the days and weeks after Bundy's execution, however, Dobson became seared by how the secular establishment, almost without exception, interpreted what they saw on the tape and how they presented what had happened in that dining room at Starke Penitentiary on the afternoon of January 23. The way Dobson saw it, his critics basically divided into three streams: those whose vocational attachment to the issue prevented them from admitting he was right; those who had a very personal stake in ensuring that Dobson's viewpoint about pornography didn't prevail; and sociocultural pundits whose supposed sophistication inevitably led them to skepticism. Of course, Dobson's skeptics said they opposed his conclusions because he was wrong and because they thought he was only trying to promote himself, his own controversial views, and his ministry.

Some experts were troubled because they discounted Bundy's analysis of his own demons. The killer's self-assessment was far less valid than that of outside experts because "his own view is biased by an elaborate set of rationalizations," wrote Dr. William Wilbanks, professor of criminal justice at Florida International University in North Miami, just a couple of weeks after the execution. He also asserted that Dobson's antipornography crusading biased his view of cause; that the porn-leads-to-violence theory had been discredited by researchers, even some that the Meese Commission had relied on; and that the idea of an "addiction" to pornography let people off the hook and helped lead to a culture of victimization that also validated "addicts" of food, gambling, and shopping.[15]

Another small portion of the expert camp entailed the serial-killer experts, who uniformly scoffed at Bundy's assertions and criticized what they saw as Dobson's spreading of yet another big lie by the clever killer. Bob Keppel, a Washington state investigator who had tracked Bundy for nearly fifteen years and met with him for several hours during Bundy's final days, said with certainty in a quote to the *Associated Press*, that Bundy's interview was "totally self-serving" and that the only remorse the killer had felt was for himself. He believed that Bundy, until the very hours before his death, was still trying to manipulate a stay of his execution.[16] Dobson countered by reminding Keppel that during the videotaped interview, Dobson asked Bundy if he deserved to be put to death. Bundy replied, "I deserve, certainly, the most extreme punishment society has."

Ann Rule, who went on to become a true-crimes author because of her friendship with Bundy, said she "didn't believe what Dobson got Ted to say." While alcohol and pornography might be catalysts to the commission of crimes by sexual sociopaths, she said "the real causes go back to their childhoods and their genetic predispositions. So Dobson's interview was nothing but glossing over the real causes with pat platitudes and surface causes that supported his teachings. Sociologically and psychologically, there were no gifts to the body of knowledge that might help us understand serial killers. To me, it was a sideshow akin to an old-time traveling evangelist blaming the devil for booze and sex and sin."[17]

John Douglass's research had helped Dobson reach his conclusions, but even the FBI profiler says that Bundy was just like nearly every other serial killer he had probed: "They never accept responsibility for their crimes; they always project blame. It's 'Poor me. Someone else, *Playboy* or *Hustler,* is the one you should go after, not me. I'm a victim.'" He noted that serial killers frequently have aspired to enter fields such as law enforcement, counseling, and even the ministry, "so they tend to know all the buzzwords and what to say and what the person is looking for" in a situation such as the Dobson interview. "But the tears you'd see from Bundy really would be tears for himself. He just couldn't identify with the people he killed." Once more, Dobson points to the actual interview: "How can Douglass assert that Bundy sought to avoid responsibility for his crime when he said specifically, 'I take full responsibility for whatever I've done . . . and I think society deserved to be protected from me.'"

Dobson opines, "That's quite an admission for a man nineteen hours from execution, if he was trying to escape the death penalty."

Not surprisingly, pornographers went on the attack. Among the mildest rejoinders was that by the publisher of the porn magazine *Screw,* Al Goldstein,[18] who wrote in the *New York Times* editorial pages: "James Dobson is a psychologist and sophisticated enough to know the logical fallacy he is promoting: Ted Bundy used porn, Ted Bundy kills women, therefore all porn-users kill women."[19] *Hustler* publisher Larry Flynt threw epithets at Dobson and singled him out for ridicule in two consecutive issues of the magazine.[20]

But not even the pornographers got as mean-spirited as media commentators. Their collective thrust was downright spiteful. Typical was Michael McWilliams, TV critic for the *Detroit News,* who smugly opined that Dobson had obtained the interview "not just to pull off his journalistic coup" but also "in order to score points for his reactionary sexual politics."[21]

H. B. London believes that professional jealousy was at work in the media as well. "The big networks would have given anything to have gotten that last interview," he says. "And here was Jim Dobson, the little Christian-radio personality, being granted it instead. The fact that he got the interview catapulted him into a whole new level in the media."

Dobson's refusal to conduct an endless round of media interviews about Bundy—and his insistence on simply letting the tape speak for itself—clearly worked against him in the media game. But he also believes that his message was ill received in large part because it put at risk the vast fortunes of segments of the media that feature sexually explicit material.

He did receive some pointed support that figured into the media coverage, including calls and letters from thousands of listeners and other fans who reacted angrily to the negative treatment of Dobson. The NBC affiliate in Denver got so much flak that the station issued a retraction of one of its stories, beginning with the words, "We blew it."[22]

And Dobson himself fired right back at what he perceived as shoddy treatment. "It amazes me that the press says [pornographic] material will not influence a psychopath like Ted Bundy," Dobson said on a radio broadcast in May 1989. "Psychologists and psychiatrists around this country ought to be ashamed of themselves for saying it."[23]

∽⌇⌁⌇∼

Nevertheless, the sting of essentially having his thesis rejected by the nation's entire secular milieu—and the even greater specific insult that somehow he had been bamboozled by a murderous psychopath—sobered Dobson greatly. He recognized that his previous strategy of trying to be as honest as possible about his views, while at the same time keeping his head down, was a flimsy duality that would no longer work if he was to remain true to his beliefs and to his calling.

"His burgeoning notoriety and name recognition made it inevitable that he'd have to speak out," Peb Jackson says. "He has a hard time mincing words, and he made the decision that he needed to be more front and center on the issues. So he determined that he would do more interviews with the press."

Dobson agrees that the episode "had a major impact on me. Before that, I was intimidated by the press. [I felt] pretty powerless to do anything. For example, after the pornography commission made its report, Bob Schieffer [of CBS News] came and interviewed me. I was eloquent, but I got just six seconds on the evening news surrounded on both sides by comments by [*Playboy* founder] Hugh Hefner. From the point of the Bundy interview on, I've not been intimidated by the press. I say what I believe and let the chips fall where they may. I am what I am."

CHAPTER EIGHT

A BORN ENTREPRENEUR

*Focus on the Family is an empire and
an army [Dobson] built one mother
at a time.*

REPORTER JOHN HOCKENBERRY,
ON ABC's *Day One*

James Dobson likes to think of himself as an eager and gifted communicator but also as an indifferent, and even reluctant, business builder. Everything about the phenomenal growth of Focus on the Family, he has said repeatedly, stems from God's blessings upon the ministry and not from some grand plan that Dobson hatched and executed to build a worldly empire.

"It was strictly a function of need," Dobson says. "We saw where the family was going and what the problems were, and we developed [programs] that addressed that. We never had a two- or a five-year plan, just like we don't now. To try to establish a long-range plan would have made something egotistical about it, and the Lord wouldn't have that."

Yet the reality is more complex than that. While Dobson certainly never set out to construct one of the largest ministries of the twentieth century, Focus grew to become that in large part due to Dobson's underlying work ethic. What drives him? A desire to affirm his father's legacy, his prodigious creative and organizational talents, and a dead-reckoning inner compass for directing the growth of the ministry. This evident success drew other highly talented people to join Focus on the Family and resourceful donors to back it, and each group made its own contributions to the ceaseless expansion of the ministry, establishing a vigorous cycle that persists to this day.

"I'm sort of a born entrepreneur," Dobson says, a description whose essential truth sometimes gets lost amid attention to his other accomplishments. He figures he got a substantial bit of this ability from his bloodline to his uncle Lamar Dobson, who helped James Dobson's grandfather run the family business of two Coca-Cola bottling plants in the South. "I loved the challenge of building this ministry. In my soul, I'm a problem solver."

His friend and early financial supporter Rudy Markmiller says that "for better or worse, the only way that Focus could have grown the way it did was [Jim Dobson's] style of leadership. And there's a lot of General Patton in him."

And springing from the very makeup of Dobson's soul, in the space of just fifteen years Focus on the Family did grow—from a tiny office and a couple of staffers to its status today as one of the highest-rated not-for-profit organizations in the United States in terms of its financial efficiency and fiscal integrity.[1]

Far beyond the daily radio broadcast, Focus on the Family also airs other regular programs, supports a huge video division, and publishes magazines that reach more than two million readers each month. The ministry provides millions of monthly bulletin inserts to churchgoers and sponsors conferences on topics ranging from the challenges of being a teenager to the angst of homosexuals going straight. Focus on the Family also supports many other ministries and influences U.S. public policy through affiliates such as the Family Research Council and state-level grassroots organizations.

"I'm continually blown away by how many things they're doing," says George Barna, a California-based pollster and the foremost researcher of America's evangelical Christian community. "It's like an onion. There really is a very strategic and very fully orbed center of activity that's going on there that even the average Christian doesn't know about."

And at the core of the onion remains what's also closest to Dobson's heart: the organization's ability to respond to the needs of many thousands of people who write or call Focus on the Family after being prompted by something they heard on a broadcast or read in a book or saw Dobson present in a cable television interview. Ministering to these people—one by one and relentlessly so—remains the lifeblood of Focus on the Family and a main reason that many staffers continue to stick with the organization. Focus on the Family's attention to other people's needs in turn generates immense gratitude and often tangible support from those they've helped. "Some people write enormous checks and others write small ones," says Tom Hess, editor of Focus's *Citizen* magazine. "They can tell that Dr. Dobson and Focus care, and that is priceless to them. People will write you a million-dollar check if you save their marriage."

As the *Focus* broadcast built an audience in the late seventies, Dobson was resolute in his belief that everything that happened on the air would be for naught if *Focus on the Family* didn't close the communication loop with its listeners. Thus, one of the most important innovations that *Focus* brought to Christian radio was the effective intensification of a two-way relationship. In fact, Dobson invented a whole new paradigm for Christian-media communications—a model that also served as Focus on the Family's main engine of growth for the next several years. And the way that Dobson accomplished this, not surprisingly, was through the written word.

Only, in this case, it wasn't *his* words that were the instigator, it was his listeners' words. Dobson believed that if someone went to the trouble of writing to his program, someone at the program ought to take the time to read and respond to every letter. So, following a formula that the Domain Agency had helped develop, early on *Focus* began offering advice brochures and booklets to listeners who wrote in and made a donation. "You had to prime the pump, to get the listener writing and including a check in the envelope, so sending back some value was necessary," Gil Moegerle says.

Mail began trickling into the Domain Agency in Illinois, and secretaries there forwarded it to Dobson in California. Applying a formula that it had developed to help broaden other ministries, the agency also initially published Focus's newsletter, conducted its fund-raising, and managed its mailing list and other activities. But Dobson, sensing the importance of feedback from listeners who cared enough to sit down and pen a letter, wanted more immediate access to the mail. That's when he asked Mac McQuiston, his former agent, to come back to Focus on the Family as his chief of staff and shifted responsibility for correspondence to the ministry itself.

In the fall of 1979, McQuiston hired five people just to open and answer the mail that had begun streaming into the Arcadia office. By Christmas, his mail-handling staff already was up to nine people, who were processing as many as five hundred letters a week. Thus began years of exponential increases in listener correspondence with Focus on the Family.

"We knew almost immediately that Focus would have to do some form of counseling, because we knew we were going to touch subjects that would cause people to cry out for help," recalls Moegerle, who was in charge of Focus on the Family's broadcast operations. "Jim is the type of guy who refuses to walk away if he touches a nerve. He wants to take responsibility for helping."

About half the letters requested some type of response, and in the first year, Dobson attempted to answer them all himself. But the magnitude of that chore soon overwhelmed him. So McQuiston's staff began composing responses based on what Dobson would usually say; he would lightly edit them, and then they'd go out. "It was a real change in the business for people to get any kind of response," McQuiston says. "We would not only respond, but if they had some need outside our area of expertise, we would research it until we came up with something that could help them."

Soon Dobson developed prototype responses that he drew up from the vast outpouring of advice he was already generating. Correspondents were free to contextualize Dobson's wisdom, of course, and to make it specific to the case presented to them, but "if we came up with what he called a 'new thought,' he wanted to approve that personally," says Diane Passno, who joined Focus on the Family as one of its original employees, then became head of correspondence and in the midnineties one of the ministry's three executive vice presidents.

The mail has just kept growing since those days. Each day for the past several years, Focus on the Family has received an average of ten thousand letters, e-mails, and calls, which are handled by a response staff that now totals more than 350 people. After Focus on the Family occupied its new campus in Colorado Springs in 1993, local U.S. Post Office officials gave the ministry its own zip code—80995—without a moment's hesitation.

As in the early days, the majority of the incoming letters and callers are simply requesting a tape of a broadcast or a book that was mentioned on the show; usually a mailed-in request will include a check for the suggested "donation" amount that Focus has specified for each item. The requests for books written by Dobson or his guests, tapes of broadcasts, and other merchandise are fulfilled promptly by staff in the organization's 153,000-square-foot operations building that stocks about five thousand separate items at a time.

About 10 percent of all incoming communications require more personal attention, asking for advice or assistance on topics ranging from gambling addiction to toilet training, eating disorders to elder abuse, rape to teenage suicide. Most of them are funneled to the correspondence department. Focus stores each incoming letter and the notes from each phone call in a constituent's file in its computers so that the organization can carry on a relationship with the writer or caller—and so that any staffer can pick up where another one left off in the dialogue. In 2001, Focus implemented new technology that allowed a piece of mail to be digitally scanned and delivered to several departments at the same time to enable efficient fulfillment of multiple requests. All in all, the ministry has built the kind of comprehensive, multichannel "customer-relationship management" system that many for-profit companies spend millions of dollars and take years trying to perfect, often without anywhere near the same level of success. "We have incredible expertise in our data-warehouse operation that I would put up against anyone's," says Tom Mason, who was until 2005 a Focus on the Family executive vice president, and a former vice president at General Motors Corporation.

Sometimes callers and writers ask for prayer, and staffers distribute their requests among colleagues for individual or occasionally group intercession. A consistent handful of requests are even more urgent and some are requests for benevolence, which Focus discreetly gives out in extreme cases. Potential suicides, spouse abuse, child molestation, and other very serious cases—about seven hundred to nine hundred weekly—are routed immediately to a staff of eighteen state-licensed therapists who counsel callers, try to deal with their immediate concerns, then refer them to someone on Focus's list of more than 1,500 recommended Christian counselors throughout North America.

All of the constituent-response departments continued to operate under Dobson's very interested, if not direct, jurisdiction until 2003, when he delegated Focus on the Family's day-to-day operational responsibilities to Don Hodel, former U.S. secretary of the interior in the Reagan adminstration. Dobson still receives a weekly numerical summary of the types of mail Focus has received (as well as a digest of listener remarks about the radio broadcast). Diane Passno makes sure that letters of a particular caliber are copied to the boss: "stomach-grabbers," she calls them. As Passno puts it, "A lot of departments at Focus became a bit removed from him, but others he remains hands-on about, and correspondence is one. He cares about what we are saying, the standards we use, the materials we send, and the decisions we make about sending benevolence. Or if someone is suicidal, he wants to make sure that our counselors are hands-on."

ༀ◌⁀◌⁀◌ༀ

It takes money to fund phenomenal growth. Dobson provided his own capital at the start of Focus on the Family, using the proceeds from his early best-selling book, *Dare to Discipline*, and the Focus on the Family film series. Then the Tyndale House seed money helped mightily in getting *Focus* broadcasts off the ground, of course, and after the radio show got traction, listener contributions provided a growing cash flow. But those two sources alone couldn't put the ministry on sound, long-term financial footing, especially as it began to extend itself beyond the broadcast. Dobson was confident that the Lord would provide it if he truly wanted Focus on the Family to prosper.

The first major financial supporter was Rudy Markmiller. Once a penniless émigré from Nazi Germany, Markmiller founded Network Courier Services in 1971, a company that specialized in delivery of time- and security-sensitive parcels, such as body parts for a waiting surgical staff or high-priced computer components. In 1979, through his agency connections, Mac McQuiston had become acquainted with Inga Markmiller, Rudy's wife, an aspiring gospel singer. McQuiston learned about Markmiller's business success and found that he was not only a dynamic entrepreneur but also a devoted Christian. Dobson's chief of staff suggested that Markmiller and Dobson get together, so the two scheduled lunch in the Occidental Towers building in downtown Los Angeles.

Although Markmiller was still building his own company, he was eager to hear about Dobson's plans. "He just asked me to think and pray about [providing financial support to Focus]," Markmiller says. "He was open about what he was doing without being demanding; and he was so sincere. I asked a lot of questions, so lunch went an hour longer than planned. But he also was open about things that were on his heart—he had just put his mom in a nursing home in Pasadena—and for him to be that open with someone he didn't know, I felt that the Lord was in it." Most Christian leaders he had met, Markmiller says, "were established and [were] maintaining organizations for the sake of growing organizations. I hadn't met anybody like Jim." Markmiller wrote out a check for $10,000, which he says, "was a lot for me, too."

Peb Jackson was an early rainmaker. The scion of a fairly substantial Southern California real estate empire, Jackson met Dobson when he worked for the agency that booked Dobson's speeches in the midseventies. Dobson asked Jackson to join the first Focus on the Family board and then to come to Focus full-time as one of the first management employees. As vice president of public affairs, connecting with donors was a big part of Jackson's job description, and Dobson allowed him wide latitude in coming up with an effective approach.

But as with operations, Dobson made sure that the ministry's method of raising money was a direct reflection of his convictions, especially as it related to the listener base. One bedrock principle was that Focus on the Family wouldn't hype a need for contributions. "The idea of creating a 'crisis' to raise money was repugnant to [Jim]," Moegerle says. "He simply thought that if he wrote a real letter about what he thought was important each month and sometimes had to say, 'By the way, we have to have your support to keep doing this,' it might work—and it did."

Dobson's monthly letters thus kept supporters informed and provided Dobson a platform to make an occasional plea for financial support. One of the first such occasions was in early 1985, when Focus's income inexplicably dropped off by 50 percent at a time that expenses were rising rapidly, producing a deficit that approached a half-million dollars. In April, Dobson wrote to let listeners know of the need, projecting that Focus on the Family soon would have to start canceling airtime and laying off staffers if the situation didn't reverse. The letter produced the largest outpouring of generosity that supporters had ever demonstrated to the ministry, reducing the deficit by about half in just a matter of a month.

When the crisis had passed, some Focus aides didn't want to tell supporters about the improved situation, fearing an immediate drop-off in contributions. But Dobson insisted on sharing the good news in his May newsletter. The higher level of contributions remained steady, just as they did the next few times something similar happened.

The sophistication of Focus on the Family's fund-raising increased over the years, producing a ready supply of donors who stepped forward to pick up the cost of many of the organization's biggest initiatives. Ed and Elsa Prince, who owned a highly successful auto parts manufacturing company in Michigan, paid the $5-million cost of the new Welcome Center on the current Focus campus, for example.

Two donor foundations in Santa Barbara picked up the half-million-dollar tab for a new television studio that allows Dobson to make appearances on *Hannity & Colmes* and other programs without having to fly to a coast to do so.

Mac McQuiston made a personal quest to develop an area that Focus had always neglected: foundation grants. From just $600,000 in such contributions in 1991, McQuiston was able to raise the total of foundation awards to Focus to more than $10 million a year by 2001.

೧೦೧೧೦೧

While Dobson kept his hand in most areas of the ministry, he knew he needed the help of others. Two of those areas became apparent during the early years of the organization's explosive growth: fund-raising and operations expertise. Peb Jackson joined the staff to handle the fund-raising, and Paul Nelson came on to give insight and experience into operations.

Nelson was a former chief financial officer of Hill Petroleum. Once part of the nation's largest private energy enterprise, the company had been devastated by the energy industry's bust in the early eighties. Burned by his experience in the high-stakes world of oil, Nelson badly wanted to redirect his career with a ministry organization, and he applied to Focus on the Family. Dobson offered him the job of putting the ministry on a sound business footing.

"They'd had geometric growth that had just swamped their computer system," recalls Nelson, who started at Focus on the Family in early 1985. "They didn't have a budget, really. The attitude was, 'No decision is final unless Dr. Dobson says so.'" Within a matter of months, Nelson got a handle on what made the organization tick and what things constituted obstacles. Then he layered a business structure onto the highly creative, growth-oriented culture that Dobson already had established. Soon after Nelson's arrival, Dobson created the ministry's first executive vice presidency and promoted Nelson to it. Soon, Dobson also hired Nelson's wife. Elaine Nelson became the ministry's first official tour guide; she eventually went on to head Focus's guest relations department for several years.

But the couple's joy at finding vocational renewal at Focus came at a price. The Nelsons quickly moved to Los Angeles and actually lived in their twenty-nine-foot travel trailer while they waited for their house in Houston to sell. Nelson never doubted the call he had perceived to come to Focus. But after waiting for more than a year with no buyer in sight, the Nelsons "moved up" to a forty-foot trailer. Major life events occurred during that period, such as the weddings of two of their three daughters. And when James and Shirley Dobson came to the Nelsons for dinner for the first time, the couples ate outside—but Nelson didn't apologize for the accommodations.

"Jim had thought I was living in something at least a bit grander, like maybe a double-wide trailer home, so we had a lot of fun as he looked around the place for the first time," Nelson recalls. "But we could have gone into an apartment. Quite honestly, we weren't hurt. It was nice weather. Nice campground. And when we finally could move out of there after three years, Elaine cried."

Always keen to seek wise counsel, Dobson also determined early on that he would try to create a board of strong, talented, godly advisers who could help him expand the ministry as well as keep him account-able. As early as 1979, for example, he had identified Ted Engstrom as a potential recruit for such a role. Engstrom had built up Youth for Christ International as its president and then achieved something similar as head of World Vision, an international Christian relief and development organization. Over lunch at the University Club in Pasadena, Dobson wooed Engstrom to serve as the cornerstone of a larger external board for Focus. The venerable Christian leader was impressed with Dobson but pleaded overcommitment.

Not to be deterred, Dobson brought a copy of *Where's Dad?* to World Vision's nearby headquarters and played it for Engstrom and a couple dozen of his senior staffers. "I was moved immediately," Engstrom recalls. "I wrote [Jim] a note in the dark saying, 'Count me in.'" The accomplished Christian leader saw Dobson's "passion for the family and for this ministry and the urgency he sensed [about] making an impact on the culture."

For the next twenty-five years, Engstrom would serve Focus faith-fully, without compensation, rarely missing a meeting.

For Dobson's part, searching for the invaluable sort of guidance that he had come to count on from his father and other elders in his life, he wanted Engstrom not only as a board member but also as a mentor and father figure. "He said, 'Keep me honest; keep my feet to the spiritual fire. I don't want to be phony. Ask me anything at all about my sexuality, money, family'—he saw the dangers of his high visibility and increasing popularity," says Engstrom, who became vice chairman of the Focus on the Family board. "We met regularly, and that's exactly what I did. He'd be honest and say, 'Here's where I'm struggling.' I never felt he held anything back."

ᘡᓂᗢᓂᗢᓂᘝ

For the first several years, Focus on the Family scrambled to stay ahead of the deluge of listener requests, frequently expanding both its staff and its facilities. When the staff grew to ten in 1979, Dobson augmented the two-room suite in Arcadia by renting additional office space a block away. In 1981, Engstrom encouraged the fiscally conservative Dobson to make a step of faith and take out a mortgage to purchase a building. Focus on the Family consolidated its staff in the building at 41 East Foothill Boulevard in Arcadia, but soon the ministry had to lease additional office and warehouse space in adjacent Monrovia. In 1984, the first structure built specifically for the ministry was erected at 50 East Foothill, but by 1987, staff growth again had been so vast that they were dispersed to seven other buildings. The constant shuffling that staffers had come to call "space wars" was "difficult to cope with but phenomenal to watch," Mac McQuiston recalls.

One alternative the ministry considered was to locate a new headquarters along with another growing ministry. Dobson scouted for sites with the leadership of Saddleback Church, a booming nondenominational congregation located in Orange County—across Los Angeles and more than an hour away from Arcadia. Dobson earlier had interviewed Saddleback's founder and senior pastor, Rick Warren, on *Focus* about reaching "unchurched" people, and the two men made a personal connection that led to their serious consideration of relocating their ministries to a joint facility.

"Dr. Dobson came down and I drove him around in my van, and we looked at a parcel that was seventy-two acres," recalls Warren, who later wrote the phenomenally best-selling book *The Purpose-Driven Life*. "At the time, I thought that we'd never need that much land, and he didn't think Focus would either. [But] we looked at homes in the area together. The Focus board came down and visited services at Saddleback. We were trying to make it happen." In the end, however, Focus demurred in large part out of its concern that the cost of living in affluent southern Orange County would be impractical for some of its employees.

Instead, Focus on the Family purchased property near California

State Polytechnic University—Pomona, about twenty miles east of Arcadia. In January 1988, a few months short of its tenth anniversary, the organization dedicated a two-story, custom-designed headquarters in Pomona, California, in the foothills of the San Gabriel Mountains. A new distribution center on the same site opened in 1989. Most staff members assumed this move to Pomona would be the last.

"I never even thought we'd use all the space in Pomona," Paul Nelson says. "If we had projected how fast Focus would really grow, we would have been presumptuous." What's more, Peb Jackson says, "[in metro Los Angeles], it felt like we were dead center where Focus should be, in part because that's where all the cultural issues we were dealing with would first show up." Remaining within a stone's throw of Hollywood had other advantages for Focus on the Family. Because of his quick success on the radio, television was also a lure for Dobson, and in the early eighties, Focus obtained a foundation grant to produce about thirteen hours of TV programming for syndication. In the end, Focus couldn't sell the series; the organization decided that television production was too expensive anyway.

But Focus had established a clear inclination to diversify its media menu if other opportunities arose. In the mideighties, for example, it expanded to include a full-service publishing house. Around the same time, it also began diversifying into initiatives targeted specifically at children, including *Clubhouse* and *Clubhouse Jr.* magazines. In 1987, the Focus film *A Man Called Norman* delivered a powerful message to teens; *Molder of Dreams* in 1989 inspired innumerable teachers to believe that they might actually be able to win their classrooms, one student at a time.

Also in 1987, *Adventures in Odyssey* came along. This high-quality, half-hour radio drama series for preteens features the fictional adventures of youngsters who visit Whit's End, a soda shop and discovery emporium run by inventor John Avery Whittaker. The program has become so popular that it now airs daily on more than 1,500 stations across North America (and a few hundred more abroad). Due in large part to its video and audio sales, *Odyssey* has attained the highest profile of any individual Focus on the Family ministry beyond those directly involving Dobson himself.

❧

Dobson is known to have a ferocious consistency, so it is natural for him to wield his problem-solving nature in his family life as well. Fighting the tendency to overwork has been a lifelong bogeyman for him. In 1979, in the fashion of earlier major shifts to his home life and career, Dobson took literally the suggestion of a board member who recommended "investing in your family." The Dobsons purchased a three-bedroom, three-bath vacation condominium in Mammoth Lakes, a resort town near Yosemite National Park, about 7,500 feet up in the Sierra Mountains.

"The kids were coming into adolescence, and I felt skiing could be a great family activity," he says. "We bought that condominium specifically so that we could ski together."

Taking off for the mountains demanded—in an era before the Internet and even fax machines—that Dobson completely disconnect himself from his vocational linkages for forty-eight or even sixty hours at a time. Soon, taking off in Shirley's white Buick station wagon, often with friends in tow, the Dobsons were visiting Mammoth Lakes eight or more weekends a year. It was a six-hour drive from Arcadia—"five and a half, if I drove," Dobson joshes—and there was fun for everyone even in the anticipation of it. That is, except for the time that Dobson asked family friend Flo Waltrip to gas up the Dobsons' brand-new, high-roofed Chevrolet van for the trip. "I drove it into a parking garage where I didn't account for the higher clearance that I would need, and you could just hear the top of the van ripping—it was stuck," she says with a grimace. After Dobson's new vehicle had been extricated by letting some of the air out of the tires, Waltrip remembers him saying, 'Don't worry, it's only a car.' But he still teases me about it. And there's still the blue paint on the overhang in that parking garage today."

In addition to the Waltrips, the Dobsons often invited other friends and family members to be their guests at Mammoth Lakes. The group would ski and play racquetball and basketball or dip into the Jacuzzi at a nearby athletic club. And everyone knew exactly what was coming on Sundays: Dobson was so resolute about observing the Sabbath that he didn't even allow any skiing on that day. It was to be a total day of worship and rest, usually with devotions in the morning and then relaxing, regenerative activities in the afternoon. Often the husbands would play chess, the wives would play baccarat, and the kids would play something noisy, like Pit. There was never any alcohol, for the Dobsons are lifelong teetotalers.

Alone or with friends, the Dobsons would cook, take walks, and read books during these getaway weekends. Then everyone climbed back into their cars for the long trip back to Arcadia.

CHAPTER NINE

COLORADO, HERE WE COME!

*The city [of Colorado Springs] is now
torn between opposing visions of what
America should be.*

ERIC SCHLOSSER, AUTHOR
OF *Fast Food Nation*

D espite the initial feeling that Pomona would be their permanent home, James Dobson and his cadre of executive aides at
Focus on the Family had learned to be prepared for mind-bog-
gling growth. So they set to thinking about a once-and-for-all headquarters facility that could accommodate just about any imaginable
exponent of expansion.

Right about then, rising real estate costs and an unsettling crime
rate were beginning to make further expansion in Pomona prohibitive.
In fact, Dobson and other staff members were beginning to sour on
California altogether, even though it had been home to most of them
and their families for many years. "Even as a non-profit organization,
Focus was paying more than one million a year in state taxes toward the
end, a figure that today would have been $4 or $5 million a year,"
Dobson says. "California drove us out."

Once they adjusted to the idea of leaving the Golden State, the ex-
ecutives were excited by the vistas that were opening up to them.
When they were still in Arcadia, Focus had considered Raleigh-
Durham or Nashville as potential sites. Now they added Seattle and
Colorado Springs to their list. Seattle was the personal favorite of Peb
Jackson, who was an early relocation scout. A group in Nashville made
a strong bid, partly on the basis of the huge attendance that Dobson had

generated there at one of his last seminars a few years earlier. But Paul Nelson spent much of the late eighties formulating his own recommendation for a new home. One of the last pieces to fall into place, he recalls, was his being convinced that Focus on the Family could have just as much national visibility in the new location as it had gained in the media petri dish of Los Angeles. "I wrote a note summarizing my recommendation on the plane coming back [from Chicago after a meeting with Focus board member Tony Wauterlek about Colorado Springs], and I was excited," Nelson says. "Once I got into the office, I slipped it under Dr. Dobson's door and ran."

In 1991, Focus on the Family was moving to Colorado Springs.

⋈⌐⌐⌐⌐⋈

Colorado Springs was hurting. The mideighties bust in high tech-businesses, which had been a significant growth driver in Colorado, hit the area hard, as did the slump in commercial real estate. The nation's general recession of 1990 and 1991 didn't help either. And the Reagan administration's expansion of military spending in the eighties hadn't benefited Colorado Springs as much as many had hoped.

Dobson believed that many of his employees were excited about the idea of starting over in Colorado. "The quality of life was good. The air was clean, and a lot of people were really tired of L.A. traffic. Property was inexpensive, so people could buy a house. And we figured that there would be an abundance of potential employees because of what had happened to the economy there." What's more, a local foundation was offering a $4 million grant that could be used for buying and building real estate. By the time Dobson and the board had finished praying and put the matter to a vote in late 1989, they had no doubt about moving to the eastern edge of the Rocky Mountains.

Pulling up roots was emotionally difficult for many at Focus, starting with the Dobson family. Neither Ryan nor Danae, who were both grown and out of the house by that time, was willing to move. Though Dobson's parents both were dead, Shirley's mother and stepfather, Alma and Joe Kubishta, were still very vital and active. Danae recalls that Grandma Alma gave her father the cold shoulder every time he'd ask her about the possibility of her moving to Colorado Springs with them. "For me, it took fifteen minutes to get used to the idea," Dobson himself recalls. "But for Shirley, it was difficult. She'd have to start over. She had envisioned continuing to make memories in the same house where [we had] raised the kids. Plus, Southern California had more culture than Colorado Springs. I brought my 'culture' with me, in Focus."

Still, because she and her husband had always communicated fully about the ministry and because her own role at Focus on the Family had grown, Shirley had long understood that leaving Southern California was always a possibility. In part, she consoled herself with the thought that she and her husband could make frequent trips back to see family members—and at least they were all in one place! Ultimately, about half of Focus's eight hundred full-time employees also packed up and moved to Colorado; this was a much higher percentage than some board members had anticipated.[1] Some of the employees accompanied the more than seventy moving vans that made the trek from Pomona to Colorado beginning in September 1991. And as the Focus caravan reached the city limits of Colorado Springs, more than ten thousand people were in the process of applying for the four hundred job openings that the ministry was bringing with it.

⁂

Colorado Springs has proven a salutary place for a lot of people over the years. Sprawling amid the foothills and arid plains that flatten out east from the edge of the Rocky Mountains about an hour's drive south of Denver, the Springs offers thrilling scenic panoramas, a temperate and dry climate, and plenty of room for enterprises to grow.

Yet during its first few years in Colorado Springs, Focus on the Family remained, in some important ways, unsettled. For one thing, in a throwback to its Arcadia days, Focus had to rent out office space around Colorado Springs for a few years until it could complete the new campus. Furthermore, the organization practically imploded from the financial strain it had put on itself to afford the new headquarters. The board that Dobson had carefully assembled over the years went the budget-watching founder one better: It insisted on financing the entire construction project without a penny of debt. Consequently, within weeks after the September 15, 1993, dedication of the new campus, Focus was nearly broke.

"By the time of the October board meeting," Dobson recalls, "we had only about four days' cash. And at that time, we had about a thousand employees. So it was really scary. The economy still wasn't very good, so giving was dropping too. I was very nervous, and so was the board. One member put some numbers up on the board that said we needed to cut $25 million out of our [annual] budget—and the whole budget was only $80 million at that time. That kind of cut would have set us back forever."

At that point, Ted Engstrom—vice chairman of the board—stood to say his piece. "He always stood when he felt strongly about something," says Dobson, who always has been willing to try to discern God's voice in the advice of his mentors. "And he basically said that God had had his hands on this ministry from the beginning and that he still did, and that we needed to push ahead on that basis. The next months, through December and January, the money came in to put us on our feet."

Another difficulty was that Focus on the Family's relationship with its new hometown got off to a mixed start. Colorado Springs is home not only to the United States intercontinental ballistic missile defenses, but also to the Air Force Academy. The city had gotten used to the overwhelming presence of military types and had actually embraced its identity as a key node in the nation's defense establishment. But the city was having more trouble culturally absorbing a fast-growing Focus on the Family and the many other Christian parachurch groups that seemed to be infiltrating Colorado Springs, despite the economic benefits these organizations offered. By 1995, for example, barely two years after its arrival in town, Focus had increased its number of employees from 750 to 1,200.

Dozens of new evangelical churches formed, some starting in storefronts, others constructing sparkling new facades. By some estimates, during the nineties the number of evangelical nonprofit organizations in the region doubled to about one hundred, although most of the newer groups were small.[2] Employees of these ministries provided much of the impetus behind the boom in the local housing market, as the populace crept north from the old city toward the Air Force Academy and Focus on the Family. New subdivisions and strip malls shot out from Interstate 25 toward the east and the west.

Yet vestiges of an earlier era in Colorado Springs remained. The city retained a core of seedy commercial establishments—and their customers—that served as a constant reminder to the ranks of eager and mostly young Christian crusaders that they hadn't moved to some kind of New Jerusalem. Pawnbrokers, adult bookstores, and tattoo parlors outnumbered churches and Christian bookstores. The Gay Rodeo Association called Colorado Springs home largely because it also was the site of the National Rodeo Hall of Fame.[3] There also was a large constituency of traditionally liberal urban residents and suburbanites who were, at best, highly suspicious of the evangelical influx and the motives of its leaders.

Focus got off to a confrontational start with its neighbors, even while it was still renting temporary space downtown, because the organization quickly entered the polarizing debate over Amendment 2. The Colorado measure, approved by voters in 1992, banned laws that would protect homosexuals from discrimination based on their sexual preference. A coalition of city-based organizations called Colorado for Family Values wrote Amendment 2. Focus donated its studio for pro—Amendment 2 commercials, and Dobson taped a Colorado-only radio broadcast with supporters of the measure.[4] The response was not entirely favorable. One opposing wag came up with the bumper sticker "Focus on Your Own D— Family." Alice Worrell, who headed the city's economic development commission, told the *Colorado Springs Gazette* that the furor over Amendment 2 prompted the city's commission to stop recruiting religious nonprofits to the area. In 2002, Dobson told the newspaper that the furor "probably laid a foundation that's taken eleven years for us to overcome" in terms of the city's perspective of Focus.[5]

The immediate effect was to put local opponents of evangelicals on high alert for other changes that the invading legions of parachurch workers might try to make to the existing texture of Colorado Springs. In 1992, Focus on the Family and local school districts had to quash false whispers that the organization was seeking lists of single teachers who might be gay. Other Focus employees and executives did get involved in local affairs: The ministry's former education-policy manager started a charter school that attracted many Christian teachers, parents, and students. And Tom Minnery, Focus's top national public policy executive, played a key role in helping social conservatives win control of the El Paso County Republican Party in 1997.[6]

The incident that most underscored Focus on the Family's high profile in the area was also the most bizarre. Kerry Steven Dore was a construction worker whose internal organs had been severely injured in 1992 when he fell sixty-five feet off the Focus administration building onto a rebar that essentially impaled him. After three surgeries, a colostomy, a reversal of that procedure, and other problems, Dore grew dissatisfied with the $180,000 workers' compensation settlement that he received from the construction company and state officials.[7] He said he had even appealed to Focus for help at one point and that the ministry had only sent him flowers. Actually, says Paul Hetrick, Dore had run through the settlement money pretty quickly and then decided that Focus should either help him financially or prevail upon its contractor to pay him more in workers' compensation. Hetrick and other Focus executives encouraged Dore to go back through the compensation process, explaining that Focus could not give him money that had been donated for ministry purposes.

But Dore wasn't able to extract anything more, and his wife, the mother of their four children, had left him. Despondent apparently to the point of suicide, Dore walked into the lobby of the Focus administrative building at about 1:30 p.m. on May 2, 1994. (Dobson was in Washington that day for National Day of Prayer activities.) Dore carried a .380-caliber semiautomatic handgun, wore a half-vest that he said contained explosives, and had a message emblazoned on his chest in red marker. As Dore shouted angrily, a security guard realized what was unfolding in the lobby; he pulled a fire alarm that initiated an evacuation of nearly all of the employees and the handful of visitors who were there. Dore took two receptionists hostage, actually jamming the barrel of his loaded gun into the neck of one of the women and threatening to blow up both himself and the building. After several minutes, two male security guards approached Dore and offered to substitute themselves for the two women. Instead, Dore took them hostage as well.

A SWAT team dispatched by the Colorado Springs police set up a command post at the nearby Focus Welcome Center to analyze blueprints for potential avenues of attack. Black-clad tactical officers began talking with Dore, who dissembled about his children, his physical and emotional pain, and his intention to kill himself. After about ninety minutes, he allowed the hostages to leave the building. A little more than four hours after that, Dore gave himself up. His vest contained signal flares.[8] At one point, Dore's gun went off, putting a bullet hole in a wall to the side of the lobby, which Focus preserved and commemorated. Dore would be found guilty of kidnapping and sent to prison for thirty-two years.

That day Focus dominated local headlines again, in the most dramatic fashion so far. Yet the ministry never came to dominate local politics or school boards as many had feared. And by the end of the nineties, the area still had the "feel of a city whose identity is not yet fixed," as Eric Schlosser put it in his 2001 book that chose Colorado Springs as an example of the cultural homogenization of America.[9] The city had lost national convention business over Amendment 2 and its aftermath, and even had picked up a reputation as a bit of a "hate capital," according to Rabbi Howard Hirsch, a professor of religious studies at the city's Regis University.[10]

Dobson himself devoted considerable time in subsequent years to trying to heal the rift. Among other things, he served with Rabbi Hirsch on a citywide panel aimed at creating reconciliation between local Christians and Jews. Its importance to Dobson was clear because he rarely serves on boards of any kind. "Now by larger and larger numbers of people here, Dr. Dobson is seen differently than the negative media portrayal," Hirsch says. "He's a righteous gentile."

∽⌒∽⌒∽

Despite a bumpy start, Focus on the Family has flourished in Colorado Springs for the past decade. The eighty-one-acre campus still commands the hill on which it was built—with Dobson's third-story office having the most sweeping view. The campus overlooks an expanding business park, the Air Force Academy beyond it, and Pikes Peak, set in the Rocky Mountain range, fills the western horizon. The administration center is built around a huge, high-ceilinged "chapelteria" where Focus on the Family holds Friday morning services, Dobson's monthly question-and-answer forums for staff, and other events. A state-of-the-art production studio on the first floor of the administration building has theater seating behind a huge glass panel for visitors. Fine oak panels and bronze trim grace surfaces throughout the facilities.

About 200,000 people a year trek to Focus on the Family, which also has its own exit signs on Interstate 25. Tours typically include the dazzling lobby, with its memorabilia-bedecked walls and grand staircase; the recording studios; and the Welcome Center across a parking lot from the main building. Originally, the Welcome Center was basically a glorified bookstore. But today it includes a wide variety of attractions, including a 10,000-square-foot retail store; a gallery packed with paintings, memorabilia, and a life-sized statue of James Dobson Sr.; and most notably, a large play area and soda fountain modeled after Focus on the Family's *Adventures in Odyssey* children's series.

Although Focus's ministries had multiplied in California, they expanded even more in Colorado as ministry leaders tried to figure out ways to cope with the ever-proliferating needs of their audiences. One of the first to help Focus fill some of that extra room in Colorado Springs was Dobson's cousin H. B. London, who had also been the Dobsons' pastor at First Church of the Nazarene in Pasadena in the mideighties. Together regularly for the first time since college, the cousins began to seriously discuss whether they ever could "work together without killing each other," as London put it. Beverley London and Shirley Dobson "didn't think it was a good idea. They thought it would work out badly because Jim would be my boss. But I saw that more of a mission for me was possible at Focus—of serving a greater, wider church than just the single denomination that I had served all my life." London wanted to help other pastors deal with their own unique set of challenges.

So in November 1991, just a few weeks after the Dobsons left Arcadia, H. B. and Beverley London moved to Colorado Springs. "The move was the hardest thing I'd ever have to do in my life because neither Jim nor I knew where it would go," London recalls. "I didn't come in as a vice president because Jim was determined that I should come in as a member of the rank-and-file staff. I took a big cut in salary and a demotion in status. He wanted me to prove myself so [my position] wouldn't be [seen as] nepotism." Within little more than a year, Dobson asked London to serve as a member of his executive cabinet, and now as a vice president, London oversees not only Focus on the Family's pastoral ministries but also several other departments.

Actually, London's domain is a crazy quilt of initiatives that illustrates how much Focus has broadened its outreach in the last several years—and how much Dobson truly let go to allow the ministry to grow, delegating many crucial functions to people he trusted. London's responsibilities alone include programs to reach African Americans, churches, physicians, crisis pregnancy centers, young people, and baby boomers.

Focus also started the Focus on the Family Institute that accommodates eighty-eight college students each semester. In 1998 Focus launched Love Won Out, a controversial ministry to homosexuals and their families. Focus on the Family began publishing separate magazines for teenage girls, teenage boys, physicians, teachers, single parents, and other groups. And Focus on the Family found more outlets for its radio content, including Dobson's sixty- and ninety-second commentaries that now are aired on thousands of North American radio stations. Ninety-second video commentaries by Dobson run on nearly one hundred television network affiliates, including stations in most of the nation's major markets.

With a presence in so many demographic pockets and the use of so many different forms of communication, synergy has been an important operating principle for Focus on the Family from the very start. Dobson's films and radio show fed followers to each other, helping each medium to grow far faster than it otherwise would have.

Dobson has never drawn a salary from Focus, in part to free him both as head of the ministry and as an independent communicator from the constraints he might feel otherwise. It's also a luxury he can afford because the success of his books outside of Focus provides him a comfortable amount in annual royalties. The arrangement has worked well because Focus on the Family benefits enormously from having Dobson at the helm; his ever-growing visibility provides continual promotion of the ministry. At the same time, Dobson the author gets tremendous marketing benefits for his books because he is able to refer to and promote them liberally on his radio show and elsewhere. To compensate for that exposure, Dobson's for-profit organization pays $60,000 a year to the ministry. In turn, Focus on the Family offers Dobson's books as "premiums," which provides no royalty to the author. *Bringing Up Boys*, for example, has brought in more than three million dollars to Focus on the Family.

Over the years, Dobson has demonstrated mastery at leveraging his dual roles. His effectiveness is often on display, for example, when he appears as the sole guest on national cable TV talk shows. He is always introduced as head of Focus on the Family. But during his full-hour appearance in September 2002 on *Larry King Live,* for example, Dobson and King mentioned four of Dobson's books nine times, including one of his latest best sellers, *Bringing Up Boys.* King promoted books by his guest after commercial breaks, but Dobson is adept at folding mentions of his books into his conversation with King and in responses to viewers' call-in questions. "What happens when a Christian man or woman would commit adultery, and what do you think Christians should do to keep that from happening in their own family?" one caller asked. Dobson answered: "I don't mean to promote my own stuff. But I wrote a book called *Love Must Be Tough,* which talks specifically about that situation. . . ."[11]

Not surprisingly, the entire organization has learned to capitalize on the synergies among the various facets of the ministry. For example, Focus began hosting Renewing the Heart conferences for women and then in 1997 launched a radio talk show with the same name. The show starred Janet Parshall, a former housewife and radio host of her own show in Milwaukee.

The founding of the Physicians Resource Council in 1987 led to the launch of *Physician* magazine. A few years ago, *Brio*, the most popular of the niche Focus magazines, began sponsoring its own short-term missions trips for teenage girls.

Life on the Edge began as a book for those between the age of sixteen and twenty-six. Then it became a series of spiritual convocations for teenagers around the country. Finally in 1997 teen expert Joe White and *Brio* editor Susie Shellenberger teamed up to create a Saturday night call-in radio show called *Life on the Edge—Live!*, which struck a significant chord with many teenagers. It was named Talk Show of the Year for 2000 by the National Religious Broadcasters.

Not everything Focus on the Family tries works—at least not in the long run. A series of Focus-sponsored basketball camps, launched as a memoriam to pro basketball Hall of Famer Pete Maravich after his death in 1988, folded after eight years. A few years ago, Focus shut down its own full-fledged book publishing operation in favor of copublishing just a relative handful of titles with established Christian publishers. A four-year flattening of contributions and other economic pressures between 1999 and 2003 led to the demise of some of Focus's magazines, including *Physician*. And that was only after Focus had stubbed its toe and ended publication of *Single-Parent Family* magazine. In hindsight, Focus editors admitted it should have been fairly obvious that many single parents would be uncomfortable having their demographic distinctiveness so underscored, even in a well-intentioned effort—and especially by such a paragon of the traditional family structure as Focus.[12]

Even as Focus on the Family has diversified so widely, it still struggles to conquer its biggest challenge in the new millennium: its perception as a baby boomers' ministry—as an organization too closely tied to one man who is very wise but is now grandfatherly as well. It's a challenge Dobson and other Focus executives constantly face. One board member recently told fellow Focus directors about an airplane flight to Denver during which he sat next to a woman who was traveling to the Colorado capital for a national convention of Mothers of Pre-schoolers. MOPS is an evangelical Christian ministry that took off after Dobson promoted it heavily on a *Focus* broadcast twenty years ago. But when the board member told her he was on the flight for a meeting at Focus on the Family, she said, "What's that?" And when the executive said, "You know, Dr. Dobson's organization," she said, "Who's he?"

"Some of these women in MOPS, [possibly including this woman], are new believers, but not to have known was pretty stunning," says Focus on the Family's Bill Maier. "What we're finding is that many of the members of young families in America don't know who we are unless they were raised on 'Doc.' And a lot of our original constituency are now grandparents. Their children know about us, but there's a broad cross section of American Christians, we're finding, who don't. We have work to do to let them know who we are and to become relevant to those families."

So Focus on the Family launched a new initiative aimed specifically at reaching young families, including a program called Focus on Your Child. At the same time, it has continued to add ministries, targeting new groups including the increasingly receptive populations of at least 168 nations. "People in the United States have a lot of information to draw upon," says Jim Daly, formerly head of Focus's ministry abroad. "But when we prepare a 'meal' of resources, people overseas generally eat it up, wherever they are. That's because there's just not a lot of solid advice on the family outside of America. They're overwhelmingly interested in and supportive of anyone who wants to help."

CHAPTER TEN

HOT PENDING

The speed of the boss is the speed of the game.

TOM MASON, FORMER EXECUTIVE VICE PRESIDENT, FOCUS ON THE FAMILY

E ntertainers don't need to have management styles; their agents and accountants can take care of the business end of things. But James Dobson is more than a multimedia celebrity, more than a social-interest megaphone. He is also the head of a multimillion-dollar business that carries the additional complications of being a ministry. And because Dobson had never been to business school and hadn't previously been a part of a private-sector enterprise, he could only run Focus his way, fully allowing the strengths and weaknesses of the organization to evolve from his own principles, experiences, and personality.

"I have a Ph.D. in child development, and I didn't have a business background, so I had to develop my own management techniques and style," Dobson says. "Fortunately, I think I have a certain intuitive organizational ability, and I believe I'm an effective leader, so I worked it out as I went along."

As Focus grew, Dobson's emphasis on high standards and quality formed a sort of managerial backbone for the ministry. Hard work and determination were highly valued, but so were creativity and innovation. The rare staffers who could bring all of those attributes to bear in a productive symphony of entrepreneurship would find Dobson delegating a lot of responsibility and authority to them. Integrity was always paramount, including a heavy sense of accountability that staffers were expected to feel toward Focus supporters, toward fellow employees, and, of course, toward Dobson himself.

"I called my management style 'mutual accountability,' and in a way it was collegial," Dobson says. "I found that if any major decision is approved by a majority, it was very safe; it was very inefficient, but it was very safe. What I observed is that many leaders of organizations get into trouble and almost inevitably say, 'I had no idea this was going on,' because the vice presidents had the authority to spend or borrow money and commit to programs that no one else knew about. This organization was growing so fast that I saw that as a threat, so I developed a 'cabinet' [of advisers] and decreed that there would be nothing of significance at Focus on the Family that wasn't known by everyone else."

But while there was an appearance of objective management over Focus, the reality was that Dobson's interpretation of these principles naturally became everyone else's. "If you want to get into trouble with me," Dobson admits, "just take off on your own and have me stumble on it down the road somewhere." Or, as Tom Mason reflects, quoting an old business aphorism, "The speed of the boss is the speed of the game. [Dobson] sets the tone from the dress code to ethical details." Mason, a long-time Focus executive vice president who left the organization in 2005 for new challenges was a semiretired former head of sales and marketing for General Motors' European operations when he was recruited in 1997 to become one of Dobson's top lieutenants. "And he's committed to doing things well."

For example, Dobson early on insisted that Focus would not install automated responses or voice mail on its phone system; he wanted to be sure that every caller would quickly reach an operator and that each phone message would get personal attention. "We do some things that are very costly, but they have a purpose," Mason says. Holding firm against the erosive wrinkle in American business culture known as "casual Fridays," Dobson also established and perpetuated a dress code that calls for all male managers to wear traditional business suits or sports coats every day and for female managers to don skirts or dresses except in wintry weather. "The dress code is contentious, especially because we have a lot of younger employees and we're located in the West, where the business culture always has been more casual anyway—we're not in Philadelphia," Mason says. "But dress codes have a way of degrading; you can never go back. Dr. Dobson wants the organization to represent the best, and he's right."

Despite such strictures, relatively low compensation levels, long hours, and the fact that Dobson absorbs most of Focus's reflected glory, the organization remains a destination ministry for many talented people. "They [Focus on the Family] don't glorify them [the employees]," says Neil Clark Warren, a regular Focus guest who himself learned about building an organization by growing eHarmony.com into one of the world's largest Internet-based matchmaking companies. "But they attach motivation to the message. And that's what keeps people there."

And Focus has in many respects become a benchmark Christian ministry, from the overall level of admiration it gets in polls of believers down to the sophistication of its communications with supporters and the integrity of its financial controls. Closely reflecting Dobson's own perfectionist ethos, Focus executives don't use the fact that they're running a not-for-profit ministry as an excuse for inferior merchandise or service. Some note the apostle Paul's exhortation: "Whatever you do, do it all for the glory of God" (1 Corinthians 10:31). "Christian ministries tend to be not so well run," says Mason. "But they should actually have the highest standards."

Moreover, while it was disruptive and often distressing to Dobson, the departure of a key executive—usually to some place of prominence in another ministry—also amounted to a compliment to Focus's founder. Other highly effective Focus executives, of course, have stayed and risen within Focus. "The size and breadth of Focus make it more of a place for grooming general leaders than most other nonprofit organizations," Mason says.

Yet the grooming process could be painful because the happy results of Dobson's management style have a distinct flip side as well: He can be as intimidating as he is inspiring, as demanding as he is devoted. "Jim was the hardest person that I've ever worked for, but he was always predictable," says Paul Nelson, an executive vice president in the eighties and nineties.

Until he turned over the reins of day-to-day management of Focus to Don Hodel in 2003, Dobson relied heavily on three main imperatives to achieve his management objectives. The first, Dobson broadly defined as "making the trains run on time," which covered not only his efforts to shape the broad agenda of Focus but also to oversee the activities of its managers and often to tweak the minutest machinations within the $100 million enterprise. The second, "smelling smoke," was Dobson's way of describing his ceaseless search for real or potential trouble within the organization, not only to ensure the fundamental integrity of Focus but also to sniff out and deal with exceptions to it. The third was Dobson's disproportionate reliance on written communications with his staff, and specifically his development of and dependence on a system of accountability memos that he called "hot pendings."

Requiring others to work as hard, or nearly as hard, as he did was one of the most important levers Dobson exercised in controlling the direction and energy level of the Focus enterprise. Dee Otte, his first employee and longtime secretary, joined him in his little two-room office in Arcadia with the understanding that "he couldn't afford to pay me for five days a week, so that I would just work four days. But," she quips, "I never did take Fridays off." And as Focus grew more successful, instead of easing up on his own workload, Dobson redoubled his efforts and naturally expected those under him to do so as well.

"The Focus culture was built for racehorses; Jim himself was one," says Paul Nelson. "Other racehorses would be attracted and stay. If you were going to go home every night and do what you wanted to do, you wouldn't necessarily stay at Focus for the long term."

This was difficult for some people who "came to work for Focus and thought they could sit around and pray all day and be counseled by Dr. Dobson," says Karen Bethany, a longtime assistant to Dobson in Colorado Springs. Echoes a high-level Focus insider: "A lot of people come to Focus expecting to get 'fed' " emotionally and spiritually. "But we need people who have support systems in place because we ask a lot of them. So a lot of people who came to work at Focus were vulnerable in that way."

Micromanagement was another important aspect of how Dobson made the trains run on time. Reflecting his immense self-confidence, Dobson indulged in micromanagement, first, because he was good at it. He believes himself gifted in being able to process the trivial as well as to make the right big-picture decisions. Others agree. "He has all the Type A leadership qualities, but on top of that he also has an intuitive genius," Nelson says. "He never steps on a land mine. I've often seen him say no and yes where I would have done exactly the opposite, but he's been right."

Hodel, the former Reagan administration interior secretary who was a Focus executive in the nineties and later returned to take the top administrative role in the organization from mid-2003 to early 2005, says that Dobson "has an incredible capacity to know what people need and want. He doesn't conduct polls or conduct surveys, because he doesn't like harassing our constituents with a bunch of surveys about what they like. All of those decisions have come from his judgment."

While business-school doctrine disdains micromanagement—and even Ryan Dobson calls his dad "a control freak"—Dobson believed that there was an absolutely sublime purpose to his unapologetic perfectionism: Focus's mission was too important for him to allow someone else to louse it up. "It wasn't details for details' sake," says Gary Lydic, who joined Focus in 1983 as director of human resources and worked fourteen hours his first day on the job. "But on the other end of every detail was a human being, and that was the bottom line."

Dobson's detail orientation stemmed from his "strong desire to create a ministry that is internally consistent. It was not good enough for me to have everyone going in different directions, each significant person saying different things and offering contradictory advice," he says. "That frustrated people. This is contrary to other types of organizations, like a magazine where an author says one thing one month and the next month a different author offers a different opinion. If I go on the air and say that I believe there's a place for Ritalin for ADD children and then some employee writes in our magazine that that's a bad thing, that creates dissonance big-time in our supporters."

Yet another reason for his thorough attention to detail was that Dobson simply perceived virtue in exactitude; he was convinced that the entire enterprise was more effective if each individual was tending to every jot and tittle—and that he could teach or goad others into being almost as punctilious as he was. "Detail, detail, detail" was a favorite mantra. "He believed that the more attention you paid to detail and to the process, the less likely you were to let something of significance fall through the cracks," says H. B. London.

Diane Passno, an early Focus employee who rose to executive vice president by the midnineties, agrees: "If you aren't a precise person, you don't want to work for him."

Once, Dobson recalls, he framed his concerns in a "harsh memo" that partially explained why Focus is "an organization that depends on detail. We get 250,000 letters a month; imagine 250,000 people standing in your front yard, and they all want something. Some want multiple things. How do you keep up with that? I wrote that if people wouldn't chase detail, they were working in the wrong organization."

In looking back at his management history, Dobson admits that his diligence in conducting the trains "made some VPs nervous, but it ensured a very high level of accountability." He remains fascinated by other organizations that manage to instill strong accountability, such as National Football League teams, where Monday-morning game films make it excruciatingly clear to everyone which players executed their assignments the day before and which didn't. "Most organizations have almost no accountability," Dobson asserts. "And many executives hide behind the notion that they don't want to micromanage—but therefore, maybe they're not managing at all. I didn't undermine the leadership of my team, because when I found a problem I went back to them to fix it. But," he adds—underscoring his sense of organizational omniscience that made so many of his top lieutenants wary—"I'm the one who found the problem."

Underlying everything was Dobson's very understandable concern that his name was on the door. Because he personifies the ministry, mistakes and problems "always reflected back on Dr. Dobson," Lydic says, "so he wanted to be involved in the details."

Dobson never forgets the people he serves. "For that woman who asks us some questions and has a certain urgency to her need, if we don't respond in a timely manner, to her I'm a phony—because I sounded like I cared, and she reached out for help," he says.

Dobson was hesitant to delegate responsibility for another reason. He once said to Rudy Markmiller, a friend and Focus's earliest significant financial supporter, "When *you* delegate to someone and they make a mistake, it may cost thousands of dollars. But when I delegate and people who represent Focus make a mistake, it may cost some people their salvation—and I won't take that lightly."

But like the driver of a car with extraordinary horsepower, having to steer all this self-generated momentum sometimes got the best of Dobson. "He didn't understand his own influence, in that people at Focus are extremely loyal to him," Nelson says. "He was high on accountability. But the level of detail wasn't always befitting. He wasted his and others' energy; he would treat with equal fervor a Thursday-morning basketball game or a [Focus] cabinet meeting. I tried to help him with time management, but that's just the way he's wired." When Dobson was still serving as president of Focus on the Family, Charles Colson urged his friend to get a second office away from Focus to give his charges—as well as himself—some space, "but he never took my advice," Colson says.

And not surprisingly, Dobson's driven, uncompromising approach sometimes caused overwhelming stress among the people who worked for him. "He would get upset, such as when we wouldn't be recording something well or something wouldn't come out right, and it was frustrating," says Gary Bender, the nationally known sportscaster who was Dobson's cohost on *Focus* for a time. "Time was so valuable; he didn't want to waste any of it."

London says his cousin simply "transfers his high expectations of himself to others. He says, 'If you make a mistake and ask me to forgive you, I will, but I don't expect you to make that mistake again.'"

Some subordinates adapted to this pressure by declining to act independently, lest they make an error for which Dobson clearly could hold them accountable. "In the early days," Paul Nelson says, "the criticism was that, 'No decision is final unless Dr. Dobson says it is,' or people debating an issue within the organization would feel free to invoke his name."

Nelson continues: "He was consistent and he was predictable; his ability to think on his feet and the consistency of his answers were strong suits. But if you'd go outside his box, you were going to get your ears pinned back. And his weak suit was that he didn't know his own strength, in a way, and how much others would really do to please him. He didn't mind sparks, but it worked against us that the staff would learn not to make themselves vulnerable."

Nelson recalls a time when a recently promoted staff member was asked to lead devotions for the Focus cabinet. "He called me just beforehand and asked if Dr. Dobson was going to be there. I told him I wasn't sure yet but asked him why he wanted to know."

Apparently, this staffer had prepared two devotions. One would be more transparent and leave him more vulnerable. "He would use that one only if Dr. Dobson was going to be absent that day," says Nelson.

Though staffers were sometimes self-protective, Dobson had other ways of keeping his finger on the true pulse of the organization. And when it came to "smelling smoke," no one had a better nose.

❧❧❧❧❧

Like anyone who understands the human heart, Dobson knew that the best way to monitor the behavior of individuals within Focus and the progress of the organization itself was to follow the money. Gary Bauer learned quickly about Dobson's hawklike oversight of expense accounts in 1988, right after he became president of the Family Research Council, at the time a division of Focus. After a taxi ride in Washington with Dobson and Tom Minnery, Focus's vice president of public policy, Bauer paid the fare of about four dollars, and everyone disembarked. No one thought for a moment about the fact that Bauer hadn't bothered to get a receipt for such a small amount—except his new boss.

"Dr. Dobson said, 'Gary, you didn't get a receipt from the cab driver,'" Minnery recalls. "He's always been of the belief that if you don't have a receipt to prove your expense, you can't be reimbursed for it. At Focus, every expense needs a receipt except tolls and tips. So Gary got his first taste of that close style of accountability."

Dobson is harder on himself than anyone else in this regard. Routinely, when Dobson boards an airliner, he will spread his seat tray with expense receipts from the trip he's just completing and fill out his Focus travel report with a sharp pencil while the events are still fresh in his mind. Focus was audited by the IRS in the nineties, and the auditors predictably crawled all over Dobson's expense reports "to see how the top guy was living lavishly. Obviously that's not what they found," Minnery says. Joking, he adds, "Someone speculated that maybe what did it was the piece of Styrofoam cup from McDonald's that [Dobson] had stapled to the receipt to prove that he had spent 59 cents on coffee."

During that audit, "the IRS was just stunned by the carefulness behind every single receipt and dollar that had been spent at Focus by Jim and everyone else," says staffer Jim Davis.

Assiduous tracking of expenses was just one important receptor on Dobson's personal smoke detector. He also relied on reports from his executive team as well as his own relationships with dozens of Focus staffers lower in the organization and the privilege he retained—for himself alone—of quizzing anyone he wanted to. "I said to our entire cabinet that if it frustrates you that I talk to anybody I want to throughout the organization, anytime I want to, about anything I want to— from a telephone operator to an operations person—you're working for the wrong man," Dobson explains. "I reserved for myself the right to do that. I wouldn't follow the traditional hierarchical approach where I had to apologize to someone for checking out smoke."

Dobson also counted heavily on his own instincts and well-honed knowledge of human behavior. "I'm really good at smelling smoke," Dobson says. "I can smell it a mile off, and when something's not working right, I know it." But Ted Engstrom, Focus's longtime vice-chairman of the board, speculates that Dobson sometimes looked for smoke because "he loves to see the dark spot rather than the bright spot." Perhaps this speaks to Dobson's Nazarene-bred pursuit of holiness, not only in himself but also in others. If someone within Focus was doing something wrong, says another significant Focus insider, Dobson would find it out. "He didn't want anybody embarrassing the organization. Integrity was very important. He worshipped at the throne of integrity; I think sometimes that he even went overboard on it. But he saw all the moral issues that other Christian ministries were getting nailed on, so he put even more emphasis on it."

Dobson also counted on another highly sensitive instrument to help him sniff out smoke: feedback from Focus supporters. For example, while he generally was hands-off with the staff of *Adventures in Odyssey,* the radio-drama ministry for kids, listener mail alerted Dobson to two or three significant instances that he felt warranted intervention. One of them came after several parents of young fans complained about an *Odyssey* character—a police officer "who was so goofy that people said he was a bad representation of police and diminished their authority with kids," says Paul McCusker, who was part of the *Odyssey* creative team. "Doc stepped in and said, 'I want you to take that character off the show,'" McCusker says. "The team was indignant," but they bounced the cop from *Odyssey.*

On another occasion, in 1990, Dobson decided that he wanted to create more synergy among the various arms of Focus to support the ministry's aims in the intensifying culture wars. In a memo, he mandated the *Odyssey* team to do its part. While the team dutifully complied with shows built on themes including the environment, evolution, and news-media bias, the *Odyssey* staff passed—wisely, they were certain—on pornography and homosexuality. But *Odyssey* hit the collective nerve of attentive parents with "Pamela Has a Problem," an episode about abortion.

"We got letters saying, 'We can't believe you did a kids' show on abortion,'" McCusker says. "And then we got another "Gadzooks!" memo from Doc and in spite of his earlier mandate, he told us to pull the show."

Still, overall, says Chuck Bolte, the first executive producer of *Odyssey*, "the great thing about working with Jim was that he gave us tremendous creative freedom once we established that we were trustworthy. It's what guys like us needed. If we'd had micromanagement in that regard, we wouldn't have created what we created, or stayed there."

In their semiautonomous state, the staff of *Odyssey* rarely received memos from Dobson, which—along with listener letters—were the other important vessel for written communication within Focus. Others at Focus weren't so fortunate.

⋈⁓⊙⌒⊙⋈

Listeners to Focus have heard Dobson get angry plenty of times, and when he does, the host can issue blistering oratorical volleys at just about any chosen target. But his oral diatribes were mere feeble arrows compared with those that arrived via Dobson's preferred delivery method: the pointed memo.

While he excels at many things, including conversation and speech making, writing always has remained the very breath of existence for Dobson—whether it is the one or two books he is always working on in the background; the extensively footnoted, four- to twelve-page monthly essays he puts together with the research and fact-checking assistance of staffers; or the stream of memos he produces as the lifeblood of his management process.

Dobson's first impulse in communicating with employees and associates was always to write a memo and to expect a memo in return. In the office, Paul Nelson says, Dobson preferred written over oral communication not because he was uncomfortable with the latter but because the former was, in his view, so much more efficient. For example, everyone at Focus knew to immediately stop what he or she was doing and focus on any memo from Dobson that bore the phrase "Gadzooks!" Dobson has used this corny tagline in memos, notes, and short replies to people ever since he can remember, typically as a way of indicating concern, chagrin, or anger. Occasionally, he'll use the phrase in a positive sense if he's pleasantly surprised or even as an indication of compassion if something has touched his heart. In 2004, Tyndale House published a book by Paul Batura, Dobson's chief research aide, titled *Gadzooks!* about Dobson's management principles.

Understanding that "Gadzooks!" is their chief's equivalent of "Holy cow!" or "This has really tripped my trigger," the folks on the receiving end of such a written spasm often tried to parse Dobson's exact meaning or the intensity of feeling that went into his usage of the phrase on a particular occasion. "I always saw it as a valve on his emotions," says Paul Hetrick, one of Dobson's top aides for more than two decades. "It was always followed by one or more exclamation marks and varied in size. From his emphasis you could draw additional conclusions about the depth of his feeling—or from the size and number of exclamation marks—and I'm sure that was his intention!"

Over time, some recipients objected to Dobson's use of the phrase because of its origins—which were unknown to him—as a euphemism for a curse. Some etymologists say that it came from sixteenth- and seventeenth-century England and Australia, where *gadzooks*—originally *od's wucks*—referred to "God's hooks," the nails that were used to attach Christ to the cross. As a result, Dobson eased off in the early nineties. "It's about as close as he ever got to swearing, which I've never seen or heard him do at all," Hetrick says.

Dobson often keyboarded memos himself, and they took various forms as Focus grew. He continually tinkered with their format so that he could optimize this crucial aspect of his command. One of the earliest he called "testing the system." If he saw a letter from a listener that, for example, criticized Focus for not being responsive to a mother who was struggling with her adolescent, he'd go to the responsible employee and say, "Show me a copy of your answer," Dobson explains. "If that person gave me a letter that was dated after my request, we had a problem. My next point then was, 'Why didn't you do it on time? Why wait for me to tell you?'"

The problem with such an approach, Dobson found, was that as Focus grew, "there was just a blizzard of paper I had to deal with because of these memos. I monitored the whole organization like that, and I couldn't keep up with everything that was expected to come back. Sometimes on Saturday I'd go through a trunk full of paper and just send notes all over the place."

By the early nineties, Dobson came up with what he decided was the perfect way to cope with the rivers of paper he had created—a system that would both streamline his own role and yet tell him what he really wanted to know, when he wanted to know it. He came to regard this "hot pending" system as essential to his management style. One of his office assistants would send out a memo designated as "Hot Pending" in the subject line, and it was understood that the recipient would make it a priority to answer Dobson, with seven days being the absolute deadline for a reply. Later, hot pendings also took the form of e-mails that were tagged with a bright red icon. The people Dobson dealt with the most, such as broadcasting and public policy managers, received the most hot pendings, while he rarely addressed the memos to accounting or information technology managers because he mostly delegated oversight of those departments to others.

When Dobson's aides handed him a list of unanswered hot pendings, he knew action was required. "And then my even more urgent question was: 'Why? Aren't you reading your stack?' I could tell who was doing a good job and who wasn't just by the way they responded to those assignments," he says.

Dobson still thinks highly of the system he devised, and Don Hodel calls it "the best executive follow-up system I've seen, bar none." But Dobson never tried to force Focus's top executives to imitate it. "I'm probably more organized than most of those guys," he says, "and besides, I had to leave some room for individuality."

Tony Wauterlek—who, as a board member, was immune from hot pendings—says he was "amused" by the system and by the reactions to it within Focus. But rather uniformly, Dobson's lieutenants hated the system. "I dreaded [hot pendings]," London says, "because they always meant extra time and effort, and you didn't know whether it would satisfy his desires or not. But I put them as a priority the moment I came in and saw them; I got to work on them immediately. It was like something hanging over your head: You knew until you got it finished that it was always something significant that you needed to finish. Did most of us like the system? Of course not. It created anxiety, and maybe even at some points you wondered if he really trusted you. This system kept everything in order, and it was a great system, but it was a very time-consuming way to manage."

Paul Nelson goes further, opining that Dobson "didn't understand his own strength" as conveyed in hot pendings and other memos. "He would already be on to the next thing as soon as he wrote it, and meanwhile the recipient [was] devastated for three weeks." Another problem, Nelson says, is that implicit in Dobson's demand for quick responses was the idea that Dobson's own priorities were the only ones of import. "I would be dealing with some significant issue and a hot pending came in," says Nelson, Focus's first executive vice president, who left the organization in 1994 after nine years. "Maybe someone at a low level of Focus made a complaint to Jim, but it was there on his desk, and so whatever he was doing in 'cleaning his room' automatically became more important than my highest priority item. But those were the rules."

Neil Clark Warren, a fellow CEO as head of eHarmony.com, believes that the zing behind Dobson's hot pending system in part reflected Dobson's own highly sensitive nature. "He can be easily hurt and frustrated by what's happening in this ministry [because] he feels a profound responsibility for [it]," Warren says. "So he's written hot and hurtful memos to lots of people. But then again, some of the greatest people in history did the same thing."

〜〜〜〜〜

By making the trains run on time, smelling smoke, and dishing out hot pendings, Dobson worked to ensure that every synapse within Focus would fire quickly at any given moment to fulfill his general or specific will. Gary Bender remembers "being down in the studio before he would appear, and everyone would say, 'Here he comes,' and put on their sport coats and ties. When he came down, everyone had to be ready to roll."

But being responsive to Dobson wasn't always enough to ensure being in sync with him. Bender had given up long-term, lucrative contracts as the regular broadcaster for the Chicago Bears and the Phoenix Suns when he moved to Colorado Springs for the job as Dobson's cohost in the wake of Mike Trout's resignation, a scandalous episode for the ministry in 2000. But within a few months it became evident, Focus insiders say, that a Dobson and Bender team didn't resonate with the audience. After a short term of service, the talented broadcaster left the organization and the search for a replacement ensued.

Similarly, Walt Larimore, the physician whom Dobson helped recruit as a vice president in 2001, departed in late 2004 after his Focus show on medical matters failed to gain traction with stations or listeners. It was difficult for Dobson to allow Hodel to handle Larimore's departure.

"I was at some distance from it," Dobson says, "which is as it should be. I shouldn't be interjecting myself even though it was a difficult issue. When I stepped down as president [in 2003], I agreed not to try to influence administrative policies, especially when it came to personnel. I kept that commitment."

Dobson's fascinating orbit and Focus's broad mission drew many devout, intelligent, and talented Christians to his staff. But by dint of his demands as a boss, the intense pace at which he expected his subordinates to work, the highly emotional nature of Focus's ministry, and the frequent travel and unpredictable schedules that are part of executive and management jobs at Focus on the Family, working for Dobson also tended to burn people out.

"I admit that my management style was not perfect," he says. "It exhausted me and was difficult for my senior leaders. Excellence is always costly to those who achieve it. But it resulted in what I believe has become one of the most well-run, efficient, prudent, and accountable ministries in the country."

Such standards, in fact, could put a strain on otherwise-troubled marriages, which occurred in the cases of a couple of Dobson's closest original aides. On the other hand, marriages remained intact for all of Focus's dozens of other executives at the level of vice president and above. Every so often, Dobson as CEO would try to relieve the strain on his executive cohorts by wrestling tactically with the issue. For example, with Dobson noting that "stress, pressure, and deadlines are taking their toll," in 1988 Focus adopted a new plan allowing each executive to work at home for one-half to a full day per week. The next year, Dobson eliminated a separate weekly time of group devotions for his cabinet of top executives, instead suggesting to them that they "take their wives to breakfast on Thursday morning or . . . spend that time together in any way" that they wished. "I really do care about you all and would never forgive myself if the workload here at Focus began to erode one or more of the marriages," Dobson said in a June 21 memo.

And in 1997, Dobson announced at Focus's monthly Friday-morning chapel gathering that the ministry was going to grant three weeks of vacation, at a minimum, to every full-time member of the staff, increased from the previous two-week minimum—in large part as an expression of appreciation for their hard work. The three-week vacation policy has remained in place until this day.

With his avuncular impulses, Dobson also tried to help individual executives control the pressure valve. When Kurt Bruner, a fast-rising manager at Focus, was offered a vice presidency in 1996, he wondered to Dobson whether he could handle the long hours he'd seen put in by other top Focus executives. As a thirty-three-year-old father of young children, Bruner was especially concerned about having to work late into the evening. But Dobson told him, "Kurt, the guys who insist on working those long hours do so despite my urging to go home. And they would do it no matter where they worked. You don't need to do that."

Bruner notes that he's been a senior executive at Focus for a decade, "and I've rarely worked more than fifty hours per week, a very reasonable amount for the role. I could work longer hours—but I don't."

Although a hard driver, Dobson never managed by fear or feint or aloofness—far from it. Most of those who work directly for him are comfortable calling him "Doc," for example, and many other Focus employees call him "Dr. D." Many staffers express gratitude, some coming to tears, over Dobson's magnanimity and generosity to them over the years. "He's interested in his staff at every level," says former aide Karen Bethany. "He always takes time with people as he walks through the building; he doesn't act as if anyone is beneath him."

One thing his staff appreciates is that Dobson doesn't mind letting loose with them from time to time. Such an occasion was his sixty-eighth birthday party at Focus on the Family in April 2004. The theme was the *Love Boat* and H. B. London played the role of "Captain." But the highlight of the day was a *Jeopardy*-style game that was stacked against Dobson, making it impossible for him to win.

Not surprisingly, for someone who likes to delve into details, Dobson managed "by walking around," a style that involved regularly mixing with employees. And when he was out and about on campus, rather than scurrying for cover or snapping to their best behavior, Bender says, many staffers "used that as the chance to get his attention and ask him a question." But Dobson's megawatt status among Focus's employees often made it difficult for him to gain truly useful information on such tours. "We couldn't get ten steps in the warehouse without someone just mobbing him," says Charlie Jarvis, a Focus executive vice president in the nineties. "So many people felt they knew him, and he's so personable with people."

But there is one place at Focus where the privileges as well as the perils of being the 800-pound gorilla more or less melt away from Dobson: the boardroom. He recruits strong board members, each a committed Christian who has achieved significant success in his or her own endeavors, and only some of them otherwise connected to a ministry. "I've served on twenty-five or thirty boards," Engstrom says, "and Focus is an unusually strong board, with strong individuals. There are no yes-persons." Dobson has good reason to pack his board with people whose egos and abilities often match his own. Just as at the beginning of Focus he submitted himself to Engstrom's mentorship, Dobson has always believed that it is crucial for him to remain accountable to other strong leaders.

Over the years, Engstrom says, sometimes the board has "had to bring him to a gray area. There's very little gray with Jim Dobson" because he tends to see most issues in black-and-white. In a number of cases, however, Dobson has proven that he's willing to swallow even a strongly held point of view and submit to a consensus of the board. "He's willing to back down on issues," Engstrom says. "He feels very deeply that he's accountable to us. And we've brought him up short on a number of ventures, especially where it has gotten into involvement with politics."

For example, though Dobson prides himself on understanding research design and always shot down the idea of surveying Focus supporters to understand what they want from the ministry, in 2003 the board disagreed and, over his objections, allocated some funds for a significant survey. And in 1985 a Reagan administration domestic policy official urged Dobson to come up with family-oriented funding proposals for the president's conservative lieutenants. Dobson suggested a modest initiative that would involve distributing his books and Focus-generated materials to inner-city families at no cost. The feds liked the idea. "But my board immediately disagreed, saying that if we ever took federal money, they would own us," Dobson says. "They worried that it would change the organization, and they didn't want that."

Still, when it comes to clashing with Dobson on how he manages the most important commodity that Focus has—his own time—no one on the board has ever had the status or the chutzpah to get him to change. Not Don Hodel nor Tony Wauterlek nor Ted Engstrom nor anyone else. On that issue, Dobson has had to wrestle himself to the ground, and it has always been a struggle to do so.

In 1998, Dobson did force himself to address the problem of his own hectic pace. He convened what he called a "blue-ribbon panel" of fourteen people who had his greatest confidence, including Shirley Dobson, H. B. London, Don Hodel, other board members, his three executive vice presidents, and Dobson's top personal assistants. Their only purpose was to streamline his schedule. The group began by using a whiteboard to list everything that he did, or could do, and each day of the year. After several meetings where they analyzed Dobson's priorities and schedule, the group agreed on twenty-one things that he was going to try to change.

Some of them Dobson accomplished easily, such as dropping off the board of Focus's Canadian affiliate, autographing fewer books, and doing less public speaking. But some of them, Dobson says, "turned out not to make any sense to change. For instance, we agreed that I should try to stay home on Fridays to work on my stack of paper. But I learned that I needed my staff sitting in front of me, so I had to come in."

Dobson also thumbed his nose at the blue-ribbon panel on another measure: personally signing Focus's letters of congratulations to Eagle Scouts. "Those kids work hard," Dobson explains. "And I can do that pretty quickly."

꿁ꪜꪜ꧀

When Dobson began building his ministry in earnest in the early eighties, he considered one of his most significant accomplishments the assembling of a team of highly capable executives to help him operate and nurture Focus on the Family for the long term. "My original idea was that I wanted it to be like Billy Graham's team that would stay together for a lifetime," Dobson says. "And for the first seventeen years, it looked like it was going to be that way."

But by the midnineties, after Focus had settled in Colorado, each of Dobson's three top lieutenants—Paul Nelson, Peb Jackson, and Rolf Zettersten—decided on his own that it was time to move on. Dobson's unique relentlessness and controlling management style, so important in many ways to the continued success of Focus, had begun to chafe and suffocate these men, each of whom was a strong leader in his own right. As they began to chart the future of their careers, they couldn't figure out how to emerge from Dobson's always-broadening shadow at Focus.

And within a period of nine months in 1994, the trio ended up leaving Focus for other ministries: Nelson, who was Focus's head of finance and operations, left in January to become head of the Evangelical Council for Financial Accountability in Washington, D.C.; Jackson, Focus's chief fund-raiser and, other than Dobson, its most familiar face to donors and other outsiders, resigned in April to help lead Young Life, a Colorado Springs–based ministry aimed at teenagers; and in September, Zettersten, manager of Focus's broadcasting and creative operations, jumped to Thomas Nelson Inc., a Christian publishing company.

Dobson felt that "a kind of malaise had begun to set in" at the top of

Focus. "There was no internal warfare or anything in particular that caused it, but those guys were feeling it. They'd done what they came to do. It was wise on both sides." In fact, Dobson came to feel that God had rather directly engineered the transition. On a writing sabbatical in London during the summer of 1994, he was sitting in a park with Shirley on a Sunday afternoon and praying "about the pressure that I felt from the demands of running Focus and about how I would handle that load without the experienced people who'd been around me," he says. That evening, the Dobsons attended a service at All Saints' Church in London, "and the preacher absolutely nailed me [in his sermon], just as if the Lord had spoken to me," Dobson says.

"His essential message was that no one was irreplaceable and that God has a plan, and that he doesn't commit himself to a man but to his plan. And when he's through with things as they are, he changes them."

But to the three executives, the end of their partnership didn't seem as simple as the inevitable breakup of a great team that had reached its natural end or as pat as God's closing and opening doors for the organization. Surely, they agreed, it seemed time for a change at Focus: "As a team, we had done what we could do to take it to that point," Nelson says. Yet to varying degrees, each of them also felt burdened under Dobson's very authoritarian yoke; and each of them, having realized that it would never change, independently came to the conclusion that it was time to go.

Peb Jackson and Paul Nelson were both concerned with the fact that Focus remained centered around Dobson's personality even after its phenomenal expansion and diversification during their time there. That persistent reality undermined the Dobsons' frequent reminders that Focus "isn't about us," during which the couple often noted that "our names are nowhere on these buildings." Actually, Dobson's greater concern was that "his name was so synonymous with Focus on the Family that he wanted to make sure the organization reflected how he felt," Jackson explains. Jackson was refreshed by the prospect of moving to a ministry that, like Focus, was achieving great things but, unlike Focus, whose leadership was virtually anonymous.

And while Nelson had accomplished a great deal in shepherding the ministry's move to Colorado, overseeing completion of the new campus, and helping Focus occupy it debt free, he felt even further away from becoming a clear second-in-command than he had been when he had joined Dobson nine years earlier. Meanwhile, as a board member of the Evangelical Council, he realized that he might be the best candidate to fill the organization's long-vacant president's chair. "I could feel the mantle lifting, but I thought at first that I was just tired," Nelson recalls. "Then Jim and I had some deep discussions about the future of Focus, until I finally concluded that my 'checker' had to move. The final confirmation of leaving was Jim's reaction. One time he looked up at me and said, 'How are you doing?' I said, 'Jim, my assignment is through here.' His answer was, 'How can I help you?' He was fabulous."

Some Focus board members, including Ted Engstrom, were concerned that the ministry had been unable to retain this high-caliber trio. Charles Colson believed that his friend's "tight control" of Focus made it prohibitive to "build a strong team." But Dobson insists of Nelson, for instance, that "it was just very clear that the Lord had his thumb in his back." And after the jolting wave of departures in 1994, Dobson says, "I just turned loose and no longer tried to hang on to everybody."

In fact, he says, "The way I believe now is that there's something about new blood and ideas and vitality that makes changes advantageous. That's the way successful [professional basketball] teams are: They change every year, and they wouldn't win if they didn't. Even when you lose outstanding people like I did, we were stronger after they were gone when a new team came in—and those guys went on to other organizations and took their ideas with them. Change like that is just part of God's plan.

At the same time, it's possible to argue that dealing with key employees would prove to be an Achilles' heel for Dobson. Sometimes he was ambushed; other times he himself simply wore down his right-hand men. The basic challenge eventually would contribute to several years of stressful uncertainty within Focus about how Dobson and the organization would ultimately emerge from his micromanagement.

In the late eighties and early nineties, Dobson's mind was fully focused on the present, on the social environment that was both contributing to and confronting the growth of Focus. His service on federal panels such as the pornography commission was only a prelude to what Dobson would encounter as the nation became increasingly polarized over cultural and moral issues.

And while the rough-and-tumble realms of public policy and even partisan politics were beckoning, they couldn't have been prepared for the entrance and impact of James Dobson.

CHAPTER ELEVEN

THE POLITICAL ANIMAL

> *Where the battle rages, there the loyalty*
> *of the soldier is proved; and to be steady*
> *on all the battlefield besides, is mere*
> *flight and disgrace if he flinches at that*
> *one point.*
>
> MARTIN LUTHER

January 20, 1993, was a sun-dappled and seasonably warm day in the granite and marble canyons of Washington, D.C., when William Jefferson Clinton took the presidential oath of office on the eastern steps of the U.S. Capitol. But outside the Lake Michigan home where James Dobson was writing *When God Doesn't Make Sense,* it was cold, and a lake-effect snow was swirling. And things were even dimmer in Dobson's heart; he was convinced that Clinton's ascension to the presidency would usher in some very dark days for the moral climate in America.

Pundits across the country had concluded that the primary issue in the presidential election that year was the state of the economy. Bill Clinton's chief campaign adviser, James Carville, had even insisted that money was the *only* issue, coining the phrase "It's the economy, stupid" to emphasize the point.

For Dobson, however, the critical issue wasn't the economy—it was Clinton's lack of moral character.

"His illicit relationship with Gennifer Flowers was front-page news, which he and Hillary Clinton denied at first and then tried to finesse on CBS's *60 Minutes*," Dobson says. "That was unsettling."

Dobson was also concerned about Clinton's appointments of Dr. Jocelyn Elders as Surgeon General and Donna Shalala as Secretary of

Health and Human Services. Both women were openly proabortion, favored condom distribution among children and teens, and held other liberal views on the social and moral issues that Dobson cared most about.

"I was also aware that as a candidate, Clinton had met privately with homosexual activists in Los Angeles, telling them, 'I have an agenda, and you are part of it,'" Dobson says. "I was concerned about what that meant and how Clinton's promise would be implemented."

As usual when pushing to finish a book, Dobson had isolated himself for a period: In this case, he and Shirley had spent a couple of weeks already at the Blue Roof House, a getaway owned by the Prince family with a breathtaking view of the austere winter beauty of the lake. Yet Dobson kept himself tapped into the news of the day, and with every reminder that Clinton was setting up shop in the White House, he sank lower and lower. Dobson thought that nothing could be more outrageous than Clinton's appointment of Elders as surgeon general. But then Clinton took the oath of office, and the same day the new president issued a fusillade of five executive memorandums, each one more politically brazen than the next, including providing federal funding for abortions in military hospitals overseas and his famous attempt to remove the prohibition on active gays and lesbians in the U.S. military.

"I'd never seen [Dobson] as depressed as he was on that day," says H. B. London, who spent Inauguration Day with his cousin. "He realized that a lot of the things that we'd worked so hard for were in jeopardy at that point."

Dobson felt Clinton's election presaged a period of decline for the nation like none previously seen. Another factor gnawing at his soul was the conclusion that character didn't seem to matter much to the American people. Columnists such as Frank Rich of the *New York Times* had written that character, or the lack of it, was irrelevant as long as a president had the qualifications to be effective in office.

"That rationale seemed to have resonated with those who voted for Clinton," says Dobson. "They knew about his infidelity with Flowers and suspected she wasn't the only dalliance in his life, yet they helped put him in office. That disregard for right and wrong was anathema to me. If a man will lie to his wife and break his commitment to her, how could he be trusted to lead the free world?"

Dobson—who describes himself as "very steady emotionally and rarely remaining agitated over anything for more than a day or two,"—

*Young Jimmy Dobson on the porch
with his mother, Myrtle*

*Jim and Myrtle Dobson
with their baby son*

*Jim, age twelve, poses
with his parents.*

Three-year-old Jimmy Dobson at home

Little Jimmy takes a spin in his very first "Ford."

Shirley Deere, six years old

Shirley, age eight, with her brother, Johnny, age ten

Jim in his National Guard uniform; he began his service in 1958.

Jim (standing, second from left) with his college tennis team in 1957

Jim and his cousin, H. B. London, during their college years

James and Shirley Dobson,
August 27, 1960

Newlyweds Jim and Shirley begin
their lives together.

Graduation day at the
University of Southern
California. Dr. James
Dobson officially receives
his Ph.D. in child
development, June 1967.

Ryan and James Dobson,
August 30, 1970

Danae and Ryan, all
dressed up in 1995

Proud parents, James
and Shirley, with Danae
upon her graduation
from Azusa Pacific
University in 1989

One of James Dobson's
favorite portraits
of Danae taken
in July, 2004

Ryan and his dad
on a pheasant hunting
trip in South Dakota
in 2004

Ryan, Danae, Shirley, and Jim at a joint-speaking event in Dallas in 2004

had a tough time shaking off his despondency. For three months, he ago-
nized over the state of his country, which he believed was in a "spiritual
free fall." He was extremely concerned "about the millions of children
who would be taught 'safe-sex ideology,' the provision of abortions for
minors without parental consent or knowledge, and homosexual propaganda taught to children as young as kindergarten," he says.

Over the preceding few years, Dobson had finally poured himself
into the public policy realm, risking much of what he had accomplished in the previous years. Now, with an activist first couple determined to attack much of what Dobson held dear, not only did it seem
as if the country was headed in a drastically wrong direction, but
Dobson's efforts to the contrary had also been helpless to prevent it.
As he shared with supporters in his March newsletter, Dobson confessed, "Nothing in my adult life has shaken me quite like the devastation we are seeing."[1]

Finally, the burden began to take its toll. One Sunday morning in
early January, the Dobsons decided not to attend church services. Instead, they drove into the mountains above their home in Colorado
Springs. As they sat in their car overlooking the city, they read Scripture together and prayed. Even though the Christmas season was over,
they read the account of Jesus' birth in the book of Luke. They revisited
the story of the angel Gabriel coming to visit Mary, telling her not to be
afraid and giving her the news that she was to bear the Christ child.

Dobson closed his eyes and prayed, "Lord, my concern for this
country is breaking my heart. I know that I am not responsible for the
moral tone of the nation, but for more than three months, I have
grieved over what is happening to us as a people. Future generations of
children are at stake as the Christian ethic weakens. Will you lift the
burden from my shoulders? Will you send an angel who will come to
me and say 'Be not afraid'?"

Two days later, Dobson received a thirteen-page letter that addressed his struggles as if the anonymous writer had been sitting in the
car with him and Shirley. "She reminded me that the killing of unborn
babies and the warping of children's minds weren't my burdens to
carry alone," Dobson concluded. From that point forward, Dobson re-
solved to do what he could to promote righteousness in the culture,
but he also knew he needed to avoid the emotional heaviness that had
weighed him down.

At fifty-seven years of age, Dobson was far removed from the days at Pasadena College when he decidedly had not perceived a call to enter formal ministry. Eventually, he responded to a different—but just as palpable—kind of calling, which over time helped explain why he never had felt compelled to become a Nazarene pastor like his father and uncle and two more generations before them, or like H. B. London. As he neared the time of life when many men are headed into early retirement, Dobson instead was driven by a conviction that he had fulfilled only part of his purpose by becoming a teacher of practical and moral truths to parents and families. His distress about Clinton's election was one of the first times, but certainly not the last, that Dobson felt God had placed an even greater mantle upon him: to become the uncompromising proponent of traditional family values in the broader social, cultural, and even political arena. Dobson had begun to understand what a ponderous burden that might be.

ဆ၁ၐြ

Ted Engstrom says that Dobson is at heart "a political animal." Dobson agrees, but with a twist. He maintains that he has always had an interest in issues of public policy, because that is where the decisions that affect the family are hammered out. From the very early days of the ministry, there is evidence of Dobson's zeal. However, Dobson claims that he didn't engage in public policy debate for political reasons, citing the fact that he never endorsed a presidential candidate until 2004, nor has he ever attended a national convention for either party.

"I have no political aspirations at all," he says. "I've turned down possible appointments in the government by both Ronald Reagan and George H.W. Bush. The driving force in my life has never been political in nature, but the great moral issues of our time. This distinction is not clearly understood."

Archibald Hart, a Christian psychologist, author, and family friend who lives in the Dobsons' old neighborhood in Arcadia, pointed Dobson in the early days to the effectiveness of Billy Graham's ministry by reminding him that "Graham's genius was his ability not to take sides between the two parties, and his influence is far more profound and far-reaching than if he did."

In retrospect, however, Hart now characterizes his advice to Dobson as "shortsighted." Looking back, he says that "it became obvious that someone had to address family concerns at the highest legislative level" and that of all the people he knew, Dobson was the best man to accomplish the task.

Dobson says that while Graham may not have felt led to speak out for the unborn, God has put in his own heart "a burning passion to defend them.

"When 1.4 million babies are dying each year, and 43 million more have been slaughtered since 1973, I can't remain silent," he says. "This is not a political issue; it is a profoundly moral concern that must be answered. This cause, and dozens of others related to it, are more important to me than my life."

The "passion" of which Dobson speaks can be traced back to 1977, when President Jimmy Carter authorized the International Women's Conference in Houston.

"He appointed the most radical feminists of the day to run the event, including Gloria Steinem, Bella Abzug, Betty Friedan, and others," recalls Dobson. "Not one conservative woman was invited to speak. Phyllis Schlafly, the conservative lawyer and activist, had to hold her own event several blocks away. The conclusions from the White House event were entirely predictable—support for the Equal Rights Amendment, abortion for any reason or no reason, special rights for gays and lesbians, and universal day care provided by the government."

As Dobson watched the goings-on from afar, his contempt grew.

Two years later, in 1979, Carter was convening a massive study group called the White House Conference on the Family. "When I heard that, I thought to myself, *Not this time, Sir.*" The government had spent millions of dollars on the women's conference, which Dobson felt did not represent the millions of women—including his wife, Shirley—in this country. He determined to make his voice heard this time.

Dobson asked his radio audience if they would like to have him represent them as a delegate at the conference. The response was overwhelming. More than eighty thousand listeners wrote letters to the office of Carter's executive director of the conference, James Guy Tucker. Tucker, in turn, invited Dobson to speak at a meeting where other prominent child development authorities were also scheduled to speak. Dobson accepted what was to be his first of many invitations from a governmental agency.

After Dobson spoke, Tucker asked if they could have a Coke together to talk about Dobson's remarks.

After they had found a place to sit down, Tucker said, "I found what you said very interesting, even though I don't agree with you on every-thing. But I want to tell you something. Until I became responsible for the White House Conference, I didn't know people like you existed. I was unaware that there were conservatives out there with university credentials in the fields of family and child development. If I am look-ing for a woman with a Ph.D. or an African American who holds to lib-eral views, I know right where I can find that person in the academic world. But you are a rarity. All I can tell you is that your ilk is not in Washington. People like you do not get asked to participate in congres-sional committees and in the National Institutes of Health. You are just not included."

That night, Dobson says he clearly recognized his mission. "I re-solved to end the boycott of conservative academics in government and to do what I could to influence the system," he says.

That very night he met with eight other Christians who shared his concerns, and a plan was hatched for what was to become the Family Research Council.

Dobson went on to serve as a delegate to the White House Confer-ence on the Family and was subsequently put on the committee to sum-marize the entire program. Carter gave him a special commendation for his work a year later.

While Dobson was trying to help bail out the USS *Family*, which seemed to be capsizing in a deluge of modernism, Washington lawmak-ers were relentlessly poking all sorts of new holes in the ship. Dobson came to believe that attempting to save the traditional family without vanquishing its enemies—who happened to be formulating opposing public policies and ways to spend billions of dollars funding them—ul-timately would be fruitless.

"Before, addressing homosexuality and abortion had been solely the purview of the church," says one longtime friend of Dobson. "It was the political arena that reached in and grabbed these issues." Dobson also saw that while evangelical churches and leadership were exploding in numbers, their growth wasn't necessarily translating into greater political clout for Christian conservatives, even in regard to the social issues they felt most deeply about.

"[Dobson] was defending his turf," says Charles Colson, who coun-seled Dobson in the late eighties about the decision to step up his politi-cal involvement. "He began to realize that he had to defend what he believed."

Still, Dobson's path to hard-hitting involvement in late twentieth-century American politics seemed far from inexorable; in some respects, he backed into it. At first, he tried to keep one step removed from personal involvement. Thus, it mainly was up to Focus on the Family's vice president of public affairs, Peb Jackson, to mine contacts in the nation's capital—relationships that Focus had developed when Dobson served on President Carter's conference, including Republican congressmen Dan Coats of Indiana and Frank Wolf of Virginia.

But by the mideighties, Dobson was growing more willing to invest his own time, energy, and reputation in the political process. And over the next fifteen years, he served on a number of federal fact-finding panels in addition to the pornography commission, including bodies on juvenile justice, teen pregnancy, abused and exploited children, tax fairness for families, child and family welfare, and gambling.

During that time, the Family Research Council (FRC) served as a listening post to track the Beltway's influence on family issues as well as to buffer Focus and Dobson himself from messiness and fallout from partisan politics. By 1988, however, with Congress not moving Dobson's way on important issues such as the tax penalty on marriage, and the FRC struggling with $2 million in debt, he decided to fortify and expand Focus's political efforts. Focus actually absorbed FRC and hired Gary Bauer, who had been President Reagan's chief domestic policy adviser for several years, as president in 1989. By 1991, FRC was so active in lobbying that Dobson and Focus felt compelled to spin it off again.

Focus also formed a formal public policy arm in 1988 that spawned state-level family policy organizations, which were operating in forty states by 2003. The Family Policy Councils (FPCs), encouraged and facilitated but not funded by Focus, became effective proxies for Dobson and Focus in countless local and state matters and as a lever for grassroots influence on specific voters in Congress. Dobson's decision to create the FPCs and, more important, to tie them closely to Focus was a considerable step of faith for him because they weren't under his direct control.

At a speech announcing the FPC initiative, Dobson said that "people had told him that Focus shouldn't be doing the councils because it could sink Focus if one of them did something wrong; [Jerry] Falwell [and the Moral Majority] had some problems like that," says Trent Franks, the first head of Arizona's FPC, who later became a congressman. "But [Dobson] realized that Focus had a good name. He said, 'God has given me a good name. But I ask myself, *Do I want to take my good name to the grave?* What am I going to do with it there? When people visit my grave, I don't want them to have a neutral attitude toward it; I want to spend all the capital that God gave me in his service. I want the last check to bounce.'"

✸✸✸✸

Ring! Rrrrinnnnngggggggg! RRRRRIIIIIINNNNNGGGGGG!

Telephone calls—lots of telephone calls. That's how individual constituents get the attention of the legislators who represent them in state capitols or in Washington. Letters, postcards, and e-mail messages also pierce the distance barrier, though not quite as effectively. And when hundreds or thousands of them are saying the same thing to the legislative aides who answer the calls, it dramatically multiplies their force.

"The reason [senators and congressmen] change opinions is because you've got callers," says an aide to one of the nation's most powerful senators. "If [Dobson] had everything the same—his 1,500 employees and his books and everything else—but no radio show and no call-ins, what he did wouldn't matter. This is all about turning out the calls that translate into Congressional votes. If you can't, you're known as a paper tiger, and people politely listen to you, but you don't change anything. If you can, you're James Dobson." This same Senate aide notes that Dobson "doesn't always get the same response" from his listeners; "they don't have equal fervor on everything that he asks them to call about, and sometimes they don't understand the issue." But overall, he says, Dobson's box score in this area is truly astounding.

In fact, Dobson may be unparalleled in his understanding of this political truth and in his ability to translate issue concerns into phone calls that resound in the halls of Congress. He certainly ranks among the most prolifically effective leaders in history on this score. Dobson has relied on his most personal and potent political weapon dozens of times over during the last quarter century. Through the eighties, he did so in a limited way, befitting his limited appetite for political wrangling. But as his interest in personally mixing it up in the political realm grew—at the same time as his capacity for making an impact there—Dobson was ready to "rain down calls on Washington" more and more often.

Examples abound. Dobson asked listeners to call Congress in 1990 in support of a federal child-care tax credit for at-home parents. Thousands responded and the bill passed.[2] More than one million callers paralyzed the congressional switchboard in 1992 after Dobson urged them to protest a bill that he believed would restrict homeschooling.[3] When Dobson announced his concern that Attorney General Janet Reno was trying to liberalize child-pornography laws in 1993, his listeners overwhelmed the White House and Justice Department with phone calls and defeated the effort.

In 1994, Dobson urged listeners to oppose President Clinton's education bill, which was intended to further federalize the classroom; they succeeded in stopping it. "You melted down our phone lines," remembers former representative Joseph Scarborough, a Florida Republican who shared the story with Dobson in late 2003 on Scarborough's late-night talk show on cable channel MSNBC.[4]

And in June 2002, after Dobson was upset that Senator Tom Daschle was blocking a vote on cloning, he asked listeners to complain to Daschle's office. After answering a few thousand calls, Daschle's staff simply changed the phone number.[5] Dobson promptly told his listeners that Daschle obviously didn't want to hear what the American people had to say.

<hr />

A confluence of developments in the nineties allowed Dobson an unprecedented opening to wield his personal influence in electoral politics. He was reluctant at first, just as he had been during the eighties about involving himself in trying to influence policy, but Dobson concluded that this step had become necessary to protect the values he lived to promote. So at long last, Dobson embraced his growing power. As a result, he helped to yank the national Republican Party back to a conservative perspective on crucial family and moral issues. In turn, this helped position the GOP for a reascendancy that culminated in George W. Bush's presidential victories in 2000 and 2004 and a historic electoral takeover of both houses of Congress in 2002, a grip that expanded after the 2004 results. But Dobson's success came only with gargantuan effort and almost as much pain.

Dobson's private embrace of a public policy role within the GOP was gradual. In part because of the federal restrictions on political involvement by not-for-profits, he had been careful through the eighties not to ally himself only with Republican legislators and positions. But in an era when Ronald Reagan's recasting of the party along conservative lines had outlasted President George H. W. Bush's presidency and reelection defeat, Dobson retained a natural accord with the Republicans on most matters. And as a "private citizen," Dobson expressed support for things that happened to be Republican.

Many in the party regretted the GOP's highly orchestrated demonstration of social-issue muscularity at the 1992 convention in Houston and in the fall campaign, blaming it for alienating moderate general-election voters from President Bush. But not Dobson. The Republican Party had lined up foursquare behind evangelicals' positions on everything from school prayer to abortion, and that's exactly where he wanted them to be, whatever effect that may have had on the 1992 race. "President Bush got a seventeen-point positive bump in the opinion polls from the 1992 Republican convention," Dobson says. "In truth, George Bush lost [the election] because he broke the only promise most voters could remember"—Read my lips: No new taxes.

From the get-go, President Clinton's domestic policies deepened the divide between evangelicals and what they saw happening in Washington. Even by 1990, as evidenced in the book *Children at Risk,* which Dobson wrote with Bauer, the stakes had clarified in Dobson's mind. "Nothing short of a great civil war of values rages today throughout North America," they wrote. "Two sides with vastly differing and incompatible worldviews are locked in a bitter conflict that permeates every level of society." Our children, they said, "are the prize to the winners of the second great civil war."[6]

In 1994 the Contract with America, forged by Republican House Speaker Newt Gingrich, helped the GOP reclaim the lower chamber of Congress. The Contract specifically addressed crime, welfare reform, term limits, the marriage penalty, and other conservative totems but glaringly steered clear of abortion, euthanasia, the homosexual agenda, and other controversial social issues.[7] Yet exit polling showed that about 43 percent of the Republican vote in 1994 came from evangelicals—a total of about nine million new voters—and most of them were pro-life.[8] And later Dobson would make the point that he "didn't hear much about the Contract with America until the Republicans had won. That wasn't what got them elected. They ran on a pro-life platform. They energized that whole community and it was incredible."[9]

In any event, the fact that the Contract mostly ignored evangelicals' biggest distinctive concerns underscored for Dobson the reality that the national Republican leadership didn't believe the way to make the GOP a truly majority party lay in the same direction that he did. Dobson was reminded of this again, he said, when Gingrich chose Christine Todd Whitman, Republican governor of New Jersey, to issue the GOP response to President Clinton's State of the Union address in January 1995. Because of her proabortion views, Dobson calls her "the absolute antithesis of everything [our] constituency stands for." He adds, "[The GOP] put a symbol of the immoral, amoral constituency up in front of the people who had just handed leadership to the Republicans." So instead of being able to assume solidarity on social policy issues with the GOP and just concern themselves with beating Democratic liberals in general elections, Dobson saw that he and other evangelicals first would have to battle for the very heart and soul of the conservative movement in Washington.

He began telegraphing his intent in a piquant series of letters and an exchange of public comments with Republican Party Chairman Haley Barbour in 1995. Barbour had "openly expressed a desire to avoid taking positions on moral issues he deems controversial," Dobson said in an interview at the time. "He wants to narrow the conversation down to issues concerning money." In the spring of 1995, the GOP distributed a half-million copies of a thirty-two-page color magazine that described the heart of the Republican Party. "There was not one single word in that magazine about values, or about families, or about abortion or homosexual rights, or anything that this large constituency cares about," Dobson said. He warned GOP leaders: "You're being watched much more closely than you think you are, and you will not be permitted to waffle on those issues. If you do, I believe there'll be a third party in 1996—which won't win. But neither will you."[10]

Dobson wrote Barbour: "I think you should warn the Republican presidential hopefuls that it will be impossible to skirt the moral issues in 1996." The candidates "will not be able to double-talk, sidestep, obfuscate, and ignore the concerns that burn within our hearts—you have my word on that."[11]

Another important skirmish occurred with Gingrich in mid-December 1995. "He'd made encouraging promises [including extending the Contract's electoral mandate to the social issues], but it began to be obvious to me that Newt Gingrich wasn't going to follow through," Dobson says. "So I went there to confront him." The Speaker had invited Dobson to a private dinner in his office along with a handful of others, including Gary Bauer, conservative lobbyist and commentator Rabbi Daniel Lapin, and Kentucky representative Jim Bunning. Lapin says it was "clear that the purpose of the meeting was for Newt Gingrich, in his role as architect of the Republican victory in 1994, to try to placate Dr. Dobson. There was no confusion at that meeting as to who was the supplicant."

Gingrich, too, was aggrieved that evening because just days before he had called Clinton's bluff and shut down the federal government for the second time in several weeks over his continuing impasse with the president over the federal budget. "With the help of the press, the Clinton administration had just killed him on that issue; he'd lost that battle," Dobson says. "He was in bad shape emotionally." And as Dobson and Gingrich's other guests pressed Gingrich "on the principles where we needed the Republicans to deliver, things grew confrontational."

But in the end, Dobson got some concessions out of the Speaker. "He gave me a list of about six things on the pro-life agenda that he thought could be accomplished," Dobson says. "He said they'd start by making it easier for women who had been abused by abortion to sue the abortion clinics. He was going to work on adoption legislation too. He was saying, 'These are some things that I think we can do. But we don't have the votes to end abortion.' " After that meeting, Dobson understood and accepted the political limitations on his goals, but he wasn't finished yet.

By late 1995, Dobson's role as the key voice for the nation's evangelicals—and, thus, as a potential GOP kingmaker—was a given. Most of the Republican presidential candidates visited Dobson in Colorado Springs, including Phil Gramm, a Texas senator; Alan Keyes, a former Reagan administration official and the party's most expressive African American voice; Tennessee Governor Lamar Alexander; and eventual nominee Bob Dole, the venerable senator from Kansas. They all realized that Dobson was constrained from openly endorsing any of them, but each wanted to be seen as aligned with him for the primary elections in the winter and spring of 1996, when the votes of the party's evangelical base would weigh heavily.

Not all of the candidates assumed a properly evangelical pose toward Dobson without chafing. Gramm had forged his reputation as a fiscal tightwad, not a social issues maven. Nevertheless, Dobson thought he saw something supportable in Gramm. "I was looking for a politician, a Republican leader, who had a chance to win the White House [and] who understood what I'd been saying," Dobson recounted in a speech a few years later. Dobson said he was looking for someone "who was willing to articulate it and willing to fight for it, and I decided that Phil Gramm just might be that man. I heard him on TV. I liked what he said. I thought that maybe he might be the one that we could get excited about."

Dobson asked Gramm if they could meet. So Dobson; Bauer; Betsy DeVos, the wife of Amway Corporation chairman Richard DeVos and a top Republican operative; and Ralph Reed, who was president of the Christian Coalition, met with Gramm in Washington. Gramm talked for thirty minutes of the forty-minute appointment. Finally, Dobson said, "Senator, we came here to share some thoughts with you. And if you do all the talking, you'll never know what they are." With that, Gramm said, "Okay, talk to me."

"I said, 'Senator, there are millions and millions of people out there, good family people, trying to raise their kids, trying to keep them moral, trying to teach them what they believe, who are very agitated and very concerned because they don't hear anybody echoing what they believe,'" Dobson recounts. "'If you would hone in on those people and speak their language and talk to their hearts and identify with the things they care about instead of just talking about taxes, the economy, and money . . . you will have millions of people following you.'"[12]

According to Dobson, Gramm responded, "I'm not a preacher and I can't do that." In his book *Active Faith,* Reed said that Gramm replied, "I'm not running for preacher. I'm running for president. I just don't feel comfortable going around telling other people how to live their lives."[13]

In any event, Dobson ended the meeting with a single statement: "Senator, you will never reach our people." Dobson's group got up and left. After the meeting broke up, Dobson walked next to Reed through the dark halls of the Russell Senate Office Building. "Dobson turned to me, his cheeks flushed with anger, and exclaimed, 'I walked into that meeting fully expecting to support Phil Gramm for president. Now I don't think I would vote for him if he was the last man standing,'" Reed wrote later.[14]

Soon after that meeting, Gramm said to a TV reporter who asked him about blowing off the likes of Dobson, "I'm not going around reinventing myself like Bill Clinton does. Or like Bob Dole does."[15] But after four more meetings with Dobson, by the time of the election-year convention of the Christian Coalition in 1996, Gramm had mellowed as he pledged his support for making abortion illegal. Still, it was too little, too late as far as Dobson was concerned. And soon Gramm was out of the race.

When Bob Dole emerged from the pack as the titular nominee by late spring, Dobson's support was assumed. But as he tried to keep up with Clinton's efforts to sway Republican moderates, Dole ignored Dobson's warnings about embracing evangelicals' concerns. And Dobson was not afraid to speak starkly about his doubts about the candidate.

"I think he felt that it was enough to make some comments about Hollywood . . . and then he had met his obligations to conservative Christians," Dobson said in mid-1995, shortly after what was supposed to be a fifteen-minute meeting with Dole turned into a three-hour session. "That isn't going to get it done. You never hear him talk strongly about abortion or funding for Planned Parenthood or a religious liberties amendment, or any of the other issues that those folks call about and talk about. He hopes to avoid those issues. In fact, I could not get him to say that he would not select a proabortion running mate, and I've attempted in the strongest possible terms to tell him that I believe it'll be political suicide for him if he does."[16] A year later, Dobson was still warning Dole that evangelical delegates, who were expected to number more than five hundred, would make trouble for him on the abortion issue at the Republican convention in San Diego. If Dole chose to thumb his nose at them, Dobson hinted again, evangelicals might just decide to launch their own candidacy in time for the general election.

In the end, the 1996 GOP platform kept the same staunch antiabortion language of 1992, and Dole chose Jack Kemp, a nominal pro-lifer, as his running mate. The Christian Coalition and other evangelical organizations accepted Dole as the better of two evils. Dobson didn't launch a third party in 1996, and he didn't urge followers to refrain from voting. But Dole declined to expound on the great moral issues of the day at the convention. "Bob Dole is a very likable and attractive man who is an admired war hero. But in the end, I could not support a candidate who talked only or primarily about the economy and money," Dobson said later. "We were in a moral crisis due largely to Bill Clinton's foolishness, and yet Bob Dole seemed not to comprehend it."[17] And true to Dobson's prediction, Dole never developed more than lukewarm loyalty among evangelical voters, one of several factors that helped doom his candidacy. "Bob Dole said harsher things about Gary Bauer than he did about Bill Clinton, and it just seemed like all the way through he was determined to distance himself from this constituency that had put the Republicans in power."[18] The 43 percent of the Republican voters who were evangelicals in 1992 shrank to 29 percent in 1996. "Where'd they go?" Dobson said later. "Some of them voted for Bill Clinton, and some of them stayed home, and some of them, like myself, voted for another candidate"—in Dobson's case, Howard Phillips, the candidate of the U.S. Taxpayers Party. It was the only time he did not vote Republican in a presidential election.

While 1996 marked the end of Bob Dole's political career, it only marked the end of another phase of Dobson's transformation into a political heavyweight.

CHAPTER TWELVE

BRINGING
THE HAMMER

*My grandmother always said that I will
let people take advantage of me and will
respond with acceptance and a smile until
I've had enough—and then, watch out.*

JAMES DOBSON

W hile Dobson and his allies felt denied the just desserts from their support of the Republican Party through the mid-nineties, they found themselves even more out in the cold beginning in 1997, as many of the Republicans they had supported failed to deliver on their promises to preserve the family or fight for the unborn. But rather than being cowed, Dobson became even more determined to follow his convictions—and to step up his efforts to get others to do the same. He threw down the gauntlet in a speech in early 1998, which was ranked by many as one of the greatest orations they had ever heard.

It was a smoldering Dobson who stepped to a podium at the Phoenician Hotel in Phoenix on February 7, 1998, to deliver the keynote address to an obscure but very powerful group of Republicans called the Council for National Policy. Formed in 1981 by a relatively eclectic smattering of both fiscal and religious conservatives, including Tim LaHaye, oilman Nelson Bunker Hunt, and fund-raising impresario Paul Weyrich, the CNP consisted of a few hundred members and a small staff in Fairfax, Virginia. Describing themselves as a conservative counterweight to the many mediating institutions of the liberal Left, they met regularly to discuss and advance their agenda. Because the CNP was created to be a place where members could feel safe to air their views and their differences about the future of their movement, it was the group's policy to close meetings to the press and other outsiders, which bothered the handful of reporters who sensed the power that resided in the group.

Dobson had practically been a charter member of the CNP, attending its second-ever meeting. But just as Dobson was severely disaffected from the Republican Party in the midnineties, he also disassociated himself from the CNP for a time, believing the organization was displaying a lack of backbone similar to the GOP's. He stopped attending the group's annual meetings in 1993.

In early 1997 CNP's executive director called Dobson to see if he would consider coming back to speak at a CNP meeting. "That felt like the right thing to do," Dobson said early in his February 7 address. "At least I can express to you what is on my heart and what I've been thinking and feeling, and then we can take it from there."[1]

Ed Prince, Dobson's friend and Focus benefactor from Grand Rapids, had died in 1995, but his wife, Elsa, was at the CNP gathering and she introduced Dobson to the audience of about 450. Dobson backed into his topic with a disclaimer, because he knew he was going to unsettle some of his old friends deeply with his remarks. "I didn't come here to argue with you or to irritate you or frustrate you or anger you or certainly not to insult you," he said. "But I am here to express some very, very deep convictions that I have that probably matter to me more than anything else in my life, and I'm going to speak to you very boldly about some of these convictions."[2] Dobson also assured the audience that he would speak as a private individual and not as a representative of Focus on the Family. He even paid his own travel expenses.

Dobson shared enough Scripture with the audience to establish his belief in an unchanging moral law dictated by God. That law was under unprecedented attack in the United States by those promoting moral relativism, he said. He explained that his listeners and other constituents were alarmed by this "moral free fall," and he cited a Luntz poll that showed 80 percent of Americans believed that the nation was in a "severe moral crisis."

It was just a few weeks after President Clinton had denied having sex with Monica Lewinsky. But Dobson did not make his speech an attack on the president; in fact, he never specifically mentioned Clinton's moral crisis in the address. Instead, Dobson veered directly toward the Republican Party's abandonment of moral issues that had begun after the 1994 election and seemed to be continuing unabated. He ticked off measure after measure that the just-elected Republicans couldn't or wouldn't prevent, each of which had felt like an abandonment of the principles on which they had run their campaigns: $900 million budgeted for Planned Parenthood to promote abortion abroad; $99 million given to the National Endowment for the Arts; only three Republicans voting against the Supreme Court nomination of ACLU board member Ruth Bader Ginsburg, "the most liberal justice in the history of the United States."[3]

As he listed each disappointment at the hands of Republicans whom evangelicals had helped elect, Dobson became more excoriating. After recounting how Clinton had recently told a gay-rights group that he believed U.S. school curricula needed to be more sympathetic to homosexuality, Dobson said he had waited in vain for a Republican response. "Where are the Republican leaders who stand up and say, 'This is outrageous. We will not stand for it'?" Dobson implored. "None of them had the courage to speak to that. They're so intimidated. They're so pinned down. It was just incredible.[4]

"[Democrats] rarely abandon their moral constituency—or immoral constituency," Dobson continued. "They're always there for them, with few exceptions." So why did Republicans leave their core in the dust? "Does the Republican Party want our votes—no strings attached—to court us every two years, and then to say, 'Don't call me. I'll call you'? And not to care about the moral law of the universe? Is that what they want? Is that what the plan is? Is that the way the system works? And if so, is it going to stay that way? Is this the way it's going to be? If it is, I'm gone, and if I go—I'm not trying to threaten anybody because I don't influence the world—but if I go, I will do everything I can to take as many people with me as possible."[5]

Of course, Dobson well understood the tremendous influence he *did* wield, and those in the room had little doubt that he could take a lot of people wherever he wanted to lead them. And he *was* threatening the Republican Party with this speech, as he was more and more wont to do. But just as certainly, the ultimatum he had proffered wasn't one that he desired to fulfill. In his inimitable way, Dobson was pleading with his audience of GOP and conservative Christian heavy hitters to heed a dire warning. And he was counting on their response.

Then Dobson finished with a subtler warning: The tide of cultural and social history was moving toward traditional morality, even if the Republican Party wasn't. Modern liberalism, he said, was akin to the

Soviet Union: "built on the sand." And if Republicans could raise up a courageous and capable leader who would take on moral relativism just as Ronald Reagan had stared down the Soviets, he exhorted, "We could win this thing, and we could do it fairly quickly." He ended by citing Deuteronomy 30:19, about the choice God gave the Israelites between life and death, blessings and curses.

"You've got to make a choice," Dobson concluded before the last of many standing ovations he had already received. "It's one or the other. There's no in-between."[6] Dobson's good friend and fellow conscience of the GOP, Charles Colson, wasn't in attendance, but he heard plenty of reviews of the speech. "I commended him for it," Colson says. "He got their attention, and he got results. He had to be the bad guy."

Several weeks after the CNP speech, on the evening of March 18, Dobson was in the same vein when he met with about two dozen House Republicans and some of their wives in the basement of the Capitol. In his after-dinner remarks, he repeated an abridged form of the same message he had delivered in Phoenix. "He said that we Republicans were pretty much just acting like politicians," says Jay Dickey, then a Republican congressman from Arkansas who was turned out of office in 2000 after he voted to impeach fellow Arkansas native Clinton in 1998.

But on that occasion in March, Dobson put an even more substantial edge on his threat to leave the party. In fact, he told the assemblage of allies that he planned to meet with reporters for the *New York Times* and the *Washington Post* the next morning, outline his criticisms of the party, and discuss the possibility that he might leave it. "I just told [the congressmen] that they hadn't kept their promises and that I was going to tell the world about it," Dobson says.

His colaborers on the Hill took Dobson's admonitions even more personally than those in attendance at the CNP meeting in Phoenix had. So the Beltway denizens did some pushing back. In fact, for much of the next two hours, until nearly midnight, several confronted Dobson about his critique. Give us some credit for our achievements was their message. "We told him that what he was going to do by despairing was to stop progress that was being made that he didn't recognize," Dickey says.

An emotional climax came when the wife of one of the representatives began tearing up and explained how she and her husband were in Washington to work hard for the same causes as he did. She explained how hurt her husband was because of Dobson's broadside at the CNP and how they'd been questioned about it by their friends. Visibly shaken, Dobson apologized to her. " I recognized that in my effort to put heat on waffling Republican leaders, I was going to make it difficult for conservatives with whom I was in agreement to get re-elected or to work for moral principles in Congress," says Dobson. "She made the point that some of them were there because of me." Sobered, he canceled his interviews for the next day.

But Dobson hadn't pulled back on the throttle enough to avoid landing on the cover of *U.S. News & World Report* in May 1998. The accompanying story discussed his campaign to return the Republican Party to the moral high ground. At least Dobson now was being clearly heard.

∽∽∽∽∽∽

Truly partisan politics remained the last frontier for Dobson as his ministry passed the quarter-century mark in 2002, and at the time it seemed likely to stay that way for a number of reasons. While clearly he favored conservative Christian, Republican candidates in most races, explicitly endorsing or disparaging politicians in partisan races was something Dobson had done rarely, even for people who were close to his heart. Trent Franks, for example, resigned as head of the Arizona FPC to run for Congress there in 1993. And while Dobson wrote him a letter saying that he hoped Franks would win, "I never released that," Franks says. "It might have helped me." Franks finished second in the Republican primary that year and finally won the seat in 2002.

Still, Dobson was willing to make a very limited number of explicit endorsements as his own sense of responsibility grew for what he calls "the defense of righteousness." In 1996, for example, Sam Brownback was in a tough primary in his attempt to leap from the House to the Senate to represent Kansas, and he asked Dobson to tape a radio advertisement for him. "It turned out to be a big boost to us," Brownback says. "I did a lot of 'retail' campaigning—walking into banks or grocery stores or downtown businesses—and people would come up to me and say that they heard Dr. Dobson was endorsing me and how fabulous that was."

As his frustration with the national GOP leadership rose in the mid and late nineties, Dobson talked more and more openly about wielding his personal endorsement—or the withholding thereof—to influence

Republican candidates and the party as a whole. Dobson's threats of trying to splinter off the evangelical vote from the GOP grew more strident, and his strength became more apparent; he also made comments about the possibility of taking periodic "leaves of absence" from Focus to further such efforts. At one point in 1998, Gary Bauer's political action committee had scouted forty races where Dobson might throw his weight on the side of a candidate in that fall's elections with an eye toward determining how to have the maximum impact in the 2000 presidential campaign.[7]

Dobson was even considering "going nuclear" against the GOP, meaning that he would pointedly withdraw his support from its candidates as leverage to deny some Republicans the thing he felt they coveted most: to remain in power. As a way of legitimating his threat, Dobson would note the number of slim congressional victories in 1996 that had undergirded the Republicans' ten-vote majority in the House. One senior Republican official in 1998 identified six districts in which he believed Dobson could make precisely that decisive difference. "I told [House Majority Whip Tom] DeLay, 'I really hope you guys don't make me try to prove it, because I will,'" Dobson said. He mused about "getting a stadium with fifty thousand seats and having Charles Colson and Phyllis Schlafly, Alan Keyes, Gary Bauer, and myself fill it at a strategic time. That gets the attention of Republican leaders."[8]

At a dinner in Colorado Springs in 1998, a group of like-minded thinkers met with Dobson, Gary Bauer, and Don Hodel to discuss the GOP nominee issue. Bauer was considering running. Dobson wrote a supportive letter but stopped short of explicitly endorsing his friend.

The obstacles facing his presidential bid were confirmed when Bauer drew only 8 percent of the vote in the Iowa Republican caucuses, and only one percent in the New Hampshire primary in January 2000. Very quickly, Gary Bauer became an ex-candidate in the election to succeed President Clinton.

Actually, Bauer caused more of a stir in the race—and unprecedented tensions in his relationship with Dobson—after he dropped out. Bauer had been relentless in pressing George W. Bush about whether Bush would select a pro-life running mate and whether, as president, Bush would appoint antiabortion judges to the federal bench. Bush perpetually dodged. "If our movement goes cheaply, it won't necessarily get us a seat at the table," Bauer said later by way of explaining his doggedness about Bush. "And we were throwing [our support to] Bush." At the same time, Bauer said, candidate John McCain, the formidable Vietnam War veteran, ex–prisoner of war, and senator from Arizona, immediately began holding out some carrots in an attempt to garner Bauer's support before the South Carolina primary, including "a commitment from him to give me a major role in picking any Supreme Court candidates," as Bauer reported.[9] And when Bauer suspected the Bush camp of being behind a telephone smear campaign in South Carolina—which brought up in racist tones the fact that McCain and his wife had adopted a Bangladeshi child with a cleft palate in 1991—he was ready to do something drastic. Evangelical leaders "should have condemned [the smear effort], although I didn't specifically ask" Dobson to do so, Bauer said later. So Bauer endorsed McCain.

Bauer called Dobson before announcing his endorsement of McCain. "He was most adamant in telling me it would be a bad move," says Bauer. "He was deeply disappointed." It would soon become apparent just how chagrined Dobson really was. On March 1—using his own name to reinforce the fact that he was speaking as a private citizen and not as Focus's CEO—Dobson expressed disagreement with Bauer's move in a scathingly aggressive press release. Dobson asked rhetorically how Bauer could support McCain unequivocally in view of what, to Dobson, was a long list of clear disqualifiers. These included McCain's votes for proabortion judges Ginsburg and Stephen Breyer for appointments to the U.S. Supreme Court, his refusal to support school vouchers, his acceptance of campaign contributions from gambling interests and gay lobbyists, and his acknowledged involvement "with other women while married to his first wife." Dobson called Bauer's endorsement of McCain "troubling" and "hard to understand."[10]

Dobson could not have more sharply rebuked Bauer, a longtime friend and ally, not to mention McCain, whose stature in the GOP would only continue to grow. It was not until the 2004 campaign season that Dobson and Bauer worked closely again.

ເວຣຣອດນ

What about the ultimate partisan political gambit: running for the U.S. presidency? If former Chrysler Corporation chairman Lee Iacocca, high-tech billionaire H. Ross Perot, bombastic Reverend Al Sharpton, radical isolationist Pat Buchanan, and silvery-tongued Reverend Pat

Robertson were considered credible candidates for the job over the last twenty years, why not James Dobson?

As the 2000 presidential race approached, more and more professional politicos were taking the idea seriously. They were looking at Dobson's multimedia popularity, the Focus mailing list of 2.5 million families, his alliances in Washington, and his vast achievements for the family as a psychologist and government policy maker, which they felt would make it more difficult for opponents and the secular media to caricature him as a religious nut. Howard Phillips—Dobson's choice for president in 1996 under the U.S. Taxpayers Party banner—believes that Dobson himself could have "done very well" as a presidential candidate that year.[11]

So did Gary Bauer. "I felt that he would be a more logical choice than I, because I believed that he could have frightened the Republican establishment more," Bauer says. "He would be an unbelievable candidate with an immediate grassroots base of very loyal folks. It would be an incredible development in American politics."

There was just one hitch in that scenario: Dobson would have none of it. "I've never considered it even for a heartbeat," Dobson says. "I wouldn't want the job; I'm not qualified for it; Shirley would have been radically opposed to it; I wouldn't want to live in Washington." Indeed, while Shirley always had fueled her husband's career ambitions, she didn't want to see him become a political candidate in part because she feared the physical and emotional strains on a man who wouldn't take anything lightly. "And," Dobson explains, "I'd be absolutely claustrophobic in that role, having people in my face every moment of the day and night. Besides, God hasn't called me to do that. I have no political ambitions at all, and I've been frustrated by the fact that people have assumed I'm not telling the truth about that.

"That would change everything," he says. "The moment you reach for political power, then your pronouncements sound like political ambitions instead of moral commitments."

⋘⋙

Dobson's presence in the national political debate actually ebbed a bit as the Clinton administration wound down and President George W. Bush moved into the White House in 2001. Part of the reason was that the nation's first recession in more than a decade, followed by the national trauma of 9/11, was taking a substantial bite out of charitable contributions, including those to Focus—handing Dobson plenty to cope with as the CEO of his ministry. And in contrast to 1996, Dobson and his evangelical allies firmly believed that their issues were in generally good hands with Bush, a professing evangelical. When Bush won election over Al Gore in 2000, Dobson felt that with such an ally in the White House, he and like-minded Christian leaders could develop significant momentum in reversing the federal policy losses and inertia of President Clinton's administration.

Actually, some suggest that Bush could have achieved a much easier victory in 2000 than the white-knuckled drama that ensued if Dobson had only taken a more proactive role in electoral politics during that campaign. Analysts suggest that Dole would have performed far worse among evangelicals in his 1996 race against Clinton were it not for the get-out-the-vote juggernaut of the Christian Coalition, whose effectiveness peaked in that election. Bush's triumph over Gore in 2000 was only close, some argue, because the Christian Coalition's influence had waned during the previous four years due to infighting and other problems.[12]

At the same time, Dobson sensed a Republican tide swelling in the background as Americans adopted a more conservative attitude, especially about the war on terrorism and the prospects of a new war in Iraq. He was acutely aware of the roles of Focus, his radio show, and their allies in helping to keep the attention on the moral concerns that he believed were an important complement to the sense of vulnerability and singleness of purpose that fell over the nation after 9/11.

By early 2002, even before evangelicals proved a vital force in handing the Republican Party a historic electoral victory in Congress in the fall elections, Dobson was in no mood to be trifled with—or taken advantage of—by people whom he considered friends on Capitol Hill. That's exactly what he believed House Majority Whip and Texas Republican Tom DeLay tried to do to him in the matter of HR 333 in the spring.

Overall, Dobson had a good relationship with DeLay, the Texas Baptist who had become the Whip in January 1995 and who had testified to the influence of Dobson's teachings on his own life. "He's one of the best friends of the family and the pro-life community in Congress," Dobson says. "But sometimes, when it comes to an issue between what's right and what's best for the Republican Party, Tom will waffle." The first such instance, Dobson says, was in 2000 when Dobson felt that he had lined up enough support in Congress to pass a measure that would have banned gambling on National Collegiate Athletic Association events. Nevada was (and is) the only state in the nation that allows betting on college sports. Dobson aired a radio program featuring legendary coach, Lou Holtz, of Notre Dame fame, as well as Senator Sam Brownback from Kansas and Senator Lindsey Graham from South Carolina. "The votes were there in the House to make collegiate gambling illegal," said Dobson, "but Tom DeLay wouldn't allow the bill to come to the floor. Why? Because the gambling industry had made huge contributions to the GOP." The bill died.

In 2002, DeLay created a further rift in his relationship with Dobson over HR 333, the Bankruptcy Abuse Prevention and Consumer Protection Act. The bill was a comprehensive reform of the nation's bankruptcy laws drafted in response to the record number of personal bankruptcies filed after the recession of 2001. Not only were more Americans unemployed, many were buckling under high levels of consumer debt. Bankers and other creditor classes were among the biggest proponents of the bill, and their Republican allies were happy to try to win this one for them. But in the spring of 2002, the liberal New York Democratic Senator Charles Schumer incited the wrath of the pro-life community by adding an amendment to the bankruptcy bill.

Schumer's amendment was cleverly disguised as a blanket prohibition against a bankruptcy declaration by anyone who had been slapped with hefty court fines in any sort of peaceful political or social demonstration but hadn't yet paid up. Conservatives right away saw Schumer's ploy for what it really was: a way to target antiabortion protesters who had been hit with multi-thousand dollar fines by judges who presumably were proabortion in their own politics. "These were quiet people who were trying to save babies, and the liberal courts slapped these horrible judgments on them—humble people with $100,000 judgments," Dobson says. "Furthermore, antiabortion protesters were the only people singled out for prosecution. Antiwar protesters and homosexual activists and proabortion people and radical environmentalists could escape [big monetary] judgments against them primarily because of the liberal judges. It was unconscionable to target one group that way."

Early in the process, the Republican leadership assured pro-life groups that they wouldn't let Schumer get away with it. But on May 5, Dobson got a call from Focus's lead attorney in Washington indicating that the Schumer Amendment had not yet been dislodged. "It was one of those you'd-better-do-something conversations," Dobson says. "So I called DeLay and said, 'You wouldn't really do this, would you?' And he said he was going to do everything that he could to stop it; he said it was terrible."

The issue receded back into the bowels of legislative process, with the banking lobby stepping up its pressure for the passage of a bill as the economy continued to sag. But the Republican leadership in the House concluded that the legislation couldn't pass the Democratic majority in the Senate without the Schumer Amendment. So instead of protecting pro-life interests, DeLay and company "were going to accommodate the bankers before we could do anything," Dobson says. "So I called [DeLay], and we had a strong exchange. He told me things that I didn't feel were accurate. I just knew too much about the details of this because I was hearing from conservative members of Congress. I had all the facts; I knew that when the doors were closed, DeLay and other Republican leaders put great pressure on Congressional conservatives."

Dobson refused to be mollified by talk of political compromise. "'Tom,' I said, 'if for no other reason to be listening to me, you've got an election coming up, and this is no time to frustrate your base.' In three days, he called me back and said, 'We've decided to pull the bill off the table. It isn't going to be voted on.' I said, 'What does that mean?' 'That's all I can tell you,' he said. 'We're not going to vote on it.' 'Does that mean when the election is over, you're going to try to do it again?' He couldn't tell me; he just said that it wouldn't be voted on that week. Then seven days after the national election, DeLay brought the bill up again and put it on a fast, but quiet, track. I went ballistic."

"Ballistic" to Dobson meant putting out a plea to *Focus* listeners and turning the screws frantically on Capitol Hill. As Dobson jettisoned regularly scheduled programming on November 13, the day before House leaders had scheduled a vote on the bill, Gary Bauer and FRC president Ken Connor were on *Focus* with Dobson, encouraging listeners to bombard their legislators with phone calls and e-mails objecting to the still-standing Schumer Amendment—and in a hurry, in time to persuade them how to vote the next day. "It was outrageous that Republican leaders would stab conversative voters in the back just one week after they put the GOP in power," said Dobson.

Still, with the vote slated for November 14, the last day of business for the 107th Congress, nobody on Dobson's side was confident that they'd been able to turn the tide. Recognizing the severity of the challenge to his leadership, DeLay worked the House floor personally, buttonholing votes along with House Speaker Dennis Hastert, an Illinois Republican. But by one a.m. on November 15, the best the duo could muster was a 204–204 tie.

The Whip had been whipped, and as soon as DeLay acknowledged defeat for the bankruptcy bill and released members to vote their consciences, so many Republicans rushed to change their votes that the clerk's office had to double- and triple-count the numbers. House leaders quickly caucused and decided to introduce HR 5745, essentially the original bankruptcy bill, stripped of the troublesome Schumer Amendment. And just before 2 a.m., thanks to the lobbying forces of Dobson and other pro-life giants, the new bill sailed through on a 244–116 vote.[13]

In California, Ken Connor had boarded a plane bound for the East Coast early in the morning of November 15, and for the several hours he was in the air, he was under the assumption that his side had lost this vote. "But I got off the plane when it landed at Dulles and called my office, and my assistant said, 'Did you hear about the vote?' I said, 'Yeah, I guess we went down in flames.' And he said, 'No, we won!' The next day I saw an article where a member of Congress was quoted as saying that people weren't talking about the calls they were getting from the business community but the calls from profamily advocates. Apparently the calls just flooded in."

Dobson says he "thanked God for all those friends out there who just hammered Congress." Connie Mackey, FRC's chief lobbyist, said the key to victory was that "we never backed down. Miraculously, what happened is the unions kicked in and some of the other blue-collar, Reaganite population kicked in, and we combined with them."

Charles Colson had warned Dobson to "have prudence" in how he handled DeLay on this issue. But other Dobson allies were happy to see him go to the mat with DeLay. "Dr. Dobson was 1,000 percent right on that," says Representative Trent Franks, one of Dobson's staunchest supporters in Washington. "The leadership tells us that as Republican members, we need to back the party on the rules, and I've always done that. But it's a two-way street, and if they put something in front of me like the bankruptcy bill, I'll vote against it. And that's what they did. So we did the right thing. The courage of Dr. Dobson and profamily legislators at that time sent a compelling and important message: We want to back the Republican leadership, and our commitment to Republican ideals is real, but the greatest hope for Republican unity is to stick to principle."

Many believe the reversal wouldn't have happened without Dobson's involvement. "I shudder to think," Connie Mackey says, "what we would ever do without it."

Dobson didn't say he was willing to forget or to forgive how DeLay had undermined him and his cause. And it wasn't until late 2004 that Dobson finally spoke to him again, meeting with DeLay for what Dobson calls "a very warm and friendly interchange. We didn't talk about the bankruptcy bill. But that's in the past, and we obviously agreed to press on." Dobson says that he and DeLay are now in agreement on all issues of substance, and the friendship has been restored.

⌘

Dobson never has sought to develop the kind of intensely personal relationships with U.S. presidents that Billy Graham did. Rather than to position himself as a personal, spiritual adviser to presidents, Dobson's motivation always has been the broader one of leveraging rapport with the occupant of the Oval Office in order to bring about change favorable to families, beginning with his successful bid to get on Jimmy Carter's Conference on the Family. But Dobson has managed to secure very good relationships with each of the last three Republican presidents.

Dobson's relationship with Ronald Reagan began after he was invited to the president's inauguration on January 20, 1981. In fact, Dobson and a colleague innocently ended up within the Secret Service perimeter protecting the new president as Reagan attended the final inaugural ball just before midnight.

Dobson also served on a White House juvenile-justice commission during Reagan's presidency. But he didn't meet Ronald Reagan until 1983 when he was invited to the White House to counsel him on the preservation of the family. Soon, Reagan wanted to appoint Dobson to a custom-designed position of federal executive director of children, youth, and families and to have him oversee a $400 million budget. This new department would examine every issue and measure for its potential impact on the family and be independent of cabinet members, reporting directly to the president. But Dobson wouldn't allow his name to come up in nomination deliberations; he thought being confined to the Beltway and smothered in federal government bureaucracy would diminish rather than enhance his work. "He has an understanding of bureaucracy from having worked in the academic world," says Charlie Jarvis, who was a top deputy to Interior Secretary Don Hodel in the Reagan administration and later a Focus executive. Dobson "exercised his sense of wisdom that it was best not to get trapped in a situation that he wouldn't have control over. And it was his wisdom to understand that it was from the private sector ultimately where he could have more influence."

In 1984, Gary Bauer, who was serving as Reagan's chief domestic policy adviser, invited Dobson to formulate a recommendation for a family-friendly agenda to submit to the president. Dobson agreed to do it. "The most valuable contribution the present administration can make to family stability and cohesiveness is for the president himself to continue providing strong moral leadership with regard to traditional family values," began Dobson's outline. He urged Reagan to increase the basic tax deduction for dependents from $1,000 to $2,000 each and actually interviewed the president in the Oval Office about that issue for a *Focus* broadcast. Congress adopted that recommendation.

Dobson also suggested that the president review federal regulations that impinged on the family, consider some way of giving the nuclear family constitutional protection, and move to end government subsidization of antifamily initiatives under the rubric of the Department of Education and other agencies.[14]

Dobson says he "admired Ronald Reagan from his early days, for his demeanor as president" and for his principled stands. But in terms of a personal relationship, Dobson was actually much more comfortable with George H. W. Bush, whom he first met as a tablemate at a state dinner in Reagan's White House. In 1988, just two months before Dobson's mother died, the two men conferred for forty-five minutes in Bush's vice presidential office. When Bush heard about Dobson's loss, he sent a handwritten note of consolation, which Dobson still has in his files. A month after George H. W. Bush was elected president, Dobson was summoned to the White House for consultation.

In 1992, President Bush even joined Dobson in *Focus*'s temporary studio in downtown Colorado Springs to discuss policy issues that affected the family. And in 1996, the former president sent a videotaped sixtieth-birthday greeting to Dobson, calling him a friend and reminding him, "I don't know that you know how much I value your ministry."

As is Dobson's tendency with principals on the opposing side, he gave President Bill Clinton practically no mind from the start of his administration and didn't bother reaching out to him in any significant way—and vice versa. "I never met him, though there were feelers on one occasion for a possible meeting with Hillary Clinton," Dobson says. "But I expressed no interest." In fact, Dobson's initially dark assessment of Clinton's election to office was compounded as the nineties unfolded, culminating in a strong public condemnation of the president as the Monica Lewinsky scandal was exposed. "We are facing a profound moral crisis," Dobson wrote in a letter to Focus's supporters in September 1998. "Not only because one man has disgraced us, but because people no longer recognize the nature of evil. And when a nation reaches that state of depravity, judgment is a certainty."

With the election of President George W. Bush, Dobson was enthusiastically invited back into the White House fold. From the start, evangelicals felt comfortable nesting there, including Michael Gerson, a Washington veteran who became Bush's chief speechwriter; and Tim Goeglein, the former aide to Indiana Senator Dan Coats who became a special assistant to the president—and Bush's principal two-way conduit to the views of evangelical leaders. John Ashcroft was a strong evangelical and Dobson ally, and the former senator became Bush's first-term attorney general. Yet Dobson insisted on evaluating the Bush administration in an ongoing way, on the basis of its actions.

In early 2002, for example, Dobson denounced Secretary of State Colin Powell for encouraging youths around the globe to use condoms in order to prevent sexually transmitted diseases. Appearing on *Larry King Live,* Dobson noted that there had been no clinical evidence proving that such diseases are reduced by condom usage. "When somebody as respected as Colin Powell stands up, not in a panel to be debated, but on MTV, and tells kids all over the world that this is going to protect them, it's just not true. It's most uninformed." After Dobson was again critical of Secretary Powell on a *Focus* broadcast the next day, President George W. Bush delivered a speech contradicting Powell's position and coming down firmly on the side of abstinence as the only dependable prevention of sexually transmitted diseases.

The most important early indication of Dobson's relevance to the Bush administration and to Bush's reelection bid in 2004 was that he made it onto the short list of Karl Rove, Bush's political mastermind. Rove occasionally floated trial balloons past his handpicked group of key conservatives, including Dobson.

Dobson's personal relationship with President George W. Bush grew throughout the first administration as well. Bush dispatched

Goeglein personally and offered his congratulations via video for Focus's twenty-fifth anniversary in 2002; the Dobsons were also guests of President George and Laura Bush at observations of the National Day of Prayer every year. This occurred as Dobson clearly warmed to Bush's performance in office; the president kept commitments to evangelicals on issues including embryonic stem-cell research, which Bush restricted in August 2001, and partial-birth abortion, a ban on which Bush signed in November 2003, with Dobson in attendance. Dobson and Bush met privately at the Air Force Academy before the 2004 graduation ceremonies, although the national media never heard about it.

ᔓᑌᐟᔐᐁᔕᔒᑕᔒ

Compared with other leaders of the Christian Right, including Jerry Falwell and Pat Robertson, Dobson possesses the unique advantage of having entered the consciousness of many in the Beltway as an avuncular family adviser rather than as a God-brandishing scold. Many on Capitol Hill "got to know him because they used his books to raise their kids, or maybe they were raised by them," Gary Bauer says. "It's a different basis, which really strengthened his hand."

Yet by the late nineties, Dobson's unalloyed assertiveness in the public policy arena had permanently altered the perceptions of many toward him. It became more and more clear not only to Tom DeLay, but also to all members of the Washington elite, that Dobson was a man who would follow his principles to the precipice—and over it if necessary—rather than bow to political niceties or engage in horse-trading. "God made me a firebrand, and I have to be that," Dobson says. Naturally, Dobson's opponents don't welcome that kind of an attitude. "Many [foes] view him as ham-handed, clumsy, and lacking in understanding of the nuances of the political process," says former FRC president Ken Connor. Nor is Dobson's intransigence always welcomed by his friends and allies. "There would be those who would say he is impolitic," Connor adds. "One of the things in our business that you have to do when you oppose someone is to conduct yourself in a way that enables you to work with them tomorrow when you agree on a different issue. It's both to his credit and to his disservice that he is direct; he is blunt; he is passionate; and when he's persuaded of the rightness of his cause, he's unyielding."

Charles Colson is a loyal friend and ally who nevertheless criticizes Dobson for this trait—and appointed himself as a constant checking influence on Dobson because of it. "We see the world differently," Colson says. "He sees everything in the political realm as crystal clear. He's less worldly wise than I am and more idealistic, which in a sense is part of his charm. I'm more understanding of the problems in it because I experienced the dark side; I was in a position to have to make prudential judgments.

"I've helped balance him when he gets too steamed up" in a number of instances, Colson says. "Sometimes he'll say, 'You're right' and back off. It's just that politics are loaded with nuances, and he's never met a nuance that he liked. He's not a nuanced guy."

Others, however, fully embrace Dobson's lack of varnish. "He passionately believes in things and carries them through," says Senator Sam Brownback. "Some would look at things politically and say, 'Let's get what little we can and not push this now,' but he doesn't operate that way. And it's a good thing he doesn't."

"Let the politicians figure out the politics," Connor adds. "The process needs people like James Dobson who are principle-driven and passionate and willing, if necessary, to suffer the slings and arrows of ignominious fortune in support of their positions."

Besides, according to Connor, the liberal Left sports a number of ideologues who are just as willing to plant a flag on a position and go down fighting if necessary.

And because he values principles over political outcomes, Connor says, Dobson isn't "afraid to lose." In 2001, for example, the Bush administration pushed and won passage of a new education policy that Dobson staunchly opposed because he believed it excessively federalized educational standards.

What's more, Dobson isn't particularly concerned about his approval ratings in Washington. "There's a sense of uncompromising integrity about him," says Rabbi Daniel Lapin, a respected conservative voice inside the Beltway. "He's not a man who's trying to win political position or social approval. He stands for things in a very unambiguous sort of way."

Some offer a view of Dobson's political behavior that is intriguing because it is essentially extrapolitical. They sense that Dobson is a modern prophet of sorts, in the vein of the Old Testament prophets. Dobson certainly has felt a strong sense of divine guidance. This explains why Dobson's social issue broadsides often are more jeremiads than position statements and why he is continually warning national leadership about the ultimate consequences of ignoring what he believes are God's desires for America.

"He's prophetic," says Bill Maier, host of Focus's weekend radio broadcast. "He calls it as he sees it and doesn't mince words or pull punches. He takes a lot of heat for that. But the prophets took a lot of heat."

In a 1988 article in *Christianity Today*, writer Tim Stafford elaborated on that theme. "People listen and are moved not so much by the content as something under the content: Dobson's concern. If you read the prophets of the Old Testament, a similar quality stands out. Their message is simple, and it tends to repeat itself. But the prophets cared. They were heartbroken over what they saw. Dobson cares about families, and he communicates passionately that they matter."[15]

CHAPTER THIRTEEN

STRESS FRACTURES

Fatigue makes cowards of us all.

VINCE LOMBARDI, FORMER HEAD
COACH OF THE GREEN BAY PACKERS,
AN APHORISM SOMETIMES QUOTED
BY JAMES DOBSON

James Dobson's heroes tend to be great champions of the Christian
faith, statesmen who famously rose to epoch-making moments and
generals who orchestrated the decisive military campaigns of history,
as well as some otherwise-ordinary people who have crossed his path and
impressed him with their passion or courage or steadfastness for Christ.
And then there was Pete Maravich. Shortly after becoming one of Dobson's more unusual but most beloved heroes, "Pistol Pete" Maravich died
in Dobson's arms at the age of forty on January 5, 1988.

It was a moment that would foreshadow Dobson's own brushes
with death over the next several years, including both a heart attack and
a stroke. These episodes greatly frightened Dobson—as they would any
man—but particularly one whose father had died at the relatively young
age of sixty-six. At the same time, Dobson also interpreted these scary
passages of pain as God's attempt to communicate with him, to slow
him down and so extend his existence and his influence, and even to en-
rich Dobson's testimony about how God dealt with him. Nothing in-
trigues people like stories, Dobson always has believed, and these
afflictions and their outcomes have provided him with some doozies.

Pete Maravich came to Dobson's attention late in Maravich's life.
Despite his lifelong love for spectator as well as participatory sports,
Dobson was not one to venerate great athletes, even the Hall of Famers
of his youth. Maravich was a sports hero whom Dobson could admire for
his accomplishments: becoming the all-time leading scorer in college

basketball and the youngest inductee into pro basketball's Hall of Fame. But even more important to Dobson, Maravich had fiercely embraced the cause of Christ in the early eighties and unflinchingly devoted the rest of his life to him.

Maravich's father, Press Maravich, was a fanatical high-school basketball coach who established one goal for his son: excel at hoops. So his son became what Maravich later called "a basketball android," and at seven years old Pete Maravich bought into his dad's dream as well. He would dribble a basketball two miles into town with his right hand and two miles back with his left; he dribbled it out the car door as his father sped up and slowed down on a lonely highway; he dribbled during solitary summer midafternoons in a movie theater. He even slept with a basketball until he was thirteen years old.[1] His unequaled skills sustained Pete Maravich through a brilliant career at Louisiana State University, where Press Maravich had become head coach, and in the National Basketball Association, where in 1970 he became the first million-dollar player and went on to rank as one of the game's all-time scorers.

But in the meantime, Maravich became an alcoholic. As he searched for deeper meaning beneath his fame and riches, he rejected Christianity even after hearing Bill Bright speak at a Campus Crusade for Christ meeting at eighteen and later after meeting Billy Graham. Only after a several-year odyssey through karate, yoga, transcendental meditation, vegetarianism, and even UFO worship did Maravich yield to Christ in a lucent conversion experience in 1982. Five years later, he wrote an autobiography called *Heir to a Dream*.

After the book was published, Dobson asked Maravich to appear on a radio broadcast. In October 1987, he and Dobson met at the Focus offices in Pomona, California, and found common bonds in their love not only for basketball but also for their fathers; Press Maravich had died just six months earlier after a painful bout with bone cancer. Maravich agreed to come back in January and tape a *Focus* show. And it was only natural that he—one of the greatest basketball players of all time—would join Dobson and other staffers in a pickup game on the morning of the broadcast.

"It was really audacious for a group of fat old men to invite someone of Pete's talents to play with us," Dobson said later.[2] "But he had largely left the game by then. He hadn't played in the previous year except in an NBA Legends game. His right shoulder had been bothering him." If the pain had been in his left shoulder, everyone later figured,

Maravich might have become concerned about his heart and had it checked.

Gary Lydic, a morning-basketball regular and the director of Focus's human services, picked up Maravich at Los Angeles International on January 4 and took him to a Hollywood studio where *Heir* coauthor Frank Schroeder was auditioning young men for the lead role in *The Pistol,* a movie Schroeder was filming about Maravich as an eighth-grade basketball phenom. The next morning, Lydic picked up Maravich and Schroeder at their hotel and drove them to the gymnasium of First Church of the Nazarene for the 7 a.m. game. "Halfway there, I knew we were going to be late," Lydic recalls. "I thought for a moment that maybe we weren't supposed to be there that day."

Actually, the same thought had crossed Maravich's mind. As a result of being hobbled and not having played for a while, Maravich proved to be only a shadow of Pistol Pete in the lighthearted competition. Guarded loosely by former Dallas Mavericks player Ralph Drollinger, Maravich "wasn't able to get the ball up over his head; he was shooting from around his belt," Dobson observed. "There was just one shining moment when he dribbled to his left and made a shot that no one was going to make if they hadn't been where he'd been."[3]

After three games that spanned forty-five minutes, the players broke for a few minutes. Most went to get a drink of water, leaving Lydic, Dobson, and Maravich alone on the court, the old star casually shooting three-pointers, talking about how he missed the game and how great he actually felt that day. "He turned to walk away from me, and I turned to walk away from him," Dobson said later, "and for some reason I turned back to look at him—and my vision picked him up when he was about halfway to the floor. He fell hard and didn't break his fall, [yet] I thought he was teasing." But as Dobson approached the prone Maravich, he saw immediately that his guest was in seizure, so he quickly knelt down to cradle Maravich's head, keep his airway open, and prevent him from biting his tongue.

After about twenty seconds, "he writhed once and stopped breathing, and he was gone," Dobson said. "One of the greatest athletes of all time was standing there talking to me and suddenly he was in the presence of the Lord."[4] Lydic dashed to call medics while the other players took turns administering CPR. Once the ambulance crew arrived, the players joined hands and prayed. But as it turned out, Pete Maravich had been born with only one coronary artery system instead of two, a nearly undetectable defect that usually killed less-conditioned men at half his age.

Everyone struggled afterward with the inevitable "why" questions, not least of all Dobson. He had coped with many of those same issues just a few months earlier, after a plane crash took the lives of Hugo Schoellkopf and three other close friends. Dobson habitually tried to make sense of God in every situation, largely because he had seen his intervention so often in his life. And false modesty was never a deterrent to explaining what Dobson saw as the obvious ways in which the Lord used him.

In the immediate aftermath of Maravich's shocking death, with his family's grief still so raw, Dobson knew better than to express the possibility that their bitter loss fit into God's greater plan. But in a later *Focus* broadcast commemorating Maravich, Dobson noted how many people Maravich's story had reached because of his untimely death. And he suggested that maybe Dobson himself had felt Maravich's dying breath for a specific reason.

"Why me?" he said. "Perhaps because I was given the task of articulating his passion to the press." Within thirty minutes of Maravich's death, Dobson said, "I was besieged by reporters, and they would have printed in all those newspapers that Pete's great love was basketball. I was able to say to nearly all of them that it was the Lord. He had an incredible commitment to both, but mostly to his Lord."[5]

Dobson also immediately made a lesson of the loss for Ryan, who was a teenager at the time, with his first "Be there!" exhortation. When he came home from the gym on the afternoon of January 5, 1988, Dobson sat his son down and warned him that one day he would get a telephone call like the one that Pete's wife, Jackie, had received that morning.

"And when you do," Dobson told his son in a moment that Ryan still recalls as a passionate connection with his father, "I want you to remember one thing above all else: Be there on the other side! I will be waiting for you; I'll be specifically looking for you just inside the Eastern Gate. Keep that appointment! Whatever else you do with your life is good and fine. Nothing else comes close to the significance of keeping that appointment."[6]

Another intersection of Maravich's life with Dobson's came about two and a half years later, in August 1990, when Dobson suffered what turned out to be a heart attack—in that same gymnasium at First Church of the Nazarene, about twenty feet from where Maravich had fallen.

Eerily, Dobson had practically foretold that occasion in 1988 on a *Focus* broadcast a few days after Maravich's death. "Did you sense your own mortality at that point?" cohost Mike Trout asked him. "My goodness," Dobson answered, "you think about that possibility. For all men, the possibility of a heart attack is like a time bomb ticking in your chest, and you don't know when it's going to go off." Though his father had died of heart disease, Dobson had never had any problems up to that point. "But I remember turning and looking at Pete on the floor and wondering if someday, somewhere, that could be me. You can't be confronted by death without realizing the brevity of life and applying it to your own circumstances."[7]

Dobson had always been a fit man, playing tennis when he was younger and basketball as he aged, through the three-mornings-a-week games at First Church of the Nazarene. He also was a practical eater, dodging saturated fats when he could. Yet Dobson did admit weaknesses for junk food and untimely snacking; he struggled, as many people do, to shed those extra five or ten pounds. Late one evening when Danae and a friend were home from college for a visit, Danae's friend had to run out for an errand. As long as she was going out, Dobson suggested, could she also pick up for him a chocolate shake and some French fries? Despite the pleadings of Shirley and Danae not to consume such awful fare so late in the day, Dobson ended up with his treat.

"Another time I came to the house when Mom was out of town, and there were takeout Mexican food containers in the trash and a 31 Flavors chocolate-sundae cup there too," Danae says. "All that was left were a few drops of chocolate around the edges." Doughnuts, cheese enchiladas, and ice cream also found their way to Dobson's palate fairly frequently.

In the days leading up to his heart attack, Dobson remembers experiencing occasional chest pains, once while he was playing volleyball in the backyard with some of Danae's friends from Azusa Pacific University, where she attended.

When he suffered the heart attack, Dobson was in pain but not debilitated; he slipped away after the game without any of the other players suspecting that something was wrong. He drove himself to the hospital and lingered outside the emergency room entrance for a while, wondering if he should go in. After praying about the alternatives, he began to break out in a sweat and experience chills, which made up his mind for him. He walked into the emergency room, registered, and called Shirley.

Dobson checked into the hospital under an assumed name, preferring not to have to deal with questions from the press during his recovery. He also wanted some time alone to think and pray about the implications of what had happened to him. He and Shirley only shared information with their closest advisers at first. They were very careful about letting phone calls through, with one remarkable exception: President George H. W. Bush called him from the presidential limousine. The president almost didn't reach Dobson: Initially the hospital switchboard couldn't figure out whom the president was trying to contact, because they had no one registered under Dobson's name.

⬭⬭⬭⬭

Dobson had no death wish, so he regretfully heeded one of the first doctor's orders for resuming normal life after recovering quickly from his heart attack: no more basketball. Physicians determined there was a significant chance that Dobson's heart couldn't tolerate the peak requirements of a sport that could be quite taxing, especially the all-out way that Dobson played it. Giving up the game was extremely difficult for him, and not just because he enjoyed playing it so much. It also had been a great mental and physical stress reliever before his workday started. "It was his ultimate outlet," Focus staffer Gary Lydic says, "because he could get on the court and forget about everything." Years later, the sacrifice of giving up hoops still haunted Dobson. "I had a dream just a couple of weeks ago about basketball," he said in early 2003. "I was hitting 13 three-point shots in a row!"

Doctors actually credited Dobson's devotion to the game with his surviving the cardiac arrest. Because his most important coronary artery had reached the point of almost 100 percent blockage, the demands of feeding blood to his limbs created by his strenuous games of basketball forced his circulatory system to improvise by building up collateral arterial routes to his heart. The blood flowing through those routes was enough to sustain him through his heart attack.

But Dobson also figured that perhaps he hadn't been disciplined enough about engineering habits into his lifestyle that might help him avoid the same sort of early death that his father suffered. So following his heart attack, he radically altered his diet to a conventional low-fat regimen. Also, on February 9, 1991, Dobson began an ambitious daily workout regimen that became a source of great satisfaction and, eventually, a testament to his own determination. On December 14, 1993, he began exercising 365 days per year—with no exception.

Almost from the start, the workout and related routine have been the same. Upon awakening each morning, usually around 5 or 5:30 a.m., he jots down in a notepad generally how he felt the day before, how much sleep he got the night before, the quality of his sleep, his weight, and other details that seem germane, often including how many calories he figures he consumed the day before. Then he often spends some time reading Scripture or recreational material—"I can't just get out of bed and exercise immediately"—before he descends to the lower floor of his townhome, turns the TV to a news or sports channel, and commences his workout. Typically, Dobson spends an hour to an hour and ten minutes a day in a combination of treadmill fast-walking and upper-body weight lifting. Then he goes back to his notes, recording how far and how vigorously he exercised and how long he worked out.

Soon after Dobson adopted this new routine, he came to the conviction that performing it each day at practically any cost was an important objective to him. Despite a schedule that never is the same from week to week, Dobson has persevered. He makes sure when he is on the road that he stays in hotels with the right equipment; and if he has scheduled a breakfast meeting or is making a morning appearance, Dobson sometimes rises at 4 a.m. to squeeze in his workout. On one occasion, a bodyguard walked the streets of Arlington, Virginia, in the middle of the night with Dobson so that he could get in an approximation of his usual workout.

"There have been many days when I didn't feel great, when I had a blister or a pulled muscle or an ingrown toenail," he says. "There were days when I had early board meetings, television appearances, speaking engagements, or other pressing responsibilities. I simply allowed myself no exceptions."

There are two reasons for what Dobson allows is "compulsivity on this score." "First, I know my own tendencies," he says. "I am an all-or-nothing person. If excuses offer a way out, I will find it increasingly easy to yield to them. The entire system will break down or be greatly reduced in effectiveness. Thus, I determined early on that there would be no compromises. There have been none."

The second reason for his rigid devotion to this regimen, Dobson says, "is that each day's exercise represents a mini stress test." And based on the detailed records he keeps of each day's activity, he hopes to "notice subtle changes that might alert me to something creeping up from somewhere."

By mid-2004, in fact, Dobson had performed some version of this workout more than three thousand consecutive days, with the exception of only five days. One of those off days occurred during 2001 when Dobson was writing *Bringing Up Boys* and, he admitted later, "I simply forgot to do my workout."

Three other missed days, permissibly enough, came during Dobson's second life-threatening health episode.

Dobson was a good 2,400 days into his consecutive workout record on June 16, 1998, feeling hardier than ever, when he was slammed by what he later called "the greatest crisis of my life": a major stroke.[8] Yet just a few days after experiencing this potentially deadly or disabling medical trauma, Dobson was back at his desk and roaming the halls of the Focus on the Family campus. Few argued with his contention that God had intervened to spare his life.

By 1998, Shirley had become a regular in her office at Focus, which is adjacent to her husband's and connected by a private door. From her office, she operates the National Day of Prayer and handles details for other ministries and causes that interest her. On June 16 the Dobsons had put in a usual twelve-hour day before driving to their home in the foothills of Colorado Springs. It was about 9:30 p.m., and knowing that his wife was hungry but too tired to cook, Dobson volunteered to fix her a hamburger. As he put the meat on the bun, he was stricken without warning. He became so disoriented that he dropped the burger and could neither find it nor respond to his wife.[9] "It rendered me unable to see clearly or even to speak," he says now. Dobson also found he couldn't move his right hand.

"When it happened, he wasn't aware of it and was frustrated by what Mom was telling him; [he was trying to tell] her not to call 9-1-1," recalls Danae. "He even knocked the phone off of the nightstand in the bedroom when he saw that she was going to call the hospital. He really wasn't thinking straight at the time, and no wonder."

Shirley, who had just seen a television documentary about strokes and new drug treatments for them, recognized instantly what was happening.[10] After summoning paramedics, she remained composed. She called H. B. and Beverley London and asked them to meet her at the hospital; she then called neighbors Dr. Roy and Carolyn Stringfellow to ask that they come and support her. She even slipped her personal telephone book into her purse and fed the dog because she realized she wouldn't be returning for many hours. Shirley's most important manifestation of mental clarity at that time, however, was to remember one of the most intriguing bits of information that she had encountered in the program about strokes: A relatively new, even experimental, clot-busting enzyme called tPA had been proving effective in mitigating the effects of strokes up to three hours after the occurrence.[11]

At the hospital, doctors quickly assessed the stroke as a treatable, pinpoint-sized clot on the left side of Dobson's brain,[12] so the use of tPA became an immediate possibility. If Dobson's stroke had resulted from a broken blood vessel rather than a clot, tPA would have been useless or even deadly.[13] Yet the risk that the drug would backfire was high, because the powerful dilutive effects of the enzyme—which had only been approved for use in 1996—not only could dissolve blood clots but also could overly thin the blood. If that happened, a leaking artery could hemorrhage, possibly leading to effects worse than the stroke—even death.

Before Shirley would approve its use after Dobson's arrival at the hospital, seven people signed the release endorsing the application of the risky drug, including the Londons, the Stringfellows, and two doctors: Procuring such an extensive agreement was standard operating procedure with a treatment as new and risky as tPA. At the same time, friends, family, and Focus staffers began to make thousands of phone calls worldwide requesting prayer for Dobson. One man was painting on a ladder when he heard the news, and he came down to pray; a Christian tour group was at Ephesus, the New Testament city located in modern-day Turkey, when word reached them and they also stopped to intercede for the Focus founder.[14]

Only about 10 percent of stroke victims recover completely or nearly so.[15] But within a few hours of administration of the tPA to Dobson, prayers were answered as hoped. At that point it had already become obvious that Dobson had sustained no serious complications from the drug. Another several hours later, Dobson's family and a few visiting friends noticed that he could string together a few words. Within a day, the slight droop on his right side and some facial paralysis had disappeared, and it became clear to all who knew him that Dobson was on a fast track to what they hoped would be a complete recovery. Just seven days after his stroke, in fact, Focus executives assembled the staff in the chapelteria for what they billed as an update on Dobson's condition. When James Dobson himself strode erect to the podium, Shirley with him, the stunned employees erupted in cheers and tears.

Before he could get to that point of celebration, however, Dobson had to reckon with one last obstacle. In the early hours after his stroke, Shirley was on the phone with Danae and describing for her what was going on in the hospital room. "At that point, the doctors were holding up little objects like a key, a nickel, a heart on a chain, and my dad wasn't able to find the words to say what they were," Danae recalls. "The grand communicator—my dad. And he couldn't speak." Shortly after being released from the hospital, where he stayed just a couple of days, Dobson said he "still had trouble finding certain words on occasion." The neurologist told him that such a problem was to be expected following a stroke, especially one that occurred in what was known as the brain's eloquence cortex—in the left temporal lobe that controls speech and creativity—and that it would disappear within a few months. But Dobson wasn't satisfied by that reassurance because he knew his life's work was dependent upon his ability to articulate.

"Everything that I like to be and like to think I am was completely dependent on that part of the brain," Dobson told reporters later.[16] On a walk, he and his wife prayed that the Lord would "return my 'song' to me," Dobson said.

Within a few weeks, that prayer—echoing what millions had prayed on Dobson's behalf during his illness—was also answered, and Dobson recovered all of his unique abilities. "I'm working harder now than I was at twenty-five," Dobson said at a Focus press conference only a week after the stroke.[17] Although he was not noticeably less articulate than before, his voice was still raspy from the tubes that doctors had just removed from his throat. "I don't drink. I don't smoke. I exercise every day. I eat right," he told reporters. "The one thing that I did do that I shouldn't do is work too hard."[18]

But soon, Dobson would start to consider ways to roll back his seven-days-a-week, twelve-hours-a-day schedule.

⁓⁓⁓⁓

Only those in his personal circle and the top command at Focus on the Family were aware that in 2002 Dobson suffered yet another major health setback. Prostate cancer is a common condition for men his age, but its appearance in Dobson presented him with his third major medical challenge in twelve years. Dobson was an otherwise healthy man; he knew he couldn't have held up through such travails without having been so robust overall.

As it happened, the microscopic sites on his prostate were diagnosed in the spring of 2002, during a time of great strain at Focus. Not only was the entire organization gearing up for its twenty-fifth anniversary celebration, but Focus was in the midst of a pronounced three-year leveling off in donations as a result of the economic strain on its supporters from the recession.

Yet Danae says she was confident of the outcome of this episode from the start. One of her mentors is Kathleen Hart, wife of Arch Hart and a Dobson family friend. Still living in the Dobsons' old neighborhood in Arcadia, Kathleen Hart prayed until three o'clock in the morning after she heard about Dobson's cancer. "She said the Lord spoke to her heart that Dad was going to be all right," Danae says. "I just clung to those words because she is a prayer warrior like none you've ever heard, and I knew that if she said the Lord had spoken to her, he had."

Indeed, doctors immediately gave Dobson an excellent prognosis, and "proton beam" treatment of the cancer went very well. He required radiation but not chemotherapy, and soon Dobson's prostate cancer was just another notch in his belt of defeated health scares.

But medical challenges weren't the only major new stresses that tested Dobson during midlife. Others arose outside his own body, even though they came from close to his heart.

∽◟◞◠◝◟◞∽

Great men cast huge shadows, attracting all sorts of other men and women into their intriguing world. But almost by definition, their disciples can't, in most ways, measure up to their leader. Dobson has proven a prototypical giant among men in this respect.

Mike Trout had been Dobson's right-hand man on the radio broadcast for more than a decade when in October 2000 he admitted to an extramarital relationship and resigned from Focus. Through hundreds of shows this silky-voiced man had set up Dobson's delivery of marriage and family nostrums and, very often, elaborated on Dobson's observations with relevant anecdotes from his own marriage and fatherhood. The contrast with the image of integrity that Dobson had always fought hard to present was too obvious for critics to resist. Focus on the Family, which the mainstream media viewed as "holier than thou," became the target of jokes on *The Tonight Show* and *Politically Incorrect*. Dobson wasn't shocked by what seemed to the comic pundits an obvious setup for humor, but he was embarrassed nonetheless.

Dobson says that he suspected all wasn't right with Mike Trout shortly before his revelation; his vice president of broadcasting, normally a highly responsive executive, had been failing to provide timely answers even to Dobson's hot pending memos. He was more saddened than angered by Trout's fall from grace. "There was never a rift between Mike and me," Dobson says. "My heart was grieved over what he did, and he himself has been embarrassed about it and admitted he'd not been truthful. He didn't blame me or Focus. We've gone to breakfast and lunch, and we took him to church. But he's gone down his own road."

Gil Moegerle remains the only ex-aide who has actually tried to take Dobson down with him. The two developed a close relationship in the late seventies and early eighties, as Moegerle filled not only the role of on-air alter ego but also of the chief shaper, besides Dobson, of the burgeoning media ministry. His smoky and decidedly unique voice, his evocative interplay with Dobson on the air, and his judgment and professionalism in directing the broadcast proved vital to Focus's growth and to Dobson's expanding personal ministry during that time.

But almost from the point of their move to California from Chicago in 1978 to join the Focus staff, the relationship between Moegerle and his wife was fracturing. And that concerned Dobson, who had developed affection for both Moegerles and their three children. Moegerle and his wife filed for divorce almost simultaneously in February 1986. And as Moegerle's marriage unraveled, so did his career at Focus.

Moegerle believes he was unfairly fired by Focus on the Family, and even went so far as to sue the ministry for wrongful termination, intention to inflict emotional distress, and other wrongs. Dobson, on the other hand, remains tight-lipped about the entire affair, citing a court order that prohibits him from talking about the particulars of the case.

And while Dobson and the Focus board probably could have put it aside as a sad but not entirely unlikely chapter in a ministry that had existed as long and had expanded as broadly as Focus, Moegerle wasn't finished. In line with his second wife's wishes, he changed his last name to Alexander-Moegerle and began to abandon some of his former evangelical views, aligning them with the more liberal sympathies of his second wife. From that perspective, in addition to his personal animus against Dobson, he began to synthesize a fear that his old mentor—by getting more involved in commentary on political issues—had begun to take a triumphalist approach to the social ills that had befallen America. Moegerle thought he could stop his old boss by writing a book that would "expose" Dobson for what he really was.

"Like many moralists who call themselves 'God's chosen,'" rails the dust jacket of *James Dobson's War on America,* "Dobson has plenty to hide." Published in 1997 by Prometheus Books, the tome is a highly personal diatribe. In the first two-thirds of the volume, Moegerle attempts to take Dobson apart as a sexist, racist, homophobic, belligerent, arrogant control freak who was a real and growing danger to the Republic. Many believe, however, that his true motives were clear in the final sections of the book where, in fine detail, Moegerle chronicles his personal difficulties with Dobson over the breakup of his first marriage, the initiation of his second one, and the complexities that they caused him in his role at Focus.

"Gil thought the whole world would be laid out for him, and he was thinking that he was almost as big as Jim," alleges a former high-level Focus insider. "And then when the silver platter of opportunities didn't come, he went ballistic." Dobson briefly condemned the book as untruthful after it came out. The book sold very poorly, just a few thousand copies.

In the years since, Moegerle's thoughts about his old boss have undergone a fascinating transformation, which he hasn't revealed in public. Much mellowed in 2003 when asked to reflect on his relationship with Dobson, Moegerle was contrite about the vitriolic nature of his attack on his old boss, with whom he hadn't communicated in over a decade. "I was caught up in times of personal outrage," he explains. "Also, there were some interpretations of facts where I got carried away and wasn't careful with language—and I wish I'd been less emotional with it." Now a public relations executive with a California utility company and recently divorced from his second wife, Moegerle adds, "It was very easy for me emotionally to extrapolate from his conduct toward me personally that the country was in for a rough ride as well. But it got too big in my head."

He says that his "bitterness is gone, and it has been for years. I don't ruminate on it; I'm not upset. I hope I have forgiven him." On the other hand, Moegerle allows, "I'm sure I wounded him in some very profound ways. It could be my friends are right who say it's too much to assume that this breech could be reconciled in our lifetimes. Through their eyes, it was unforgivable."

For Dobson's part, he says that "God really used the Moegerle experience to teach me that I don't have to fight all my own battles; the Lord dramatically led me to let him handle it. But it was very hurtful to me personally. And," Dobson adds, "it was in the same era where, if people got you in the spotlight, they could really hurt your ministry."

Moegerle's regret is intensified by vivid memories of his early days at Focus, when the staff could barely keep up with the interest Dobson was generating. "We had something really special," he says of Dobson and the handful of Focus staffers and devotees at the beginning. "We had experiences that are once-in-a-lifetime experiences. We had over-the-top joy, a sense that somehow, by God's grace and blessing, we were putting something together that met some gigantic needs, and letters would come pouring in that would make us weep. It was just an extraordinary experience."

CHAPTER FOURTEEN

THE DOBSON DIFFERENCE

If it doesn't adhere to his principles,
it won't adhere to his game plan.

GALAL GOUGH, FRIEND OF JAMES DOBSON

"Topping out" is a major milestone in the construction of a building, typically marked by the crew with a little celebration. So in January 1993 when the contractor finished the structural steel roof of Focus's new administration building—in a vista still punctuated by a Christmas tree that construction workers had dragged up there—Focus bought pizzas and Cokes for the several dozen hard-hatted celebrants.

Focus Executive Vice President Paul Nelson was a veteran of construction sites from his days in the oil refining business. He briefed James Dobson on the importance of the occasion as they drove the several miles from Focus's temporary downtown offices out to the new digs.

A cold wind blew through the building shell, and the workers were milling around gnawing on pizza, when their foremen told them that Nelson and Dobson were coming by. The two business-suited executives donned hard hats when they arrived, but neither banality nor bonhomie was going to cut it in this setting.

"Construction sites hadn't been Jim's background, so I could tell that he didn't know his audience," Nelson recalls. "It looked like this was going to be a dud of an occasion. Here he is, and these guys are kind of looking at us and pawing the dirt. And I flopped with my introduction. I asked the guys if they knew who Focus on the Family was, and they really didn't. Then I started to try to find common ground, asking who had families; they were unresponsive. Then I asked them if any of them had mothers! Finally, I introduced Jim by saying here is a man who is concerned about all of that, a big man who's taking time to thank you. But I got nothing out of them.

"Then he came up there, with the same crowd I was talking to, and over the next fifteen or twenty minutes, I watched him totally win over these guys who had no idea what or who he was," Nelson says. "This was an audience that was completely foreign to his typical message, but I saw him turn them around that day."

Dobson began his remarks by referring to the peril involved in their jobs and by sympathizing with Kerry Dore, the construction worker who had been impaled on a rebar not fifty yards from where Dobson was talking (and who later would return to the scene of his injury threatening violence). Dobson talked warmly about the importance of their work, their roles as breadwinners in their families, and in particular about the significance of the building they were finishing. Dobson explained Focus's plans to broadcast his radio program from studios that would be completed just about where they were standing that day, beaming messages to satellites that would spread positive family prescriptions across the country and around the globe.

"After taking it into their world and expressing appreciation in a way that communicated with them, he made them feel that this wasn't just another office building they were putting up—that it had a special mark," Nelson says.

The initially stoic crowd warmed up, and soon several came forward to talk with Dobson. One worker mentioned that his wife listened to the Focus broadcast regularly but he'd been embarrassed to admit that publicly; others said Dobson's comments on the family had touched a chord within them. Nelson, who has seen Dobson speak in many different settings, was reminded of Dobson's skill in reading and connecting with his audience. "I just stood there in amazement. It was one more confirmation that this guy is something else," Nelson says.

⊱⋇⊰

When people try to take the measure of Dobson, they often list his talents and attributes, concluding that he possesses a rare combination. For example, "he's a remarkable combination of entrepreneur, biblical thinker, detailed administrator, stunningly effective communicator, and visionary," says Charlie Jarvis, once a senior staffer at Focus and later Gary Bauer's presidential campaign manager. "Those almost never all exist in a single person. That almost always has to be a combination of people. He is all of those things and at the same time he's personable." Yet the story of Dobson and the hard hats goes beyond any mere listing of aptitudes, illustrating his elemental appeal and an even deeper reason for his longevity as a sage and communicator. This is the essentially unnameable quality that continues to confound friends and enemies, fellow conservative leaders and rank-and-file employees alike. Call it "the Dobson difference": the ability of a man who often provokes extreme responses to find the shrewd middle in so much of what he does.

The Dobson difference emerges in many ways—through the truths by which he lives his life, his words and actions, and the way people react to him. This singularity may seem paradoxical, but it actually reflects a deep and studied complexity about a man who isn't at all internally inconsistent. For example, Dobson is a doctrinaire Protestant yet has great ecumenical appeal. He is, more than anything, a man of principle, yet he is capable of great pragmatism. He hits a sweet spot with female readers and fans yet easily touches chords with men as well. Dobson is uncompromising in his political goals, yet effectively Lincolnian when he has to be: Just as President Lincoln utilized strategy and compromise to vanquish slavery, Dobson knows when to take a stand and even occasionally when to step back in order to make his point most effectively or to win a broader victory.

Though Dobson books sell millions and he runs one of the largest Christian ministries in the world, his personal and organizational financial stewardship is a model of restraint and responsibility that even further sets him apart from many of his contemporaries. And while he makes enemies, many don't really enjoy being at odds with him.

⁓⌇⌇⁓

Dobson's fan base is not limited to evangelical Christians. He has also developed broad appeal among traditional Catholics and conservative Jews. "There are lots of people who might not agree with him theologically and certainly wouldn't consider themselves evangelical, who nonetheless enjoy listening to him and find his advice on families to be cogent and useful," says John Green, an expert on religion and politics at the University of Akron.

Despite the strong vein of anti-Catholicism in his own Nazarene tradition and in evangelicalism as a whole, Dobson has made inroads particularly among Catholics. To be sure, he sometimes takes a step backward in that relationship. In 1994, for example, Dobson notably decided against signing on to a high-profile effort led by Charles Colson called Evangelicals and Catholics Together, which was designed to come up with a document emphasizing all the things that evangelicals and Catholics could agree on. "He was afraid of the Baptist reaction," Colson says, explaining that among Protestants, Baptists take particular theological exception to some tenets of Catholics; Baptists also make up a huge core of Dobson's audience. Advised by his board of directors not to sign, Dobson says he wasn't sure what position to take on Colson's invitation to him to be a signatory but that the Focus board made a unanimous decision against it.

By the midnineties, however, Dobson was nurturing ready and steady Catholic allies including William Bennett. "He's found common cause with Catholics because in some ways, Catholics have been more appreciative over the years of the importance of cultural issues and battles, and Jim has shown a remarkable appreciation of that," says Bennett, one of the nation's best-known conservative Catholics. Another leader of conservative Catholics, Father Robert Sirico, head of the Acton Institute, a Michigan-based think tank, observes that Dobson has come to be seen by many Catholics as a leader "in an unintended ecumenical encounter that's afforded by the crisis in the culture. James Dobson is coming to know a lot more about Catholicism and is making a distinction between cultural and serious Catholics." Dobson himself acknowledges his serious theological differences with Catholics but says, "I really believe that the stand they've taken on cultural issues is absolutely critical, and we'd have been in a bigger mess if they hadn't."

In fact, when Sirico helped organize an international conference in Rome in 2000 on the family, he suggested that the Vatican invite Dobson and Colson because he believed they saw eye to eye with the cardinals on most family issues. So along with about two hundred family experts, theologians, politicians, and others from Europe and the Americas, Dobson and Colson and their wives attended the weeklong gathering in November 2000, and as Colson recalls, became the first two evangelicals ever to address an audience at the historic Synod in the Vatican.

The Dobsons and the Colsons also received *prima filia,* or front-row, first-aisle seats for a general audience with Pope John Paul II, a privilege that is reserved only for highly important figures such as heads of state. And while the honor thrilled Dobson, the anticipation of it also made him uncomfortable. He believed he would be expected to kneel down and kiss the ring of Pope John Paul II, perhaps appearing to compromise his belief that the papacy deserves no more homage than any other human institution of the church. So he was relieved to find out just beforehand that non-Catholics are given a pass from paying that kind of homage.

Ironically, however, Dobson ended up kneeling before the papal authority anyway. The Pope was becoming so infirm that he now sat during these public audiences rather than standing as he had done during his earlier days. And at six feet two, Dobson had to kneel down just to utter a few words to the pontiff; Shirley did likewise. It was a bit of pragmatism that he was only too happy to practice.

ဆင်္

Just as Dobson increasingly finds accommodation with Catholics but not with Catholicism, he also manages to navigate the crosscurrents that swirl within Protestantism. Though he did write one essentially theological work, *When God Doesn't Make Sense*, and though interviewers such as Larry King often seek to draw him out on theological fine points, Dobson is always quick to point out that he is "no theologian" and has had no specific training in the subject. And though he was raised in a denomination with boundaries deeply set in tradition and theology, Dobson manages to file off his own doctrinal edges for public consumption. He even places his fervent opposition to gambling—a vice to many conservative denominations for doctrinal reasons—instead in the context of sociological concerns about the impact of gambling on families.

In fact, Dobson has purposely chosen to avoid many issues that stir divisions within the diverse world of conservative Protestantism, especially those that have little to do with the protection of the family. Despite the strong influence of his own highly sectarian upbringing on his beliefs, Dobson almost completely avoids discussions about denominational differences. Instead, he engages his readers, radio listeners, and the culture at large as a sort of evangelical everyman and finds himself generally recognized as such. It came as little surprise, then, when the Southern Baptist Convention invited Dobson, a noted Nazarene, to deliver the keynote address to their annual conventions in 1998 and 2001.[1]

Dobson has surprised and disappointed some of his supporters over the years by taking a moderate or no position on issues that many Christians believe call for a response. For example, unlike many Christians who crusade against the use of Ritalin and other drugs for treating attention deficit hyperactivity disorder and similar maladies, Dobson believes that such drugs are often very helpful. Likewise, he has never dipped into the topic of racially mixed marriage.

Dobson always advises parents not to expend too much parental capital trying to stop their kids from masturbating, because he has determined that the practice doesn't lead to aberrant behavior later on in life and because he figures parents have little chance of succeeding anyway. After early broadcasts addressing birth control pills—which he does not object to theologically—generated controversy, Dobson decided that there was no reason to dwell on a topic that unnecessarily creates so much division among his listeners.

And while his traditional views about family life imply condemnation of mothers working outside the home, Dobson has never been strident about that point, always acknowledging that economics and other life circumstances dictate the need for many mothers to work. "Even early on, he wouldn't say that women absolutely should stay at home," says Ginger Shingler, a friend of Dobson dating back to Pasadena College days. "For a Christian leader of his status to take that position—that shows a lot of respect toward women."

In fact, Dobson's genius in a way follows the methods of the world's best retailers. Like them, he knows that women make the vast majority of consumption decisions in American society, including what station remains tuned in on the kitchen radio. And he clearly understands that they tend to be the heart of the family.

It isn't that Dobson disregards men. He has aimed books at them, such as *What Wives Wish Their Husbands Knew about Women*; he talks widely about his interest in hunting and in sports; he devotes considerable attention to male roles in relationships; and his rough-and-tumble tactics in the political realm certainly bespeak a man's man.

"A lot more men listen to *Focus* than we once assumed," says John Fuller, Dobson's cohost beginning in 2001. "He becomes a role model for many men, and they need that."

But there is no doubt that in his work, Dobson displays a particular empathy toward women, something that family members and longtime friends believe he developed because of his background and upbringing. "His mother must have rubbed off on him, because he can really put himself in the shoes of a woman," says Dobson's friend Arch Hart. "Part of it is coming from the Nazarene denomination where women have a lot of influence, where you don't find the machismo that you find in the Baptist church, for example." In 1936, the year that Dobson was born, there were only fifty-seven men in the Nazarene denomination for every one hundred women.[2] Among other things, the crucial role of women in the Nazarene church was exemplified by pastors' wives, who were expected to play major social roles in what was essentially a co-ministry. Certainly, Myrtle Dobson was exemplary in that way.

Later on Dobson strategically embraced this appreciation for women and made it a foundation of his success. Still true today, married women between the ages of twenty-nine and fifty-nine with children make up the majority of *Focus*'s audience; and the majority of the audience (men and women combined) have a college degree, according to a recent study compiled by the Barna Research Group.[3] Time and time again, Dobson communicates with these female readers and listeners in ways that tell them he understands their concerns like few others, that they can trust him to see things from their point of view, and that he will deliver messages that are relevant to their lives.

One memorable passage in *Night Light: A Devotional for Couples* illustrates Dobson's understanding of life as women experience it. Women typically express their feelings and thoughts better than men, Dobson says, and are often irritated by their husbands' reticence to talk with them. "God may have given a wife 50,000 words a day and her husband only 25,000," Dobson writes. "He comes home from work each day with 24,976 already used up and so merely grunts his way through the evening. He may even descend into watching *Monday Night Football*— and all the while, his wife is still dying to expend her remaining 25,000 words."[4]

"He is a master at that," says Dean Merrill, a former Focus executive and an author. "Millions of women have felt authenticated by him and squared their shoulders and said, 'Here's a man with a Ph.D. who thinks who I am, and what I'm doing, is important.' His exaltation of them was the key."

Ginger Shingler believes that Dobson understands that "the greatest things women want are to be loved and to have a sense of security."

Colleen McDannell, a University of Utah history professor, came up with an incisive thesis about how Dobson managed to leverage his sensibilities about feminine concerns into the huge base of female support that he and Focus now enjoy. In 1999 McDannell researched and wrote the treatise "Beyond Dr. Dobson: Women, Girls, and Focus on the Family." Her main argument was that a primary reason Dobson and Focus enjoy such popularity with women is that they deliberately avoid controversy whenever possible, in large part because "women and girls respond differently to conflict than men and boys."[5] While men respond to arguments based on critical thinking that is impersonal and perfectionist, women prefer to learn through collaboration and empathy.

"Women and girls find in the Christianity of Focus on the Family a religion that is unified, connected, practical, and relational," McDannell said. "Rather than engage in theological speculation or ethical argumentation, Focus on the Family is silent on any issue that would divide or demand an analytical response. Women, who find that they cannot easily disconnect their family lives from their working and religious lives, may find this type of Christianity more in tune with their emotional outlooks. . . . The success of James Dobson's message and his organization may be more due to his emphasis on relationship and empathy than a fundamentalist wish for 'clarity, certitude, and control.'"[6]

While Focus's broadcasts use empathy to appeal to listeners, Dobson brings much more certitude to the political arena. He rarely spins things so that they go down more easily with any constituency. And he doesn't triangulate from his principles to some kind of mushy midpoint so that he can be acceptable to the masses or to focus groups. What Dobson does is demonstrate an uncanny ability to know which matters and which positions to emphasize, to understand when to singe and when to couch, when to nudge and when to parry, and in the end to recognize which hills he wants to be found standing on and which to retreat from.

His allies as well as his enemies attest to it. "We've made it through some pretty substantial disagreements," says William Bennett. They've had differences, for example, over how to approach abortion, with Bennett sometimes favoring less dogma than Dobson in the interests of achieving partial gains for the antiabortion movement. "It's been a matter of discussion and debate, but even when we differ at the end, mutual respect," Bennett says. "We've had some strong and intense conversations and have been very direct with each other. But he doesn't pout about it afterward. He's direct and manly, and we move on."

Yet as averse to sacrificing a matter of principle as Dobson is, he is still capable of assuming a posture of openness to compromise that sometimes surprises even his close associates. One such case was Dobson's reaction to President George W. Bush's decree on stem-cell research in August 2001. Focus and most other evangelicals were opposed to any research involving embryonic stem cells from aborted fetuses because it essentially involves using a dead baby as a laboratory specimen. Early in Bush's presidency, Christian conservatives—including Dobson—were putting tremendous heat on Bush to ban the research despite the potential benefits in treating a variety of serious conditions and diseases.

When Bush made it clear that he intended to show his hand on stem-cell research by late August or early September of 2001, Dobson prepared to do a *Focus* broadcast right before or after the announcement. One thing the Focus brain trust didn't yet know, even at that late date, was what Bush was actually going to declare; the president was keeping his proposal very close to the vest. What was clear from Focus's contacts in the White House and on Capitol Hill, however, was that a presidential proposal of an outright ban on all stem-cell research using embryos would have been overturned by Congress, recalls Walt Larimore, a physician who was one of Focus's experts on prenatal life. "We were assured that a veto-proof margin for overturning such a ban was already in the bag in both houses and that if President Bush decided to take that road, it would have in essence condemned millions of embryos to destruction."

Larimore urged Dobson to wait until a date expected to be closer to the president's announcement to air a program so any call to action would have more impact. But Dobson said he sensed the Lord telling him to record a program right away, even if it was just to educate *Focus* listeners about the issue in advance of the president's decision. So on Tuesday morning, August 7, Dobson and Larimore recorded a *Focus* program about stem-cell research that concluded with a call to pray for the president to have wisdom in making such a momentous decision. The program was scheduled to air that Thursday. And on Thursday morning around ten o'clock, the White House announced that Bush would outline his actions related to future stem-cell research in a speech that evening. Shortly thereafter, a producer for *Larry King Live* requested that Dobson appear on the program immediately after the president's speech to respond to what he had said.

"Now the pressure cooker really went on," Larimore says, "because we would be talking to literally a worldwide audience. And we still didn't know what Dr. Dobson was going to say to all those people, in part because we couldn't get the White House to tell us first what the president was going to say."

A few minutes before the presidential announcement, Dobson received a phone call from Karl Rove in the White House. He gave Dobson a "heads up." Dobson probed for details, and was assured that the president would not allow any live embryos to be killed on the federal dime.

Focus had requested that its employees spend part of the afternoon praying about the issue, and the Dobsons, Walt Larimore, and a few others closeted themselves to pray not only about the issue but how Dobson himself should address it.

"We prayerfully considered the various points of view," Larimore says. "But finally, Dr. Dobson said that he understood that incremental change—and at times even understanding the political process—requires wise compromise." According to Larimore, Dobson decided about fifteen minutes before the president went on that he would support most of the president's position. He was especially pleased that President Bush was the first president in history to openly express his belief that life begins at conception and that life at all stages was valuable. About that point Shirley Dobson—by now a frequent member of her husband's inner counsel—opined that the president "needs a bouquet."

An hour or so later Dobson was sitting in his studio at Focus, hooked up via satellite, and ready for Larry King's interview. King's other guests were Mary Tyler Moore, the actress who advocates broad stem-cell research in her role as international chairman of the Juvenile Diabetes Research Foundation, and Christopher Reeve, who was an even more ardent backer of stem-cell research until his death in 2004. Both Moore and Reeve essentially condemned the president's plan.

Then King introduced Dobson, who said, "There are still some aspects to [Bush's decision] that we want to look at, but I think he found a good solution for this stage." He expressed gratitude that the president hadn't called for "federal funds to be expended to take human life, to kill those little embryos" and that Bush at least had "implied that life begins at conception. And although we grieve the loss of the babies that were sacrificed for those cells that now exist, they are now gone, and these cells are there. And I think we can live with that."

Dobson went on to express empathy with Reeve and others who advocated unimpeded stem-cell research in the hopes of quicker cures for diabetes, paralysis, Alzheimer's, and other conditions. "But we don't support research that takes a life," he said. "Once you start doing that, it is a slippery slope down which humanity will slide, and I am grateful that the president did not do that tonight."

King challenged him on whether parents of "unused embryos" should have any say in the disposition of those bodies. In response, Dobson reached for an anecdotal illustration of the sort that often reduces opponents' arguments to a heartless heap. First, Dobson mentioned Moore's reference to these embryos in earlier congressional testimony as resembling "little goldfish." He continued: "I tell you what, two days ago I held a little two-year-old 'goldfish' on my lap, and she sang a song to me. She said, 'Jesus loves the little children, all the children of the world.' We must not forget that they are human beings. You and I started that way, as did our children, Larry—and we must protect them."[7]

<hr/>

Dobson is anything but Lincolnian when it comes to money. As he made his own livelihood from book royalties and used the contributions of millions of listeners to build Focus, Dobson has always understood that financial matters could just as easily kill his ministry and his reputation as buttress them. And he believes that it was absolutely necessary for him and Focus to differentiate themselves clearly from many Americans' perception of Christian ministries as money-grubbing monuments to the founder's self-aggrandizement.

Dobson has spent much time studying what the Scriptures say about money. "Show me the way a person handles money, and I'll tell you a great deal about what that person really believes," Dobson says. "If there's an ethical weakness hidden somewhere, it'll probably involve money in one way or another. Money is very dangerous. Jesus talked about it more than any other subject—most of it in the nature of a warning or something negative. It can get ahold of you and control you and make you control others."

Of course, Dobson isn't the first observer to note the power of lucre. But he and Focus came into their prime during the eighties, when many other Christian leaders allowed greed and deeply sinful behavior to derail their ministries and their careers. Dobson was relentless about drilling a sense of fiscal responsibility into his lieutenants, constantly reminding them that even Focus was vulnerable to a financial scandal that could greatly damage or even destroy the ministry.

Dobson's convictions about spending Focus funds also are on display in his attitude toward his air travel. It would be easy to make the argument—and some associates and Focus board members certainly have—that Dobson is an ideal candidate for a private jet. The demands on his time are as great, or greater, than those even on many Fortune 500 CEOs and U.S. senators. And he has more daunting geographic challenges than most because he has to make frequent trips to both coasts from the relative remoteness of Colorado Springs.

But while he occasionally agrees to private flights donated by Focus supporters, Dobson never has been open to the possibility that the ministry could purchase its own jet or even own a time-share of a Lear jet. He's painfully cognizant that it would make him vastly more efficient and certainly fresher upon arriving at his destinations. But the importance of utter fiscal responsibility—and just as crucial, of making its exercise apparent to Focus supporters—overrides any of those other considerations.

When Dobson makes such decisions, associates say, he draws his bottom line from the biblical widow who donated her two mites, small-denomination coins that represented most of her possessions, to the church (Mark 12:42). Focus has plenty of supporters like her. "Some of our contributors live on Social Security," Dobson says. "To spend money that way wouldn't be right." It's not just a matter of the difficulty of communicating the need he would have for a private jet, he points out. "There are certain things expected of you when you're in this kind of leadership," such as making do on commercial flights, although his board has insisted that he fly first class. The board felt that first class offered a better environment for him to read or catch up on paperwork during long flights.

Early on, Dobson also took pains to establish a structure for separating personal from ministerial proceeds that has never been seriously challenged, either within or outside Focus. Book proceeds had provided a good income for Dobson by the early eighties. Just as Focus began growing in its financial dimensions, so Dobson drew a line between the two revenue streams: He alone would harvest royalties from his books sold outside of Focus, but he wouldn't draw a salary or any form of compensation from Focus. You could argue ad infinitum about whether Dobson or Focus was benefiting more from the symbiosis between his popular persona and the growing organization, but there didn't seem to be a need to wrap such a discussion around a precise financial equation.

At the very least, Dobson made sure that he did everything possible to build and observe a fire wall between his writing career and his ministry. He hired Karen Bethany as an administrative assistant once Focus moved to Colorado Springs in 1991, for example, and personally paid 50 percent of her salary even though all of her work was actually for Focus. "He didn't want . . . there [to be] any misunderstandings about whether it was appropriate," Bethany says. "And if there was ever an error in an expense report or something, he wanted to err with the expense on his personal side. He was very conscious that he would rather pay for things than risk that it would come out of Focus funds."

This conservatism is also a reflection of Dobson's attitude toward administering his own resources. "We don't live extravagantly, and I wouldn't be comfortable doing so," he says. Thus, friends often needle Dobson to buy a new suit or perhaps a luxury wristwatch or two to complement the utilitarian models he favors. "I have a plain gold wedding ring that hardly has been off my finger in forty-three years," he adds, "and Shirley is very conservative in her jewelry. That's the way we're supposed to live, and we've tried to do that. You have an obligation as a ministry leader to live to a certain modest standard, and I don't like showy kinds of materialism anyway."

Part of Dobson's sensitivity to such matters stems from how he got burned over a red Mercedes that he owned in the eighties. Even before Focus was off the ground, he says, a friend who went to Europe brought him back a bright red Mercedes-Benz sedan from Germany. It would have retailed for far more in the United States, and his net price was actually a lot lower because he was able to write it off as a business expense. He kept the vehicle for seven years and wove into many a conversation an apology for the showy appearance that the Mercedes created. Some supporters and associates began criticizing his ownership of the car.

"They were saying that I had a flamboyant lifestyle," Dobson says, now able to joke about a matter that caused him some distress for a few years. "So I sold it for $15,000 and bought an Acura, which cost more, but those people were happy." His latest car, another Acura sedan, and Shirley's Ford Explorer are late nineties models, Dobson notes.

Even Dobson's homes have been modest. The family's beloved house on Harvard Drive in Arcadia hardly bespoke the financial status that Dobson enjoyed by the time he moved out of Southern California in the early nineties. His Colorado Springs condominium is one of many cookie-cutter townhouses in a pleasant development; the family's vacation condo in Palm Springs, California, which they bought after leaving the state for Colorado, is a two-bedroom hideaway of only about a thousand square feet.

The Dobsons also give generously from their income. They support a variety of ministries including churches, Christian colleges, pro-life organizations, and Prison Fellowship, founded by Charles Colson.

More significantly and unusually, however, Dobson is also often ready to provide individual and even extemporaneous benevolence. He frequently authorizes his aides to send a book or tape gratis to someone with a particular need. "He'd say, 'I met a waitress last night, and she's a single mom,'" Bethany says. "'We need to send her a book.'"

And on a 1997 trip to South Africa, several associates observed just how spontaneous Dobson could be in his generosity. A handful of Focus board members had traveled there on a fact-finding mission connected to the ministry's office in that country. During dinner one evening at a game reserve, a South African staff member told about his upcoming nuptials to another staffer. The problem for this young man was that he had to produce a dowry of eleven cows in order to secure his bride's hand from her father, and he had only managed to acquire seven cows at that point.

"When Dr. Dobson got up from the table later, he told me that he wanted to give this man a personal check for another cow, which amounted to about $300," recalls Karen Bethany. "He didn't have to be interested in this young man or his needs. But that's just the way he is."

Such a philosophy also has afforded Dobson the very real pleasure of knowing that his financial integrity never can be questioned. He remembers talking about the issue with his son, Ryan, in 1993, when the ministry of evangelist Robert Tilton was collapsing amid allegations of egregious financial abuses such as his purchase of a $450,000 yacht using proceeds from supporters.

"There was a news helicopter that flew over all of this incredible real estate [Tilton] had," Dobson recalls, "and Ryan said to me, 'Yeah, Dad, if they do an exposé on you, they'll fly over your condo here and say that you live in the eighth brown one from the left.'"

❧❧❧❧❧

Perhaps it is this "Dobson difference" that sometimes disarms even his ideological enemies. They understand that there always will be diametric opposition between them on spiritual, social, or cultural matters. But it might be that people of all political and relational persuasions sense that Dobson and his organization really are interested in and capable of relating to them. In any event, there are some who by all rights could despise Dobson and Focus but can't bring themselves to do so.

For example, in her 1998 book *Ferocious Romance: What My Encounters with the Right Taught Me about Sex, God, and Fury*, author Donna Minkowitz—a self-described "lesbian, feminist, and sex radical" who has won awards for her coverage of social issues for the *Village Voice*—told about a series of visits she made to churches, Christian events, and parachurch organizations in order to get a better feel for her political and social enemies. She went to a service at the church of the "Toronto Blessing," sneaked into a Promise Keepers rally, and then went to Focus on the Family to visit with Paul Hetrick; Larry Burtoft, who was then Focus's resident expert on homosexuality; and Bobby Ace, a former gay man who was on the Focus periodicals staff.

"Focus is more influential than the Christian Coalition and about six times as sympathetic," she wrote as she introduced her visit to Focus. "The influential Focus men who have filed into this lovely conference room to have coffee with me are very nice behind their ties and their clean shaves: Niceness, in so many ways, is what Focus is about, and the reason you probably haven't heard of it, despite its power."

Minkowitz entered the room full of cheek and ice but soon mellowed somewhat when she realized that she and the men from Focus both opposed such things as violent pornography. They had a long, reasoned, and respectful discussion of homosexuality, and finally one of them shared a hug with Minkowitz. In the end, she found that "I respect these people. I don't know why, but it feels so liberating that I don't have to hate them at every moment and in every way. In the peace and openness of this clunky exchange, it's as though I've taken a knife out of my own *kishkes,* not theirs."[8]

And in a February 2003 column in the *New York Observer,* Eileen Kelly revealed yet another aspect of why it's difficult to hate Dobson and Focus. Jogging through Prospect Park one day with her Walkman, Kelly wrote, she tuned in to *Focus.* "It's antichoice, antigay, antifeminist, pro—corporal punishment," she wrote. "I would tell anyone—I tell *myself*—that what I hear outrages me. And it's true. But also—really!—I am tranquilized."

A self-described feminist and stay-at-home mother, as she pondered the very different roles that she and her husband had chosen within their marriage, Kelly found herself drawn to "the honeyed tones" of Dobson on the broadcast and attracted by his exhortations to traditional family values. "Does anyone besides me sometimes need to reaffirm her existence by listening to Christian talk?" By the end of the column, Kelly had decided that she doesn't really need to listen to Dobson in order to feel better about her life. But at the same time, she admits that she was compelled by his message.

"The truth is, I do need to have faith—just not Dr. Dobson's brand," Kelly ended. "I know that. Really. But for the time being, I don't mind his company."[9]

CHAPTER FIFTEEN

TRANSFORMED LIVES

I can't thank you enough.

P aul and Stephanie Consbruck of Jacksonville, Florida, are one of several hundred married couples who met via eHarmony.com, which in 2003 became the world's fastest-growing online match-making service. The Consbrucks owe their wedded bliss to Neil Clark Warren, the Christian psychologist who founded eHarmony.com in 2000.[1] His goal was to apply his life's study of marriage dynamics to the business of helping people find true soul mates using the Internet. Warren credits his company's success in large part to James Dobson, his colleague of more than twenty years, who featured the entrepreneur on a *Focus on the Family* show in August 2002. At the time, Warren's company was still trying to break out of a gaggle of digital matchmaking start-ups.

"No one has been more helpful for my entire career," says Warren. "He has built such a mighty communications base that if he looks favorably on something, he'll move people. And after our show in August [2002], we got ninety thousand new referrals to our site, which overwhelmed any previous level of activity we had had." From there, Warren says, eHarmony.com began to acquire enough proceeds from new members to fund national radio and television advertisements that became ubiquitous in 2003. Its expanded marketing enabled eHarmony.com to begin to seriously pursue the Rupert Murdoch–owned giant, Match.com, in the size of its membership roll in 2004.

Warren is one of a long line of individuals whose lives have been significantly affected—and in many cases actually transformed—through a relationship or contact with Dobson and his books or with Focus on the Family and its multimedia output. Instead of the mawkish handful of people who appear at the end of the movie *It's a Wonderful Life* to toast George Bailey, the movie's hero, imagine a stream of individuals whose testimonials about Dobson and Focus could fill three or four full-length movies.

There is plenty of evidence for this conclusion. Even people who have only heard the man once or read one of his books say that Dobson changed their life. Close friends attest to the same. And there are all sorts of testifiers who find themselves somewhere in between.

ಲಾಗಾದ

Lourie Staton of Moscow, Tennessee, heeded Dobson's advice in the early nineties to shield her "late-blooming" offspring by homeschooling them if necessary, and by 2000, she credited the move for her son's successful academic and emotional development. Native American missionary Robert Disque of Guffey, Colorado, lauded a Focus staffer in 2002 for sending a box of pamphlets on suicide and other personal issues; the material was instrumental in converting to Christianity several members of a tribe in Wyoming where Disque was serving. And Debra Brinkman of Arlington, Minnesota, credited a Focus counselor for "helping me think through things rationally" after she found out that her seventeen-year-old daughter was pregnant; Brinkman was happy to report in 2001 that her eighteen-month-old grandson was bringing "delight to the entire family."[2]

Often it takes awhile for the respondent to recognize the catalytic effect of Dobson's ministry. "Back in 1992, you aired a program where a girl shared her testimony about life as a foster child" begins a typical retrospective, offered by Terry Goodman of Oak Grove, Missouri, in 2003. "At that time, after sixteen years of frustration, my wife and I had given up our dream of ever having children. But when we heard this broadcast, we were riveted. Emotions began to well up inside us, and we realized that God might have another plan for us. God used that girl's story to change our lives forever. One year later, we adopted our first child and are currently in the process of adopting our fifth! The impact you've had on our family cannot be put into words."[3]

Greg LaRance of Roseburg, Oregon, wrote to Focus in 2001 about a transformation that began several years earlier. "I am an alcoholic, and several years ago my drinking brought my family to the brink of despair,"

LaRance said. "I lost a highly respected, well-paying job in the medical profession, and my wife of sixteen years was seriously considering following a counselor's advice to take our five young children and file for divorce. During this time, she came across Dr. Dobson's book *Love Must Be Tough,* and it gave her the wisdom and guidance she needed to handle the issue. I broke down before the Lord on June 22, 1996, and gave my life to him—and I haven't had a drink since. God has restored my marriage, my family, and my career. I can't thank you enough."[4]

Occasionally, Dobson and his staff draw kudos for helping in situations that are so extraordinary that they sound like the raw material for a country-and-western song. "Several years ago, I bought a copy of *When God Doesn't Make Sense,*" began a tribute offered by Beth Rogers, of Springfield, Illinois, in 2002. "A few days after that purchase, my eighteen-year-old niece died of a brain hemorrhage. Your book helped me during the ensuing period of grief. About eighteen months ago, my mother passed away; again, I found comfort in your words. Shortly thereafter, while we were at a Christmas Eve service, our house burned down—all four of our dogs were killed in the fire and we lost most of our personal belongings. While sifting through the rubble of our home, I found your book: smoke-damaged but readable, and once again a source of strength."[5]

Especially notable are those who have been drawn into Dobson's closest spheres of influence and whose response has, in turn, affected still more people.

Consider those who chose Christian radio as a career, largely after being exposed to Dobson. In the midseventies, Janet Parshall was a stay-at-home mother of four children in Wisconsin, looking for validation in the role she had chosen instead of responding to her pangs for career satisfaction. "I could have daily messages in my home from Dan Rather and Tom Brokaw or I could turn on Christian radio," Parshall says. Dobson's was "the voice that resonated with what was going on in my heart." After confronting attempts at her kids' public school to introduce New Age practices of the sort that Dobson had been warning about on the air, "in one afternoon I became a member of the knee-jerk, radical Religious Right." As her kids left the nest, Parshall began hosting a daily talk show on a Christian radio station in Milwaukee; and within a couple of years, Concerned Women for America recruited her to Washington, D.C. to be its president. At the same time her husband, Craig Parshall, joined the staff of the Rutherford Institute, a Christian legal organization. More recently, Parshall hosted her own weekly program for Focus, *Renewing the Heart,* and now she fills in for Dobson on *Focus* occasionally.

Bill Maier trod some of the same ground Dobson did at Childrens Hospital in Los Angeles, both in his psychological training and even in hosting a radio show in California. Still, joining Focus as one of its "other voices" in January 2002 was a difficult decision for Maier. He and his wife, Lisa, were particularly concerned that when they had children she would be able to remain home with them, but taking the Focus job required Bill to take a pay cut from a lucrative radio and television voice-over career in Los Angeles. Then the Maiers traveled with Dobson to Nashville in February 2002 for the National Religious Broadcasters convention, where Dobson delivered a spirited challenge to his audience to engage the culture. After recounting how homosexual activists were infiltrating public schools and how postmodern culture was discounting the value of preborn life, Dobson challenged his 3,500 listeners to follow in the way of saints and martyrs stretching from John the Baptist to Martin Luther King Jr.[6]

"It was one of the most powerfully convicting messages I'd ever heard," Maier recalls, "and I saw a lot of blue-haired old ladies from the Midwest express shock and horror at the facts he presented." Dobson's oratory certainly stirred Maier, who was very quiet afterward in his hotel room. When Lisa Maier asked why, her husband said that God had confirmed their decision to join Focus through Dobson's speech. "I felt the Lord was saying, 'I want you to learn from this man and make a difference in the lives of America's children,'" Bill Maier told his wife.

Many politicians also find themselves swayed by Dobson, probably because they're uniquely empowered to do something about the sources of his alarm. Many of them have even been motivated to run for office because of Dobson's urgings.

Sometimes Dobson strikes really close to home. David Schultheis had been Dobson's neighbor since the midnineties when he and his wife, Sandra, and their two daughters and sons-in-law moved to Colorado Springs because of reversals in his real estate business in California. Before long, they and another couple were getting together regularly with the Dobsons to have dinner and watch old movies. In 1998, the Schultheises attended the Council on National Policy meeting in Phoenix with the Dobsons, where Dobson launched his oratorical bid to reclaim the soul of the GOP.

Schultheis heard his friend loud and clear, and in a way that he didn't expect. "It was a defining moment in my life," Schultheis recalls. Later, at a reception in the suite of former vice president Dan Quayle, Schultheis announced to those in attendance that Dobson's speech was "so profound to me that I've decided I'm going to strongly consider mounting" a campaign for state representative from Colorado Springs. After two elections, Schultheis won the seat, and Dobson became one of his constituents.

Likewise, Dobson was a significant reason that the number of committed Christian conservatives on Capitol Hill in the early years of this decade reached a modern high. "We've counted a couple of dozen who've been heavily influenced by [Dobson] and a handful who went there directly because of him," says Tom Minnery, Focus's head of public policy.

Trent Franks is one of the former. He was twenty-two years old and running his own oil-drilling contracting company in Texas in 1980 when he saw Dobson featured along with Pat Robertson, President Reagan, and others in an inspirational film called *Assignment: Life*. He was so impressed with Dobson's message that he bought a copy of the film for $1,800 and began showing it at churches in the Dallas area. Several years later, in large part motivated by Dobson's plea for Christians to run for political office, Franks got elected to the Arizona state legislature. He later ran the nation's first Family Policy Council in Arizona. And in 2002 Franks won his first term in Congress, where he's been a Dobsonian stalwart ever since.

Frank Wolf was one of the heavily influenced. The native Philadelphian and father of five was elected to Congress out of Virginia in 1980, and he admits that he soon allowed career demands to begin to squeeze out his family. That is, until the evening when some House colleagues talked Wolf into attending a showing of *Where's Dad?*—Focus's recently released TV special. "It starts very slowly, and I was telling the guys that I really had to get back home because I'd taken some meat out of the freezer," Wolf jokes. "I said to myself, *What am I doing here?* I really was going to leave, except I'd promised these guys."

Then in the film, Dobson turns to one of his favorite rhetorical devices: reading the lyrics of a popular song as poetry. In this case, it is the words to "Cat's in the Cradle," a ballad about a father's unwillingness to pour himself into his son's life—a message that was especially poignant because its author and singer, Harry Chapin, had been killed in a car accident in 1981. "It had a major impact on me," Wolf says. He "immediately made the commitment" to become a better husband and father and followed through on it. And in the ensuing years his closer attention to Dobson's concerns greatly influenced Wolf's activities in Congress, where he subsequently helped create the national task forces on pornography and gambling. Dobson served on both. Wolf still slips copies of *Where's Dad?* into the hands of new colleagues and pulls the tape out once a year to watch himself. "I hate to think [what would have happened] if I hadn't gone to see the film that day," Wolf says. "It's had a major impact on my life."

By 1996, Alan Keyes had become a rare entity: an African American who passionately and boldly articulated the conservative agenda. An accomplished Reagan administration diplomat and talk show host, the exceptionally eloquent Keyes had run for the U.S. Senate in 1988 and 1992 against liberal Democratic incumbents in Maryland, losing both times. Nevertheless, he was running for president in 1996 and getting the nominal news coverage that every declared candidate was being afforded in advance of the New Hampshire primary in January. Then something happened to his campaign: James Dobson noticed him.

"I gave a speech in New Hampshire that was televised on C-SPAN, and [Dobson] saw the speech and responded to it very favorably and very strongly," says Keyes, who is Catholic. "It was just an eight-minute thing that I gave at a dinner that night. But he put it on his broadcast, and the response to the speech essentially was responsible for the rest of my campaign. People from his audience wrote letters and sent e-mails and started organizations around the country for me, which became the basis of a grassroots campaign."

Although considered by some to be an extremist, Keyes went on to establish himself as a credible candidate in 1996 and received even more support when he ran again in 2000. After a brief stint on MSNBC as a talk show host in 2002 and another unsuccessful run for the Senate in 2004, he remains one of the most intriguing figures in the Republican Party.

༺༻

Linda Bruce was seated at Dobson's table at a luncheon in Denver in 1984, and the two started talking about the loneliness that often plagues mothers of preschool children. The Littleton, Colorado, housewife told the curious Christian psychologist about a volunteer ministry she had started to try to combat that sense of isolation. Bruce had been developing the MOPS (Mothers of Preschoolers) program on a volunteer basis for more than a decade, she told him. Fascinated and ever prepared, Dobson whipped out a tape recorder and recorded a conversation with Bruce on the spot that he soon ended up airing on Focus. Intrigued mothers, pastors, and others flooded Focus with inquiries about MOPS; ministry leaders appeared on later Focus shows; and by the end of 2003, there were more than 2,200 MOPS groups in the United States as well as seventeen other countries.

The galvanization of MOPS is one of many examples of how steady attention from Dobson and Focus has helped to transform institutions as well as individuals over the last quarter century.

Promise Keepers was a national influence in the midnineties, filling stadiums all over the country with hundreds of thousands of men pledging to redevote themselves to God and to their families. Bill McCartney, the former University of Colorado football coach who founded Promise Keepers, has said that his appearance on *Focus* in 1992 was the "launch" of the movement.[7] The growth of Moms in Touch, then a fledgling ministry of mothers who met weekly to pray for their schoolchildren, accelerated in 1988 after founder Fern Nichols and more than a dozen women who headed local groups were on a *Focus* broadcast. More than ten thousand letters streamed into Focus after it aired.

Many homeschooling families credit Dobson with that movement's increasing popularity. By 2004, about 1.1 million American children, up 29 percent in only five years, were being educated in their living rooms and basements by stay-at-home parents.[8] The vast majority of homeschooled students are being brought up in evangelical Christian families that have come to disdain what they consider to be the dumbing down and the extreme secularization of U.S. public schools. Homeschoolers have distinguished themselves by their academic superiority to other students while defying critics who warned that they would be socially maladjusted.

But homeschooling was the practice of only an obscure few parents in 1980 when educator and author Raymond Moore appeared on *Focus* to promote his then-controversial ideas. Such was Dobson's interest and the response of his listeners that the host brought Moore back repeatedly over the next few years. Each broadcast helped the movement gain momentum and fueled the confidence of parents who latched onto the reassuring affirmations they heard from Dobson about the very challenging undertaking of homeschooling.

"Dr. Dobson got on board with this during the eighties and nineties when Focus was growing by leaps and bounds, and we gave a voice to Moore and his ideas that would have been very difficult for him to get any other way," says Bobbi Valentine, executive producer of *Focus* for many years. "We even got it to the point where a whole new generation of leaders arose to take it to the next level."

◡◠◡◠◡

Dobson's shrewd sense for which new Focus ideas are worthy of his support is one of his most impactful talents, albeit an underappreciated one. The radio-drama series *Adventures in Odyssey* is one of the best testaments to this truth.

Not unusually, *Odyssey* began with Dobson's notion that Focus needed to play a role in combating a social ill. By the early eighties, he'd become alarmed by the slow but sure drift of Saturday morning TV cartoons, first into mere vacuity and then into the exploration of morally questionable material that often subtly promoted such harmful influences as the occult. "They were becoming dark and weren't celebrating anything of goodness," recalls Paul McCusker, one of Focus's earliest radio-drama hands.

At the same time, Focus's small pool of creative staffers was itching to take on the challenge of producing radio dramas. (Dobson and other Focus executives had remained wary of undertaking TV production because of the vast resources required to do it creditably.) So the creative team came up with a dozen half-hour radio dramas called *Family Portraits,* with the intent of reviving the old-time format in a Christian context—hoping to get families to listen together, to use their imaginations, and to end up talking about the real-life issues involved. The adult-skewed *Family Portraits* ran as fill-ins for Dobson on the regular *Focus* broadcast and became an immediate hit.

The creative team was confident that its members could leverage their fresh success with *Family Portraits* into a different radio-drama series aimed specifically at eight- to twelve-year-olds. It would run on Saturday mornings on the many Christian stations that surely would welcome fresh programming in those relatively dead hours.

"People told them it wouldn't happen and couldn't happen because kids had to have visual stimulation, and they wouldn't listen to radio anyway," says Chuck Bolte, the first executive producer of *Odyssey*.

But two keys proved the skeptics wrong about *Odyssey*. First, as with anything to which Dobson set his hand or his reputation, the show would have to be done well—or not done at all. Second, as with any good serial drama, every element the *Odyssey* cadre created for their show was strong and sustainable. It went on the air weekly in November 1987 and became a daily show in 1992.

Its creators set the series in the mythical small city of Odyssey, giving it an indistinct location somewhere in the Midwest but placing it squarely in the real world of late twentieth-century America. The tone of the program ranged from the playfully comic to the tensely dramatic. *Odyssey*'s plots took off in many directions, but biblical values were always conveyed. For writing, acting, and production, the Focus team happily drew upon the top-shelf talent who lived all around them in Southern California.

And most important for the show's continuing success, the team filled *Odyssey* with a memorable ensemble of regular characters whom they conveniently supplemented as people visited and moved into and out of Odyssey. In many ways, in fact, the handiest analogy for *Odyssey* is the sixties-era TV sitcom *The Andy Griffith Show*.

So it was fitting that all of these promising strains came together most harmoniously in *Odyssey*'s key character, John Avery Whittaker, who had made his first appearance in the *Family Portraits* series. An avuncular and at times grandfatherly widower and former schoolteacher, John Whittaker operated a local ice-cream parlor called Whit's End, where his main mission was to mentor the town's kids and win and keep them for Christ. "Whit" was a technical genius, generous, gentle, humorous, and above all wise—and in his past lurked great wealth, international intrigue, profound sorrow, and other elements that could be handily dredged up for dramatic purposes. As a protagonist, he couldn't be beat.

Bolte was able to add a *real* touch of Mayberry to the show when he landed Hal Smith—who had played the town drunk, Otis Campbell, for several years on the *Griffith* show—as the mellifluous voice of Whit. Actually, though his distinctive voice wasn't a component of his *Griffith* character, Smith had mainly made his living with his pipes: as the original Barney Rubble in *The Flintstones*, before he was succeeded by the inimitable Mel Blanc; as the dog Goliath in the popular Sunday-morning, Lutheran-produced TV series *Davey and Goliath,* an innovative precursor to Claymation technology; occasionally as Winnie the Pooh; and late in his career as Philippe the Horse in the Disney movie *Beauty and the Beast.*

Smith made such a convincing Whit that his performance even managed to quell reservations about whether he was spiritually oriented enough to portray the Christian father figure. While convinced he was a believer, the Focus team saw Smith as "of the generation that, you could tell, was uncomfortable talking at length about faith," McCusker says. It also became clear that Smith didn't understand the American evangelical subculture. For example, he would break into a deep and meaningful tone whenever citing Scripture to the kids in *Odyssey.* "It was indicative of where his faith was," McCusker says. "We'd say, 'Hal, we want it to be conversational, as much a part of your speech as anything else you'd say.'"

Chuck Bolte recalls "philosophical criticism" from within Focus over the issue of Smith's playing so prominent a role. "People said, 'How can you expect unspiritual people to do spiritual things?' But . . . I wanted to hire the best actors we could get; I didn't even care that they were Christians. We wouldn't hire someone who was antithetical to what we believed, of course. But the impact that we had on some of the actors' lives was profound—Hal, I think, included." In any event, Smith was so integral to *Odyssey* that the show faced its biggest crisis in 1994 when he died of a heart attack at the age of seventy-seven, while he was listening to the radio. "It was devastating" to the show, McCusker says. "For a while, we weren't even sure that the program would survive. Some of the team was ready to call it quits: He was the heart of the show. We thought it was over. We had loved him so dearly."

Quickly, however, the Focus team rallied behind the continuation of the show, which in turn led them to a tactical *sine qua non*: "We couldn't kill off the character of Whit because it affected so many different things," McCusker says. Instead, Chuck Bolte's group literally pieced together a show using old clips of Smith's voice and had Whit leave for a mysterious adventure that evolved from the previously undisclosed fact that he had been a CIA agent in his youth. Meanwhile, the producers set off on a frantic search for someone—anyone—who somehow could fill the huge shoes left by Smith's death.

Nearly eighteen months later, no replacement had been found and the producers were growing frustrated. So when the manager of a

Christian radio station in Seattle called with a local nominee who was a freelance voice-over actor, "Chuck and I were looking at each other like, 'Oh no, here's another Bigfoot sighting,' " says McCusker. "But then I got Paul Herlinger's answering machine, and he said, 'Hello'— and that's all I heard, and then I think I swooned. It sounded so much like Hal that it just stopped me. I almost couldn't leave a message, because it was like Hal from the grave."

Odyssey's listeners, too, took extreme ownership of the show. "I'm still humbled when people approach me about *Odyssey*," says Bolte, who left Focus in 1996 to head the ministry Childhelp USA and currently consults for various Christian organizations. "Second and even third generations of children are now being affected by it. I was in Minnesota at a MOPS convention recently, and people were quietly pulling me aside and thanking me for the spiritual impact it has had on their children. They were practically falling down on their knees . . . because of how *Adventures in Odyssey* had changed the nature of the long car ride."

Dobson may not have been clairvoyant about the specific impact that *Odyssey* would have in the life of many thousands of children and families. But as is so often the case, following his convictions about the worth of a ministry led to many more transformed lives.

CHAPTER SIXTEEN

FRIENDS OF JIM

They are antidotes in life.

SANDEE FOSTER, ON HER FRIENDS
JAMES AND SHIRLEY DOBSON

James Dobson felt he had made the right decision about kneeling to speak with Pope John Paul II at the Vatican in 2000, but Charles Colson still chuckles as he notes that his friend may have made the wrong choice about where to stay during that visit. Colson and his wife, Patty, accepted Vatican officials' invitation to spend their week ensconced in Casa Santa Marta in Vatican City. The $30 million hotel was built in the eighties to house the College of Cardinals during the next papal election (which ended up occurring in 2005), but in the meantime church officials used it to accommodate honored guests. It is suspected that the walls of the rooms inside Casa Santa Marta are too thin to fully protect the privacy of conversations during crucial proceedings. But the small suites are comfortable, and the copious marble throughout gives the place a regal sheen.

The Dobsons were invited to stay at Casa Santa Marta as well, but they had already agreed to stay in an apartment owned by Priests for Life, a pro-life organization based in Staten Island, New York, and headed by Father Frank Pavone. The small apartment was located in Rome's Trastevere neighborhood, a quaint sector on the Tiber River. And while it couldn't provide amenities like those at Casa Santa Marta, Shirley concedes, "It was Jim's heart to stay there. No way could he have turned those priests down. We care a lot about them."

But the Dobsons had no idea how spartan their arrangements would actually be. The three-room apartment was tiny; the shower could barely accommodate an adult. There was practically no furniture, and right away the Dobsons noticed that it was very cold at night. It wasn't until midweek that they discovered that the windows, for some reason, had been constructed in a permanently open position. They finally got their hosts to close the windows temporarily and to bring in a space heater. But by then the week was almost gone, and the Dobsons had gotten very little sleep.

"Here I was staying in the most palatial quarters in Vatican City during one of the most exciting weeks of our lives," Colson recalls, laughing, "and Jim was bringing in heaters just to get by."

Still, their shared time in the Vatican was one of the most memorable in the history of a bond that became very important to both men. Tony Wauterlek had introduced them shortly after he became chairman of Focus's board in 1982. He had forged a relationship with Colson in Naples, Florida, where the two ex-Marine officers lived close to one another. And because he understood the loneliness that's often felt at the top, Wauterlek soon recognized the benefits his two high-profile friends could bring to each other in a friendship of their own. Colson flew to Arcadia to meet Dobson, and what had been scheduled to be an hour-long session went on and on. Before Colson left, he and Dobson even went into the *Focus* studio and recorded five straight programs on the use and abuse of power. Mutual admiration took root almost immediately.

But it would be another several years before the two stoked their acquaintance into a true friendship. Over a period of months, Wauterlek convinced Colson and Dobson to talk regularly on the phone.

"People who are powerful and self-made tend to be alone in many respects and don't have a close cadre of friends and confidants whom they can go to and bounce ideas off of and let their hair down with and talk as peers," says Wauterlek, who has also been an adviser to Colson's Prison Fellowship ministry. "I saw in both of them the need to have close friendships where they didn't always have to be 'on' with the people around them."

Finally, in 1989, Dobson flew to Florida for a weekend with the Colsons, and the two men spent most of one day simply talking, baring their minds and hearts. A strong friendship began to develop, formed from an extreme intellectual attraction, spiritual concord, complementary personalities, and a highly effective political alliance.

"They do sharpen one another," says Wauterlek. Dobson agrees that Colson "has been a godsend in my life." And on a *Focus* broadcast, Dobson once said, "I listen to him as much as anyone else in the country, and I thank God for that man." Such was his regard for his friend that, when it came time for Dobson to select a keynote speaker for Focus's twenty-fifth anniversary celebration in 2002, his first and only choice was Charles Colson.

ᘐᗯᗰᗰᘗᗯᘈᗰᗯᗰ

A man's man, Dobson seems to make a special impression on many men because of his directness. Sometimes that comes across via an apology. "He does know when he's wrong," says Rudy Markmiller. "It may be a half hour later when he admits it. But when he does, he sets things straight." His friend Mike Williamson remarks on another "great characteristic" that he got to appreciate while he and Dobson were young careerists: "If you started talking when he approached you, he'd keep his eyes focused on you; you had his attention. Even if there were our little kids around who would stir, he'd say 'Excuse me' and deal with it. And he'd be right back to you."

In a later context, Rabbi Daniel Lapin was struck by the contrast between Dobson's typically locked gaze and the wandering eyes of President Clinton, whom Lapin also knows. "I'll never forget how, no matter whom Clinton was talking with, his eyes were constantly darting above and around the room to see whom else he *should* be talking with," Lapin says. Dobson, on the other hand, "is only focused on the person he's talking with."

As with many men, interest in sports is a glue between Dobson and many of his friends. But while he enjoys watching sports with friends—especially a football game involving his beloved USC Trojans—Dobson prefers the more proactive give-and-take of athletic participation. In high school and college, Dobson's intense interest in playing tennis helped him forge relationships with classmates such as Wil Spaite, his predecessor as Pasadena College singles champion.

Crossing rackets with Dobson also helped Peb Jackson take the measure of his new boss in the early days of Focus. "I was very athletic, but even though he had less talent than I did, he won every time," Jackson says. "He could play with your head, and he was very consistent. He would draw me to the net, and I would run ragged all over the court. But he had a good serve and he could place the ball well." At one point in the eighties, Jackson says, Dobson was thrilled to rally with budding tennis star Andre Agassi a few times.

But as he aged and as the Focus staff grew and became more collegial, Dobson turned his athletic energies toward skiing and especially basketball. His ranginess and innate athleticism came in handy in hoops, and Dobson relished the intense bursts of action, the overall aerobic benefits, and the fact that he could easily forget about everything else while he was playing a brisk game of basketball. Before long, he had developed a certain expectation of his male colleagues, friends, and *Focus* guests: Unless they were lame, he expected them to join him in the regular pickup basketball games that he played.

At first, Dobson invited friends and new employees to play three-on-three games on his driveway at home. It quickly became apparent that the Dobson grounds at 348 Harvard Drive were not really equipped to accommodate six or eight grown men still trying to prove their athleticism. Once Dobson's friend and colleague Jim Davis, a former college All-American, who was six feet four, collided with another player, a six-feet-six former crew athlete, near the basket. Davis fell into the door of Dobson's garage and splintered much of it to smithereens, producing ten minutes of guffawing all around—including from Dobson—before play resumed.

In the mideighties, after H. B. London became pastor of the First Church of the Nazarene in Pasadena, Dobson was able to gain access to the church's gymnasium. Thrice-weekly five-on-five games at 6 a.m. became a quasiofficial institution within Focus. As they became more and more a part of Dobson's routine, the contests also revealed his tendency toward micromanagement. "I was responsible for making sure we had enough guys each morning," says Gary Lydic, a longtime Focus executive who at that time headed human resources. "I'd give him the list the night before of who was to be there, and he'd often call me at home to go over it. And he wasn't happy when someone showed up late."

Dobson could become fast friends by sharing bounce passes and floor burns with someone, as Pete Maravich would have testified. Dobson also got to know Don Hodel on the floorboards, a venue that the former interior secretary hallowed as much as Dobson did. Hodel and his wife, Barbara, attended a National Religious Broadcasters convention in Washington, D.C., in 1987 so that they could catch Dobson's speech there. During his speech, Dobson told an anecdote about playing basketball with a much younger man who ended the game by saying, "Boy, you sure must have been something in your prime." The amused Hodel invited Dobson to play a pickup game the next time he came to D.C.

Yet the niceties of friendship couldn't douse Dobson's competitiveness, which consistently blazed forth in the free-throw lane, Dobson's territory on the court. He still maintained some spring in his legs from his days as a high school hurdler. Usually taller and often heftier than fellow combatants in these pickup games, Dobson didn't mind using those physical advantages to jostle his defenders and try to create some space for himself so he could make easy baskets close to the hoop. In fact, Hodel would tease Dobson, " 'Since when did they abolish the three-second rule?' He did camp in the lane a lot," Hodel says. But Dobson also was a decent shot with a soft touch, so he often would come out ten to twelve feet from the basket, catch a pass, turn in, fade away a bit, and shoot what Hodel calls "an awkward-looking jump shot." In fact, because he brought the ball back over his head an unusual distance, Dobson's shot could sometimes be blocked from behind. But because of his offensive versatility, defenders usually tried to deprive Dobson of the ball in the first place.

Going for loose balls, rebounding, and playing defense, Dobson threw himself around quite a bit. One time while playing at First Nazarene, he and Mike McGee, who was then athletic director at the University of Southern California, both chased a ball that was headed out of bounds. McGee had been a lineman for professional football's Cardinals, but Dobson outpursued him to the ball—and accidentally elbowed McGee in the face on the way. "If it had been anyone else, I would have been more aggressive going for the ball," McGee maintains. "But I didn't expect to get a black eye out of it."

Rudy Markmiller came up with an antidote to his friend's aggressiveness on the court. "There were a few times I got clobbered by him going to the basket, or he'd elbow me," Markmiller says. "But I wasn't afraid to call fouls on him."

❧❧❧❧❧

Dobson acquires friends like habits: He picks them up easily, and they never quite leave him. He believes he inherited much of that tendency from his maternal grandfather, "Little Daddy" Dillingham, a gregarious, humorous, and much-loved man. Shirley Dobson considers herself a social person but considerably "more private" than her husband. "He loves people; he doesn't get tired of people," she says. "He does get tired, and there are times when he likes to pull away and get his space—but he's not tired of people. Because he's an only child, and I have only one brother and we're a small family, too, friends are like our family. That's why the move to Colorado was very hard on me. I think that without friends, life gets lonely."

H. B. London says, "Once you're Jim's friend, you'll always be his friend. You may not have been in touch with him for all that time, but when he sees you and greets you, it's as if you haven't been apart. He has an ability to make people feel special and honored."

Dobson has his share of friends who have risen to prominence in the secular world, including Focus patrons such as Steve Reinemund, chief executive officer of PepsiCo, Inc. Herb Fisher, a shopping-center magnate from Pennsylvania, met Dobson on a ministry retreat in Elk Canyon, Montana, in the midnineties, and he and his wife, Dona, became friends and traveling companions of the Dobsons. Barry Meguiar is head of a family-owned company that is a global leader in car-care chemicals and lives on an island in Newport Beach, California; their friendship dates to Dobson's Southern California days. Dobson also has made many friends in his twenty-seven years of broadcasting and while working shoulder to shoulder with allies in the public-policy arena. "It has become a cliché on *Focus* for me to start a broadcast by introducing 'my great friend' or 'my good friend,' and at first I didn't realize I was doing that," Dobson says. "But the truth of it is that I see those people that way."

But relationships with old family friends are some of Dobson's deepest, and many of these are economically ordinary people who "knew him when." Sandee Foster met the Dobsons in college and later went to church with them. "When [my daughter] Kristen was growing up, I would call and ask him for advice, and he still took such time with me," says Foster, whose daughter is a contemporary and friend of Danae Dobson's. Eyes glistening, she adds, "And he was right on about everything he told me." In 2002 Dobson called Foster when she was in a California hospital. "He said he knew just what I was going through and that he was praying for me," Foster recalls. "A few weeks later when I was in there again for extensive tests, he called again and asked, 'Sandee, are you afraid?' He encouraged me in my faith and in the fact that he had gone that way before. He said that I would be fine. It made all the difference."

Galal Gough met Dobson at Pasadena College. Later, he served as a U.S. Army medic in the Vietnam War near Quang Tri, where some of the bloodiest fighting of the conflict occurred. Dodging incoming mortar fire at night, Dr. Gough helped to run a hospital and treated thousands of wounded Vietnamese soldiers and civilians. He also delivered approximately one hundred babies during his tenure. "I'll never forget how, when I got home, Jim told me that he had prayed for me almost every day while I was gone," Gough recalls, tears trickling down his cheeks. "Those kinds of things have a big impact on you." Gough also worshipped with Dobson at First Nazarene Church of Pasadena and went on to become an obstetrician, giving away more than eighteen thousand copies of *Dare to Discipline* to his patients. Dobson used to follow Gough around USC's County Hospital when they were both students, watching the doctor deliver babies and treat patients.

During many of their frequent visits back to Southern California since Focus moved to Colorado, the Dobsons get together with Jim and Flo Waltrip, who still live in Pasadena. Dobson called the couple to console them when he received news that one of the Waltrips' grandchildren had been diagnosed as autistic. Dobson also continues to remind them and other friends when he is scheduled to appear on national television and asks for their prayers in advance. "He asks us to watch him and let him know what we think," Flo Waltrip says. "He waits for our fax and wants the input. He has time for you even when he doesn't have time for you."

Dobson is keenly aware of the gratitude he engenders in friends by maintaining strong ties with them despite his celebrity status and the ceaseless demands on his time. "The more visible you become, the more a phone call or a letter means," he says. Danae agrees. "Even if my parents haven't spent a great deal of time with someone, [friends] still feel close to them because they know that they matter and that my parents do take time to pray for them—and that they would pray for them right away if they knew they had a concern." H. B. London says that "a lot of old friends write to him because of his fame, and whether he does it personally or his staff writes it, there's always a response to them. He never just lets a greeting go unacknowledged. If you lose a loved one or have success and he finds out about it, he responds to that."

Naturally, celebrity has also brought regular requests from friends for favors, not just greetings. In 1996 the president of MidAmerica Nazarene University (previously Mid-America Nazarene College) in Olathe, Kansas, asked Marge Smith, a close friend of Dobson's parents', if she might be able to get Dobson to give the school's twenty-fifth anniversary commencement address the next spring. "I said I didn't think he would, but I would ask," Smith remembers. "When I called Jim, he said, 'You know I don't do that. I can't start that.' And I said, 'Well, do it for someone—me or Myrtle or your daddy,' and he laughed it off like a joke. But within a week, he called me and said he'd come to speak, and that he was doing it for me and me alone."

There are even more extreme circumstances when people believe it a privilege to be a friend of James Dobson: personal crises. At least a few times a year, Dobson tries to accommodate friends who have requested counseling intervention. The most common requests involve his help in holding a marriage together. "I've done more counseling on the theme of 'love must be tough' than any other issue," he says. "There's usually one person within the marriage who wants to hold it together, and one who wants to get out."

Especially in Focus's early days, Dobson also received many calls from listeners and other strangers who simply *had* to talk directly with the doctor or they wouldn't be satisfied. "My books thrust me into the role of crisis intervention where people I'd come into contact with would look to me for guidance," says Dobson. Because of his many years of counseling work at the university and hospital, he was, of course, qualified to help out. "Sometimes it was overwhelming because it came in addition to everything else."

But as the demands on his time grew, Dobson began screening such pleas. He designated Dee Otte, his first employee and later office manager, as his first line of defense when Focus was based in California. One of her most valuable skills, in fact, was the ability to distinguish strangers and mere acquaintances from true friends needing help. She directed the first group elsewhere for help but knew when Dobson would want to personally help a friend—or reach out to someone in a special situation. "Everybody thought that only *he* could help them," Otte says. "I would refer them to people on the staff, usually. But sometimes I would just get a desperate call—there was one from a family in Colorado who had just lost someone in a plane crash—so I put them through. After a while, though, I could size people up pretty quickly. Some people would just fake things. I would pray for the right thing to say at the right time."

As Dobson's circles and his fame grew, the challenge of whom to counsel—and whom not to—became exponentially more difficult. His increasing time crunch was one reason. Another was that he got calls for help from what amounted to a who's who of the Christian world as well as an occasional secular celebrity.

Patsy and John Ramsey are evangelical Christians and Dobson fans, as well as victims of worldwide notoriety. In one of the most infamous crimes of the late twentieth century, their six-year-old daughter, JonBenet, was beaten and strangled inside the couple's Boulder, Colorado, home on the day after Christmas 1996. Police and public suspicion immediately descended on the Ramseys as complicit in their own daughter's murder, and Americans' condemnation of them only strengthened as weeks dragged into months without an arrest in the case. By mid-April 1997, the Ramseys felt as if they simply had to escape somewhere and relax. So with their nine-year-old son, Burke, they slipped away and took a two-hour drive to Colorado Springs and checked into a hotel under an assumed name.

As they discussed painful matters such as how they might honor their lost daughter with a memorial or a foundation in her name, Patsy Ramsey felt an impulse to call Dobson and see if he would counsel them. Both Ramseys had read some of Dobson's books and frequently listened to *Focus,* but they'd never met Dobson and had no expectation that he would drop everything for them—despite their backhanded fame.

"But he surprised us and literally said, 'Come on over now or tomorrow,'" John Ramsey recalls. "Here 70 percent of the world, according to a Gallup Poll, thought that we had murdered our daughter, and yet [Dobson and Focus staffers] were very welcoming and open and compassionate. He treated us as parents who'd lost a child when the rest of the world was treating us as murderers. There wasn't a hint of suspicion or skepticism; he was just very open and welcoming and kind." Dobson also gave the Ramseys practical advice about handling skeptical and even hostile news media, a constituency with which he had considerable experience.

Several Focus executives and other staffers lunched with Dobson and the anxious couple, but only Dobson, the Ramseys, and Focus executive Charlie Jarvis remained in Dobson's office for an extended conversation. "We prayed with them and just listened to them, and they were overwhelmed," Jarvis recalls. "You could sense the crushing weight on them, but he drew them out lovingly and expressed what they were struggling with and their befuddlement at this whole experience: 'How could anyone think that we had done anything to that little girl?'

"When they left, you could actually sense that that massive weight had been lifted off them. The Lord was using Jim in yet another case where people were in emotional extremis. It was an extraordinary thing for me to see and be a part of because you could just see the changes on their countenance."

Confirms John Ramsey: "It made a big difference in our lives."

Dobson has done less and less of this sort of intense personal counseling in recent years. "But I still get pulled into the lives of donors to Focus, of people who have an especially serious need, or a teenager who's going off the deep end," he says. "I do less of it now, but it's still there."

ᗠᘓᗜᘓᗜ

Dobson's friends see all sides of him. Many are amazed that he has time to explore deep avocational interests in hunting and fishing, reading about World War II, studying the lives of twentieth-century giants such as Winston Churchill and Douglas MacArthur, and plumbing cosmology and geology.

"One time he bought a *Living Bible* and read through the entire thing and only underlined the stuff that had to do with Creation and the earth; he was just that interested in it," says Jim Davis, a friend and Focus colleague. "He has intense curiosity about some things."

Perhaps surprisingly, the Beatles long have been an object of Dobson's curiosity and appreciation. During the sixties, he grew to admire their musical styles and abilities, only to see his interest spoiled toward the end of the Beatles' tenure by their distressing turn to glorification of the drug culture. "I still like their 'saner' music," he says.

Often friends get glimpses of the compassion that helped suit Dobson for his lifelong role as a helper. At the end of a long day of depositions in the Gil Moegerle case in 1990, for example, Tony Wauterlek came down with what turned out to be food poisoning, barely making it back to his hotel room near Los Angeles. Dobson, who had been planning to drop off the Focus board chairman and then go to dinner with his daughter, decided instead to tend to his stricken friend. He also called a physician he knew to come and check on Wauterlek. Dobson "sat there at my bedside for three to four hours until the pain subsided, when he had plenty of other more pressing things to do, like prepare for his radio show the next day," Wauterlek says.

Dobson's compassion for his friend only confirmed a soulfulness in him that Wauterlek first had experienced in 1979. On the last day of an outdoor retreat weekend, while everyone else was taking a refreshing dip in an alpine lake, Tony Wauterlek stayed back at camp. He was craving some time to study, pray, and contemplate the beauty of Yosemite National Park, but the investment banker also wanted to ponder an offer to become the first outside board member of Focus on the Family. Wandering with his Bible about a hundred yards down a path into the woods, he was startled to spy another man up ahead. Approaching the sandy-haired figure quietly, Wauterlek was still a hundred feet away when he realized it was the long frame of Dobson—on his knees, next to a dead tree, glasses removed, pressing his forehead to the ground and, as Wauterlek found out later, praying for God's direction of his life and his ministry.

"It confirmed to my heart and my mind that if this was the way he built a foundation, on the ground in prayer, then this was a ministry I needed to be involved with," Wauterlek says.

Dobson's respect for the sanctity of the Sabbath is legend among friends who have spent weekends with him and Shirley and have observed it firsthand. Their retreats to the Mammoth Lakes condominium were built around his prohibition of skiing on Sunday. Spending money on the Lord's Day proves problematic as well. Herb and Dona Fisher, the Focus donors from Pennsylvania, were shopping with their friends in Durango, Colorado, one Sunday several years ago when Dobson spied an antique toy train from his father's era.

"He'd been hunting for a train like that for a long, long time," Dona Fisher recalls. "But because it was Sunday, all he did is take the man's name and phone number and say that he would contact him later to buy it. We told him, 'We won't tell'—and he just looked at me weirdly and said that it was something that he couldn't do in his soul. He wouldn't violate his convictions."

Friends universally describe a playfulness in Jim and Shirley Dobson that made it easy to be around them even after they had reached unmistakable celebrity. Dobson has a penchant, for example, for attaching nicknames to friends as well as family members. His wife, for example, is "Shirl-zeez," and Joey Paul, a Christian-publishing executive and friend of Dobson's, is "Joe-sie."

"It's an affectionate thing that he knows will be a part of our relationship and no one else's," Paul says. "It's a very effective thing in a friendship. And it's the kind of thing that a great politician would take advantage of too."

Friends also understand that Dobson's sense of humor is integral to his personality. This was demonstrated memorably to Charlie Jarvis, a top Focus executive in the nineties, on one occasion when the ministry was renting the resort at Elk Canyon, Montana, that is provided for Focus use by a major donor. Focus was hosting a number of significant contributors to the ministry for a few days of relaxation, including trout fishing, white-water rafting, skeet shooting, and other activities. Sometimes, quite naturally in such an atmosphere, the camp became a little bit like a college fraternity.

"One time a staffer covered the toilet bowls surreptitiously with Saran Wrap underneath the seats," Jarvis recalls. "Everyone else discovered it one way or another and didn't respond too nastily. But one man who was an extraordinarily world-renowned executive came to our session the next morning and began to describe how he thought there was a drum playing in the bathroom and how he couldn't figure out what was going on in the middle of the night. It was hilarious, because Jim then launched into five or six stories that had the whole place rolling in laughter. He was just riffing on the experience that this man had had with the Saran-covered toilet. He showed a wonderful sense for taking a moment that was hilarious but intense—and where some people were wondering how a bunch of evangelicals would react to this crude prank—and not only handling it but really applying it to life. He has a masterful way of seeing several levels at one time."

Though not a classical practical joker, Dobson also enjoys playing a trick or two of his own on his buddies. Christian author and literary agent Robert Wolgemuth and his wife, Bobbie, vacation regularly with the Dobsons and constantly are on their guard for these playful expressions. One time, on a crowded elevator ride down to a hotel lobby, Wolgemuth felt someone behind him gently tweak his ear. Then it happened again. "*The nerve*, I thought," Wolgemuth recalls. "But I didn't want to turn around. So when the doors opened, I moved straight toward the bell stand. At that point, Jim ran up behind me and almost tackled me to the ground like a kid on the playground—like some mischievous boy looking for trouble."

Yet Wolgemuth and others tell how Dobson has been known to carry things too far, sometimes belying the tonal perfection that they naturally expect of him in all interpersonal relationships. The Wolgemuths and their daughters were in Colorado Springs in 1994 to record a *Focus* broadcast about Robert Wolgemuth's just-published book *She Calls Me Daddy*. Over an Egg McMuffin breakfast that same morning, Jon Schrader asked Robert Wolgemuth for his twenty-three-year-old daughter Missy's hand in marriage. Before the broadcast, Wolgemuth shared that confidentiality with Dobson. When the interview was done, Dobson opened his microphones in the gallery outside the Focus recording studio and asked if anyone had any "questions or comments for the Wolgemuth family." Schrader stepped to the microphone and hesitated just a moment.

"Then Jim, thinking that Jon was going to propose to his girlfriend in the radio presence of seven million people, picked up the cue and blindly went where no man should have gone," as Wolgemuth tells it.

"Is this it?" Dobson chirped. "Is this *it?*" he repeated with even more enthusiasm. Then Wolgemuth turned toward his host "and shot a visual dagger straight to his eyes, telling him with body language not to say another word. He got it and deftly changed the subject. But later, in private, he whined to me that Jon 'could have asked Missy to marry him in front of millions of people.'"

Instead, Schrader decided to take Missy Wolgemuth into the foothills above the Focus campus and proposed privately.

Shirley Dobson also has what her daughter describes as "a bit of a crazy side, especially when she gets tired." The Wolgemuths have seen this side of Shirley firsthand. In July 1985, for example, the Dobsons were headed from the East Coast to their California home and stopped for a few days of vacation with the Wolgemuths near Nashville. Because Dobson is a voracious student of American military history, their hosts took them to a Civil War battle site and spent several hours with Richard Fulcher, one of middle Tennessee's most respected historians. Afterward they went to a popular local diner for some lunch.

As the hostess was leading them to their booth, they passed a table where a man was sitting alone, holding a hamburger with both hands and preparing to take a bite. Something inspired Shirley to stop at his table; he looked up wondering who this woman was and why she was standing there. He squeezed out a smile wondering if, perhaps, this may have been a friendly someone from his past.

"Hi," Shirley said to him. He did not speak. There were several Tater Tots and a dipping pool of bright red ketchup on his plate. "Are the Tater Tots good here?" she asked. Still no response from the man. Then she reached down to his plate, picked up a Tater Tot, dipped it into the crimson puddle, and popped it into her mouth. The man's eyes widened. "Yummm," the mischievous Shirley said with a smile. "They're delicious. Thanks." With that, she turned and joined her husband and the Wolgemuths at their booth.

But good humor isn't the only emotion that comes readily to the Dobsons. Friends also describe Dobson as a man whose anxieties and even his temper sometimes get the best of him, especially when he feels that others aren't meeting standards that he has set for himself. Mike Williamson, his colleague and friend from USC days, describes a tug-of-war that he and Dobson frequently had because they traveled so often together. Upon landing at an airport, Williamson says, Dobson typically would direct his friend to get the baggage while Dobson rented a car. "It was just natural for him to take charge of a situation, and there was no point in arguing because there would only be a scene," Williamson recalls. "I schlepped the bags around all over the country! He'd say, 'This ship needs a captain,' and one time I said, 'Let me be the captain.' But I started driving and I missed a turn because of how on-the-spot I felt. It was ridiculous for me to try to compete with his need to lead."

As an old friend, Markmiller has witnessed a few episodes as well where Dobson's patience has worn thin. One time a number of friends were at the Dobsons' home in Arcadia for a dinner party before the group was departing for a movie, and the caterer was running late. "The later it got, the more impatient [Dobson] got," Markmiller says, "and finally he just said, 'We're going.' But Shirley kind of went over to him and said, 'Jim, this lady worked on this all day; we're going to wait.' He said, 'I don't like this at all,' but he sat down. Ten minutes later the lady showed up, and the evening took on a better hue."

Sometimes, too, the great self-assurance Dobson is known for— and which many times is his biggest asset—can trip him up. William Bennett and Dobson became allies and friends during the eighties as the two social commentators found unity in their opposition to abortion and other issues. But in hindsight, it became apparent to his followers and critics alike that Bennett always carefully sidestepped commentary on one vice: gambling. Not only had Bennett, a Catholic, grown up with a predilection to gamble, but for several years he had been a rather surreptitious big spender at casinos in Las Vegas and Atlantic City. When *Newsweek* reported in 2003 that Bennett's career gambling losses had exceeded eight million dollars, disgust from many conservative quarters piled on him more quickly than poker chips on a high roller's table.

As an ardent and outspoken opponent of gambling and its social toll, Dobson was deeply pained by news of Bennett's habit. It would have been an effective occasion to raise the profile of his own views on the issue by attacking his friend, but Dobson didn't even consider that. He decided to take a more nuanced approach, issuing a statement that said he regretted Bennett's apparent "addiction" to gambling and praising Bennett's decision to quit. Yet Bennett took strong exception even to that approach.

"He called me ahead of time and told me he was going to issue a statement, which I expected him to do, but I took issue with that statement and directly with Jim," Bennett says. "It's not an addiction; even my wife said so, publicly. People in the practice of psychology should never diagnose from a distance. It's unprofessional."

Dobson made no further comment to Bennett.

⚬⚬⚬⚬⚬⚬

The Dobsons decided to honor many of their friends on the occasion of Focus's twenty-fifth anniversary in 2002 by inviting them to their Colorado Springs condominium for a private party on the Wednesday evening before the official four-day celebration. The Dobsons greatly anticipated and then savored the occasion for reconnecting and recollecting.

For Shirley, the backyard party was a reminder of gatherings that she and her husband had enjoyed with many of those same people decades earlier, when most of them were new careerists and young parents. "We had about thirty close friends who would come over to our house during the summer [or] on the Fourth of July and play volleyball and Ping-Pong, for example," she says. "We would do lots of entertaining."

The affair also brought back some painful memories. One of the unfortunate early by-products of Dobson's fame, for example, was that some friends had difficulty handling their pal's rather sudden and clearly inexorable success. Actually, that was commonly the case in Southern California in the seventies and eighties as Dobson's career and reputation flourished.

"When we graduated from college and we were in one another's weddings and had our babies together and started out in life, we were all kind of at the same level financially and socially and in every way," Shirley says. "But when things started happening to Jim, with *Dare to Discipline* and being on talk shows and the radio, the gap began widening a bit, and some of our friends had difficulty with that. I'm not sure if it was jealousy; I'm not sure what it was. I would tell them to tune in because Jim was on *The Dinah Shore Show* or something, and I could tell from their body language and demeanor that there was resentment there. Jim didn't see it, but I did. We found that it was easier for friends to be there in moments of pain, but in moments of exploding success, they can start resenting you. So we just started being very sensitive about that. If anyone wanted to know anything, we'd wait for them to ask us. Since then, many of our friends have gone on to be successful in their own ways, so that has gone away now."

The Southern California contingent formed the rank and file of the attendees at the Dobsons' home-grilled soiree. "I was expecting to see a who's who of Christianity there, and we did recognize Bill and Vonette Bright," says Nancy Hawley, who attended with her husband, Wendell, the longtime marketing vice president of Tyndale House. "But other than that it was people like their neighbors and Sunday school class, people from their church."

And at the Dobsons' party, fond reminiscence cast its mellowing effects over everything, including the hamburgers that Dobson himself prepared. He and Shirley stood together at the front and, one by one, explained their relationship to each of those assembled. They sang a few of the classic Bill Gaither hymns and praise songs that so many of them loved. And the Dobsons invited them to a slide show at Focus the next day where they would continue to relive past memories or old relationships.

"We had lots of laughter and tears and fun," Dobson says of the two-hour affair. "It was an absolute highlight of my life."

CHAPTER SEVENTEEN

A SILVER THREAD

I've seen dramatic answers
to prayer in my life.
SHIRLEY DOBSON

I f ever a setting was designed to intimidate a speaker, surely this was it. On the morning of May 5, 2005, the 54th annual National Day of Prayer, Shirley Dobson prepared to take the podium on a small raised stage in the East Room of the White House. The world-renowned St. Olaf College Choir had just finished a stirring rendition of "Abide with Me" and "My Soul's Been Anchored in the Lord," bringing stout applause from every corner of the place. About two hundred members of a Who's Who of America's faith community—ranging from evangelical Christian leaders to prominent orthodox Jews, from Catholic clergy to the president's own Methodist pastor and even a Muslim cleric—waited expectantly in rows of chairs in a semicircle stretched out before her. A few feet in front of Shirley, and slightly to her right, sat the president of the United States and the first lady, George W. and Laura Bush.

If Shirley had thought about it long enough, the physical setting alone might have caused her knees to knock. Known simply as the most famous room in America, the eighty-foot-long East Room is a shrine to decorum and elegance, from the red marble at the bases of the pilasters to the three massive crystal chandeliers that hang above its finely polished marble floor. This breathtaking national treasure is the largest room in the White House, and the one where Lincoln, Kennedy, and five other presidents who died while in office laid in state. Over Shirley's left shoulder hung a portrait of George Washington by Gilbert Stuart, the only item that has remained in the White House since it was built.

Or Shirley Dobson might have been frozen by the significance of the moment. Of course, affairs in Washington can always be counted on to provide a buzz-filled backdrop to any event. On this morning, President Bush had squeezed a precious half hour out of his schedule to host the annual National Day of Prayer event at his home, immediately after which he would wrap up preparations for a four-day trip to Russia and former Soviet states.

The knives were out in Congress, this time for Tom DeLay, the House majority leader and a friend of Shirley and James Dobson, whose travel accounting was being scrutinized by the ravenous Washington press corps with help from willing Democratic sources. Senators of both parties were trying to triangulate toward a deal that would avoid Republicans' fateful invoking of the so-called "nuclear option" to change the rules of the Senate, block Democratic filibustering, and finally bring several of the president's important judicial nominees to a vote. And just to top it off, the two days of gatherings that Shirley Dobson had organized as chairman of the National Day of Prayer represented a coming-out party of sorts for those in the Christian Right who had played a role in keeping President Bush in office and improving the Republican margin of control on Capitol Hill in November 2004.

But dressed in a tailored, cream-colored suit with navy blue trim, Shirley was the epitome of poise and sophistication as she stepped behind the podium. Over the past fourteen years, the National Day of Prayer had become the one time each year that, reliably, Shirley cast a shadow as large as that of her husband, and she was about to live up to the occasion again this time.

"That's one of my favorite hymns," she said to Anton Armstrong, the St. Olaf choir director. Then she looked at the Bushes, saying, "Good morning, Mr. President, Mrs. Bush, and distinguished guests." And that was homage enough paid to the dignity of the most powerful office in the land.

"We found out who the real speaker in the family is," she said in a relaxed and playful tone, with a knowing smile to President Bush. Some in the audience began chuckling in recognition of where their speaker was about to go next. "And I'm sorry, Mr. President—it's not you." Laughter came again from the crowd as they shared the full realization that Shirley Dobson had just chosen to tweak the president of the United States—in his own domain, at that. She was referring to Laura Bush's much-celebrated performance of the weekend before, when the first lady had roasted her husband at the White House Correspondents' Association dinner, making fun of everything from his early bedtime to his incorrigible mispronunciation of *nuclear.*

"Laura," Shirley Dobson concluded her aside, "you were fantastic."

It's a long road from where Shirley Dobson started life to a safe zone where she could feel completely comfortable razzing the president of the United States.

As the wife of James Dobson, she certainly has learned the ropes of public life. And she deserves the credit for transforming the National Day of Prayer celebration from an afterthought on America's calendar to a red-letter day for prayerful patriots across the land. But Shirley Deere began life way back in the pack, as far from the dream of headlining a White House event as the Atlantic is from the Pacific.

Shirley was born into a dysfunctional family, headed by an alcoholic father whose addiction perpetually kept the family in financial and relational peril. Eventually his drinking fomented a divorce, before Joe Kubishta became the earthly salvation for Alma, Shirley, and John Deere. Shirley's sensitivities about her upbringing have evolved over the years. Early in her speaking career, she talked about the economic and emotional circumstances of her childhood in the direst terms. But later on, she interpreted the time somewhat differently, focusing more on the fact that, while the family felt poor, somehow their financial want never made them feel impoverished.

"Money was tight and we had to get used to living on a shoestring," she recalls. "But my mother's strength of character made the most out of what we had, and after separating from my father, she worked very hard to give us what we needed."

Just as important in the long term, Shirley believes, her early travails also caused her to turn directly to God for solace. "As a child, I was very tender to the Lord and didn't want to displease him," she says. She says she encountered Jesus Christ in a personal way at a little Nazarene church in Torrance, California, bowing at an altar one Sunday morning when she was eight years old. Shirley prayed regularly from an early age, and she sat for countless hours at the piano making up her own renditions of hymns as well as the popular songs of the day. Her church youth group also became very important to her, and Shirley attended all the church-related activities she could, including Christian summer camps.

Neither did the challenges keep her from enjoying some of the

freedoms of childhood—she liked to play softball in the vacant lot behind her home with her brother and friends, for instance—nor from
developing her other gifts. And so, though wounded, Shirley Deere
was a confident and capable young woman when she walked onto the
campus of Pasadena College in 1956, became a major personality on
campus, and met and wooed her future husband, James Dobson. In addition to being elected homecoming queen and senior class president,
she was selected by the faculty for "Who's Who in American Colleges
and Universities."

When she graduated from Pasadena in 1960 with an elementary-
education degree and a teaching certificate, her soon-to-be husband already was enrolled in graduate school at the University of Southern
California. Shirley immediately became a schoolteacher—and the
family breadwinner. But she always assumed that such a role would
only be temporary, and by the time the Dobsons brought home baby
Danae from the hospital a few years later, Shirley was even more comfortable with her husband's career path and with her own plans for
traditional motherhood.

"She was going to be a schoolteacher, and he was going to be a psychologist in private practice, and that was going to be their life," Danae
says. "She was going to be happy with a quiet and tranquil lifestyle.
That's her basic temperament." Until Ryan left the Dobson household
in Arcadia after high school, Shirley focused almost exclusively on
home, hearth, and church, and on nurturing the family's relationships
with relatives and friends in Southern California.

Another important by-product of Shirley's happiness in the home,
of course, was that it helped solidify Dobson's traditionalist views
about family roles, and his marriage relationship served as welcome
fodder for the broad themes behind his burgeoning writing and speaking career. The couple's inside jokes even became public because of
how much Dobson put his own family and relationships into his books,
radio repartee, and other outlets. After Dobson would make a revelation about their marital relationship, for example, Shirley often would
quip that his remark "means we only have three secrets left, and if you
ever tell those, I'm out of here!" The couple didn't actually keep count
of how many big secrets they still shared—"It is just a representation of
the fact that I'm open and she's closed," Dobson says—but Dobson's
fans got to know the "secrets" rap.

On one occasion, Ryan was asked to speak after his dad had just told the familiar bit. The son walked to the podium and said, "My folks have only three secrets, and I'm one of them!"

As her husband's profile rose inexorably, a more public life certainly wasn't what Shirley wished for. "He's a lot more open than I am," Shirley says. "My life choice wouldn't have been a public ministry, but I never fought it. I always felt we were a team and just accepted it." Yet one of the most fortunate things about the Dobsons' marriage was that Shirley found she *could* adapt to an increasingly public role as James Dobson's wife—in fact, she seemed to handle it, for the most part, rather effortlessly.

And as their nest was emptying, the unrelenting spotlight on her husband tempted Shirley to think that perhaps her role might not remain completely in the home. "She began saying to me: 'I know who you are, tell me again who I am,'" Dobson recalls. "That wasn't an unusual identity problem for spouses of very visible, very successful men. 'Shirley,' I would say, 'God has his hands on you and has given you primary responsibility for the kids right now. And when this is over, you'll see—he's got a new assignment for you.'"

After Focus's move to Colorado Springs, when she was separated from their adult son and daughter, Shirley became more involved in her husband's ministry. She set up an office adjacent to Dobson's and began to write books, such as one on establishing family holiday traditions, *Let's Make a Memory,* that she coauthored with Gloria Gaither.

Then one day, with a phone call from Vonette Bright, Shirley Dobson the housewife, mother, and dutiful spouse of a famous Christian leader began to embrace an additional role—as Shirley Dobson the evangelical mover and shaker.

∽∾∾∽

Prayer is a silver thread of grace and power that has run through Shirley's life for as long as she can remember. "I learned to talk to Jesus at an early age," she says. "I would kneel each night by my little bed and pray for my family. I've thought many times, *Why would the God of the universe care about the prayer of an eight-year-old?* I don't know, but I've seen dramatic answers to prayer in my life."

One of Shirley's fervent prayers was for the family that she would someday help form. "She would cry out to the Lord and express her sadness and frustration and she even prayed for her future husband as a little girl," Danae says.

This predilection to prayer came along with Shirley into that family. She and James Dobson prayed together regularly when they were dating. When their kids were young, the couple focused their regular prayer time on Danae and Ryan, always including a request that they would commit their lives to God and be productive in doing so. "I can't count the number of times I've come home and found my mom and dad on their knees at the side of their bed praying for us," Ryan Dobson says. "She's always been a force to be reckoned with when it comes to prayer."

In the evangelical tradition, Shirley even keeps a closetlike space in her Colorado Springs townhome, an area where she can kneel in private prayer.

Shirley testifies that she has seen many palpable results from her prayers and others', and that God's answers come in many different ways. Sometimes, she believes, God has responded to her prayers quickly and specifically. That was certainly the case, she says, when he preserved her husband during his heart attack and stroke. Another time many years earlier, Shirley recalls, Danae was out with a friend one night as a teenager. Shirley was alone and working in the kitchen when she suddenly had a strong urge to pray for Danae. At first, she ignored the prompting, "but it was so strong that I put down what I was doing and prayed right then for Danae's safety, calling for a legion of angels to protect her." Turns out that Danae had been in an accident about that time on a mountain road, with the car ending up on its roof and skidding to within a few feet of a five-hundred-foot precipice. Neither Danae nor her friend were seriously hurt.[1]

Other times, Shirley believes, her prayers don't yield such immediate answers, but she is able to see God's provision over time. She was very broken up about having to leave Southern California for Colorado Springs when Focus moved, for example, and Shirley prayed for God to help her understand the reasons for it. Within a few years in Colorado, he did. She had stretched and grown in ways she couldn't have foreseen; many of the couple's old friends had moved out of Southern California as well; and the Dobson clan got together about as much as it ever had.[2]

Shirley also is an enthusiastic exponent of forming prayer "partnerships" with friends who pray together in person or on the phone and uphold one another before God. Tru Lincoln, for example, got to know Shirley in Southern California when she helped design the interior of a Focus building there, and later she worked with an architect on the inside of Focus's new administration building in Colorado. Lincoln got to understand more about Shirley than the fact that her favorite colors for decorating are raspberry and rich blue; the two women met weekly for about five years as part of a Bible study and prayer group in Colorado Springs. "She's especially good at having a connection to the Lord and then being able to express herself about it," Lincoln says.

Another prayer partner, Marilyn Hontz, has been struck specifically by the passion that Shirley demonstrates in prayer for her country and its future. Hontz is a pastor's wife and author in Holland, Michigan, and she and Shirley had been friends for several years in the midnineties when the two got together for lunch at Hontz's home. They also had been long-distance prayer partners for that time, so they savored this occasion when they could actually be together in person and pray. It was then that Hontz first was struck by her friend's passion in prayer for a particular concern.

"She knelt down in our living room and she began to pour her heart out for our nation, and I'd never seen anybody pray like that for our country," Hontz remembers. "And then she started weeping. So we were on our knees just crying out to the Lord on behalf of the entire United States. And it just stuck with me: her passion for God to touch the heart of America."

God showed that he knew what he was doing in tapping Shirley Dobson for her next assignment.

ᴑᴄ⌒ᴄ⌒ᴄ⌒ᴄᴜ

Recognizing the national tradition of covering the endeavors of American presidents and armies with prayer, President Truman signed a joint resolution of Congress in 1952, declaring an annual national day of prayer. But it remained an obscure footnote to the national religion until the early seventies, when various groups of Christian women around the country began praying for their country, many of them influenced by a 1969 Billy Graham conference in Minneapolis. Their interest focused on raising awareness of the national prayer day that was already on the books, and in 1982, Vonette Bright was asked to head a task force to formally elevate the observance. The wife of Campus Crusade for Christ founder Bill Bright and a partner with him in that worldwide ministry, Vonette Bright steadily raised the profile of the tradition. Then she spearheaded an effort to get Congress to dedicate a specific day each year to the event, arising many days at 4 a. m. in California to call congressmen repeatedly and urge them to support the initiative. In 1988, Bright succeeded, and President Ronald Reagan signed the law that permanently affixed the first Thursday in May as America's National Day of Prayer.

In 1990, after Vonette Bright had nurtured the effort for several years, the Brights were moving to Florida, and she felt that "the organization needed some new blood." Bright had grown "NDP" but with no particular ambition to expand it to some next, higher level. She saw a hunger for ministerial impact in her younger friend that convinced her that Shirley Dobson would make a particularly fitting successor. "Dr. Dobson had been so responsive to me in allowing me to be on his program, and I had come to see Shirley kind of as I was: supporting my husband and being involved in his ministry without similar strong commitments of my own," Bright remembers. "I felt that she had what it took, and her visibility through Focus on the Family made it a natural."

So after checking with James Dobson, whom she knew at that point much better than she knew Shirley, Bright approached Shirley about taking over. At first, Shirley demurred. But a bit later, in prayer about the opportunity, Shirley says she "laid out two fleeces," an expression from an Old Testament character's test of faith:[3] that her husband would say yes and that Bright would ask her again. Both were affirmed quickly. "God obviously called me to be the chair of the National Day of Prayer," she says now.

As it turned out, the decision to answer God's call was easier than Shirley's first days at the helm of NDP. "I had six thousand dollars and one volunteer staffer to start with," Shirley says. Dobson acknowledges that while his wife "had worked in the church and the kids' schools and neighborhood things, all of a sudden she was in charge, and she had to develop confidence in that area because she didn't know what the business world was like. She had never seen a business budget, but she got in there and learned it."

Shirley became "the heart of this thing," confirms Jim Weidmann, a former top sales manager for IBM who joined Focus in 1997 and has become vice chairman of NDP, splitting his time as an executive between it and Focus. "The thing she does is that she shares at a high, high level what she wants. She wanted it in the public square, and she wanted national media for it. Her vision was to communicate with every American family the need for personal prayer and repentance and the need to pray for our nation and its leaders. And every year she spends a lot of time praying through what the theme will be."

At the same time, says Weidmann, Shirley is happy to pat a few backs and twist a few arms for the cause. "She has amazing boldness about that," he says, "because she believes that everyone should have this kind of love for his nation. So she'll just pick up the phone and call anyone." In 2005, for example, Weidmann had come to feel that Christian media in general weren't supportive enough of NDP. "So Shirley called the president of PAX TV [Lowell Paxson] and said, 'We're really trying to promote prayer for the nation, and we'd like you to consider airing these commercials for free.' And he said, 'Sure.'"

Her leadership of what has become a vast ministry still puts a lump in Shirley's throat from time to time, however—despite the smoothness and comfort she projects as NDP's leader. "It hasn't always been easy for her, because of her personality," says Anne Ryun, Shirley's friend, the wife of Kansas Congressman Jim Ryun, and a frequent guest on *Focus*. "She loves people, but she usually loves them in milder, kinder, and gentler ways than extroverts like Dr. Dobson do. And actually, that draws people to her, because she's not in your face."

Shirley Dobson and Weidmann have overseen explosive growth in the NDP franchise. It now has a $1.5-million budget. More than forty thousand separate prayer meetings occurred across the nation on May 5, 2005. Given how NDP has become a phenomenon locally as well as nationally, by 2001, the event was generating fourteen million "hits" in news-media coverage, a ubiquity that mushroomed to forty-four million hits in 2004. And the apex of NDP activity each year, two days of observances in Washington, steadily has gained importance because of the rising political clout of evangelicals. Several senators and congressmen joined a few hundred Christian leaders in attending Shirley's reception at the JW Marriott Hotel in Washington on May 4, 2005, the eve of the formal NDP observance.

At the 2005 observance, the growing prominence of NDP was underscored because of the fact that it occurred in the midst of high-profile efforts by Democrats in Congress, and their allies in the mainstream media, to skewer Tom DeLay, the House Majority leader, over alleged violations of lobbying laws. On the morning of May 5, a story in the *Washington Post* even suggested that DeLay "ducks around the Capitol like a fugitive these days, using back doors and basement passages to avoid television cameras."[4] Yet on the evening of May 4, DeLay certainly didn't seem like a man in hiding. Instead, he was among friends at the annual NDP reception. Shirley introduced him as a man "who's been under fire lately" partly because "he's effective in what he does."

DeLay took the podium and recounted the role of Bill Bright in "bringing me back to Christ" two decades earlier. "I don't think I've ever been as close to the Lord as in the last few months," DeLay said, but then allowed: "When I ask him to defeat my enemies, his timetable could be a little quicker." His audience ate up the quip, and then they prayed for DeLay.

So each year for a couple of days in early May, Shirley becomes the epicenter of attention of American evangelicalism while she runs NDP in Washington, and her husband willingly takes a backseat. He's still very visible, and Shirley gives James Dobson prominent podium time during the two days of events. In fact, following Shirley's remarks in the East Room in 2005 at the White House NDP program, President Bush quipped that he was "glad to see you brought your husband, Jim, with you," breaking into one of his patented half chuckles.

But it's clear to all assembled that NDP is Shirley's stage. And she usually uses it to throw a loving barb or two at her husband in front of all his friends in the capital. "We don't have a perfect marriage," she said from the stage more than once during the 2005 observance. "Because Jim's not perfect." Audiences could almost hear a rim shot in the background as James Dobson pretended to take offense from his seat in the crowd.

And because of her role as head of NDP, Shirley playfully maintains, "Many times in the airport, I'm recognized before [my husband] is. People talk to me first and then say to him, 'Then you must be Dr. Dobson.' It happens a lot, actually. He jokes about it. But he's proud of it, for me."

CHAPTER EIGHTEEN

INSIDE THE FISHBOWL

It's not a facade.

DANAE DOBSON, ON HER DAD
AND HER FAMILY LIFE

Most well-known and admired men and women are evaluated on their accomplishments, not the success of their personal life. Fans judge whether an actress such as Julia Roberts has succeeded by considering the quality, box-office appeal, and staying power of her films, or whether a professional athlete such as Michael Jordan has achieved a worthy career by considering his statistics, championship rings, and most-valuable-player titles.

But Dobson watchers know that his legacy can't be gauged simply by the number of books sold, radio programs recorded, or federal policies influenced. Instead, as the preeminent family-relationship guru of our time, Dobson is judged by how good a husband and father he is. How well did he do in establishing and nurturing his own marriage and in rearing his own children? How is it all turning out for them? Is he as advertised as a husband and father?

In the case of the Dobson family, the real answers are the apparent answers: James and Shirley Dobson enjoy a strong, loving, and vibrant marriage by all accounts—an achievement all the more remarkable because of their extremely high public profile as individuals and as a couple. Danae and Ryan Dobson are talented, economically independent, well-adjusted individuals living in Southern California. They have their own thriving careers, yet are comfortable enough in the context of their father's fame to have pursued similar vocations. And they remain devoted to God, their parents, their extended family, and their longtime family friends.

The Dobsons endured plenty of issues and stresses along the way, just as any family does, including Dobson's workaholic tendencies and medical episodes, Shirley's adjustment to a very public life and their move to Colorado. But by the time the Dobson offspring were forging their own path during the eighties, his family had emerged as perhaps the strongest real-life testimony to the efficacy of Dobson's teachings.

⚬⚬⚬

James and Shirley Dobson were infatuated with each other in their youth certainly, but with the passing of years their regard has grown into a mature and complete appreciation for each other. "He's one of the most remarkable people I've ever known—an incredible man of integrity and passion," Shirley says unblushingly. "He's one of the greatest blessings in my life. He's disciplined and hardworking and very bright. He's always been open to me giving him advice. He doesn't have a lot of faults."

Dobson family friend Marge Smith believes that James Dobson "carried out his parents' model by picking Shirley, because she has the same devotion to Jim that Myrtle had for [James Sr.]. And he chose a girl who was very intelligent to help him."

Dobson describes his wife as "a very strong woman, a very feminine lady who recognizes and acknowledges my leadership and doesn't try to overwhelm me. But also she's just a very strong individual who knows what she believes and has a real good compass as to where she wants to go."

It took Shirley awhile to develop that compass, however. After she quit teaching school and Danae was born, Shirley became "a full-time, absolutely committed mother until Ryan was gone," says her husband, and it was a role that she really relished—especially because of her own rocky youth.

"You always try to put into your kids' lives and your family what was missing in yours," Shirley says.

Her kids testify that their mother succeeded, a truth that became more and more evident to them as they grew older. Ryan recalls his mother's cleverness. "She knew the importance of fitting in and she knew that part of it was how you dressed," he says. "So her way of picking out 'cool' clothes for me was to go to a clothing store and look for a girl she knew I'd think was cute. Then she'd walk up to her and say, 'I have a son about your age—what would he like?' How cool is that?"

When she bought Ryan's first skateboard, Shirley rounded up some neighborhood kids, took them to the local skate shop, and had them select the board they liked for him. "To this day," Ryan says, "I can name every part on that board."

Danae is still impressed by the devotion to their needs that Shirley demonstrated, even as her kids were rustling to leave the roost. When Danae was getting ready to start a fall semester at the University of Southern California, for example, and had a lengthy to-do list, Shirley left a note where Danae would find it. "I know you've got a lot going on and I just wanted to let you know that I can be your feet and walk around campus and help you get things taken care of," the note read. "Just let me know what you need." Even though Danae didn't take her mother up on her offer, she says, "I saved the note just because I was so blessed by it."

Today, the Dobson household no longer generates anecdotes about child rearing. In fact, friends can't help but see the irony in the fact that James and Shirley Dobson have no grandchildren who could benefit from their attention and expertise. But Shirley isn't concerned. "I don't sit around and worry about it or be depressed about it," she says. "I share the joy of friends who have grandchildren."

Friends confirm that expression of grace. Robert Wolgemuth notes that Dobson "has been very open, even on broadcasts, in talking about this. But never has he made me feel self-conscious" about Wolgemuth's own five grandchildren.

Bill Maier lends a different perspective. "Who are the [Dobsons'] grandchildren right now? They're the children of America who are under attack from so many different directions."

◦◦◦◦◦

Dobson assiduously nurtured his relationship with his kids, both before and after they left the roost. At Focus headquarters in Colorado, for example, he installed a private telephone line so they could reach him quickly and easily. Yet there has always been unresolved tension over Dobson's long hours at work, even after he stopped traveling a nationwide speaking circuit. Ryan Dobson, for example, says his father works too much. "When he said he stopped traveling in 1977, he stopped traveling and he went to work," Ryan says. "There is a huge difference between being home all the time and being in the office all the time. But Focus is where it is today because of the time he spent in the office."

Besides, Dobson adds, his son's characterization shortchanges the yeoman-like efforts that he had made over the years to stay connected and involved with his children, especially in their formative years. Day to day, for example, the Dobsons loved to surround themselves with their kids' friends, and they often bought pizzas and hosted volleyball parties in their backyard. "My friends were always comfortable being around my parents," Danae says.

Ryan adds, "I can't believe how much noise my parents put up with when I was growing up. My friends and I built skate ramps in our backyard and skated there until all hours. My friends were always welcome at our home. That was part of the deal, that if there wasn't anyplace to go and hang out, we could always go to our house."

Dobson also strove to make plenty of time for family vacations and getaways. "I've got six thousand slides in my computer, and if you go back and look at [the ones] from 1977 to 1991, you have documentation of all that we did," including vacations to Hawaii and the East Coast in 1977 alone, Dobson says half-seriously.

The trips didn't always go smoothly. With the bemusement that only the passage of time can bring, Dobson tells of a "writing vacation" in Hawaii that the family took in 1973. It was going to be the first time flying on a mammoth Boeing 747 for any of them, and everyone was enthused. Once they were on board, Shirley excused herself to go to the lavatory. But then she realized that she had left a book she was reading in the airport lounge, so after checking with one flight attendant, Shirley dashed off the plane to fetch it. Unfortunately, the message was not relayed to the other flight attendants, and before Shirley could return to the plane, the 747 took off without her.

No one in her family knew that Shirley had left the aircraft. When she didn't return to her seat after a few minutes, Dobson asked the flight attendants to check the plane for her. "I was nervous as a cat and even took a photo of Shirley's empty seat," Dobson says. "We were halfway to Hawaii when the airline finally radioed the plane and said that my wife was at LAX. [They] couldn't tell us when she'd be able to come. Ryan got deathly ill on the plane, and once we got to Hawaii, we had to spend all day at the airport just waiting for her plane to come in."

The trip back to the mainland wasn't much easier. It seemed to Dobson that thousands of people were jamming the airport at Maui for Sunday flights back to Honolulu and then on to California. But Dobson's need to return was urgent: He had to give a speech on Monday.

Under threat of being bumped from the flight he needed to be on, Dobson managed to squeeze his family onto the approved passenger list and get all four tickets validated—or so he thought. When they tried to board, the flight attendant noted that only two of the tickets were actually valid—only two family members could get on that flight.

"I said, 'That's not my problem,' and I pushed right past him," Dobson recalls. "The four of us headed across the tarmac with him yelling for the police. But there were four planes on the tarmac, and I didn't know which one was going to Honolulu. Then Danae got on one of the planes, and we didn't know which one." So while Dobson was checking all of the planes to see which was headed for Honolulu, Shirley checked the others for Danae. Finding her, she emerged onto the tarmac with Danae and Ryan in tow. "That was fortunate," Dobson says, "because by that time, the police were out there, but they were looking for four people, not three. In those pre-9/11 days, airport security was not nearly as tight as it is today."

Shirley and the kids slipped onto a plane, and to the delight of everyone, it happened to be the one that Dobson was on—and it was headed for Honolulu. They all hunkered down and kept a low profile for a long trip home.

⁊⌒⌒⌒⌒⌒⌒⌒⌐

Danae Dobson was an early beneficiary of Dobson's attention, which naturally was clinical as well as personal: He often included stories here and there about his young daughter in his early books, under different names. She knew from the start that her father was "very special and very unique," Danae says, and that creativity was one of his strong suits. Even when she was as young as three or four years old, she remembers him playing games to get her to brush her teeth or do other necessary or unpleasant things.

Marked early on by her father as a gifted writer, Danae earned the distinction of becoming one of the youngest authors ever represented by a significant publisher. Word published *Woof!: A Bedtime Story about a Dog,* "by Danae Dobson, age 12, with a little help from her dad, Dr. James Dobson." She had been fascinated by stories about a dog named Woof and his unpredictable adventures that her father made up while carpooling her and her friends to school once a week. They were unpredictable because Dobson composed them extemporaneously while navigating Southern California early-morning traffic. But *Woof* gave them life outside the carpool lane.

In high school, Danae got involved in her dad's ministry, working after school and during summers. "I was in the correspondence department, and I would read the letters that came in about, for instance, women whose husbands were hooked on pornography," Danae recalls. "My eyes were kind of opened at a tender age to all of the things that could go wrong in a marriage." But later in high school, she told her parents the demands of homework, extracurricular activities, and her job were just too much, so they allowed her to quit working at Focus and paid her an allowance instead.

At the same time, Danae insists she wasn't bothered by her father's frequent absences when he was giving speeches and building his career during her earliest years. "I'm a very self-sufficient person; I don't need a lot of emotional catering," she says. "The love of my parents was very important to me, but I'm not the type who needed a lot of my dad's time. I never resented Focus. And any time I asked my dad to help with a manuscript or a homework assignment, he always did. Maybe not always on the spot, but he'd do it within a couple of days."

Danae says that her strong will and emotional and spiritual maturity helped her avoid thinking of herself as a "follower" of peers during high school and college. "I'm totally comfortable in my own skin," she says. "Having that strong-willed streak was helpful in that regard."

As an adult, Danae's writing career has flourished, and she now has twenty-two titles to her credit. "I'm aware that my opportunity came as the result of my dad, but it's up to me to be able to write something that sells and that enables the publisher to get their money back—so it's a ministry, but it's also a business," she says. Danae has built on her early success of writing children's books and recently came out with a title for teenage girls called *Let's Talk!* "Now that I've written a nonfiction book, I realize that I like to be able to express my ideas and opinions in regard to different Scriptures and various stages of life that people go through," she says.

At the same time, she has become involved in a variety of personal ministries, such as visiting nursing homes. "She doesn't just sit around and wait for life to happen to her," Shirley says. "She makes it happen. Much of what she is I think is from me, but I see a lot of her dad in her too, because Jim is very resourceful. And she's always got something going on." Her daughter is "stable," Shirley says, "not down very often. In fact, she's in a prayer group where they call her 'Joy' because she brings so much joy to people."

Danae has been involved in a number of serious relationships. But she acknowledges the difficulty of any potential husband measuring up to the standards she sees in her father—or passing his muster. "It only takes one person," Danae says. "It's not a hurdle as far as the Lord is concerned." While her daughter would "love to be married and have a family," Shirley says, "she wants to go on with her life."

ᴔᴄᴂᴄᴂᴃ

Ryan Dobson's adoption wasn't mentioned in Dobson's early writing and speaking, though he and Shirley told their son about it even before he understood the meaning of the word. Since then, "it's been a story they let me tell, because that's personal to my life," Ryan says. Much more integral to his life and development both as a boy and as an adult is the fact that Ryan suffered from attention deficit hyperactivity (ADHD) disorder. "I was so restless even when I slept that I would wake up just starving," Ryan recalls. "I was frantically hungry. It was so tough for my mom because I'd wake up mad—because I was hungry. She taught me to cook when I was six years old. That skill helped me get my first jobs during college when I worked as a cook in Chinese and French restaurants."

Dobson recognized that his son had a problem when Ryan was very young, but in the seventies the only available medications were too sedative. And in keeping with professional understanding of the condition at the time, Dobson believed that his son's restlessness would disappear when he reached puberty.

Like many a boy growing up, especially one as rambunctious as he, Ryan enjoyed nudging his father into pushing the envelope a bit. When Ryan was fourteen years old, in 1984, the two rappelled down high cliffs in the Sierra Nevadas with Rudy Markmiller. And while Ryan "bounced down the mountain and didn't have any trouble with it at all," Dobson remembers, "I was praying all the way down."

When he was a junior in high school, Ryan attended Summit Ministries, a "mountaintop" week in Colorado Springs that confronts teenagers with the challenge of deepening their relationship with Christ. "It was one of the greatest experiences of my life," he says, "where I found out there was something out there beyond my own nose."

Though Ryan never expressed much interest in going to college, Dobson insisted that his son enroll in Olivet Nazarene University in Bourbonnais, Illinois—Dobson also provided for his son's best friend, who was fatherless and had financial needs, to attend Olivet. Not only did Dobson arrange and pay all the expenses for his son and his friend, but he also managed to secure the release of Ryan's buddy from a four-year obligation he had made to the U.S. Navy just a week earlier. "That was one of the first times that I thought my dad's power was very scary," Ryan says.

Coming from metropolitan Southern California, he felt like a fish out of water in rural Illinois. Ryan struggled at Olivet, whereupon his parents did the best thing they knew to do in such a situation: apply tough love. They pulled him out of school, helped him move to Colorado, set him up in an apartment with a month's rent and a security deposit, and then told him he needed to fend for himself. Once he was able to apply his intelligence and ambition in a nonacademic environment, Ryan excelled at a handful of jobs and finally talked his parents into giving him one more shot at higher education, enrolling at Biola University in metro Los Angeles. "He said that if I got another D, he'd never send me anywhere again," Ryan says of his father.

At first, Biola didn't work out well either, and Ryan began to despair. That Thanksgiving, Ryan remembers, "I had more stress and angst in my life than ever before. It was right when we were taking our family photo for Christmas, and I looked like everyone else in the picture—I faked it real well." He asked his father if he could see a counselor, and Dobson sent him to the dean of Rosemead School of Psychology, the Biola-affiliated graduate school that had been founded by Clyde Narramore, one of Dobson's mentors. After a battery of tests revealed a genius-level IQ along with strong disabilities in math and languages, the psychologist told Ryan that he had ADHD.

"I told him my dad wouldn't believe him, but he said, 'I've got proof,'" Ryan recalls. "And he said that if Dad wouldn't ease up the pressure on me, he was going to recommend that I quit college."

When Ryan's doctor explained the test results to James Dobson, the father was aghast at how this evaluation about his own son could have evaded him for all those years. "He said that when he was getting his Ph.D., authorities on child development had all taught that when a child hit puberty, the hormone changes ended ADHD," Ryan says. "It just hadn't occurred to him that his son could have been ADHD. But discovering that changed lots of things in our relationship. It took the pressure off and said that 'whatever happens, happens'—which was a big deal." Now that his past and current behavior made more sense,

Ryan relaxed and began taking Ritalin; his grades improved as his concentration improved, and he graduated from Biola in 1995. "I couldn't believe how understanding my parents were during what had to be a very difficult time," says Ryan. "I wasn't a very good student, and my parents accepted me no matter what my grades looked like. They just wanted me to graduate."

Though more able to enjoy his relationship with his parents, Ryan still experienced some difficulties. While his gift for public speaking began to evidence itself at that point, he wasn't able to settle on a career; he worked for brief stints with the Family Research Council and in Saddleback Community Church's youth ministry program.

"I went through a major life crisis when I moved back to California," he commented. "I had quit my job and at the time I just didn't care if I got another one. My weight dropped down to 130," he recalls. "I lost my pride, some friends, and was quickly losing every cent I'd ever hoped to earn."

But Ryan believes that God used three things to turn him around. The first was discovering surfing, a sport that Ryan says brings him into closer communion with God than anything else he's done. The second was that others began to recognize his speaking talents, garnering him a contract with the Ambassador Agency, a Nashville-based group that represents many of the leading speakers in Christendom. The third crucial development was that Ryan was asked to help with a Focus event that had been the bailiwick of the just-departed Mike Trout: Focus's National Bike Ride for the Family, a fund-raising mechanism for the ministry that culminated on the twenty-fifth anniversary in 2002. The stint not only engaged Ryan in a fulfilling activity but also gave him a new appreciation for his parents and their ministry.

"It got me meeting people whose lives had been changed by Focus on the Family, who were on the brink of suicide, whose marriages had failed, who were out of control—but they turned on the radio and my dad's voice gave them hope and help and ideas. All the anger"—at personal disappointments, at the late recognition of his learning disability, at his early career woes—"got washed away doing those bike rides, meeting people who said, 'I just couldn't have done it without your dad.'" He further reflects, "What really brought me around was the love and support of my parents. When I was at my lowest point, they stepped up to the plate. They made it clear that my well-being was the most important thing to them. I'll never forget my dad telling me that nothing mattered more to him than to see his kids succeed. Some will think he was talking about business or wealth, but my sister and I know that success in our family has to do with spiritual well-being. My parents made it very clear to me that they would do whatever it took to see me through that time. From that point on, everything was different."

෴

The Dobsons didn't play a real family on television—they were a real family, living in a fishbowl that was created by James Dobson's celebrity status. Exacerbating the situation were expectations by many of Dobson's fans and supporters that they would only observe scenes of peace, beauty, and utter control inside the Dobson aquarium—and that they could tap on the glass whenever they wanted.

Such inevitabilities began to surface for Danae when she was in college and for Ryan when he was in high school. For example, Ryan had a substitute teacher who initially and rather obnoxiously doubted his claims that he was the son of Dr. Dobson, only to ask her student to have his dad sign ten of his books for her as soon as she was convinced that he had been telling the truth. "It seemed cheap to me," Ryan says. A junior high administrator once suspended him, saying he was punishing him for talking in class, but actually, Ryan argues, the teacher or administration "was trying to make a point to my dad."

When they lived in California, the Dobsons would have to leave church early whenever Dobson wanted to avoid being detained for an hour or more after the service in impromptu minicounseling sessions in the lobby. Even more problematic, Ryan recalls, was "being interrupted at virtually every meal at a restaurant for years. You'd be at dinner and someone would say, 'I don't want to bother you,' and my first thought was, *Then don't come over here and say anything*. And my dad has never cut a conversation short. Part of it he enjoys, and part of it he feels as a responsibility to people. But it was tough for me to always be interrupted." Although Danae says she was not bothered by such scenes, Ryan says that "my sister has mellowed out a lot in her feelings about Focus and growing up in the limelight. She was more negative five years ago."

On one occasion, a fan acted out a scene that literally could have come from a TV sitcom: He came and sat down next to Shirley and actually scooted her over just a bit as he proceeded to corner the Dobsons through three-quarters of their dinner at a local restaurant. But for the most part, well-wishers were kind and respectful, and the Dobsons gave them their due. "Even if the kids were whining, he would give that person their moment," Shirley says. "If people stop coming up to us and thanking us, it means we're not touching their lives."

When Dobson is handling Focus-related duties, Focus's board and his handlers do as much as they can to keep a shield of isolation around him, providing him with one or two assistants on most long trips who multitask as security people, drivers, and gofers. But their assignment is made especially difficult on airplanes, where James and Shirley Dobson make themselves highly approachable.

"One time the airline attendants moved him up to first class, and us with him, and he was sitting a couple of rows ahead of me," recalls one former high-level colleague. "And about four or five of these attendants were around him talking about family issues. It was every guy's dream: They were all attractive. The guy sitting next to me said, 'Who is this guy? And what's he got that I don't have?' He strikes such a hot button—or a raw nerve—everywhere he goes, people want to tell him things that are profound."

But as Dobson's celebrity and his list of critics grew, his family began to actually fear for his safety as well as regret the constant inconveniences. Bulletproof vests and bodyguards at public events, even sometimes for family members, became part of the currency of being a public figure. The family first realized that Dobson's views might get him into danger during his stint on the federal pornography commission, which ended up probing Mafia control of much of the hard-core porn industry. "I knew he was in Satan's domain," says Danae. "Our family prayed a lot, and so did other people, against enemy attacks on all fronts"—the spiritual as well as the physical.

In fact, a specific threat did materialize after Dobson delivered the keynote speech at the National Religious Broadcasters convention in 1989, just a few weeks after the Ted Bundy interview. Dobson was still behind the podium answering questions from the crowd when the hotel's head of security turned him around briefly and told him that someone had called in a death threat against Dobson. "'Two guys came in with long knives on their belts, and they didn't come in together,' he whispered to me," Dobson recalls. "'And one of them is right in front of you, behind the lady in red. As soon as she moves, we're going to close you off.' Then the guy fled."

The results of their father's fame can be jarring to the private life of

Ryan and Danae Dobson in other ways as well. "We're just a regular family like everyone else," says Ryan. "I can be in a fight with my dad, and then have someone say to me, 'I wish I had your parents.' It happens all the time, because my parents parented tons of people out there. And for my mom it's got to be tough to have women out there who would be standing in line for my dad if something ever happened. It's like being on tour with a rock band."

Being the Dobsons, Ryan concludes, indeed produced a distorted reality—but one that has failed to divide a family whose members actually lived the father's principles pretty closely.

"The crazy thing is that he's exactly who he says he is," Ryan says. "I've known many ministries out there and the ins and outs of many families and skeletons popping out of everywhere. As far as I know, he doesn't have them. I do; he doesn't."

CHAPTER NINETEEN
BLACK AND WHITE
AND RED AND BLUE

> *If we choose to use any "warfare"rhetoric,*
> *it would be prudent of us to employ it . . .*
> *with humility, good will, and compassion.*
> *We who are proponents of a gospel of*
> *reconciliation do not want ourselves*
> *to be needlessly divisive.*
>
> HISTORY PROFESSOR JOHN WOODBRIDGE,
> IN A 1995 ESSAY THAT LED TO A DISPUTE
> WITH JAMES DOBSON

The national headquarters of People For the American Way is surprisingly nondescript, a modest suite on the fourth floor of an office building in the northwest quadrant of Washington, D.C., about two miles from Capitol Hill. Not much distinguishes its accoutrements from those of an insurance brokerage or a computer-sales office except a few large wall posters featuring some of PFAW's favorite heroes: actress Kathleen Turner; Martin Luther King Jr.; and Norman Lear, the television producer of *All in the Family* fame who founded the group in 1981.

But if there's anything that stands in diametric opposition to everything that James Dobson and Focus on the Family represent and strive for, it's PFAW, which Lear established specifically to become a political and cultural redoubt against what he saw as the dangerous spread of Christian conservatism. Several other organizations have joined PFAW in various causes, including the National Organization for Women, the National Abortion Rights Action League (known since 2003 as NARAL Pro-Choice America), and Americans United for Separation of Church and State. In fact, Barry Lynn, executive director of Washington, D.C.–based Americans United, has made criticizing Dobson the sound track of his career.

"Every time I turn around, he's whacking me for something," Dobson says. And sometimes Dobson takes the trouble to pound Lynn as well. One indicator: Between 1985 and the end of 2003, no fewer than 110 articles in which both men appeared ran in U.S. newspapers and magazines.[1]

Yet PFAW, which pegged the number of its members and activists at 750,000 in mid-2005, is the only organization whose very purpose is to battle the Christian Right across the many fronts of what Dobson often calls a "civil war of values." Increasingly, Lear and his allies in Hollywood and the secular news and entertainment media have made it clear that they feel the same sense of urgency about the conflict Dobson describes. So PFAW opened an office in Denver in the early nineties just to monitor the boom in parachurch activity in Colorado after Focus moved there. Its researchers regularly listen to Dobson's broadcasts, and for several years, PFAW agents produced written analyses of Dobson's organization and effectiveness. Its Web site carries a thorough dossier on Focus and on Dobson, including quotes that PFAW finds the most provocative, such as Dobson's description of the homosexual agenda from his book *Complete Marriage and Family Home Reference Guide*.[2]

And just a few months after Dobson feted supporters at Focus's twenty-fifth anniversary in July 2002, which featured a video message composed expressly for the occasion by President Bush, PFAW's faithful congregated in Hollywood for their own commemoration. It was Lear's eightieth birthday, and in November liberal leaders from politics, entertainment, and academia flocked to honor the man who had institutionalized production-studio leftism. Providing his own video greeting, likewise warmly recorded just for that event, was former president Bill Clinton.

As they plot against a Christian Right they believe has been strengthened through the 2000, 2002, and 2004 elections, two key PFAW executives acknowledge that they have Dobson more in their crosshairs than anyone else does—but that they don't quite know how to bring him down. "He's really persuasive because he's not just political," says Peter Montgomery, communications director. "He really builds loyalty from those who listen to his ministry. He builds goodwill that lends credence to what he says. And his ministry allows him to pretend he's not political."

Carol Keys, PFAW's director of research, describes Dobson as "very confrontational. Either you agree and are totally for his position or you're totally against him; there's no middle ground. He would be more successful if he were more open to compromise; although maybe I would compromise too much. What makes him more and more effective in spite of that, though, is that he doesn't speak as much about issues in political terms as he does in moral terms: He makes moral pronouncements about political issues."

Other Dobson foes also understand the power of Dobson's appeal. "Focus on the Family is one of the most powerful special-interest groups in this country," says Wayne Besen, a gay activist, speaker, and writer. "When James Dobson talks, leaders in Washington don't just listen— they jump and react. That makes his positions very dangerous."[3]

The fact that these opposition leaders so lucidly understand one of their top political enemies underscores concerns that some Focus board members first harbored when they blessed Dobson's divergence into politics in the mideighties. "We've tried to remind him that he's a lightning rod," says Ted Engstrom, vice chairman of the Focus board. "We've said, 'Be careful.'"

Actually, Dobson would be surprised if he wasn't drawing massive fire from enemy forces, because the continual fusillades are confirmation that he is sticking to his own guns. As long as he isn't open to valid criticism for some sort of personal failing or Focus hasn't egregiously mishandled something, Dobson can abide attacks on his ideas and views. He also often gives his rhetorical opponents credit for being as honest and sincerely motivated in their polemics as he is—the difference is, he believes, they are just wrong.

It's not that Dobson enjoys being vilified—by anyone. In fact, it is a point of pride for him that critiques rarely veer into an attempt to ridicule him as a person. "I just love people, and I try to treat everyone with respect, even those with whom I disagree," he says. Dobson is especially pleased that many of the ideological opposites who sat with him on the presidential pornography and gambling commissions "said they liked me as a man." And H. B. London observes, "You'll never ever find that even the liberal media has been able to find Jim in a lie or being vicious; you've never seen him in a vengeful spirit. He might respond to attacks on his character, but he never does it in a spirit of revenge."

Nevertheless, his rivals for the moral high ground in American society, culture, and politics charge that Dobson insists on seeing everything in black-and-white. There is a lot of truth in the assertion, Dobson admits. But increasingly, his lens also has tints of red and blue.

Thanks to the results of the 2004 elections, by now the terms "red states" and "blue states" have become a part of America's broad cultural vernacular. Red states are those that were won by George W. Bush, as they were depicted on the electoral maps by television networks. John Kerry's conquests were colored blue. Most of the blue, Democratic-leaning states were those on the east and west coasts and in the North, while most of the red states were found in the interior and the South. Republican-red voters also dominated the suburbs and rural areas across the country, while Democratic-blue voters were strong in the cities.

"Red" and "blue" first became shorthand for social pundits in describing the "two Americas" that seemed to emerge more clearly during the long, tense chapter of national introspection known as the 2000 presidential election. The unprecedented closeness of the 2000 popular vote first caused commentators to fixate on the red-and-blue divide and conclude that the American people as a whole had become split into two almost exactly equal-sized politico-cultural groups, one represented by each color. The primacy of "moral values" as a concern of voters in exit polls on Election Day 2004 amplified the continued importance of this crucial cleft in the American body politic.

But to Dobson, the handier distinction isn't among geographic territories but instead among individuals who have a red-state mentality and those who have a blue-state attitude, between the God-fearing who generally support conservative (and Republican) positions on moral and social issues and the secularists who typically favor liberal (and Democratic) attitudes. There are many other correlative indicators, of course, but strong agreement with Dobson's ideas is a very reliable sign that an individual is a "red," while basic opposition to his views alone likely puts someone in the "blue" column.

Yet while the electorate seems to be increasingly "red"-minded, Dobson believes that the "blues" still control the mediating institutions in this country that crucially determine, in large part, how the civil war of values is interpreted by the American people. Their continued dominance of most colleges and universities, most courts, the federal civil service, and the news and entertainment media assure that their views prevail. This status quo remains little endangered by the success of Rush Limbaugh, the rise of the conservative Fox News network, and even the greater respect accorded the Christian marketplace in the wake of the success of Mel Gibson's 2004 blockbuster movie, *The Passion of the Christ*.

Many believe Dobson's frustration over this reality has fueled his continuing hostility to these elite institutions and his growing determination over the last couple of years to try to counter them by raising his own profile.

Dobson blames the national news and entertainment media for a large share of America's deteriorating social fabric since the sixties, in particular because of its open advocacy of liberalism and secularism. Dobson also harbors a more personal grudge against marquee news organizations because of how they treat Focus on the Family and its cause. Dobson has been calling attention to the obvious tilt in the news media for at least two decades, a campaign he intensified after the 1993 publication of the infamous *Washington Post* article referring to evangelical Christians as "largely poor, uneducated and easy to command."[4] The article was published during the very early days of Clinton's presidency and in the wake of several other examples of journalistic trampling of Christians that outraged Dobson.

"It is open season on any Christian who has the courage to stick his head out of the foxhole," Dobson said in his March 1993 newsletter to supporters. "Indeed, I believe we are seeing the beginning of an era of serious repression against believers. . . . Leading a large conservative ministry today is reason enough for ridicule."

In fact, the rising media vitriol against evangelicals was lapping more and more at Dobson's own heels. Around that time, for instance, an Associated Press story falsely implied that Dobson had tried to hound homosexual teachers out of Colorado Springs, even though three local superintendents signed affidavits asserting that there was no truth to the story.[5] And while Dobson wasn't suggesting that Dan Rather and Peter Jennings and other media personalities had targeted him personally, he did claim that they and their liberal colleagues in the secular media were both openly and subtly hostile to conservative and Christian ideas and leaders, and that Dobson naturally caught some of that flak.

But there was something more afoot as well: The reporters, editors, and producers who were increasingly observing and interpreting Dobson and his words and actions had little idea who he really was. "In his style and language, [Dobson] clearly appeals to and is a very comfortable figure for the reds and is a weirdo to the blues," explains Jeffrey Satinover, a Yale-educated psychiatrist and political author, as well as a member of the Focus on the Family Physicians Resource Council. And despite his ubiquity in the vast evangelical subculture, his indisputable influence inside the Beltway, and his outsized role in reshaping the Republican Party, many members of the political media knew little about Dobson.

Christianity Today published several long and insightful pieces about Dobson throughout the eighties and nineties, as did several other Christian publications; yet just a few mainstream media organizations sensed and conveyed his significance, such as the *Washington Post,* which dedicated several hundred column inches to him over the years. But as recently as 2004, experienced national reporters still made the mistake of calling him "Reverend" Dobson, exposing their ignorance about the leadership of one of the most influential segments of the American electorate.

"It doesn't help," Dobson told the National Press Club in his first appearance there in June 2004, "that Larry King has been calling me 'Reverend' for twenty-one years on his program."[6]

Many journalists and media personalities have purported to understand Dobson and his milieu, but it's a difficult task. At least Hanna Rosin wrote in *GQ* in 1999 that Dobson "embodied the man-eating demons haunting [Newt] Gingrich."[7] And Margaret Carlson, columnist for *Time,* seemed in the know in 1998 when she called Dobson "the country's most powerful Christian activist." But then Carlson couldn't resist the temptation that often plagues secular pundits: condemning a mind-set because she doesn't share it. She questioned how "Christian" Dobson and the Christian Right really were: "The golden rule doesn't include gay bashing and divisiveness," she opined.[8]

Dobson became a favorite target of Frank Rich, arguably evangelicals' greatest media scourge. Formerly a theater critic for the *New York Times*, Rich became an editorial page regular and then a featured Sunday columnist, and he has referred to Dobson as "the Godzilla of the Right"[9] and compared him to Ku Klux Klan leader David Duke.[10] Over the last few years, Dobson has returned the favor by pointing out that Rich and his opinions are among the most vicious in the media toward evangelicals.

In Dobson's view, TV-network news operations and on-air personalities may be even more irredeemable than elite newspapers. Episodes
he finds despicable include the time in 1999 when Katie Couric, cohost
of the *Today* show, even linked the death of Matthew Shepard—the
young gay man who was brutally murdered in Laramie, Wyoming, in
1998—to "people like" Focus on the Family, the Family Research
Council, and the Christian Coalition (whereupon thousands of people
complained to NBC about Couric's statement).

As someone skilled in broadcast production himself, he also remains very wary of being interviewed for any pretaped, edited pieces
about himself or Focus because of how much "control goes to those involved in the editing process," says Paul Hetrick. And because he has
reached the point where he can insert himself fully in the public-policy
debate on his own terms, Dobson has refused to cooperate with a number of network producers and anchors who want to interview him. He
snubbed Public Broadcasting Service's iconic Bill Moyers, for example,
in 1993, and NBC in 1997 and again in 1998.

Dobson's longest-running game of cat and mouse occurred with
CBS's venerable news-magazine show, *60 Minutes,* which attempted in
1996 and again in 1998 to gain his cooperation for interviews about
various aspects of evangelicals' involvement in politics. In the process,
Mike Wallace, the show's senior and best-known correspondent, did
what Dobson would refer to as "blowing smoke" at his quarry in a 1996
exchange of letters. After Dobson formally declined Wallace's request
for an interview, citing "many examples of bias and misrepresentation"
by *60 Minutes,* Wallace objected in a letter of response: "My politics, my
views on some current social issues may be somewhat closer to your
own than you imagine, but I have always, on *60 Minutes,* tried for dispassionate, accurate and fair reportage."[11] Fruitlessly, he asked Dobson to
reconsider.

Such tactics, Charles Colson says, are one reason that the news media "haven't been able to make him into a caricature. [Dobson is] too
smart for them. He's picked and chosen his spots."

On one of the rare occasions in which Dobson did agree to be interviewed by a network reporter, the result was the lengthy segment that
ran on the ABC magazine-style show *Day One* in September 1995. The
piece was fairly dispassionate, and Paul Hetrick says that, "overall, we

were pleased with it." But like nearly every other secular reporter who addresses the Dobson phenomenon, John Hockenberry threw in a few twists—and at least one outright falsehood—apparently designed to make his subject look extreme. And the piece ended with speculation about Dobson's very honesty about political ambition.

The *Day One* depiction opened with Dobson walking down the steps of the U.S. Capitol next to Gary Bauer, towering over his much shorter companion, as Hockenberry described him as "one of the most powerful men in America," yet one whose name few people knew. In the obligatory interview with Barry Lynn, his arch foil said that Dobson "likes to be a kingmaker" and that his support of a national political candidate had become more important than that of "[Jerry] Falwell and [Pat] Robertson combined."

In a snippet of his interview with Dobson, Hockenberry baited him with questions about abortion and creationism, but Dobson responded obliquely and along the lines of his own agenda. "John, we're involved in a civil war of values [between] two worldviews that center around whether God exists or whether he doesn't." Hockenberry then described Focus's correspondence system, which he called "a machine for dispensing advice that runs on Bibles and the advice of kindly ladies."

Yet, Hockenberry allowed, the demographics of Focus supporters "aren't as Ken and Barbie as you might think." For instance, there was a full-blooded Navajo woman whose son had died of a brain aneurysm but who was greatly comforted by materials and advice from Dobson and Focus. "He could come and live in my house if he needed to," the woman said in an interview.

Then Lynn essentially accused Dobson of abusing the trust of people like the Navajo woman. "These are names of people who call in because of a trauma," he told Hockenberry, "and now they're on a mailing list." Hockenberry led him on: "So [Dobson] has turned a family crisis hotline into a political army?"

"That's right," concluded Lynn.

"But can he deliver?" asked Hockenberry.

"There is evidence" that Dobson could indeed, "more than [Robertson's] *700 Club* [show]," said Lynn. "His folks respond quickly and directly to whatever he urges."

Hockenberry reported that such "political hardball tactics delight his followers" but then intoned that "some of [Dobson's] political ideas are bizarre." He asked Dobson whether he had actually warned parents that allowing their teenaged daughters to go away to college would turn them into "lesbian lovers," then gave Dobson a chance to respond. Dobson straightened him out: "I didn't say that a university education" per se would have such a dire effect. "I said that [college] women's studies programs have that flavor." Answered Hockenberry: "Do they cause lesbianism?" Dobson didn't budge: "They can encourage it."

Then Hockenberry shifted to the 1989 Bundy episode as more evidence that Dobson demonstrated "paranoia about [people] being lured into some dark sexual world." Said Dobson in a sound bite from the interview: Pornography "is a curse, and Ted Bundy knew it." Hockenberry said that the Bundy video brought Dobson almost one million dollars in contributions and then incorrectly alleged that Focus "gave away the proceeds of the video after being criticized." Actually, in an agreement worked out with Bundy's lawyer ahead of time, Focus distributed most of its proceeds to antipornography organizations, retaining only what it required to cover the cost of production and distribution.

Hockenberry wrapped up his taped piece with a philosophical comment by Dobson that explained his urgency. "The side that wins gains the right" to teach children, he said. "And in one generation, you change the whole culture."

Back in the studio after the piece ran, ABC coanchor Forrest Sawyer asked Hockenberry, sitting with him on the air, if Dobson had political ambitions. The reporter said that Dobson "claims he has no [such] ambitions." Chimed in coanchor Diane Sawyer, sitting at the same desk, "Do you believe it?" Hockenberry's apparently extemporaneous response was appropriately balanced. "He's an amazing figure," Hockenberry said. "It's possible that power will push him over the threshold. [But] I believe [Dobson]. I think it would be tough for him as a candidate."

Diane Sawyer concluded sloppily, confusing Dobson with those he was trying to influence, by saying that, in the meantime, Dobson was "giving an obvious lesson . . . to other politicians."[12]

꧁꧂

Dobson strongly believes that the institution that became his first career love, the study of child development, can't be trusted any more than the news media. He blazed trail after trail in combining psychological precepts with a Christian context, and many credit Dobson with making it acceptable for evangelicals to see a psychologist or psychiatrist. But Dobson is highly displeased with the secular evolution of psychology. And mainstream psychology and its proponents certainly return the favor.

Dobson's suspicion of the motives—if not the methods—of secular psychology took root under the tutelage of Paul Culbertson, his mentor at Pasadena College.

Culbertson "wasn't down on secular psychologists and psychiatrists," says Wil Spaite, Dobson's classmate and also a student of Culbertson's. "But he realized that the source of healing had to be God. And where secular experts thought all the answers lay in psychology, [Culbertson] believed that they were missing a whole dimension of the person."

Early in his career as a highly regarded practitioner in the very secular realms of a medical school and a teaching hospital, Dobson made some tentative moves toward accommodation with the mainstream psychological community. In 1978, for example, he joined the American Psychological Association and attended one of its conferences. "But then I looked around and said, 'These folks don't represent me. They believe things I don't believe,' and I never went back," Dobson says. Indeed, as it developed during the twentieth century, psychology "tended to draw from liberals and their ideas, among them a very antireligious viewpoint," explains Neil Clark Warren, a Christian psychologist and longtime Dobson associate.

Another aspect of his estrangement from his greater profession was the chasm between his training and his approach. Dobson was specifically trained in child development, not in clinical psychology, but the holistic approach he took as he began to build Focus on the Family required him to straddle the two. "He wanted to be seen as more of a pediatric neurologist," Warren says. "He feels a little inferior *and* a little superior in psychology circles. As researchers, psychologists try to be good scientists. But I don't know that he sees himself that way. And he's a bit like a fish out of water with Freudian theory; he doesn't really have a therapeutic orientation. He's very pragmatic: He cares about what works and how to change the culture."

Dobson says that he also is troubled by the increasing tendency of psychologists to focus on communicating with their peers rather than with those outside their erudite cloisters. "Most people who have terminal degrees think in terms of writing for their colleagues, to impress those who have similar degrees. But their books are boring to laymen," he says. "I had to decide early on if I wanted to cast my tent with them and climb that ladder in secular circles or whether I wanted to try to influence parents and husbands and wives and the general public. And I specifically chose the latter." In aiming at popular consumption rather than academic dissection of his ideas, Dobson says, he was actually imitating Benjamin Spock. "That's the same thing he did."

Not surprisingly, psychology found ways to strike back at Dobson over the years. For example, Fuller Theological Seminary in Pasadena, a bastion of evangelicalism, didn't particularly embrace its close neighbor or his ideas, even though Dobson was essentially defining Christian psychology, says Warren, who was dean there for a time. Most of the faculty members were unaware of Dobson even as late as the early eighties. Others didn't respect his academic background because it wasn't in clinical psychology. And some were biased against the spiritual shadings in Dobson's ideas. Only when Arch Hart, an already identified supporter of Dobson, was appointed dean of psychology in 1982 did the seminary begin to hold Dobson in higher regard. "The time is long past when Fuller should be doing a careful analysis of his writings," says Hart.

And the secular psychology community does not respect Dobson at all, says Jeffrey Satinover. "There's not a pediatrician type of individual with the possible exception of [T. Berry] Brazelton with a larger constituency of parents who pay attention to him, and yet universities around the country and the national media make no effort whatsoever to include [Dobson] in discussions of psychology," Satinover says. "I believe it's just gross prejudice that he [and Focus] are not taken more seriously." In the arena of secular psychology, Satinover has concluded, Dobson's "biggest sin is being a Christian and letting people know that."

For at least two decades, running parallel to Dobson's estrangement from secular psychology, there has been a continuing campaign by some religious thinkers to undermine Dobson's shaping of a Christian approach to psychology. Critics ranging from the renowned to the obscure have been attacking Dobson since he first went public with his ideas in the seventies.

The general problem, as these critics see it, is that Christians should rely always on God's healing power rather than on the probings of a therapist who has been trained in the godless science of psychology. And specifically, they scorn Dobson for what one skeptic calls "his belief in the false gospel of self-esteem." They accuse Dobson of placing too much emphasis on low self-esteem and self-hatred as "the basic causes of virtually every social malady." Clearly, this critique goes, Dobson's underlying belief is "in the 'medical model,' which treats people as innocent victims rather than culpable sinners."[13]

Obviously, Dobson disagrees. "The doctrine of sin and the remedy provided by Jesus Christ on the Cross are central to my beliefs. Anyone who knows me or my work must be aware of that fact."

Actually, Dobson sometimes irritates people within the evangelical Christian community almost as much as he does those outside of it, just as he sometimes makes as much trouble for Republican politicians such as Newt Gingrich and Tom DeLay as he does for his enemies on the Left. Dobson usually has plenty of allies among religious reds in attacking outright sin within Christendom. But he becomes more of a maverick in his critiques of fellow leaders in the broad church. Dobson often feels compelled to speak out because of his deep sense of conviction and rectitude, born of his Nazarene upbringing, his father's posthumous blessing, the growth of Dobson's ministry that he interprets as a continuing endorsement by God, and the always-rising sense of urgency he feels about the erosion of the family and the culture.

In 1996, for example, Christian Coalition director Ralph Reed spoke positively about the presidential prospects of Colin Powell, even though Powell's views on abortion and other issues clashed with those of evangelical leaders. Dobson criticized Reed in a private letter, accusing him of succumbing to the temptation to compromise bedrock Christian beliefs in a bid for political influence. The letter was leaked, apparently by someone in Reed's camp, and the two men's disagreement quickly became public.

At the same time, it's also in such conflicts that Dobson can demonstrate a characteristic that really gripes those he has been prone to attack: a thin skin. The perception that Dobson can't take it as well as he can dish it out may have grown unfairly; his sharp rhetoric is often interpreted as defensiveness. But Dobson's run-ins with any number of evangelical leaders and organizations highlight the fact that he's not afraid to go on the offensive with them if necessary—or to vigorously justify his actions afterward.

The firestorm over Today's New International Version of the Bible, called the TNIV, is illustrative. Zondervan/HarperCollins kicked off a huge battle within evangelical Christendom in the nineties with the decision to create a "gender-corrected" version of the New International Version that, among other things, would make passages gender neutral where scholars judged that the changes wouldn't affect their meaning. The publisher believed that the TNIV would prove relevant to many potential Bible readers who were put off by the masculine-pronoun dominance of the NIV and other translations. But Dobson and other critics of the plan feared that the publication of the TNIV would represent a hijacking of Scripture by liberal scholars. So at a meeting at Focus on the Family in 1997, the opponents managed to obtain an agreement from the International Bible Society, which owns the NIV translation, and the president of Zondervan to abandon the gender-corrected version.

Thus, when Zondervan executives changed their mind and announced in late 2001 that they were coming out with the TNIV after all—citing their responsibility to spread the gospel as widely as possible—the translation's opponents blew gaskets all over the country. One hundred of them, including Dobson, Charles Colson, and Pat Robertson, placed an advertisement in a number of Christian magazines that proffered a scathing and detailed critique of the TNIV. And a number of independent bookstores and even entire chains of Christian stores decided not to carry the TNIV. The ban continued to be an impediment to TNIV New Testament sales as Zondervan prepared for the debut of the TNIV Old Testament in 2005.

Often, too—without provocation—Dobson becomes the object of criticism or opposition within the evangelical community simply because of the breadth of his influence. One such instance revolved around Dobson's establishment of the Alliance Defense Fund in 1994. Although the original purpose of the American Civil Liberties Union was libertarian—to preserve the many forms of individual freedom in this country—increasingly through the eighties and nineties Dobson and other evangelicals began to see things differently. In their view, the ACLU had become a puppet of liberal special interests whose main purpose was to interfere with Christians' attempts to influence government and politics and to oppose any reference to God in the public square. That put the ACLU squarely in Dobson's way. And so he personally, as well as Focus, helped fund the start-up of the Alliance Defense Fund, an organization of lawyers whose objective was to become a significant counterweight to the ACLU and defend Christians and the principles of the faith in courtroom skirmishes across the land.

"Dr. Dobson told me that he was extremely committed to this idea and very serious about it," says Alan Sears, a federal prosecutor who had befriended Dobson as a member of Ed Meese's pornography commission in the mideighties. "That was the turning point for me to accept the job to run ADF."

The problem was that there *already* was an ADF of sorts. Constitutional attorney John Whitehead had withdrawn the last two hundred dollars from his savings account and founded the Rutherford Institute in 1982 for essentially the same purpose. Over the years, Rutherford had scored a number of legally and politically significant victories in matters such as the advancement of school-choice programs, the rights of Christians in public schools, and parental rights in cases of social-services intervention. Not surprisingly, Focus became a large donor to the Rutherford Institute, and Dobson put Whitehead on his broadcast several times. So when Whitehead got wind of the formation of ADF, he wrote Dobson a series of strongly worded letters taking exception to Dobson and Focus's role in starting what Whitehead considered a rival organization.

Whitehead saw ADF as competition for attention and resources, Sears says. Dobson told Sears not to worry about the Rutherford Institute's criticism. "They're throwing stones, but just do your job," Dobson told Sears. Dobson explains that he "saw the Rutherford Institute as having a different mission" than ADF, because ADF mainly trains and deploys Christian lawyers, while the Rutherford Institute focuses on where its own staff can have the most impact in the courtroom. Nevertheless, Dobson concedes, "I became persona non grata" with the Rutherford Institute.

As Dobson became more aggressive about public-policy statements and his political involvement in the nineties, several prominent voices rose in opposition to his approach. In early 1995, in a cover story in *Christianity Today* called "Culture War Casualties," John Woodbridge singled out Dobson for hurting the church by using the rhetoric of warfare to describe evangelicals' struggle against the culture, as in Dobson's phrase "a civil war of values." The professor of church history at Trinity Evangelical Divinity School in Deerfield, Illinois, criticized Dobson and other politically active evangelical leaders because, he asserted, "culture war rhetoric" tends to exacerbate rather than solve conflicts with enemies and "leads us to distort others' positions." It makes Christianity's message seem more about politics than about the gospel, Woodbridge asserted, playing into the hands of leftists who want to paint an extreme picture of the Christian Right and creating divisions among Christians.[14]

While Woodbridge mentioned Dobson only once in the article, his focus on the latter was intensified by the fact that Woodbridge didn't mention by name any other Christian leader of the era. So Dobson felt entirely justified when, a few months later, he responded in *Christianity Today* with his own essay, defending his use of "fighting words." Dobson cited the long history of warfare language in the Bible and in church history. And while most of those references have to do with spiritual warfare, Dobson noted that today's cultural war is "simply a continuation of the age-old struggle between the principles of righteousness and the kingdom of darkness."[15]

Dobson also took exception to Woodbridge's characterization of Christians who use the language of war as unpleasant and vindictive people, especially because Woodbridge cited no other leader in his article. "It doesn't matter what people think of me," Dobson wrote. "My concern is that Dr. Woodbridge may have reinforced the argument of those who do not think people of faith have a right or obligation to address issues of public policy." By the time the contretemps was over a few weeks later, Woodbridge had responded to Dobson's response. But neither man's position had much changed.

Perhaps emboldened by Woodbridge's attack, syndicated columnist Cal Thomas and Reverend Ed Dobson struck a similar theme in their 1999 book *Blinded by Might: Why the Religious Right Can't Save America*. Thomas had experienced the limits of political power on behalf of the gospel when he worked as communications director for Reverend Jerry Falwell's Moral Majority. That organization had burned brightly across the political skies in the early eighties and then faded as ideological enemies and an unsympathetic news media succeeded in caricaturing many of Falwell's views. One of the lessons Thomas learned from that episode was that Christian leaders and organizations ought to focus mostly on the gospel and less on public policy in doing the work of the Kingdom on earth. As senior pastor of Calvary Church, a megachurch in Grand Rapids, Michigan, Ed Dobson (no relation to James Dobson) had long been preaching a similar message. It seemed natural for them to key on James Dobson for their critique. "Underneath Dr. Dobson's highly commendable zeal is a potential zealotry that is eating away at the benefits that can come with rightly applied zeal," wrote Thomas in the book's chapter on Focus. "His increasing zealotry is hampering the very goals he—and we—seek." Thomas asserted that Dobson's aggressiveness allows him to "be painted an extremist" and alienates "the vast middle of the body politic" where elections in America must be won.

"We would like to see Dr. Dobson serve one term in the United States Senate," the pair wrote. "He would have to adopt different tactics if he were ever to have any hope of reaching his goals." They concluded by conceding that Dobson and Focus had "done more than anyone else or any other organization to strengthen the family in our nation" but feared that "his current focus on politics will derail and dilute the good he is doing through Focus on the Family" and "obscure the central message of the gospel, which is about personal, not political, redemption."[16]

Very recently, another friend also publicly turned on Dobson, ostensibly also because of the latter's growing political involvement. As in the cases of Cal Thomas and Gil Moegerle, Dobson didn't see this betrayal coming—and it stung him badly.

Because Dobson and Focus had been so instrumental in helping him take eHarmony.com to a new level of business success, Neil Clark Warren had been effusive in his praise of both his friend and the organization, even in media interviews, through early 2005. But as the success of his company grew, Warren believed, so did the pressures on him and eHarmony to catch up to his still-bigger rival, Match.com. And the way to do that, he believed, was to stretch eHarmony way beyond its original focus on evangelical Christians, which he had come to see as a liability to the company's business potential. For example, Warren had started out marketing eHarmony as "based on . . . Christian principles"; and Focus published—and its identity was prominently displayed on—three of Warren's ten books.

In the spring of 2005, Warren finally concluded that his longtime affiliation with Focus on the Family was getting in his way. He bought back the titles to his books from Focus. "He wasn't political when I knew him," Warren said to a *Los Angeles Times* reporter about Dobson for a story published in May. Pointing to the Focus on the Family banner on his book Warren said, "That's a killer to us." Several days later, *USA Today* carried a profile of eHarmony and Warren in which he made much the same case. Warren said he no longer would appear on *Focus* broadcasts. "We're trying to reach the whole world—people of all

Before addressing the crowd, Dr. Dobson surveys
the 1993 Promise Keepers event in Boulder, Colorado.

Jim and Shirley in March 2005, while visiting the Reagan Ranch in California

Jim Dobson with friends Chuck Swindoll (center) and Peb Jackson on a Canadian fishing trip in the 1980s

Jim and Shirley skiing at Mammoth, California, in the 1980s.

*Focus on the Family Institute students pack Dr. Dobson's office
for a question-and-answer session.*

*Dr. Dobson chats with some young
visitors to the real Whit's End Soda
Shop in Focus on the Family's
Welcome Center.*

*January 1988. Dr. Dobson
commemorates ten years of ministry
at the Pomona dedication.*

Dr. and Mrs. Dobson spoke in Phoenix on September 29, 1983. More than thirteen thousand attended the event at Arizona State University in spite of heavy rain.

A standing-room-only crowd of more than fifteen thousand came to hear about biblical family values in Seattle.

Dr. Dobson was honored to carry the Olympic torch on its way to Salt Lake City in 2002.

On May 5, 2005, National Day of Prayer chairman Shirley Dobson and her husband, James Dobson, are escorted to their seats in the White House for the day's events.

The view from the engineer's console. Dr. Dobson in the studio circa 1987 with Dave Spiker at the controls.

Dr. Dobson receives the National Religious Broadcasters (NRB) Golden Mike Award at his induction into the NRB Hall of Fame in 1991. In 2002, he received the NRB Board of Directors Award, which honors Christians who demonstrate integrity and creativity and make a significant impact on society.

Jim Ryun (in plaid vest) and his family join Dr. Dobson in the studio.

Ted Bundy met with Dr. Dobson the night before his execution to explain how pornography impacted the course of his life.

Dr. Dobson poses with frequent broadcast guest Charles Colson in the broadcast studio, circa 1988.

President George H.W. Bush joined Dr. Dobson in a temporary studio in downtown Colorado Springs in 1992 to discuss policy issues that impact the family.

Dr. Dobson interviews President Ronald Reagan in the Oval Office for an upcoming radio broadcast.

Both Dr. Dobson and Shirley have met with President George W. Bush to encourage his stand on pro-family and pro-life issues.

spiritual orientations, all political philosophies, all racial backgrounds," Warren explained in the interview. "And if indeed, we have Focus on the Family on the top of our books, it is a killer. Because people do recognize them as having a precise political position in this society and a very precise spiritual position."

Marylyn Warren claims that both reporters "were determined to cast a bad light on Neil's long-term relationship with Jim." But, she explains, "Jim is operating in a very strategic and polarizing role at the moment and Neil was trying to get beyond that." Marylyn Warren insists that her husband "continues to be enormously appreciative of the wonderful boost that Jim gave to eHarmony" and that Warren hadn't changed his "great regard for Jim and Focus . . . one iota."

But to Dobson, Warren's comments to the two newspapers told a different story. Hurt and perplexed, Dobson deliberated on the matter for several days. Then he sent his friend a letter in which he recounted with sadness the end of their twenty-year friendship and professional relationship, noting the highlights of their association. And on a *Focus* broadcast about another topic in late May, Dobson sandwiched in his explanation of the contretemps for listeners who may have wondered. He said that after Warren had associated himself so closely with Dobson and Focus over the years and had credited them with much of eHarmony's success, Warren now "says he wants to distance himself from Focus and me." Dobson read some of Warren's published comments to his readers and opined that Focus's sharpened political identity was "the rub" for Warren. The host also said that he was disappointed by Warren's new reluctance to take a moral stand against abortion, premarital sex, and same-sex relationships.

"Dr. Warren is anxious to change his direction, and we'll accept that and go our separate ways and do that with reluctance and regret," Dobson concluded.

✂✃✄✁

In 2002 Dobson assumed a central role in a controversy that tore at the heart of the National Religious Broadcasters organization and brought down a new president-elect before he could even take office. Wayne Pederson was executive director of the NRB and scheduled to be installed as president at the group's national convention in Nashville when an interview with him appeared in the *Minneapolis Star Tribune*. Pederson told his hometown paper that when people thought of the NRB, "they think of the political right, and I think that's unfair. We missed our main calling with that. But what's probably more disturbing to me is that evangelicals are identified politically more than theologically. We get associated with the far Christian right and marginalized. To me the important thing is to keep the focus on what's important to us spiritually. . . . We need to not be pulled into the political arena."[17]

Pederson's pronouncement on politics was anathema to Dobson and other stalwarts of the Christian Right who had been largely responsible for building the NRB. So they immediately moved to block his ascension to the presidency of the organization. Dobson set up an initial phone call with eighteen other conservative members of the NRB board "to see if they were equally concerned about the effort to move the organization away from what [Pederson] has called the 'political right.'" He says that the group concluded nearly unanimously that Pederson "had lost his consensus to lead, and that he could help avoid conflict in Nashville by stepping down."[18] Soon, Pederson tendered his resignation.

Dobson maintains that he wasn't critical of Pederson except in the closed forum of the ad hoc meeting of board members and that throughout the brouhaha he "expressed love and support" for Pederson repeatedly.[19] But Pederson's supporters weren't so easily appeased. Robert Neff, vice president of the Moody Broadcasting Network, wrote a letter protesting the decision, targeting certain "power boys" and "600-pound gorillas" in the organization who were quick to pick up their marbles and leave when things didn't go their way.[20] In his own letter of response, Dobson called Neff's accusations "vicious and entirely uncalled-for." And he called the fracas "a tragic escalation of what began as a policy issue and has deteriorated into a full-scale split in evangelicalism."[21]

Jerry Rose, a friend of Dobson's and president of the NRB in the mideighties, says that Pederson's remarks essentially violated the organization's long-standing philosophy of dealing lightly with the widely varying political and denominational orientations of its members. "Both sides could have been more Christian" about the aftermath, Rose says. "But in Jim's case, he's very intense, a conviction-deep person, and when he believes in something, it's 100 percent or nothing. And if he does, he'll go to the mat with it. . . . That's a battle mentality. The difficulty for people like him is to understand when you don't need to fight a battle but to sit down and work through some things."

But Charles Colson believes there was more than a fighter's mentality at work in his friend's actions in the Pederson affair. Dobson "tends to be extremely sensitive to things like this because he sees them as an attack on his integrity," Colson says.

In a way, Dobson was responding to all of his critics from the previous several years when he took the podium at the NRB annual convention that March, where Pederson originally was to have been promoted to president. In March 1993, in his message of angst at President Clinton's election, Dobson had issued a challenge "to those who suggest we retreat to our Christian enclaves" with a series of pointed rhetorical questions: "At what point will you rise to defend what you believe? Is there anything worth putting your reputation or your life in jeopardy? Will you rise to speak if every tenet of your faith is legislated against in Congress and in your home state?"

Nine years later, with an audience that he thought should know better, Dobson felt compelled to do pretty much the same thing. After recounting how homosexual activists were infiltrating public schools and how "postmodern culture" was discounting the value of preborn life, Dobson addressed "those of you who [feel] that the church has no responsibility in the cultural area"—implicitly calling out those who had criticized him on this score over the previous decade.

"You have tended to feel our job is to preach the gospel and all the rest of these things will kind of fall into place, and you haven't felt it is something that you should devote yourself to because that's something somebody else is called to," he continued. "Let me argue with you for just a moment."

Dobson then challenged his audience to put themselves in the place of a pastor in the South during the Civil War who didn't want to deal with the issue of slavery; or Martin Luther King Jr. sitting in a Birmingham, Alabama, jail in 1963; or Dietrich Bonhoeffer, awaiting his hanging by the Nazis in 1945 for having tried to protect Jews from the gas chamber—or even John the Baptist fingering King Herod for having his brother's wife. "Since when," Dobson summarized, "have we become timid about addressing the moral issues of our day?"

The speaker went on to assure his attentive audience that "the easiest thing to do would be to quit" in the face of public criticism, including being labeled extremists. "But God has called us to stay in the field and we will do that as long as we have breath in our bodies," he concluded. "And I beg those of you who are here to do the same."

※∽∾∾○○

Although Cal Thomas "keeps ripping off the scab with columns every once in a while" that criticize Dobson, says Focus public policy chief Tom Minnery, the two men basically made up on a personal level shortly after the publication of Thomas's book. And Ed Dobson says that he had an all-day meeting with James Dobson and that they've "become friends, though we certainly don't see eye to eye on all of the issues. I have a great deal of respect and love for him."

Just as with his ideological enemies, many within evangelicalism who have differed sharply with Dobson often reach rapprochement. Many in both groups simply lose their starch, finding themselves incapable of sustaining animus toward him. Perhaps this effect is produced by the fact that Dobson hasn't backed down from his own views despite all the blistering critiques. Or perhaps the demonstrably growing electoral importance of evangelicals to conservatives and the Republican Party has made it clear that Christians indeed have succeeded in acquiring substantial real-world political clout over the last several years.

But some of Dobson's allies suggest yet another reason: It's more and more clear that Dobson is correctly interpreting events, they say. American culture in many ways has grown more sordid over the last decade, making Dobson's pleadings seem ever more urgent and the solutions he proposes ever more sensible.

Charles Colson puts it another way: "He has stood, sometimes practically alone, against the church's disengaging from this battle. And he, in fact, has kept the church from disengaging."

CHAPTER TWENTY

A CRUCIBLE
AND A GAUNTLET

*Bruce is a great Bible teacher, but he can also
get carried away. And I thought he might have
been totally out of line that morning.*

MAC McQUISTON, ABOUT BRUCE
WILKINSON'S 2002 SPEECH AT FOTF'S
TWENTY-FIFTH ANNIVERSARY
CELEBRATION

James Dobson had just received word that he had prostate cancer, and
Focus on the Family was in the midst of one of the most financially
difficult stretches in its history in July 2002, when the ministry celebrated its twenty-fifth anniversary. The four-day affair had been pared
back a bit from the original plans, but it still constituted a personal and
professional hallmark that Dobson enjoyed thoroughly.

One of his finest moments came on Saturday, July 27, in front of a
crowd of some fourteen thousand Focus supporters who had packed
the Pepsi Center arena in Denver. The program of music and commemoration was to be the highlight of the entire long weekend. Dobson and his wife entered the arena like rock stars: Behind a wedge
provided by three vested bodyguards, Dobson entered to the cheers
and shrieks of fans who recognized him as soon as he appeared from
behind the stage. Michael W. Smith and Steven Curtis Chapman, two
of the biggest names in Christian music, led the crowd in worship
songs and provided entertainment along with the Colorado Springs
Symphony Orchestra. Charles Colson was the keynote speaker. Governor Bill Owens of Colorado showed up. Timothy Goeglein, the
White House's liaison to the U.S. evangelical community, dropped by

to introduce a video tribute from President George W. Bush himself. And then it was the Dobsons' turn to express their gratitude, to reminisce, and to ham it up just a bit with each other in front of thousands of their closest friends.

But clearly the most fun Dobson had on the stage that evening was in telling the story about how he finally got to snub Phil Donahue. Dobson had come a long way since that 1978 day when he had received such poor treatment on Donahue's nationally syndicated TV show. Donahue had quit TV in 1996, but in early 2002 he resurfaced on the air just a few months before Focus's celebration.

"Guess who called me yesterday?" Dobson said to the arena crowd that night. "That's right: Phil Donahue," he answered with relish, as chuckles began to ripple through the adoring throng. "He asked me to be on his MSNBC TV show. Guess what I told him?" Laughter swelled from an audience in anticipation of what Dobson would say next. "No way, *Jose*." Donahue's show was canceled just a few months later.

 споскраски

The entire anniversary observance was a sentimentally draining experience for Dobson. Beginning with the huge party for close friends that the Dobsons threw at their condominium on Wednesday night, all the way through a rousing Sunday morning service on the Focus grounds, the celebration was filled with emotional hooks that tugged at the founder from every direction. But the one that really snagged Dobson was something he couldn't have anticipated: the unveiling of a bronze sculpture of his father that had been secretly commissioned and funded by the Focus staff.

The idea of surprising Dobson with a statue of his beloved father originated with Beverley London who, as the wife of H. B. London, was intimately familiar with both Dobsons. With planning for the anniversary in full gear during 2001, Beverley London and Lisa Crump, a Focus human resources staffer, surreptitiously collected donations of ten-, twenty-, and fifty-dollar bills from Focus staffers to come up with the tens of thousands of dollars required for the statue.

London and Crump had considered a handful of candidates for the commission, but in January 2002, they selected their early favorite: Greg Todd, a Christian sculptor and professional firefighter from Greeley, Colorado. He specialized in realistic bronze life-casts of people and animals. A couple of years earlier, he had crafted *More than*

Words, a tender depiction of a young mother reading to her two small children about Jesus the Good Shepherd, which Focus installed on campus between the visitor's center and administration building. Like so many of Dobson's listeners, the fifty-two-year-old Todd already felt that he knew not only the psychologist but also his late father. He listened to *Focus on the Family* nearly every day while working in his studio.

"I was aware when his dad passed away, and I knew stories about his dad taking him on hunting trips and the times they shared that way, and I remember how he was comforted by his dad when he came home from school and his dog had died," Todd says. "So from my perspective, I felt that I really knew them well." From the start, because Dobson Sr. was an evangelist known for spending hours on his knees in prayer each day, London and Crump "wanted him depicted in an attitude of prayer," the sculptor says. "And in one of his books, Dr. Dobson talked about how his dad wore out the toes of his shoes before his soles because he was on his knees in prayer so much. So that was something we wanted to try to achieve."

What Todd cast is a life-size depiction of the Nazarene evangelist in a suit and slightly loosened tie, crouching on one knee, with a Bible in his right hand and his index finger placed inside to reference a Scripture. Under Beverley London's purview, Todd managed to create a highly accurate visage of a sixtyish Dobson Sr., scruffy-browed and dimple-chinned. Interestingly, Todd initially sculpted the evangelist with his eyes open in order to provide a full likeness. "I [thought I] would close them later on," he said. But London liked the effect of being able to look into the man's eyes even as he was in prayer. And, of course, the toes of his shoes are well-scuffed. Titled *He Prayed,* which is also the epitaph on Dobson Sr.'s gravestone in Kansas, the sculpture is about six-and-a-half feet tall including the base, which cites the twenty-fifth anniversary as "a living witness to God's answer to the prayers of James Dobson Sr." It now resides in a James Dobson Sr. gallery inside Focus's Welcome Center.

But on that Thursday morning, as more than 2,500 Focus staffers and guests gathered under a huge white tent that had been set up in a parking lot, *He Prayed* was hidden safely in the bowels of a nearby storage building. Despite the sprawling size of the campus and the fact that employment there had reached more than 1,400, it was still difficult to keep anything of consequence secret from the hands-on Dobson. So in addition to the excitement of the opening ceremonies of the anniversary observation, an extra buzz was running through the crowd due in part to the collective sense of satisfaction for having pulled one over on the boss.

Christian pop artists Steve and Annie Chapman, Steve Green, and Rebecca St. James performed and led some worship music. Henry Blackaby, the influential Baptist theologian and author of the popular *Experiencing God* Bible study, delivered the main address, praising Dobson for "faithfulness [that] in the long haul has literally changed the lives of millions of people" and exhorting him to allow God to continue to "make a difference through you as you go." And then, near the end of the two-hour affair, Focus Executive Vice President Diane Passno took the stage and explained that the Focus staff had "wanted to give something of historical importance" on the occasion.

Passno briefly distracted Dobson and his family by asking them to look at a monitor above them, and the veiled statue was quickly wheeled in. Just as quickly, the shroud was pulled, revealing the gleaming objet d'art. "Since I was two years of age, I've never found myself speechless before," Dobson said as he beheld the gift of love, tears gathering and trickling down his face. "But I am now. I can't tell you what this means to me. My good father, as you know, had such an impact on me. He never compromised. He was not a perfect man, but he never compromised. I never saw him one time violate what he believed or fail to stand for righteousness. And somehow, I think, I hope, I pray that he's here today. I think maybe he is here. And you know what? The Lord has been here today. I cannot express what this means to me."

Then, flashing his quick wit through his tears, Dobson finished: "I'm going to cherish [the sculpture]. We're going to put it in our bedroom at home," he quipped, with a quick and playful glance at Shirley.

The emotional nature of the moment was easy to understand. Here was a man who had risen to heights that are rare not only in Christian ministry but in any endeavor, giving him a worldwide impact far beyond anything that he or his father could have imagined. And Dobson was certain, in an extremely visceral sense, that this vast, prosperous, highly influential enterprise was above all the direct result of God's affirming answer to his father's prayers and of a dynastic prophecy that reached back four generations. That is a very compelling conviction and—because it burns within a man of such obvious talents—an extremely powerful one.

Yet while the importance of Dobson Sr.'s legacy remains clear, some believe that Dobson's continuing identification with his father becomes a complication for the ministry at times.

During the Saturday night affair at the Pepsi Center, for example, Dobson discussed the family history. And even before *He Prayed* found its place there, the visitor's center included a small but substantial gallery just off the entrance devoted entirely to the artifacts of Dobson Sr. The gallery includes several of his landscapes, some of his Western-themed paintings, a portrait of his son with a couple of marbles and a model race car, his painting of the dog Penny that Dobson Jr. adopted at thirteen, and Dobson Sr.'s Christmas coat—the only article of clothing that fit the son, who wore it during the Christmas holidays for more than two decades after his father's death.

"In my heart somewhere, I think that there's an overstatement by Jim, that he defers to his dad more than he really needs to," H. B. London said of his cousin shortly afterward. "His dream started with his dad and was fulfilled in [Dobson Jr.]; I do believe that. And Jim feels that way. But I do think it makes a better story this way."

This concern is more than incidental. It also speaks to the inherent tension within Focus over the continued usefulness of its perpetual, close personal identification in the public mind with the Dobson family. With one eye toward succession and another toward how to most effectively motivate the Focus staff, Dobson has tried mightily in some ways recently to carve an identity for the organization that goes beyond his own personality. Yet repeatedly linking the ministry's ongoing success with Dobson Sr.'s encounter with God a quarter century ago can act at cross-purposes with such efforts. This paradox was apparent as Shirley Dobson addressed the Pepsi Center crowd. "You won't see our names on any of the buildings" at Focus, she said, "because we realize we had very little to do with the growth of this ministry. We're just willing vessels."

Dobson Sr.'s legacy weighs on Focus in another dimension that is more subtle but just as significant. A few years ago, some people close to Dobson sensed that as he neared sixty-six, the age at which his father died, the son was growing almost fatalistic about following in his father's footsteps, perhaps even all the way to an early grave. At that moment, the Dobsons knew—but had not yet shared—that he had been diagnosed with prostate cancer and would soon be receiving treatment in Southern California. Because of his brushes with death or severe disability during the previous several years, the question of his mortality had become far less abstract. Just a few days before the anniversary celebration, the Dobsons had gotten word that the cancer afflicting Joe Kubishta, Shirley's stepfather, was terminal. For the second year in a row, annual contributions to Focus had failed to keep up with inflation in 2001, thanks to the continued recession and the aftershocks of 9/11, and Dobson still hadn't come up with a satisfactory plan for his eventual departure from the ministry.

Thus, it also seemed God-ordained that while the affair began with a stirring tribute to his father—a reminder to Dobson of his own mortality—the final event of the anniversary celebration provided a different twist on that issue. On the morning of the last Sunday in July 2002, under the same brilliant-white tent where the sculpture of Dobson Sr. had been unveiled just three days earlier, Bruce Wilkinson used his sermon to encourage Dobson to look beyond both the past and the present, to lift his head from any doubts he had about his own longevity, and to focus instead on hope for his future prosperity.

Dobson was sitting in the front row, on his home turf, at the end of a four-day love-in, surrounded by thousands of family members, friends, employees, fans, and well-wishers. Anyone who would go beyond merely tweaking Dobson in that situation would have to be sure of what he was doing. But Wilkinson—former head of the Global Vision missionary agency, author of the best-selling *Walk Thru the Bible* study and, most recently, the wildly popular best seller *The Prayer of Jabez*—might have been one of the few people who were up to it at that moment. "I'm going way outside the box here: I think the greatest days of the Dobsons and Focus on the Family start in about two weeks when you get your energy back," Wilkinson said to Dobson, who was sitting a few feet away. "It's so easy for you to just say, 'Whew!' And it's at that moment that I want to encourage you to change completely from that point of view and take the vision and make it much larger: to aim for the whole world before you're seventy-five." Wilkinson then cited the example of Bill Bright, founder of Campus Crusade for Christ who would die in 2003 but who, at that moment, remained active in his ministry even at the age of eighty-one.

"And, Jim, when you turn your face and you say, 'Lord, I don't know how to do that,' remember [that you didn't] know how to do any

of this either. [Say 'Lord,] you did this when I aimed for your marriages. Therefore, will you let me do the whole world for you? And
show me how to do it. Let me get on TV all the time, not just radio.'
What do you think about that, ladies and gentlemen?

"I know TV's a pain in the neck. It means you've got to get makeup
on your face, the lights are there—and it means you'll reach many
more people, Jim. The Dobsons need to break out of this box called radio into—everything. They need to break through that uncomfortable-
ness. 'I'm not comfortable with this; I'm comfortable with radio.' I
know—so? The biggest sin of my life, Jim, is called unbelief—that I
know God wants this done but I don't really believe that he wants it
done enough to help me do what he wants done.

"I hear your voice. I see you. I read you. I see the whole staff tri-
pling, growing four and five times because, when people go for that
kind of vision, heaven opens up. And people walk up and say, 'Here's
fifty million dollars. Go get it.' That's how it happens."

When Wilkinson was finished, Dobson ascended to the podium,
before a crowd that clearly had been electrified by the gauntlet that had
just been thrown down by the high-energy, in-your-face Wilkinson. After a pregnant pause or two, Dobson began his response, clicking in at a
much more languid pace than his guest and revealing in less than a minute his unique mastery of microphone and message. "Have you heard of
preachers preaching to *you*?" he said to relieved laughter throughout the
tent. Then, smiling, to Wilkinson he said, "C'mon, Bruce, I'm *tired*,
man! That message is going to resonate for a while. I know a little
phrase: 'How am I going to do that?' That'll take a miracle.

"So bring the fifty million," he said with a half chuckle, "and we'll
talk."

∽∾∾∾∾∽

No one disputed that Wilkinson had been greatly used of God over the
course of his career. But initially, and for months afterward, some people close to Dobson basically shook their heads or grumbled at the in-
decorous chutzpah involved in what Wilkinson had said to Dobson and
how he had said it.

"Bruce is a great Bible teacher, but he also can get carried away, and
I thought he might have been out of line that morning," says Mac
McQuiston, Dobson's original speech-booking agent, later an aide to
Wilkinson, and until recently, a Focus vice president. "He's always giv-

ing grandiose comments about what people should be doing, and when you sit and think it through, it doesn't make a lot of sense. I've watched other people attempt to do what he said to do, and they fell flat on their face. It just gets you riled up; there's not a lot of substance as to whether it can be done. I felt it was out of line."

Vonette Bright was similarly put off. While her husband, Bill Bright, lay ailing at home in California, she had followed Dobson to the podium after Dobson's response to Wilkinson and toward the very end of the concluding session of Focus's twenty-fifth anniversary celebration. In her extemporaneous remarks that morning, Vonette Bright emphasized that Dobson would need lots of help from those assembled there to have any hope of fulfilling Wilkinson's challenge. But she wishes she hadn't been put in the tough spot of having to sublimate Wilkinson's blunt remarks.

"I felt it was God's place to tell Dr. Dobson what to do, not Bruce Wilkinson," says the Dobsons' friend and Shirley's predecessor as head of the National Day of Prayer. "I felt he laid too heavy a load on Jim at that moment, and I was afraid Bruce was trying to send him on a guilt trip about doing more—when he already was doing a great deal." She was one of a small group of confidants who met with Dobson in his office after the morning program and prayed with him about how he should interpret what Wilkinson said.

Yet others close to Dobson and Dobson himself weren't so put off by Wilkinson's rhetorical firecracker. "When you're making decisions about important stuff as he was, it's good to have different sources of input from the body [of Christ], " Danae Dobson says. "[My father] filed it away with other comments that had been made and thought about it and prayed about it."

And nearly three years later, after seeing not only a recovery in Focus's finances but also an overwhelmingly successful financial start for Focus Action, the ministry's political-action arm, Dobson himself waxed philosophical about the incident. "I appreciated his heart and what he was saying," Dobson says in 2005. "Actually, it turned out to be kind of prophetic."

CHAPTER TWENTY-ONE

A WEEK IN THE LIFE

His every moment could be booked.

Tom Minnery, Focus on the Family
vice president

On February 1, 2003, death and bad news permeated the air. But it was business as usual for James Dobson as he boarded the United Airlines flight that regularly runs from Colorado Springs to Los Angeles. In the small DC9, before he could gather his lanky six-feet-two-inch frame into one of the tiny coach seats, he bumped his head on the overhead luggage bin.

An annoyance, yes. But definitely the least of Dobson's concerns as he buckled in, ready for his scheduled two-and-a-half-hour flight on that sunny Saturday morning. His mood had been set just a few hours earlier, when the space shuttle *Columbia* exploded in midair over Texas, riveting the nation in horror. Dobson saw a report about the accident on TV during his morning treadmill workout.

The day before, a reluctant Dobson had presided over the layoff of thirty people and the elimination of sixty-six more unfilled positions at Focus, the result of a few years of "static" income. It was the first time the organization had ever been forced to lay off any of its loyal staffers.

And just that morning, Dobson had decided to have his aging and sick dog, Mitzi, euthanized. He had been waiting to catch a plane to Washington, D.C., when he received a call on his cell phone with the news that Mitzi seemed to be near death.

More grave than any of those things for Dobson personally, however, was the main reason for his flight to California that day: He was going to visit Joe Kubishta, Shirley's stepfather, for what he thought

might be the last time. Long ailing, the ninety-year-old Kubishta was
fading fast in a Long Beach hospital. And while Dobson was grateful
that he apparently would have most of a weekend to spend with the
gentle and generous man—the man who had rescued Dobson's future
wife and her family from brokenness in the early fifties—Dobson was
sobered by the prospect of saying his final good-byes.

At the same time, Dobson couldn't afford to allow all of his attention and energy to be absorbed by everything that had transpired during the previous couple of days, or even by what might lie ahead in the
next two. On Tuesday, he would be flying to Washington, D.C., to host
receptions on Capitol Hill for new senators and representatives who
were friendly to the cause of the family. He would also attend the National Prayer Breakfast on Thursday morning and, in between, visit allies and lobby for new issues. There wasn't even a thought of doing any
fresh radio broadcasts that week or finding time to work on a list of
pressing writing projects.

Meanwhile, Larry King's people were jockeying with Dobson's
people over whether Dobson would come to the CNN studios in Hollywood that Monday or Friday to make the next of his regular appearances on *Larry King Live*. If the appearance was delayed until Friday,
Dobson faced a second wearying transcontinental flight in one week.

Dobson never had been one to dwell on his sorrows, even when
they were considerable. This week wouldn't give him much time for
doing so anyway.

∾∾∾

The apparently avoidable destruction of the space shuttle *Columbia*,
which left a broad path of disintegration over the Southwest, was a terrible case of déjà vu for the American people, not to mention a horrific
spectacle for the families of the crew. But when the great wounded ship
blew to pieces on the morning of February 1, the event also had a particular poignancy for the staff of Focus on the Family and for Dobson
himself. The forty-five-year-old commander of *Columbia*, Rick Husband, had been a big fan of the ministry and an outspoken Christian
witness inside the highly secular technoscientific culture of the U.S.
space program.

In fact, a few months earlier, Husband had written to Dobson and
invited him to attend the shuttle's launch on January 17. "We have been
blessed by your ministry for years," he wrote. "I would like to recognize

the influence that Focus on the Family has played in my life by flying an item from the ministry on my mission." The item needed to be light and not composed of wood, glass, or metal, so Dobson autographed the bill of a Focus on the Family baseball cap and sent it along for Husband to take on his mission—and to autograph for Focus upon his return. Dobson also sent his regrets and said he wouldn't be able to attend the launch at Kennedy Space Center.

In typical fashion, Husband and fellow crew member Lt. Col. Michael Anderson, another professing Christian, were focusing on their faith right up until liftoff. When Husband gathered the crew and their spouses on the night before to discuss final details of this mission, he finished by reciting Joshua 1:6-9 from memory, which closes with these words: "Be strong and courageous. Do not be terrified; do not be discouraged, for the LORD your God will be with you wherever you go."[1]

Dobson thought of Husband immediately after hearing about the *Columbia* on that Saturday morning but quickly dismissed the possibility that it had been Husband's flight; he assumed Husband would be in charge of a later one. But shortly after he arrived at the baggage claim at LAX, Bruce Hoover, Dobson's head of security and driver, shared the news with his boss that the *Columbia* had, indeed, been Husband's command. A look of shock quickly passed over Dobson's face, then anguish. "I hadn't made the connection," he said softly.

Dobson quickly added Husband's family to his list of urgent concerns for that weekend. By Saturday afternoon, Dobson left a message for Husband's wife, Evelyn, to offer his condolences and any assistance that he could. Finally, on Sunday evening, Evelyn Husband returned Dobson's call. "I talked to her and to [their] eleven-year-old daughter and tried to comfort them," he says. Dobson invited the family to come to Colorado Springs to be on his show anytime they wanted to talk about the wonderful husband, father, and hero they had just lost. Also on Sunday, Dobson called Larry King's producer to suggest that the show book Evelyn Husband as well.

Later in the week, Dobson's aides confirmed that, indeed, Husband had worn the Focus cap at various points during the flight. Now, the keepsake cap with Dobson's autograph lay in tiny pieces on the ground, perhaps spread over several square miles somewhere under the flight path. Or perhaps it had been vaporized—like the hopes, dreams, and lives of the *Columbia* crew.

೨ഌ഻ൟඁൟඁ

Upon landing in Los Angeles, Dobson got good news about Joe Kubishta. Shirley had been able to bring her beloved stepfather out of intensive care to a convalescent hospital, and she said he was demonstrating much more coherence than he had in several days.

But Shirley's mother, eighty-nine-year-old Alma Kubishta, was also ailing, so she and Danae had had their hands full over the previous week. Dobson planned to spend most of the next couple of days helping them and enjoying some final time with Joe Kubishta.

Kubishta became like a second father to Dobson after the death of James Dobson Sr. in 1977. But Kubishta's role in the Dobson family already had proved salutary nearly three decades earlier when the bachelor married Alma Deere, lifting her and her children, Shirley and John, from the economic ravages of divorce. By that time, Kubishta had established his own ceramic-tile setting business.

Kubishta had grown up poor on a farm in North Dakota, with eleven brothers and sisters. His mother had died when he was nine, and his father was an abusive alcoholic who often would disappear for days at a time. When Kubishta was in eighth grade, he dropped out of school to work in a coal mine. Eventually, in the midst of the Great Depression, he migrated to California with others from Midwestern farms, setting bowling pins, working on a potato farm, and simply doing whatever was necessary to stay alive. He proved himself a member of what news anchor and author Tom Brokaw termed the "greatest generation" in World War II, serving aboard the battleship *South Dakota* at Guadalcanal, Iwo Jima, and Okinawa, and receiving a navy commendation for heroism at Guadalcanal.[2]

Over the years, Dobson realized why the navy veteran had fallen in love with Alma: She possessed many of the traits that Dobson found so endearing in her daughter, Shirley. These included frequent displays of a feisty sense of humor. During one visit, for instance, Dobson observed his mother-in-law padding around her small ranch house in her slippers, holding a transistor radio to her ear. "But she wasn't listening to me," Dobson recalls with a chuckle. "She was listening to Rush Limbaugh! I asked her, 'Alma, why don't you listen to me anymore?' And she said, 'Oh Jimmy, I've heard everything you've got to say.'"

Even after James and Shirley Dobson left Southern California for Colorado Springs in 1991, the Kubishtas' home remained a popular gathering place for their grandchildren, Danae and Ryan. It was a place they could hang out with their friends, play games, and get fed. One of their friends loved the Kubishtas so much that, when he had to move away, he drove sixty miles to their house with a rosebush to plant in their backyard so they wouldn't forget him.[3]

ᴄᴏ⌒ᴀ⌒ᴏᴄ

In November 2002 the Dobsons had learned that Kubishta was in the end stages of leukemia, meaning among other things that it was time for Dobson to make another "Be there!" approach to his stepfather-in-law. Over the decades, Kubishta had made inferences about having come to a genuine, saving faith in Christ. At the very least, Kubishta managed to fit neatly into the evangelical subculture that included his in-laws by regularly attending a nearby Baptist church and sometimes even leading family prayers. But the Dobsons and Alma Kubishta never were entirely sure that he had grasped the concept of salvation, even after Dobson took him to lunch one day specifically to talk about it.

Now, with the doctor's prognosis, the matchless eternal stakes for Kubishta became immediate as well. Dobson came to his bedside and confronted him: "Joe, do you know for certain that you will be with us in heaven when you die?" Kubishta wept quietly but didn't respond. A few days later, Kubishta prayed what is known as the sinner's prayer—a simple acceptance of salvation—with his Baptist pastor, and he rejoiced to share the news with his stepdaughter and son-in-law.

"Jim, I'm saved! I'm saved!" he said. Dobson recalls how the next day, the usually stoic Kubishta looked up through his tears and said, "I feel so clean, Jim, so clean." He died at about 1:30 in the morning on February 19, 2003. Dobson finally has no doubt that his adoptive father-in-law will be with his family in heaven.

ᴄᴏ⌒ᴀ⌒ᴏᴄ

During that first weekend in February 2003, there remained a good chance that Larry King's production assistants would still call and ask Dobson to come to Hollywood to do the *Larry King Live* show on Monday evening. But that possibility was looking less and less likely as King's team began to factor coverage of the shuttle disaster into its plans for the next few days.

Finally on Sunday, King decided that he wanted Dobson to appear on his show at the *end* of the week, on Friday evening. That switch would necessitate Dobson's having to fly coast-to-coast again on Thursday night so that he could prepare for the broadcast. Focus aides asked King whether Dobson could appear on the show remotely, from Focus's studios in Colorado Springs; he had done so a couple of times before. But this time, the producers balked at the idea, stressing the importance of the in-person chemistry between King and his guests. Dobson knew he'd be severely fatigued even before appearing on King's show in Hollywood, not to mention afterward. But weighing the significance of his relationship with King and of worldwide exposure on CNN, Dobson said yes.

❧

Dobson had carved out a huge portion of his schedule for the week— parts of three days and two nights—so that he could begin to capitalize on what he saw as a once-in-a-generation opportunity in Washington, D.C. At the very least, it would require Dobson once again to demonstrate his mastery of lapel-to-lapel lobbying.

Dobson was especially enthusiastic this time, pointing out that the 108th Congress was the most family-friendly that Focus and its allies had ever dealt with (until the 109th, which would be seated after the 2004 elections). Dobson's allies were positively electric with the sense that the new Republican majorities could allow them to make immediate progress on long-tabled issues such as further restricting stem-cell research and advancing President George W. Bush's stalled nominees for federal judgeships.

To kick things off, the Family Research Council had booked conference room S-116 in the West Wing of the Capitol for a light breakfast get-together with senators Wednesday morning. There, Dobson spent an hour reuniting with stalwart allies, such as Sam Brownback of Kansas, as well as a promising smattering of newer friends, including Senator Saxby Chambliss, whose unexpected defeat of incumbent Democratic Senator Max Cleland in Georgia had been one of the most breathtaking results of the 2000 election. Ten senators in all showed up to spend some time with Dobson.

After the senators were seated around the room's huge oval cherry table, and as late participants filtered in, Brownback introduced his old friend. Dobson apologized to the senators for his somewhat froggy voice, explaining that he was suffering jet lag from his flight the day before and from having arisen at 4 a.m. that day. Then he shifted into a mode that goes a long way toward explaining the success of this child psychologist, utterly untrained in politics, in the most important political realm on earth.

First, Dobson politely explained a bit about himself and the background of Focus, ostensibly for those who didn't understand who he was. It was as if he were some kind of bit player who nevertheless had managed to assemble fully one-tenth of the most powerful legislative body in the world to spend an hour meeting with him. It must have struck at least some of the senators as false humility. But quickly, Dobson let them know that he recognized his power as a player in Washington and that he was in the room with them to wield it openly.

Dobson began by challenging the senators about how they were handling the nomination of President Bush's federal court nominee Miguel Estrada. In part fearing that the pro-life Estrada could jump on a fast track to an eventual Supreme Court nomination, Senate Democrats were trying to vanquish him by using a filibuster, a legislative maneuver in which one party tries to wear down the resolve of the other by holding the Senate floor hour after hour, day after day, even week after week. (In fact, the Democrats' fierce opposition finally would defeat Estrada in September 2003, when the nominee withdrew his own nomination.)

But in early February, it was only just becoming clear that Estrada was a target. And Dobson made no attempt to hide his frustration about the fitness of the federal judiciary, so he was in a mood to lecture the senators a bit about the importance of saving the Estrada nomination. If the Democrats were going to break traditional protocol and filibuster Estrada, Dobson said, Republicans "ought to make Ted Kennedy read the New York City phone book" to get through the filibuster. The Capitol Hill visitor next opined that "the Democrats are a lot better at playing hardball than you guys are. Ginsburg got ninety-seven votes," he said, referring to the confirmation vote on Supreme Court Justice Ruth Bader Ginsburg in 1993, when there were forty-four Republicans in the Senate. "She's an ideologue of the first order and an ACLU board member. It seems that it's not a level playing field."

Feeling a bit challenged, Senator James Talent of Missouri countered, "We take our constitutional oath seriously." Dobson shot back, "Would you vote for Ginsburg if she was being considered today?" Equally unhesitating, Talent said, "Yes. . . . It's God who raises rulers up." Dobson didn't respond.

Then Dobson turned the tables a bit, asking for the senators' advice on the strategy that pro-life groups such as Focus should pursue when it comes to judicial appointments. He told the senators that he was encouraged by some markers in the broader picture of abortion. "For the first time in thirty years," he said, "I'm really starting to see a cultural shift. But I'm not just concerned about the whole enchilada," meaning overturning *Roe v. Wade* or otherwise making abortion illegal. "If we can save just a few babies, it's worth it."

Finally, Dobson shifted to one of his favorite rhetorical devices: the telling anecdote. This one was about his attendance at President George H. W. Bush's inauguration in 1989. "I sat next to Jesse Jackson for two hours," he began. "And at one point, I said to him, 'You know, there is a racist element to abortion' because of its disproportional occurrence among minority women. 'So why haven't you spoken up?' Jackson responded, 'I'll talk to you about any *other* subject you wish, but not that one.' That was the end of the conversation," Dobson said, implying that Jackson had admitted his own hypocrisy on one of the biggest issues on the liberal agenda. "He knew."

At that point it was 10 a.m., but Dobson had only just begun a schedule that would require every second of what he and his aides matter-of-factly call his "twelve-hour energy." Along for the day were Shirley Dobson; Colorado representative David Schultheis and his wife, Sandra (Dobson's neighbors in Colorado Springs); Tom Minnery, Focus's vice president of public policy; a scheduler; and an aide. Dobson's entourage would crisscross Capitol Hill, call on congressional friends in their offices, brush past enemies, and end their lobbying blitzkrieg late in the evening with a gathering of freshman House members in a format similar to the earlier meeting with friendly senators.

The first stop was the office of Kansas Republican representative Jim Ryun, a legendary track star who had gained fame as the first American high schooler to break the four-minute mile nearly forty years ago. He had been one of Dobson's biggest allies during his eight years on the Hill and has appeared on the *Focus on the Family* radio broadcast, so the informal session had a bit of a reunion quality as Shirley and Anne Ryun, Jim Ryun's wife, hugged and caught up. As the Dobsons sat on a couch in Ryun's private office, Dobson filled in his friends on the condition of Joe Kubishta, holding his wife's hand as he spoke. The two men lightly discussed a few issues, but Dobson felt no need to go deeper because he knew Ryun was in accord with him on everything of importance.

Before Dobson's group departed, someone mentioned that Ryun had just been voted the greatest-ever American high school athlete in a poll on ESPN.com. Practically out the door by then, Dobson laughed and joshed, "But do they know about *me?*"

The next stop was the office of Representative Frank Wolf of Virginia. The protocol was much the same as it had been in Ryun's office, except that Wolf's family wasn't there. The group discussed the evils of gambling and pornography, and then Wolf hit Dobson with an issue that had been hounding him: how to relieve the ravages of ongoing famine in Ethiopia. He showed Dobson's delegation a video that depicted immense human suffering amid the famine, and Wolf decried the lack of global attention to it. "President Bush spoke about it in his radio address on Saturday," Wolf said, "but the *Columbia* [accident] overshadowed it." Dobson offered to devote a *Focus* broadcast to the issue and then, after a few more minutes of watching the video, winced and said, "Frank, this is so tragic I can't watch it."

By now, after covering the equivalent of a mile or so in the Capitol, Shirley said her feet were bothering her and asked the aide for some softer shoes from the bag he was carrying. She and Dobson walked hand in hand for much of the day. Conveniently, her chairmanship of the National Day of Prayer provided her a somewhat official platform on which to greet legislators, and she was able to promote her event as well as support her husband in his lobbying.

Before lunch, Dobson had decided to squeeze in an extemporaneous appearance across Capitol Hill at a press conference sponsored by evangelical groups to announce their creation of what they called a "Manifesto on Biology and Human Dignity." The purpose was not only to express opposition to cloning and to stem-cell research on embryos, but also to provide a "comprehensive framework for bioethics policy." An entire roll call of evangelical leaders was scheduled to appear in support of the statement, but Dobson hadn't signed on until it was too late to be included on the printed program.

"It's crazy what happens when he schedules a trip to Washington," Minnery explains. "Word gets out and his every moment could be booked. He tries to avoid that. But he felt strongly enough about this that he wanted to get to it."

A top aide to one of Dobson's senatorial allies quickly led the group through the labyrinth of tunnels and walkways that laces subterranean Capitol Hill and onto a members-only tram that took them to the press conference room. By the time Dobson arrived at the preconference meeting, Charles Colson, who was chairing the group, was just heading out to meet the press.

A number of print and electronic journalists were ensconced there. Evangelical leaders who had shown up for the announcement included Colson, Gary Bauer of American Values, Joni Eareckson Tada of Joni and Friends, and Sandy Rios of Concerned Women for America. As a latecomer, Dobson wasn't introduced, even though he was perhaps the most recognizable face at the front of the room. Speaking passionately without notes or an outline, Dobson said, "We signed this manifesto on behalf of Focus on the Family and perhaps a million of our constituents. I cannot imagine a culture that will sanction the creation of little human beings and then the cannibalization of them [for research]. It's audacious to interfere with God's design in that way."

⋙⋘

Besides Dobson's genuine affection for the friends who help him accomplish the legislative aims of his ministry, one other thing was clear from his working the Hill on February 5: He doesn't waste much time humoring his enemies.

As he disembarked from the tram on the way to the press conference, for example, Dobson brushed almost within hugging distance of Senator Tom Daschle, the Democrat whom he would help vanquish from the Senate in 2004. At that moment, Daschle had just been knocked from his perch as majority leader by the Republican victories in November 2002. Each man—the towering Texan and the short-of-stature South Dakotan—recognized the other, but neither gave any indication of that in their silent passing.

As Dobson shared a late lunch after the press conference in the intimate senate dining room with the rest of his delegation, only two other tables were occupied. In one corner sat Democratic senator Joseph Lieberman, who had been Al Gore's running mate in 2000; in another corner sat a guest with Senator Joseph Biden, the Delaware Democrat. Many sworn enemies in such a situation would have at least exchanged pleasantries, but Dobson had none of that.

"He's comfortable being a leader within evangelical Christendom, and that's who he is," explains Minnery. "He doesn't think there would be much to gain by small talk with Joe Lieberman."

∽∽∽∽∽

Perhaps reflecting their status as new members of the junior chamber, the first-year congressmen and congresswomen who greeted the Dobsons at a Focus-sponsored reception that evening were giddy compared with their more sober-minded counterparts in the Senate that morning. The several new members who attended included Marilyn Musgrave, a Colorado homemaker who had been inspired to run in part by Dobson's pro-family messages and who would go on to spearhead efforts to amend the Constitution to forbid gay marriage. Also attending was newly elected Representative Katherine Harris, an evangelical who had been Florida's secretary of state during the 2000 election, when her determined stand on ballot-counting issues helped George W. Bush to his eventual Supreme Court–ordered victory.

The next morning, it was Shirley's opportunity to shine. The National Prayer Breakfast is a separate annual event from the National Day of Prayer. But obviously the two events have hugely overlapping constituencies. Sponsored by the little known Fellowship Foundation and chaired by Republican Representative Ray LaHood of Illinois, the prayer breakfast at the Washington Hilton attracted 2,500 people from 154 countries, including three heads of state, twenty-one cabinet ministers, eleven members of Parliament, fifty-four ambassadors, fifty-six U.S. senators, 245 U.S. House members, most of Bush's cabinet members—and the Dobsons.

"In this hour of our country's history, we stand in the need of prayer," President Bush said in his nine-minute address. "We pray for the families that have known recent loss. We pray for the men and women who serve around the world to defend our freedom. We pray for wisdom to know and do what is right. And we pray for God's peace in the affairs of men."[4]

After the prayer breakfast Thursday morning, Dobson met briefly at the Hilton with Tim Goeglein, the main White House contact for evangelicals. By that evening, James and Shirley Dobson were back on another coast-to-coast flight, this one from Washington's Dulles International Airport to Los Angeles.

Friday morning brought a phone call from Karl Rove, President Bush's chief political aide, asking for feedback on the mood and concerns of America's conservatives. And by Friday evening, Dobson was to be ready to match wits with the inimitable Larry King.

৩৩⌒৯৬৩

As usual, Dobson prepared very seriously on February 7 for that evening's appearance on *Larry King Live*. Back in Southern California again, Shirley spent most of the day visiting the Kubishtas. That morning, as is the routine, Larry King's researcher contacted Dobson to discuss the general topics the interview would cover, so that she could prepare the blue, five-by-seven-inch index cards that King shuffles when interviewing a guest. Dobson spent the day reading the day's newspapers and other materials, updating himself through conversations with peers and aides, and readying his messages for the program.

Dobson's appearances on *Larry King Live* are consistently among the show's most popular. The host would like to have Dobson appear about every six weeks, says Paul Hetrick. And while Dobson tries to accommodate King, his appearances over the last few years have averaged more like once every four to six months.

The show also makes a great forum for Dobson. First, it is broadcast live, not taped and edited. Second, Dobson is almost always invited on alone, allowing him to avoid what he believes are the distortions that often affect a multiguest format, including intense disagreement. Third, it is an hour long, giving Dobson a fair chance to discuss issues fully. Fourth, doing the show allows Dobson to address millions who don't regularly listen to Christian radio or buy his books. *Larry King* airs live, then is rebroadcast three hours later and again six hours later; it is simulcast or "proximity aired" on many radio stations nationally and is seen in 220 countries, which covers just about all of them. A thirty-second commercial on the show costs about $25,000.[5] By appearing on the show, Dobson gains thousands of dollars' worth of exposure for his ideas and Focus on the Family. And while King usually gives him a rhetorical workout, Dobson is at his best extemporaneously, where his sincerity and his crinkly-toned voice are tremendous allies.

Still, the squeaky-clean, God-talking Dobson doesn't exactly seem like Larry King's kind of guy. King, a poster child for the secular high life, has been married five times and seems to depend greatly on the show's guests for his philosophical training. Every time he's got Dobson in his hot seat, King demonstrates curiosity not only about child-rearing and social issues but also about theology. Dobson gets the opportunity to connect not only with his host but also with the presumed millions of viewers who think like King.

King often flies wildly from topic to topic, spending only about 60 percent of each show on the expected lines of questioning, according to Paul Hetrick. He's been known to ask Dobson questions about areas that his guest is uncomfortable discussing, or unprepared for, such as foreign policy. More often, King asks Dobson "Why does God . . . ?" questions, though Dobson's answers are pretty consistent. In other words, when he's interviewing Dobson, King exhibits all the hallmarks of a person on an honest spiritual search. Dobson usually responds with reassurances that he gets from the Bible, and when King tries to bully him into an explanation of the inexplicable, Dobson isn't afraid to say that he's glad God has a handle on the things that no human being can fully understand.

The February 7th show fit the pattern. Much of the week's *Larry King Live* programming had been devoted to reporting on and memorializing those killed in the shuttle explosion, with the notable diversion of one hour with Elizabeth Taylor. The night before, former president Bill Clinton had been King's guest, and they had talked about Iraq, North Korea, President Bush's tax cuts, Clinton's planned presidential library, and more. But immediately after *Larry King Live* began on Friday, it was evident that King was bothered by several things and hoped that Dobson could help him get to the bottom of them.

After allowing Dobson to report on his activities in Washington, King focused on the challenges of fighting terrorism and demonstrating vigilance in domestic security; these issues were hardly Dobson fortes, and he dealt with King's questions cautiously. Then King switched directions radically, moving into one of his theological probings, as their discussion came to focus on the fate of the *Columbia* astronauts.

"Why do bad things happen to good people?" King asked. "Why did these seven people . . . have to die?"

"We can't answer [that]," Dobson responded. King then wanted to know how Dobson "continues" his faith "when you don't get the answer?" Dobson replied, "Because the Scripture tells us to lean not on our own understanding." With one of the remarks that has gained him a reputation as a sharp interviewer, King then challenged Dobson. "That's a crutch," he said. " 'Don't let it bother you. Someone else will worry about it.' "

Making the clear declaration of his faith that he tries to utter at least once on each *Larry King Live* appearance, Dobson then told King that he had confidence in "God and in my Lord, Jesus Christ, and I believe he has the answers even when I don't."

Brief conversations about AIDS, racism, Dobson's book *Bringing Up Boys*, and the National Day of Prayer followed before King began taking viewers' questions by phone. As is typical, a few were challenging; a handful, clinical; and several, simply complimentary. Dobson handled them all smoothly, with King helping to keep each questioner's segment relatively concise. The questions also provided a framework for King to take on Dobson about abortion and the justification for war.

And near the end of the broadcast, just a glimmer of their personal connection shone through. "Always good seeing you. Stay well," King said to Dobson as they neared sign-off.

"Feels like home," Dobson replied.

"Thank you," King said. "A high compliment."

CHAPTER TWENTY-TWO

MAYBE BRUCE WAS RIGHT

[Dobson] pounded the White House staff pretty hard.

CHARLES COLSON, ON JAMES DOBSON'S
LOBBYING IN FAVOR OF ABSTINENCE
LEGISLATION

The problem with any huge success is that it demands an encore. How to provide a credible sequel to the quarter century of ministry at Focus became an increasingly urgent question in the new millennium as Dobson neared, and then exceeded, normal retirement age without a clear plan in sight. The reigning assumption from the start was that no one man would ever again presume to run the entirety of Focus, overseeing both the ministry and media sides of the organization. Yet that consensus still left the brain trust to figure out two monumental issues: how Dobson would hand over the administration of Focus as an enterprise and the more difficult challenge of providing a ministerial successor to the outsized persona of Dobson himself.

One thing was clear: Dobson was ready for some relief. "In the past, I would have thought that he would have had a difficult time relinquishing control of the ministry to anyone else because he has a wonderful ability to 'smell smoke'—as he likes to call it—within the ministry," says Danae, exhibiting a second-generation mastery of some of her father's favorite clichés. "He also likes to make sure that the trains run on time. So in order to make sure the trains run on time and to smell any smoke, he's always felt that he needs to be at the helm so he can oversee everything.

"But he's done this for twenty-six years, and he's tired." Besides, she adds, Focus had only constituted the most recent several chapters of her father's career. "He's worked hard all his life. He deserves to have some time to himself. He loves to read and spend time with my mom and maybe take a vacation here and there. So he's more open to sharing the load."

Actually, Dobson had been trying to anticipate some sort of handoff for nearly a decade. Through the late eighties, even though he was moving into his midfifties, he had hardly thought about a successor. But the board began to discuss succession lightly in 1989. The topic suddenly heated up after Dobson's heart attack in 1990 and even more so in the wake of his stroke in 1998. The 1994 departures of three original top aides—Paul Nelson, Peb Jackson, and Rolf Zettersten—hit Dobson like a blow to the solar plexus.

In 1995, Dobson and the Focus board took a first stab at building some sort of bridge to a future without him. Three years earlier, they had hired Dick Mason, CEO of the popular Radio Bible Class based in Grand Rapids, Michigan, and in 1995 the board handed Mason the title of executive vice president and chief operating officer. Their hope was that he would be able to take over the business administration responsibilities that weighed so heavily on Dobson.

But the attempt was doomed from the start because Dobson needed a chief of staff, not a COO. Mason "came in with one set of expectations, and Dr. Dobson had a different set, and that's a formula for a problem, which eventually surfaced," says Don Hodel, Dobson's pal from the Reagan administration who joined the Focus board in 1994. Mason, a talented administrator, "thought the board had brought him in to be the manager, the decision maker," Hodel recounts. "But then people in the organization who weren't happy with some element of a decision he had made would communicate that to Dr. Dobson, who became increasingly distressed. And besides, while he attempted to take his hands off, Dr. Dobson really wasn't prepared at that point to relinquish his responsibilities and obligation to God for management of this organization."

Dobson's view was that Mason "had a very different agenda than me and was following a very different drummer. I found myself therefore going around him on some of the issues that I cared about. That was frustrating to us both. There are times when things just don't fit." Mason resigned in 1995.

Hodel himself then served a voluntary stint as Dobson's executive vice president and chief of staff from early 1996 through the middle of that year. He stunned a grateful Dobson with his dedication and talent as an administrator, particularly in the way in which Hodel streamlined Dobson's decision-making process. "My perspective was I never made a decision during that period, and his is that I made 90 percent of the decisions," Hodel says. What Hodel did is boil down the issues facing Dobson into one- to three-sentence summaries plus a one- to three-sentence kicker describing what Hodel would do. "He was very comfortable with that relationship, and he increasingly trusted decisions that I made and ended up approving them without spending a lot of time on them."

But since Dobson wasn't yet ready to give up control, Hodel determined that a big part of his job would be to design and implement a management structure that would work more efficiently under a boss that some viewed as stubbornly imperial. He created a hierarchy that included three executive vice presidents who reported directly to Dobson—a structure that worked smoothly from the start.

It was 1998 before Focus seriously addressed the succession issue again. And in February 1999, the board adopted an official "succession strategy" that for the first time envisioned a permanent division of labor in the post-Dobson era between a CEO and a "chief articulator." The plan assumed that "the CEO role will be the easier position to fill by acquiring an experienced executive with a craft honed in the business world." But the board conceded that "the creative and teaching responsibility promises to be more challenging," and they laid out requirements for fulfilling it that, understandably enough, looked like an outline of Dobson's résumé. The new chief articulator would have to be a scriptural, moral, and cultural conservative; be above reproach in his personal Christian walk; have a stellar family life; have a thorough knowledge of the Bible; possess an advanced degree in psychology or medicine or some other "helping science"; wield a "highly developed ability to communicate" in speaking and in writing; and display "a pleasing radio voice and skill as an interviewer." Also on this highly demanding wish list were "ceaseless compassion" and "potential to serve as a moral and spiritual leader in the nation."

Not surprisingly, no one emerged, and Focus soon shifted subtly into an attitude of simply not wanting Dobson to retire. The succession issue faded over the next several years until contributions to the ministry leveled off in 2001. Dobson became preoccupied with the very immediate task of righting the ship. Yet Hodel became so frustrated at the organization's failure to deal with the problem of ensuring future leadership that in early 2002 he asked Dobson to name him chief of staff at Focus so that he could relieve some of the administrative overload. He had already successfully pulled off a similar structural change when he was secretary of the interior under President Reagan. When Dobson said he just couldn't let go yet, a frustrated Hodel announced that he wouldn't stand for reelection to his fourth two-year term on the board.

"Since [Dobson] wasn't willing to relinquish the management obligations of the job, I wasn't willing to stay on the board and watch him kill himself," Hodel said later. "The idea that he was going home on Friday night with a two-foot stack of paper and coming back Monday morning having gone through all of it over the weekend meant that he had no rejuvenation time. I believed that he could kill himself. He'd already had a heart attack and a stroke, and here he was still carrying a workload that would have killed a younger man already. That's all I could think of during board meetings, so I quit."

Hodel's departure and the post–9/11 challenges to the budget added to a somber tone felt at Focus through 2002, a pall that partially darkened even the twenty-fifth-anniversary celebration. Focus had to change the planned venue for the Saturday night celebration from the Air Force Academy football stadium, for example, to the much smaller Pepsi Center as fewer supporters than had been anticipated demonstrated enthusiasm for attending the event. Overall contributions to the ministry continued to be static for four consecutive years.

By October of 2002, a beleaguered Dobson was finally ready to turn the administration over to someone, and he told Hodel so. "I enjoy administration, and I enjoy making the trains run on time," Dobson says. "I enjoy being the boss. So I was very reluctant to let it go. But the Lord put his thumb in my back, and my wife's thumb was somewhere in the same neighborhood, and my board began to be concerned. It had to come and the moment comes to all—so why not do it in an orderly fashion so that way it might be a model, rather than waiting until the president dies or is just too tired to continue?

"Once I got to that point—and it took about two weeks to do it—I had to come to terms not only with the fact that Focus on the Family would be led by someone else but that someone else would recast the organization in their image. Once I accepted that and became comfortable with the fact that my successor didn't have to be me, he can be him, then I was prepared to let go, and to do so without consternation."

To friends and associates who had succeeded in the world of business, Dobson's decision to surrender daily operations and be comfortable with the move, especially after his history of hesitation, was remarkable enough. Such a transition "doesn't happen easily" with most classic founder-entrepreneurs, says Tony Wauterlek, a longtime Focus board chairman and investment banker who knows many highly successful entrepreneurs. "They find it very difficult to agree that perhaps their way isn't the best way to run everything or that the organization should change a way of doing things that they've been outspoken about."

Wauterlek had thought that Dobson would "prove more resistant to it than what he has been. The board had been at [the succession problem] for longer than a decade, and when you've done that, you begin to think that it's more or less of an academic exercise because nobody really foresees it happening. But when you put feet on it finally, there can be a lot of emotion. I'm surprised that he's been as willing as he is to do it. But it is characteristic of the way that he can process things. You don't know what he's thinking, and he'll surprise you by ultimately making a change more easily than you think he might."

The difference-maker was the availability of Hodel for the job. "Jim has absolute confidence in him, and he has proven himself with his integrity and his loyalty and love for Jim," says Wauterlek. Wauterlek, a friend of Charles Colson's, also served on a transition committee for Prison Fellowship that in 2002 hired a new president and chief operating officer. In the same way, Wauterlek says, Dobson "had to have someone he could trust implicitly."

Hodel had uniquely earned that trust with Dobson through both their previous working relationship and their friendship. Hodel and his wife, Barbara, had sustained a terrible loss in 1974 when their son committed suicide on his seventeenth birthday. "After we'd seen portions of one of the Dobson videos at our church," Hodel recalls, "we commented, 'Boy, I wish I'd known about him and this video series before we lost our son.'"

In 1987, several years after Barbara and Don Hodel had recommitted their lives to Christ and thirteen years after their son's death, Hodel finally crossed paths with Dobson in person. Hodel and his wife attended a National Religious Broadcasters convention in

Washington, D.C., so that they could hear Dobson's speech there. Afterward, Hodel invited Dobson to the sacred ground of camaraderie—the basketball court—and the friendship was solidified. The Hodels accepted Dobson's invitation to talk about their son's death and their subsequent Christian commitment on a *Focus* broadcast. And after the Hodels left Washington in 1989 and moved to Silverthorne, Colorado, in the heart of Rockies ski country, they began participating in the annual ski trip that the Dobsons enjoyed in Vail as guests of a couple who had been the largest Focus supporters.

In the meantime, Hodel also had added to his already-impressive résumé by serving as president of the Christian Coalition from 1997 through 1999, succeeding Ralph Reed. Persuaded that Dobson finally was serious about a management restructuring, Hodel rejoined the Focus board in late 2002 so that he could help execute it. Although it wasn't a fait accompli at that point, by February 2003 it had become clear that board members wanted Hodel himself to take the new chief administrator job, even if it was just temporarily in order to oversee the search for a permanent occupant. When Hodel decided that he was actually "being called to be here and manage as long as the Lord has me do so," the rest was easy. On March 28, 2003, the board named sixty-eight-year-old Hodel as president and chief executive officer and created the new title of chairman and founder for Dobson. The board asked Dobson to retain responsibilities in broadcasting, writing, and public policy. And he would still work from his office at Focus.

A new era for Focus on the Family was underway.

⊱⌒⌒⌒⌒⊰

Hodel wasn't scheduled to take over until May 15, but Dobson seemed immediately unburdened. "He backed away very quickly," says former Focus vice president Walt Larimore. "The transition really took place in April. I would sit in meetings where someone asked him something that, two weeks earlier, he would have answered instantly—and which he still was fully capable of answering—and he'd say, with that smile, 'It's not my job.'"

And within a month, even before he had finished handing over duties to his new CEO, Dobson had the opportunity to test his newly cut, longer leash. A bill that fleshed out President Bush's new global AIDS initiative was set to be voted out of the House—but not before Dobson could put his mark on it.

AIDS prevention in the United States had never drawn much support from Dobson and most of his social-conservative allies. They opposed control of HIV mitigation programs by liberal interests who they believed were more interested in justifying the homosexual lifestyle than in seriously battling the disease. But in his State of the Union address on January 28, the president radically broadened the landscape on the matter when he dropped a bombshell proposal to spend $15 billion to try to help sub-Saharan African and Caribbean nations eradicate the scourge of AIDS. Besides its obvious appeal as a great humanitarian gesture, Bush's move was a political masterstroke because it was a palpable expression of his "compassionate conservatism" that also happened to be applied to a matter of great concern to black Americans.

But while evangelical leaders were prepared to consider backing the president's plan, they would insist on certain conditions if he was going to garner their support as his AIDS program went to Congress. Their sine qua non was that much of the funding be spent to promote abstinence. They pointed to a program in Uganda, the ABC model, which had reduced the growth rate for new HIV infections from 21 percent a year down to 6 percent annually.[1] In some areas of the country, the number of pregnant women with HIV had fallen by half.[2] The program emphasized Abstinence first, Being faithful in marriage, and using Condoms only as a last resort. In the United States, of course, condoms were already being freely distributed to high school students, a practice that conservatives felt only fanned the spread of HIV and other sexually transmitted diseases. But the Ugandan government provided condoms only to prostitutes, giving prophylactics no official role in AIDS prevention.

The problem was that the version of the bill that had been ushered out of committee in April by Representative Henry Hyde, the usually reliable conservative Republican from Illinois, made practically no mention of abstinence and earmarked virtually none of the $15 billion to promote it. In view of Uganda's well-documented success, Christian conservatives simply couldn't tolerate that. Neither were they mollified by the fact that Hyde's bill foresaw evangelical mission arms and other faith-based groups executing much of the real work of the program among the people of Africa and the Caribbean; as it was, the bill would force even these groups to distribute condoms along with other assistance. Their worries snowballed as Hyde's bill, with an apparent endorsement by the White House, came up for consideration in the last week of April.

"We'd been told by people at the White House to get on board or get out of the way and don't muck this bill up over abstinence," says Ken Connor, who was president of the Family Research Council, which had been promoting its own amendments to rectify the bill's shortcomings. "We were in a very uncomfortable position, strenuously opposing the bill of a popular president."

James and Shirley Dobson were already in Washington, D.C., on April 28 in order to finalize preparations for the National Day of Prayer scheduled for May 1. But that evening, Franklin Graham called Dobson at his hotel. He asked Dobson if he would meet with him, Charles Colson, and other evangelical and social-conservative leaders the next morning at the White House. They planned to confer with presidential aides and make a last stand for abstinence before President Bush's speech at 2 p.m. Dobson, liberated by the realization that he didn't have to remotely manage affairs back in Colorado Springs, shifted gears immediately.

Later that evening Connor says, "We had a chance to tell Jim that it was important that [the White House] not use him and his position as a means of advancing a bad bill. We didn't want him to let the White House manipulate him. If he was seen as willing to go into the tank on the amendments that we were pushing—for the conscious protection of abstinence—if he was there when the president made his speech and was in the photo, and Franklin Graham and Charles Colson and he appeared to be on board, then that would make it easy for them. But to his credit, he pitched a fit."

In fact, as soon as Dobson got to the White House on April 29, it was clear that he was going to be in for a long day. "To my utter dismay, the fairly low-level staffers who came in gave us a briefing and spoke in glowing terms about this global AIDS bill, which actually would have been just a big windfall for Planned Parenthood and condom distributors," Dobson recalls. Colson says that "in a process that went on all day, Jim was crucial in softening up the [White House] staff."

By early afternoon, it still wasn't apparent to the allied conservative forces what the president was planning to do. Colson, Graham, and Cardinal Theodore McCarrick, archbishop of the Roman Catholic Diocese of Washington, D.C., were the only conservative religious leaders invited to the meeting headed by President Bush, along with a handful of his staff people—Colin Powell, Health and Human Services Secretary Tommy Thompson, and the Ugandan ambassador to the United States. Dobson wasn't invited to that meeting, supposes the FRC's Connie Mackey, because he already had come to cross-purposes with the administration's junior staffers on the issue.

In any event, in the wake of that meeting, Bush seemed to end up siding with the forces of Dobson and Colson.

"Congress should make the Ugandan approach the model for our prevention efforts under the emergency plan," Bush said in his speech, which was delivered in the East Room of the White House.[3] The rhetoric cheered conservative leaders in the room. But by the end of his brief remarks, the president had gone no further in praising the Ugandan model and didn't promise a fight to ensure that Congress wouldn't go off in its own direction.

Dobson had been sitting off to one side of the room that was packed with reporters and TV cameras, and Karl Rove noticed him before the speech. After the president's remarks, Rove pulled a disturbed Dobson into the adjacent Blue Room to assure him "why he thought this was going to be okay, which had to do with the president's executive powers to administer the funds in the bill as he thought appropriate," Dobson says. "But I was concerned about what happens when Bush is out of that office, in two years or in six years."

Without assurances that they already had won the day, Dobson, Colson, Graham, and others spent the rest of Tuesday afternoon lobbying House members and senators on the phone and in person on Capitol Hill. Dobson himself met with Bill Frist—the Senate's majority leader and, as a physician, a leading figure on the AIDS issue in that chamber—for more than an hour. "In a very real sense, we had planted, Jim watered, Chuck harvested," says Connor. And when the bill sprouted and was dissected in the House on Thursday, the swarming conservatives had gotten what they wanted, including a requirement that a whopping one-third or more of the bill's HIV prevention funds would go toward abstinence programs.

"On Tuesday, the House was going to pass that bill without the abstinence provision," Dobson said shortly after his trip. "But we made a lot of noise the morning we met with those staffers, and Colson had an opportunity to talk directly with the president; that could have been the turning point. Some of us spent seven hours working on that bill. And on Thursday, the amendments we wanted passed. It was a $15 billion bill, more than anything that ever had been spent on this, and we had almost lost everything."

In the wee hours of May 16—just one day after Dobson officially dusted his hands of responsibilities for Focus's benevolence budget, unreturned hot pendings, and fallout from February's layoffs—the U.S. Senate approved the AIDS bill with the conservatives' amendments intact. Dobson's "influence was terrific," says one congressional aide who was at the hub of the action. "It was a critical part of all of this."

Given Graham's eleventh-hour plea for help on that Monday night in Washington, Dobson may have done exactly the same thing even if he had still been president of Focus. "But he would have been more fatigued in the process and very well may have been less effective because of the fatigue," Hodel says. "What thrills me is that by doing what we're doing, we're freeing him up to take those opportunities, and I know as long as the Lord gives him breath, his passion for the impact of public policy on the family is going to drive him."

Indeed, if this was what relinquishing control of Focus was going to be like, Dobson thought, the possibilities excited him.

⋘⋙

By the end of 2003, Hodel had already launched an even more sweeping reorganization that he hoped would finally put Focus's management structure on a twenty-first-century footing. The idea was to tighten up coordination of Focus's activities among its many ministries.

Hodel spent much of the first several months in his new position simply trying to recreate Dobson's intuitive genius for leadership of the organization that he had founded, nurtured, and finally let go. "As long as he's with us, we can still rely on his sensing ability," Hodel says. "But we need to develop a system in which people who don't have his sensitivity can achieve substantially the same end result in terms of relating to our constituency. It's artificial intelligence, in many ways."

Hodel's return to the apex of Focus in May 2003 had also cast a different light on Bruce Wilkinson's stunning demand that Dobson redouble his efforts in the ministry. With the addition of Hodel, the course that Wilkinson had presumed for Dobson finally began to make more sense. Dobson had calculated—based on a "numerical analysis" of memos and appointment schedules—that he would move about 30 percent of his previous workload to Hodel. "I want to just go at a slower pace, and maybe what has happened here will save me Saturday and Sunday work," he said. "That's not a windfall of time, just a return to more reasonableness."

A Dobson liberated from operating responsibilities might actually have an even bigger public impact than before. For example, Dobson said that he would spend more time writing. "For me, writing is very invigorating and exciting."

And shortly after the change, Hodel said he could already see new energy in Dobson. "It's very easy to forget how burdensome it is to be doing global things and then have to come back to your desk and deal with a two-word change in the vacation policy. It may be important to the organization, but compared to saving the world, it's hard to get your mind on it."

Indeed, board members had sensed in February that, rather than beginning to phase out a fading James Dobson, bringing in Hodel might actually unsheathe a revitalized James Dobson. So in making their announcement in March, they changed their terminology for dealing with this issue. They and Dobson no longer called Hodel's appointment the beginning of a "succession" process. It was instead the start of a "transition." And while no one was yet ready to send Wilkinson a bouquet of flowers, the difference would prove to be far deeper than mere semantics.

CHAPTER TWENTY-THREE

THE THIRD WAY

*There is no way we can replicate
James Dobson.*

DON HODEL, FORMER CEO
OF FOCUS ON THE FAMILY

T he leadership of Focus on the Family has never discounted the possibility that God could raise up someone remarkable to shepherd all aspects of a post–James Dobson ministry. But by 2003, they weren't expecting someone else of Dobson's prodigious intelligence, talents, integrity, spiritual sensitivity, and ready stature to emerge to take over seamlessly for him. Don Hodel's assumption of the day-to-day reins of Focus had solved half of the total challenge, at least for the foreseeable future.

And when the board appointed Jim Daly to succeed Hodel as CEO in February 2005, Focus took another step toward an orthodoxy of succession that for many years had seemed like a pipe dream.

Hodel hadn't promised Dobson that he would administer Focus indefinitely. Having implemented his reorganization plan, Hodel had achieved his main goal besides that of easing Dobson's burdens. He was growing tired of the weekly two-hour commute to the Homewood Suites Hotel in Colorado Springs, where he and Barbara stayed, and back home again for the weekend. And after putting many of his own personal and professional obligations on the back burner—and nearing the age of seventy—Hodel was ready to bring up his own successor. He would remain on the Focus board.

The forty-three-year-old Daly emerged as a natural choice for Focus's first "homegrown" leader. An orphan at the age of twelve, Daly was comforted by Dobson's broadcasts even during his college days.

After becoming a top sales manager for International Paper, Daly jumped at the chance to work for Focus when he was offered a position in 1989. He slid up through the hierarchy, working in public affairs, marketing, and the international division, eventually becoming chief operating officer. But Daly's promotion signified more than just a personal achievement; he also represented the ascension of Focus's self-described "twerps," a cadre of internally developed executives who contrasted themselves to the "geezers," including Dobson, Hodel, and executive vice president Tom Mason.

"We weren't just handing off the baton to Jim," Dobson says, "but the responsibility for Focus to our younger generation."

Nevertheless, while by 2005 the new succession mechanism already had worked twice for Dobson's former administrative role, the other half of the challenge remained.

"Who's going to *replace* Jim [Dobson], ultimately, is a whole different question," explains Tony Wauterlek, board chairman. "And it's much more difficult."

Focus's leadership had begun addressing the issue of creating an heir to Dobson the Articulator several years earlier. They boiled down the potential solutions to three types. One was a version of the classic "horse race" strategy often used by leaders of organizations to designate a successor. The second would be to anoint someone who clearly had no competition.

The third way initially seemed the most far-fetched possibility. But soon it proved the most likely of all.

⋙⋘

When there is no heir apparent in a large organization, the soon-to-retire chief executive officer often sets up a formal or informal "horse race" competition among two or three candidates to determine who will succeed him. They can be career-long company executives, ringers brought in from outside to raise the level of competition, or a combination thereof, but these "horses" understand exactly where the finish line is. Typically, after a year or two—and several months before the CEO's retirement party—one crosses that line first.

That's part of what Focus did in 2001 when it established its "other voices" strategy and began bringing in a handful of Christian media personalities to stack up against the board's 1999 description of Dobson's articulator role. Immediately, although not explicitly, these other voices became candidates to someday take over Dobson's golden microphone and the other responsibilities of being the face of Focus. Some of the other voices included Janet Parshall, whose weekly syndicated show for Focus ended up being canceled during the February 2003 budget crunch, and Jim Weidmann, who came to head a weekly broadcast called the *Family Night Guy* and earlier became vice chairman of Shirley Dobson's National Day of Prayer organization.

But from the start, the thoroughbreds in this race were Bill Maier, a Christian psychologist from California, and Walt Larimore, a Christian physician from Florida. Larimore joined Focus in February 2001 as vice president of medical outreach; he developed and became host of a syndicated Saturday morning medical call-in show for Focus as well as daily TV and radio commentaries. Maier came to Focus as vice president and psychologist in residence in January 2002 and became host of Focus's *Weekend Magazine* show. Each also began guest hosting for Dobson on the main *Focus* broadcast, appearing as experts on a variety of topics, and handling media interviews.

A family doctor, Larimore had practiced for four years in the rural Smoky Mountains and wrote a book about his experiences before cofounding a larger family practice in Kissimmee, Florida, in 1985. Over the next fifteen years he extended his media credentials by hosting daily live cable TV talk shows about health on Fox and other networks. Focus employees could see that Larimore had been polished by his media work but remained genuine. He is known to be a quick study with a ready wit, and his versatility immediately came in handy at Focus. When the early 2003 budget cuts eliminated his weekend show, Larimore poured more energy into his daily *Focus on Your Family's Health* commentaries that aired on more than eighty-five TV and radio stations across the country, most of them secular.

From his college years, Bill Maier almost literally followed in Dobson's footsteps, graduating from Point Loma Nazarene University in San Diego, the Nazarene school that had been Pasadena College. But Maier spent the next twelve years in radio, cohosting *The Bill and Sylvia Show* in morning drive time on KBIG-AM in Los Angeles. Heeding a call to Christian psychology, he got his master's and Psy.D. at Rosemead School of Psychology. He also worked a practicum at Childrens Hospital, where Dobson had spent seventeen years. Other clinical work followed. Maier's *Weekend Magazine* program gave Focus its first all-original general programming for the huge weekend market and adopted a magazine-style format similar to that of National Public Radio. One of Maier's favorite features of the program was "New Dad's Diary," inspired by the birth of his first child in early 2003.

But neither Maier nor Larimore immediately champed at the bit to make the "race" much more than a trot in the park. "No decision has been made or even considered on whether there should be one or more voices who would take over if and when Dr. Dobson is unable to speak or chooses not to anymore," Larimore said diplomatically in 2003. "My position is to be here as a servant and not to be involved in a decision as to how my service will play itself out. Dr. Dobson is irreplaceable. And if anyone thinks they can replace him, they've immediately disqualified themselves."

Likewise, Maier said that he didn't see the situation as a horse race. "My speculation is that Focus will move away from being a one-man show to being Focus on the Family, coming alongside you as a parent or a spouse and providing a variety of experts who can speak to the different family issues that concern you. But there isn't any horse race. As I see it now, no one could ever replace Dr. Dobson. This will always be his organization and based on his core teachings."

Indeed, Maier was expressing something that had changed even during his relatively brief period at Focus: Rather than fading as the public face of the ministry, Dobson's public exposure only increased following Hodel's addition.

And as Dobson's persona continued to dominate the public face of Focus once Hodel took the administrative reigns, the very idea of a horse race to succeed Dobson the communicator began to fade. Dobson and Hodel discontinued the media-outreach training that Larimore had been conducting for Focus managers and executives. They declined to develop Larimore into a protégé with cable-TV networks and other national media and canceled his show. By Election Day 2004, Larimore had left Focus.

So for then and well into the future, it seemed, Focus's "other voices" were to remain exactly that: other voices.

◗◖◗◖◗◖

Many have wondered about the possibility of Ryan or Danae Dobson replacing their dad at the helm of Focus on the Family. One aspect of the Dobson legacy that seems secure with his children are the first two family callings: writer and speaker. Both Danae and Ryan have taken up the pen and the microphone. Not surprisingly, given their contrasting personalities and life stories, they have followed in their father's enormous footsteps in these disciplines at different times in their lives and in varying ways.

An early psychology major, Danae switched to communications after catching a bit of inspiration from the work of novelist Danielle Steele. Her adult writing as represented by *Let's Talk!* is reminiscent of her father's subject and style: extremely relational and very anecdotal.

"I learned a lot from him just in his editing my manuscripts," says Danae, a reddish blond like her father whose bright beauty is most similar to her mother's looks. "For example, he'll often write several lengthy sentences in a paragraph and then end with a three- or four-word 'power sentence'—something that has some punch. I've copied that sometimes in my writing."

The family name and her accomplishments as an author have also garnered Danae a speaking ministry. Initially, she focused on Christian schools and younger children. But after publication of *Let's Talk!* she began to receive more invitations to address teenage girls. Although she's single, Danae says she intends to delve further into marriage and other family relationship topics in her writing and speaking. And it wouldn't be surprising, Focus insiders say, to see Danae someday assume a portion of the ministerial legacies of each of her parents. After hearing a 2003 *Focus* broadcast in which Danae discussed *Let's Talk!* Larimore credited her with inheriting gifts from both her parents. "She's a lot like Shirley in that her natural temperament is more quiet and nonpublic, but after that show I wondered, *Is God preparing Danae for something like what happened to Shirley with the National Day of Prayer?*"

By the end of 2003 Ryan Dobson had become one of the nation's most sought-after speakers to Christian youth. And he was heavily booked with speaking engagements, mostly addressing Christian high school classes, benefits for crisis pregnancy centers, and other evangelical events.

But he didn't arrive at that point in the straight line one might assume for the son of James Dobson. "My parents never pushed me to go into ministry," says Ryan, who's blond and wiry and buff—although much shorter than his adoptive father. "They never even hinted at it. It was just, 'Do what you want to do in life, the right thing, and what God is telling you to do.'" A short stint in the nineties working for the Family Research Council in Washington didn't work out for either party. And after that, Ryan only dabbled in speaking as he served for three years as a youth minister at a huge church in Orange County, California.

Then a mentor sat him down and asked, "Why are you working in regular jobs? God put you in this world to be a speaker." The Ambassador Agency of Nashville signed him to a representation contract. And in 2002, after wrapping up his responsibilities with Focus's annual bike ride program, Ryan began to fully grasp the opportunity before him, as if finally assuming a birthright. He did so with the understanding that entering the family occupation also created certain assumptions.

"Tomorrow night," he said in late 2003 before giving a speech at a crisis pregnancy center in Tampa, "people are expecting someone as good as my dad on stage. I'm thirty-three; he's sixty-seven—but they're still expecting him on stage. I do the absolute best with what God has given me, and in the past three years I've turned into a pretty good speaker."

While James Dobson's delivery has always been a bit like Thanksgiving dinner going down, Ryan's style—burning with the liveliness of his youth, the conviction in his message, the urgency of his generation, and the gratitude forged from an up-and-down life—is more akin to a bean burrito.

At first glance, Ryan's career as a writer seems to have been as disparate as possible from his father's—and his mother's and his sister's. It is short; theirs are decades long. The title and tone of his first book are anomalously sassy: *Be Intolerant: Because Some Things Are Just Stupid,* published by Multnomah Press in 2003. In fact, he didn't actually "write" it. No endless scrolls of handwritten prose underpinned this production; Ryan provided the substance for the book, based on his speeches, then recorded himself talking about the topic. Finally he turned over the tapes to a writer who produced the manuscript and then reviewed the result to make sure the book sounded like him.

It's difficult to reconcile Ryan Dobson's almost-growling visage on the book's cover with the smiling James Dobson that graces so many of his own books. "My parents hated [the cover] because I looked really angry, and it's black and silver and white, and a little bit scary-looking. And it's a big stretch for Multnomah, too, because it's abrasive in a way. But God has called me to a sort of John the Baptist–type role," he says—sounding clarion calls to youth about the rewards of genuinely embracing Christianity and the consequences of falling away from the faith.

Yet with a closer look, and not too much distortion of perspective, striking similarities emerge between *Be Intolerant* and *Dare to Discipline*. Just as Francis Heatherly had to plant the idea with James Dobson to write his first book, Multnomah executives went after Ryan after hearing him speak about absolute truth on a *Focus* broadcast. "I wanted someone to seek me out," Ryan says. "I could have had a book contract a long time ago; it's not that hard when your name is Dobson. But it would have seemed cheap; I hadn't earned it. And I didn't have anything to say."

More important, in their first efforts, each Dobson elected to rail against a leading mantra of their time. When James Dobson wrote *Dare to Discipline,* such was the predominance of Spock's permissive parenting philosophy in America that it was really a bold step for Dobson's readers to assertively channel the behavior of their offspring. Similarly, by exhorting readers to "be intolerant," Ryan took on the golden chant of the early twenty-first century: There are no absolutes, so everyone is right; respect diversity above all other values.

And just as Tyndale House quickly tied up James Dobson for his next book even as *Dare to Discipline* was coming down the chute, Multnomah moved rapidly to publish Ryan's second book, *2Die4*, in 2004.

ᔕᦉᦉ

It may seem obvious to assume that the mantle of leadership of Focus on the Family is being fitted for Ryan, but the son says he doesn't feel called to succeed his father as head of Focus on the Family and doubts that he ever will. His father agrees, though until very recently, according to Ryan, the two had never even discussed the subject. Many Focus insiders also don't believe that such a thing would ever occur, citing the simple fact that just as no one else has proven to be another James Dobson, neither has his son.

But stranger things have happened, and the strides that Ryan has made in ministry over the last few years have changed his handicap in this matter considerably. Besides, no other worthy successor to James Dobson has become obvious. And there is a precedent of sorts within high-profile ministries for Ryan Dobson to succeed his father. It is the case of Franklin Graham, the oldest son of Billy Graham. Once a college dropout, Franklin Graham says that he perceived a call on his life to succeed his father and executed a radical about-face. Suddenly Graham was appearing on *The Tonight Show* in his motorcycling outfit, cutting a more contemporary figure than his father. Still, a dignified Franklin Graham demonstrated highly effective leadership of the international relief agency Samaritan's Purse. Then he garnered international headlines in the wake of 9/11 by branding Islam "an evil religion." While faltering from Parkinson's disease, Billy Graham has lead occasional crusades even in his eighties; however, the transition of the Billy Graham Evangelistic Association to Franklin Graham is clearly well underway.

Naturally, because the public feels such ownership of Focus on the Family, there are expectations about what Ryan Dobson should be doing and how he should be doing it—and he chafes at those. He says some strangers have gotten angry with him because they don't feel he has expressed enough ambition about succeeding his father. And in the evangelically flush culture of Colorado Springs, both Danae and Ryan have garnered significant local media attention, even though neither one has ever been a long-term resident of the area.

In 2001, for example, the *Gazette* calculated Ryan's earnings from Focus by using records that the not-for-profit organization must file with the federal government. It showed his earnings that year at about $34,000 in independent-contract work, hardly the stuff of scandal. In the same article, the *Gazette*'s beat reporter on Focus expressed the certainty that neither of the Dobson children would be taking over Focus.

"I just figured a long time ago that I'm not going to be most people's idea of James Dobson's son, and I'm sure I'm not that," Ryan says. "That's okay, because God told me that's okay. And people will figure that out and be okay with it themselves and we'll get along; or they won't."

Yet even though he's not following a diagram from Focus's playbook, Ryan is already reaching the twenty-something audience that Focus has targeted as absolutely crucial. And at the end of a conversation about James Dobson's legacy, Ryan does warm a bit to the thought of someday treading the same ever-narrowing path toward righteousness that was hacked out by his great-great-grandfather, beaten down by his great-grandfather, grooved by his grandfather, and paved by his father.

"I know now what God had ordained for my life—the legacy of James Dobson Sr. and of James Dobson Jr., my dad, who talks to 2.8 million people a day," he says. "There's a legacy of sorts in that I definitely feel called into the ministry. I have no idea where that's going to go. But the difference between me and my dad in some ways is very slight."

And representative of other Focus insiders with similar views, Larimore opines that the "saga of Franklin and Billy Graham is incredibly parallel" to that of the Dobson men. "They're also very different people, like the Grahams, but equally passionate." Larimore says he thought it "would be a good thing if the Lord led" Ryan to probe the possibility of taking over for his father some day. Were both Ryan and Danae "led to be a part of Focus on the Family," Larimore concludes, "my sense is they would have a dramatic impact."

Upon further reflection, however, Ryan backs away from comparisons with his father and the possibility of a calling to succeed him in a recognizable way. He just doesn't have the same background, he notes. And philosophically, he believes that orchestrated passings of the baton are a bad idea because ministries aren't truly dynastic—even Focus on the Family.

"God created one James Dobson for a reason," Ryan says. "Focus is here for a season. I shouldn't pick it up."

His father agrees. "Ryan and Danae are forging their own ministries, which is as it should be," Dobson says. "To install one of them at the head of this vast organization would be unfair to them and unwise for Focus on the Family. That will never happen."

❦

So as Focus on the Family searched for the missing piece of its succession strategy, it became apparent that both the horse race and family-legacy strategies faced limitations. "The problem with succession," Hodel says, "is that there isn't another James Dobson out there. There is no way that we can replicate James Dobson. Therefore, if that's our model for succession, we are doomed to failure."

Instead, Dobson and Hodel formulated a bold yet remarkably simple alternative: a third way that would be built around an as-yet unexplored strategy. *The successor to James Dobson,* Focus's leadership decided, *is going to be James Dobson.*

"Focus on the Family needs to become the repository of the wit and wisdom of James Dobson, and the communicator of it," Hodel says. "We have his views and his speeches and his writing based on his commitment to Scriptures that cover almost everything that the family could encounter, at least to this date. These are essentially unchanging truths. They may need to be packaged a little differently, and lead to other ministry thrusts. But fundamentally, there is no reason for that to change any more than Scripture changes."

Dobson notes that "the post-Dobson era isn't my problem, and it shouldn't be." Yet, he says, "If the ministry can make effective use of my teachings and my ideas and illustrations through the last twenty-six years on into the future, that's fine. I've addressed just about everything relative to the family at this point. I'd hate to see it go the way of all flesh."

There aren't many precedents—maybe none—for attempting this kind of multimedia, living-legacy, wit-and-wisdom strategy. None of the great evangelists, preachers, or Christian media kingpins of the late twentieth century offer a model because almost all of them are not only still alive but also very much in business. But Focus's brain trust has forged ahead, confident that the wit-and-wisdom approach might work for several solid reasons. First, in a way, Dobson already has been using this approach. Focus counts heavily on wisdom that he formulated long ago. Its continued appropriateness is integral to many aspects of the ministry, such as the building blocks of Dobson's written thoughts that correspondents use to construct answers to letter writers seeking advice.

"The correspondence system is a direct reflection of Jim Dobson," Hodel says. "The astonishing thing is that people can't find many inconsistencies between what he said twenty-five years ago and what he's saying now."

Second, Dobson always tries to avoid dating his material whenever possible and works assiduously to update books and other output that require it. In the past decade or so, he has already written new versions of three of his original best-selling books, including *The New Strong-Willed Child,* which was published in 2004.

Third, on his own initiative, Dobson has already launched an effort to create new materials that combine old highlights with fresh output, producing finished results with a deliberately timeless quality. More time for creative pursuits has given Dobson leeway to come up with more such materials. For example, Dobson has already been working on a project called *You and Your Child,* a curriculum consisting of thirty-eight videos that update all of his early work on child development and child rearing, while adding some animation, interviews with parents, and snippets of Dobson himself.

Fourth, Hodel is convinced that new digital technology will allow Focus to create and manipulate virtual replications of James Dobson that will help make the wit-and-wisdom strategy perpetually successful. He has in mind a much broader and more sophisticated version of what was attempted by the ministry of J. Vernon McGee, one of the era's great expository radio preachers who died in 1988. Because the drawling Texan's method was simply to go through the entire Bible from front to finish, book by book, chapter by chapter, his organization was able to continue to provide the half-hour tapes of McGee's sermons as if he were still alive. And by excising the clearly dated references in his programs, McGee's ministry was able to continue posthumously well into the new millennium.

Perhaps, Hodel says with a chuckle, digital manipulation could even help Focus modernize Dobson's first video series, *Focus on the Family*. One of Dobson's favorite bits of self-deprecation is to point out how strange the wide ties and long sideburns that he wore back then appear today. "Except for that, those videos are timeless. But with the increasing technological capabilities to colorize movies and morph people," Hodel jokes, "it's probably even possible to shorten his sideburns and narrow his ties.

"Our mission," Hodel explains, "is to evangelize the world by encouraging and supporting the family, and I think that the future lies with an organization that continues to propound the views of James Dobson. So I'm hoping that our other voices can be increasingly steeped in how Jim would have answered this question or that question, and their writings measured against it, and incorporate references to it. We would be spared this horrible problem of trying to shift our constituency."

This third way could carry inherent problems, including the "dangers of falling into the cult of the personality," says Hodel. "We'd have to make sure to avoid that by always tying everything back to Scripture, as Dr. Dobson has done."

This strategy also puts shackles on other voices that remain in the ministry. If the interactions of Focus's other spokesmen with the news media and other outside constituencies "are only those that involve the recitation of a core orthodoxy, such as only from the works of Dr. Dobson, then people who can do that would be the equivalent of the press secretary at the White House," Larimore says. "But if Focus desires to have interaction with the public, both general and Christian, that allows spontaneous questions and answers and rapid responses to issues, then it has to have spokespeople who have the ability to do that—sort of like a [former Secretary of State] Colin Powell or a [Secretary of Defense] Donald Rumsfeld to President Bush. There is more fluidity with the latter. They are at a different level professionally and in leadership."

In a significant departure from when Larimore and Maier arrived, in 2003 the ministry switched to a strategy that disallows such "minor prophets," as one Focus insider says. "We didn't want other experts commenting on things and making new 'policy,' maybe about things that Dr. Dobson hasn't even commented on yet."

Larimore says that the wit-and-wisdom strategy also will pose a continual challenge—and one that will grow over time—of trying to ensure that the views of a retired or deceased Dobson still make sense. Though Focus will always hew to the biblical and moral principles that underlie everything Dobson teaches, new issues inevitably will arise that will challenge the application of those principles. Consider, for example, the difficulties that even Dobson had in coming up with Focus's positions on some aspects of stem-cell research in 2001. It could also be a mistake to assume that Dobson's persona will continue to be the best tool for reaching generations of parents that are further and further removed from his own.

But if Focus can effectively deal with such factors, Hodel says, Dobson's body of work should grow in significance rather than diminish, even in the years after he retires and has died. Despite the recent controversy over whether the handlers of C. S. Lewis's works have allowed new interpretations to water down the vibrant Christianity that was integral to his worldview, for example, Lewis "has a broader reach now than when he died" in the sixties, Hodel notes. "That's because someone has seen to it that his ideas will be communicated to the world as C. S. Lewis's views.

"That's what we could do with James Dobson."

ఎా ఎా ఎా ఎా

Michael Medved offers other examples and another view of the possibility of success for this approach. Look at Oprah Winfrey, he says, when pondering whether it's possible for Dobson's body of work to serve as the basis not only of a legacy but also of a continuing ministry even after he's gone. Winfrey, the talk-show host turned multimedia megapersonality and avatar of a big-tent spirituality, is already a living legend with her own movie production company, popular magazine, and a now-informal book club that can make a new title an instant best seller.

"In a sense, she's the anti-Dobson," says Medved. "At some different level, yes, she's a good person or trying to be a good person or at least struggling with it in a New Agey way. She sells out huge venues at $185 a ticket for people basically to listen to Oprah talking about life and what's important. The interesting thing is that this is a lady who's never been married, is terminally single, and now never will have kids—telling people how to live life."

Follow Medved's logic lower down the totem pole of virtue, to what he calls "the dark side of the force: another 'doctor,' who happened to be a doctor of lepidopterology [the study of butterflies], Alfred Kinsey," founder of the Kinsey Institute. "He never trained as a psychologist or physiologist, never studied people at all, never had an academic background in people, and was as personally corrupt as possible. He created all this fake science, such as the canard that 10 percent of the population is gay based on a survey where about 30 percent of the respondents were prisoners. Yet he left behind the Kinsey Institute, which is still very much alive and still has this poisonous, disgusting, malign influence years and years after his death—and he was the subject of a 2004 movie starring Liam Neeson. [Kinsey] was a liar, a pervert, and a child abuser, a really horrible guy. But he's a huge force long after his death.

"If evil and corruption can continue to redound so long after the death of a very, very bad man, surely it's possible that his sanity and decency can continue to resonate long after the departure of a very, very good man like James Dobson."

᠊᠊᠊᠊᠊᠊

If the wit-and-wisdom strategy is going to work, Dobson's *Bringing Up Boys* video series may be a prototype for how Focus plans to make that happen. The eleven-part *Boys* series, taped on Focus's campus in Colorado Springs, affirmed one more time that Dobson's old formula for making presentations is effective even with younger parents who grew up with the quick pace and frequent cuts of modern TV shows, movies, and even video games.

Though more than twenty years older than when he filmed the original *Focus* series, Dobson again was clothed in a light suit, wearing a tie, standing effortlessly erect behind a simple wooden lectern with his outline in front of him. The audience was packed in, alert, and responsive.

And within the first several minutes, it was clear that Dobson had the audience in the palm of his hand, following a plot that he has used hundreds of times in a variety of media. His goal was to drive home quickly and effectively the point that boys really *are* different from girls despite the culture's efforts over the previous generation to prove otherwise. He began with a wry story about an anonymous four-year-old boy, then followed up with another humorous tale. "Everybody's got a boy story," he said, "and I'd like to hear yours.

"Just keeping them alive is often a challenge," he continued. Then Dobson offered a story about his son as a four-year-old, running through their backyard in Arcadia with his eyes closed, then tripping and falling on a metal stake that gashed his forehead almost to the bone and missed piercing his eye by a fraction of an inch. "Ryan knew the emergency room staff at the hospital quite well by the time he'd grown up," Dobson said. Next, he backed up to a story about himself as a ten-year-old boy, a time when he fantasized about becoming a real-life Tarzan but crashed painfully to the ground at the end of a rope that he had tied to a tree limb—and then left too long.

Any student of Dobson could have anticipated what was coming up: an anecdote about how his father was a red-blooded American boy, too. In Dobson Sr.'s case, the proof was that he'd taken a dare from his buddies, tried to crawl through a narrow length of pipe that was nearly a block long, and then got stuck at the shoulders for a distressing length of time before finally wriggling his way not only out of the cylinder but also out of big trouble with his parents. "It was another event in the life of a boy; you all have them too," he said.

Having softened up his audience with stories that connected them to his theme and to his own life, Dobson shifted almost seamlessly to framing the reason that he was talking with them in the first place: A secular culture run amok on feminism and liberalism had declared that boys weren't special enough to deserve different treatment from girls, and he was there to fight that notion until the bitter end.

"In the late sixties, a really crazy idea came along, that males and females were identical except for their ability to bear children, and boys and girls were only different to the degree that they had been raised differently," he said. It was called the unisex movement, and it lasted nearly twenty years. Not surprisingly, Dobson's old nemesis, Phil Donahue, had been involved in promoting this outrage. "He was talking over and over on his show about this, and then his wife, Marlo Thomas, wrote a book called *Free to Be You and Me*," whose point, Dobson said, was to shame parents into raising androgynous children. Feminists Gloria Steinem and Germaine Greer, the latter in her book *The Female Eunuch,* joined the fight. "And soon they were pressuring toy manufacturers not to differentiate between boys and girls.

"Listen carefully," Dobson said by way of summarizing his hook. "And why hasn't the media said it? [The] people behind this movement weren't married, or mothers; hadn't raised kids; didn't like men; had no academic training in this field . . . [yet] influenced a whole generation of parents and just about everything else" in the culture, including schools and the entertainment industry, to believe a hugely destructive lie—"that boys and girls are identical."

Ten-and-a-half videos and dozens more anecdotes later, Dobson the Orator remained at the top of his game. It was the sort of performance that made it clear why the visage of James Dobson will forever represent Focus on the Family.

CHAPTER TWENTY-FOUR

NO SMALL FEAT

*He's been open and honest all the way
through, and he's seen discouragement
and fought through it and faced the
wind. And he's still soaring above it.*

Jay Dickey, former Republican
congressman from Arkansas,
on James Dobson

One of James Dobson's greatest heroes is Winston Churchill.
He has devoured a number of biographies about the mid-
twentieth century statesman, and he has visited Churchill's
home in Chartwell and the bunkers in London from which Churchill
directed much of the war. A portrait of Churchill hangs prominently in
Dobson's office at Focus.

Dobson admires the Churchillian doggedness and determination
that so inspired the British people during the darkest days of the Ger-
man bombing and ultimately led them to share in the Allied victory. He
has also come to appreciate the savvy that allowed Churchill to assess
the wide swings in circumstances at different points of World War II
and then to shape and deliver rhetoric that helped secure the only acceptable outcome in one of history's most important conflicts.

As an acknowledged leader and key rhetorician on one side in a different—although in many ways just as significant—kind of war, Dobson personally identifies with what Churchill went through. He feels
passionate about the state and the future of the traditional family and,
therefore, is sometimes not sure how to depict it. "The struggle to preserve parenthood and the family is complex and multifaceted, in constant change," he says. "Let's compare it with World War II. The Battle
of Britain resulted in London's being devastated, and many thousands

of innocent people were killed. It was a terrible time. But it also was a turning point in the war, because Hitler failed to bring the British people to their knees.

"So . . . whatever you discuss first sets the tone for your overall assessment of the situation. The same is true of the fight against cancer: You can talk about the millions of people who are dying horribly, but also about some encouraging signs in medical research."

The collective status of the North American family, Dobson says, remains mixed as well and is wide open to arguments about whether the glass at the moment is half-full or half-empty. The glow of conservative Republicans' victories in the 2004 elections is coloring his view more optimistically these days than in a long time. But Dobson believes the ultimate fate of the traditional family still very much hangs in the balance.

In fact, many serious followers of Dobson's rhetoric, and indeed some close allies, assume that his net view of the situation tips toward the bearish. He has given them plenty of reason to make that assumption over the years, partly because in trying to rally defenses of the family, he must constantly make the case that the family urgently needs defending. But Dobson surprised even some Focus insiders by sounding decidedly pessimistic about the nation's moral climate at what could have been a moment for pure celebration: his address at the climactic observance of Focus's twenty-fifth anniversary weekend on July 27, 2002.

"We're in a moral free fall," Dobson told the crowd of more than fourteen thousand, in a moment that sobered them. "Wherever you stick the thermometer into the American culture, you'll find corruption—the Catholic church, the Internet, the gambling addiction that's taking place. . . . Whatever it is, [it's] wherever you test the system. The Abercrombie & Fitch catalog for your kids has nudity and distasteful pictures. They're attractive, but their purpose is to twist your children. Wherever you look, you'll see it."

Dobson later explained that he took such an approach that night partly out of a desire to remind Focus employees and supporters not to get too self-congratulatory over the organization's milestone—that traditional moral values still face daunting challenges, particularly those affecting the family. Yet Dobson reiterates that he does harbor fundamental reasons for expressing such a dark view of the difficulties of the family, believing there is "every indication that [the family] is continuing to lose ground, that the family as we know it is dying. That's what I reported at the twenty-fifth [anniversary], and it's more true now than it was then."

The pessimistic case, Dobson says, begins with the simple statistics showing that the traditional nuclear family—a man and a woman united by marriage, raising their own children—is crumbling as the basic building block of North American society. In 1960, the zenith of the *Ozzie and Harriet* era, nearly half of all American households included at least one child. But today children occupy fewer than one-third of U.S. households, and Census Bureau projections suggest that by 2010 households with children will comprise little more than one-quarter of American households, the lowest share in a century. In turn, the most important reason for that trend is the growing endangerment of marriage, the institution Dobson believes is the sustenance of every other vital aspect of the traditional family. One particularly startling statistic cited by Dobson: Since 1960 there has been an 850 percent increase in the number of cohabiting couples who live with children, and an estimated 40 percent of all children are expected to spend some time in a household with a cohabiting couple during their growing-up years.[1]

The routine acceptance of divorce has been particularly destructive to the institution of marriage, he says, and to the long-term mental and physical well-being of the offspring of divorced couples. But the troubles of childhood aren't restricted to the children of divorce, Dobson notes, in part because of a contemporary American culture whose norms, demands, and expectations hammer away even at families that are relationally healthy. These include entertainment media and a public education system that use both blatant and subtle messages to deteriorate the traditional family by devaluing it.

Even more important, Dobson told Larry King on the host's TV show in March 2002, "The biggest problem facing the family is nothing more complex than fatigue and time pressure. We are working ourselves to death, literally. We don't have time for each other. We don't have time to talk together and be together. We don't even have time to have sex together. We don't even know each other and we frequently don't know our kids. Then what happens is you begin to drift."

Another facet of the disintegration of traditional marriage and family arrangements, Dobson observes, is the fast upward spiral in both voluntary and involuntary single parenthood. The proportion of un-wed births among American women aged twenty to twenty-four rose to 61.7 percent in 2001 from 48.2 percent just eleven years earlier.[2] Dobson blames the media for much of this, pointing to the many televi-sion programs and movies that coronate volitional single motherhood as an acceptable, even laudable, lifestyle. While many divorced or un-married mothers have no choice but to go it alone, many of today's Hollywood celebrities have the economic luxury of deciding to birth and raise kids without a father—and are proud to tout it. According to Dobson, this represents the fulfillment of what then vice president Dan Quayle warned about (and was pilloried for) in a May 1992 speech in which he criticized the title character of the TV sitcom *Murphy Brown* for "mocking the importance of fathers by bearing a child alone and calling it just another 'lifestyle choice.'" Dobson and his mother invol-untarily endured eleven years without Dobson Sr. around the house much of the time, but it never was a circumstance they would have cho-sen.

"The discouraging fact is that the younger generation is being effec-tively propagandized and manipulated to accept all of these things, in-cluding cohabitation, promiscuous sex, condom usage, and the homosexual lifestyle," Dobson said recently.

And while the typical mother is moving into an even more intense relationship with her offspring in part because of the rise of single motherhood, Dobson notes, the opposite has been occurring with America's fathers. The proportion of children living apart from their biological fathers has increased sharply, to 24 percent in 2000 from 17 percent in 1960.[3] This trend has been unmistakable even as a growing minority of fathers are highly involved in their children's lives, many because of Dobson's direct influence on their approach to parenting.

But Dobson saves his sharpest alarm for the rising support of gay marriage in North America. "My greatest concern is for the relentless attack by homosexual activists who are determined to destroy the in-stitution of marriage," he said in 2003. "And there are very few conser-vative leaders who are willing to stand up against this most powerful lobby, which has the passionate support of every branch of the media." Just after the decision, in his speech in Montgomery, Alabama, at the pro–Ten Commandments rally in August 2003, Dobson noted that "the majority on the [U.S. Supreme] court appears to be headed straight as an arrow for the sanction and supposed constitutionality of same-sex marriage."[4] And even after President Bush's reelection, there clearly was no guarantee that the composition of the U.S. Supreme Court would change significantly enough, and quickly enough, to divert that arrow from its mark.

The undeniable reality of it all seems to mock everything that Dobson has worked for. But fortunately it comprises only half the picture he sees.

Largely in the background, Dobson has also been formulating a much more optimistic view of the future of the American family, based on "some encouraging developments." There is a movement back toward full-time motherhood, for example. The divorce rate has continued its slow but steady decline since reaching its height in the early eighties, and violent crime and drug use by youth have dropped or remained relatively stable in recent years.[5] From 2000 to 2002, the percentage of children in two-married-parent families inched up nationwide by about one point, from 68 percent to 69 percent—the first reversal in decades. Teen pregnancy and birth rates have steadily declined for the past twelve years, thanks variously to increasing devotion to abstinence and to birth control among youths. In 2003, there were 41.7 births per 1,000 kids between the ages of fifteen and nineteen, down dramatically from 61.8 in 1991, according to the U.S. Centers for Disease Control and Prevention. And the percentage of teens who have had sexual intercourse dropped from 54.1 percent in 1991 to 49.9 percent in 1999.[6] The mostly strong economy and welfare-reform measures over the last decade, which enabled and encouraged families to fend together as they stayed together, also have contributed to the basis of Dobson's positive thesis.

This more sanguine perspective also gives some credit to the work that he, Focus, and other evangelical Christian leaders and organizations have been doing over the last generation. They have worked hard to get a hearing for family-friendly viewpoints not only by the culture at large but, more important, by individuals as they make moral and ethical decisions affecting themselves and their families. Also, Dobson believes, the family recently has gotten help from an unexpected source: the secular news and entertainment media. "The rise of the conservative talk show appears to be having a rather dramatic effect on millions people who in the past would have heard only liberal nonsense," he says, citing

Fox News and Internet-based information outlets as examples. "And some of that influence is changing the way people view morality, marriage and children, and other factors related to the family. The net effect of these alternative information sources, I'm convinced, is a rise in conservative values."

On the issue of abortion, for example, "pro-lifers gradually are winning the battle for the hearts and minds of the people," Dobson says, despite the continued support of abortion by liberal elites in the news and entertainment media, education, and elsewhere. The U.S. abortion rate itself has fallen to its lowest level in twenty-nine years, plunging more than 19 percent between 1973, when *Roe v. Wade* legalized abortion, and 2000, according to the Alan Guttmacher Institute, a liberal "family-planning" research organization.[7]

Moreover, an attitudinal shift against abortion appears to be portending even greater gains in the future. More than 20 percent of Americans had views that were less favorable toward abortion than they held ten years ago, according to a Zogby International poll released in January 2003.[8] This pro-life shift was most pronounced among younger Americans, with one-third of those aged eighteen to twenty-nine saying that abortion should never be legal, while about 23 percent of those ages thirty to sixty-four held the same view and 20 percent of those over sixty-five years old also agreed with that statement. That finding was echoed, Dobson notes, by a *Time/CNN* poll around the same time that found 53 percent of women of childbearing age, eighteen to thirty-nine, "saying flat out that abortion is murder. That wouldn't have happened five or ten years ago," he says. "And the younger generation is rejecting abortion at a more rapid pace than would have been anticipated as baby boomer women who came through the late sixties and bought into that extremely liberal lifestyle are getting older. Something's happening here."

Actually, given his penchant for studying history, it's characteristic that Dobson favors another major historical development as a metaphor for his alternative, more hopeful thesis about the eventual fate of the family in Western culture. "In 1988," he says, "there was no indication that the Soviet Union was going to collapse. Great diplomats and historians alike—no one—saw it. But it was a complete house of cards: What looked to be a monolith that threatened the entire free world was actually corrupt and bankrupt and disintegrating, but people didn't see it. I believe that liberalism is like that."

Michael Medved, talk show host and perhaps the nation's leading spokesman for Jewish conservatism, explains this dynamic another way. Profamily and antifamily forces are "like two express trains speeding in opposite directions, and the center cannot hold. I don't think that we're about to see the collapse of the family as we know it; but we're also not going to see the end of the other train right away either. Once the squishy center of Americans get on board one train or another, we'll see that the numbers on the express train to sanity will be so much higher than those that get on the other train. And that other train will grind to a halt or fall off a cliff. In any event, it'll look somehow less formidable than it does today."

More prognosticators have begun to express the same hope in the wake of the 2004 election results, which seemed to constitute among other things a statement by the American public against further encouragement of moral decline by the nation's laws, politicians, entertainers, and culture.

These positive prospects also depend on even wider communication, from more sources, of exactly the kind of advice and encouragement that Dobson and Focus on the Family have been dispensing for nearly thirty years. That's the main reason he has dramatically stepped up the frequency and breadth of his appearances on national cable television in recent years. He's more motivated by the fact that Shirley has urged him to broaden his exposure than by Bruce Wilkinson's directive in 2002. But it's clear that Dobson is determinedly raising his profile via cable television.

The tens of millions of Americans who regularly see Dobson on these programs—including not only *Larry King Live*, but also *Scarborough Country*, *Hannity & Colmes*, and others—are a growing part of his audience.

Dobson's greater visibility on cable TV is as strategic as other major moves he has made over the years to broaden his exposure and influence. Also, the social issues in which Dobson specializes have found greater currency in the news-media climate, and demand for the voluble Dobson has been high.

Cable TV is a handy venue for Dobson for several reasons. First, it isn't network television, where Dobson's distrust of journalists and dislike of the sound-bite format provide little temptation. Second, Joe Scarborough, Sean Hannity, and Bill O'Reilly are happy to have Dobson on their shows frequently. Third, these hosts generally allow Dobson to occupy either his own segment or the entire hour. Certainly, part of the reason Dobson favors having the stage to himself is that he doesn't have to brook debate with anyone.

But it isn't that simple. "So much of what is done on cable when they bring in a bunch of people with differing opinions turns into a circus," Dobson says. "Instead of an actual debate where there is an exchange of ideas, there is shouting and a *Crossfire* kind of thing, and it's disrespectful. I don't want to be a part of it. And why should I, if I can be on myself and hold the whole show?"

Even with such ground rules, Hannity says, Dobson "always has strong ratings" on his show. He also has a way of disarming Alan Colmes, the show's resident liberal, whose own affability seems to mesh with Dobson's playfulness and allows them to disagree without gritting their teeth at each other. "There's no equivocation with Dr. Dobson," Hannity says. "He has strong opinions and the ability to articulate those opinions, and he doesn't back down. People admire that conviction, agree or disagree."

But ultimately, of course, a real reversal of fortune for the American family depends on millions of individual, life-changing decisions that his ministry facilitates every day. Dobson understands that even his apple-pie-à-la-mode form of persuasion is no antidote to the hardened hearts of culture and a society that has rejected what it considers the strictures of Judeo-Christian morals and ethics. "While culturally and politically we may see victory soon," he says, "ultimately, only a spiritual awakening will save us and preserve the family."

 споскои

No doubt, Dobson's impact on individual lives and families will prove his greatest legacy, and the collective benefits of his timeless advice on relationships probably will grow in the years ahead even as he is destined to fade someday from his current pivotal spot in the public arena. Yet regardless of what direction the institution of the family takes, there is little debate that Dobson has played a monumental role—perhaps even the single greatest individual part—in whatever vitality the family has retained in the cultural and political realms at the beginning of the twenty-first century.

Dobson himself is hesitant to discuss the impact of his ministry and modest in the self-assessment that he does offer. "Without being falsely humble," he avers, "I've probably played a minor role in the grand scale of things. I'm sure I have helped to reinforce conservative Christian values at a time when there were few alternative voices out there. Through the seventies and eighties, I had an impact on those of Christian perspective. But as for what difference that impact made, someone else will have to make that evaluation."

Many give Dobson much more credit than he claims for himself. "It's unclear what the long-term effects are, but the arguments of conservative Christians are taken seriously now," says Professor John Green of the University of Akron, an expert on evangelical politics and culture. "I doubt very much if conservative Christians and Dobson will ever get everything they want; ultimately, that's the nature of living in a pluralistic society. But at least their arguments are out there now, and [Dobson] deserves a great deal of credit for making it happen."

Senator James Talent calls Dobson "the most influential and respected leader on public policy issues in the [evangelical] community." The Missouri Republican says Dobson's status reflects, among other things, the fact that "he knows what's going on in Washington and the players there, but he also knows where listeners and people who follow Focus on the Family are coming from. If you want to know what the evangelical community thinks, he's the guy to talk to."

According to Dobson, Talent, who is Jewish, "found a personal relationship with Jesus Christ while listening to a *Focus on the Family* broadcast. At the end of an interview with Dr. Luis Palau, I suggested that those who were driving in a car and didn't know Jesus pull off the road and give their hearts to him. Talent did just that, and has been a born-again Christian from that moment to now."

Kansas Senator Sam Brownback entered the Senate in 1996, he says, "when the Republicans were still dominated by more of the business wing of the party. They just tolerated social conservatives. But today, the GOP caucus is a solidly social-conservative caucus, a strong majority that has embraced the desire to carry this movement forward." Speaking from Washington, D.C., he adds: "I am here, and we're engaged in culture-war issues, and we're winning some of them, in no small part because of James Dobson."

While the steadfastness of his convictions continually loses Dobson style points with some evaluators and at times diminishes his effectiveness in the political realm, it also continues to be the most remarkable and differentiating characteristic of his leadership in the marketplace of ideas. "He's extraordinarily principled," says Steve Reinemund, Dobson's friend and chief executive officer of PepsiCo, Inc. "He doesn't shoot from the hip, but he thinks through issues and understands why he believes what he believes, and that perspective sometimes ends up being one of the bookends that can be helpful to me in framing an issue."

"There's a sense of uncompromising integrity about him," says Rabbi Daniel Lapin. "He's not trying to win political position or social approval; he's a man who stands for something in a very unambiguous kind of way, and that's primarily what contributes to his effectiveness. I've certainly never seen him give any impression at all of weighing out the implications or political fallout from a statement; he says what his passion and his faith compel him to say. This might well create difficulties for what in the political world would be his handlers, I don't doubt. But I also think it's what endears him literally to millions and millions of people."

Given that, it's even reasonable to compare Dobson to an early-nineteenth century figure who risked as much in the public square on behalf of Christian principles as nearly anyone in the last few hundred years: William Wilberforce, the British statesman, whose resolute opposition to slavery finally wore down its supporters in 1807, when the House of Commons voted overwhelmingly to abolish the slave trade. Unlike Wilberforce, Dobson isn't a statesman; and history certainly will render its own verdict on the comparison. But clearly, Dobson and Wilberforce were woven from the same moral fiber.

"In the case of every question of political expediency, there appears to me room for the consideration of times and seasons," said Wilberforce, who embraced evangelical Anglicanism and then struggled politically against the barbarism of slavery for twenty years before the vote that vindicated him. "At one period, under one set of circumstances, it may be proper to push, at another, and in other circumstances, to withhold our efforts . . . [B]ut in the present instance, where the actual commission of guilt is in question, a man who fears God is not at liberty . . . Be persuaded then that I shall never make this grand cause the sport of caprice, or sacrifice it to motives of political convenience or personal feeling."[9]

That sounds very much like Dobson's conduct and words amid the sometimes smoldering, sometimes searing heat of any number of social-issue debates over the last ten to fifteen years. Some observers say Dobson reminds them of Francis Schaeffer. Schaeffer's 1976 book *How*

Should We Then Live? The Rise and Decline of Western Thought and Culture, launched an entire new era of effective evangelical criticism of modern Western philosophy and practice. Dobson sometimes sounds very much like Schaeffer in his prophetic pronouncements. But while Dobson is no less intellectually gifted, says Ken Connor, former president of the Family Research Council, he communicates similar ideas even more effectively than Schaeffer.

"[Schaeffer] had a great influence on me," Dobson says. "He was so right on target with where we've ended up today. He was the first one to see the links between abortion, infanticide, and euthanasia." Dobson never met Schaeffer, but he could have. In 1984, when Schaeffer was ailing badly with cancer and living in Santa Barbara, California, Dobson had an opportunity to visit this giant of Christian thought and record a *Focus* broadcast with him. "But I just didn't have the time to go up there; it would have cost me a whole weekend," Dobson remembers. "So I didn't go, and I've regretted it ever since. He died right after that. I could have been honored with some of his last thoughts."

⋘⋙

Actually, over the last ten years, many see James Dobson as a *primus inter pares*—first among equals. He has been called the most influential advocate of the traditional family, and many believe he's the unparalleled leader of American Christian conservatism—outshining Charles Colson, Pat Robertson, and even Billy Graham among what might be called the Big Four of popular modern evangelicalism. That evaluation takes into account not only their regard within the evangelical community but also their reputation outside of it. "Jim is clearly the most influential evangelical leader in North America," Colson himself said in late 2004.

One of the subtle strengths of the evangelical movement in North America is that it responds to multiple, overlapping leaders here on earth while recognizing the ultimate headship of Jesus Christ. So in addition to their own church pastors, individual conservative Christians typically turn to a variety of prominent preachers, authors, and other interpreters of the faith to inform their views and help them shape their allegiances. And while Americans devote much of their attention to the Big Four, there is also an important second tier of leaders who have not ascended to a higher level either because they remained limited in some way or because they lost a bit of their luster.

Gary Bauer, for example, reached his high-water mark of influence with evangelicals in 2000 when he made a credible run for the Republican nomination for president; he no longer heads a large organization. Ralph Reed made himself a formidable force in Republican politics by heading the Christian Coalition's political wing for several years, but by 2002 he had crept into the background to become a reelection adviser to President Bush. Jerry Falwell, after jump-starting the rise of the movement in the eighties by founding the Moral Majority, has retreated since then under the weight of a media-created caricature that he occasionally lives down to. Conservative Catholic William Bennett generated a huge following among evangelicals with his outspoken support for traditional values and authorship of best sellers such as *The Book of Virtues*—but news-media vetting of his high-stakes gambling habit in 2003 nicked his credibility.

Chuck Swindoll, Bill Hybels, Robert Schuller, Tim LaHaye, Max Lucado, Charles Stanley, John MacArthur, Joyce Meyer, Bruce Wilkinson, and others lead huge churches or multimedia ministries, but they're somewhat confined by their pastoral niches. Pastor Rick Warren's profile has risen considerably as sales of *The Purpose-Driven Life* have soared to rarefied levels, and some secular pundits have bestowed on him the title of America's most influential evangelical. But Warren has yet to produce an encore, and it's too early to determine his staying power. Phyllis Schlafly is the head of her own activist group, Eagle Forum, and has a devoted following, but the architect of conservatism's victory over the Equal Rights Amendment in the seventies doesn't have the media reach of Dobson. A bevy of other experts have tried unsuccessfully to equal Dobson's impact on relational issues without adding the political element, including Dennis Rainey, Gary Smalley, Stephen Arterburn, and John Trent. Other highly influential evangelicals include Josh McDowell, Philip Yancey, and Ron Blue, but they're mostly print personalities. Another of the last true giants of American evangelicalism, Bill Bright, died at the age of eighty-two on July 19, 2003; he was founder of Campus Crusade for Christ, an organization that has been influential in the born-again experiences of millions of Americans, and author of the well-known evangelization tool called the Four Spiritual Laws.

So that leaves the Big Four: Dobson, Colson, Robertson, and Graham. In a way, it could be considered unseemly to argue that any one of them is more influential at this moment than any other—sort of like the apostles quarreling over who's going to be greatest in heaven. Evangelicals wouldn't be where they are today without the contributions of each one of these leaders. And clearly, this is not an argument that these men have about or among one another. The entire discussion makes Dobson uncomfortable, as though "stature" and "greatness" have motivated him for the past twenty-eight years.

But if only to benefit the future of the evangelical Christian movement in North America, it is worth considering the current impact of Dobson and his approach compared with those of the other major leaders of the Christian Right.

Billy Graham is sure to be remembered as the most revered and influential evangelical of the twentieth century, beloved by believers the world over. His star has been dimmed during the last decade only by his declining health, which has led to severe curtailment of his involvement in his globe-trotting crusades and to a growing role in the ministry for his son, Franklin Graham. Yet even at the zenith of his prowess for Christ, Billy Graham was in some ways a leader of narrower scope than any of the other members of the Big Four. For all the public attention accorded to his role as adviser to presidents, beginning with Dwight Eisenhower, Graham always emphasized the spiritual nature of his discussions with the leaders of the free world and mostly left politics and social-issue discussions to the professionals. Now eighty-seven years old, the great evangelist never made a priority of applying the imperatives of the Gospels to public and social policy; Graham was always focused on stirring the individual heart.

Robertson in some ways is the closest parallel to Dobson because the charismatic preacher created not only a multimedia ministry that remains a force, with shows such as *The 700 Club,* but he also deliberately and very effectively entered the public policy arena. Along with Falwell, he did so unapologetically in the eighties; but unlike the Moral Majority, Robertson's political action organization, the Christian Coalition, managed to give evangelical voters a powerful and unprecedented conduit to electoral success. Robertson's own stock as a statesmanlike figure peaked with his run for the presidency in 1988. Since then, he has continued as a mainstay on his own Christian Broadcasting Network.

But Robertson's legitimacy in the eyes of the secular culture always has been suspect and has diminished even more over the years as he has claimed credit for steering hurricanes away from his Virginia Beach, Virginia, headquarters, including Hurricane Gloria, which in 1985 caused millions of dollars of destruction in many states along the East Coast. Robertson and Falwell found agreement with many believers but also made some fellow evangelicals wince when they attributed the 9/11 terrorist attacks partly to God's judgment on secular America. And in the heat of the election season in October 2004, Robertson caused some grief for President Bush when he made a point of saying that he had warned the president before the Iraq war began. Robertson said he had "deep misgivings" about the war and that the Lord had told him it was going to be a "disaster" and a "messy" conflict in terms of casualties.

Dobson and Colson are both known for their ability to understand their times and their ability to reason and communicate with the secular world. As founder and chairman of Prison Fellowship for almost thirty years, Colson has established strong credentials of servant leadership. Having learned to work the Beltway as a Nixon Administration insider (and a Watergate conspirator), Colson enjoys clout about equal to Dobson's in Washington. They complement each other nicely: Colson's lawyerly background, cool reasoning, and deal-making ability, and Dobson's passion, wit, and huge constituency. Thus the two have become effective allies on issues ranging from stem-cell research to federal funding of abstinence programs in Africa.

But they diverge significantly in that Colson is best known for his explication of the Christian worldview and for his strength in apologetics, appealing largely to a relatively intellectual subset of Christians. Dobson, meanwhile, enjoys unparalleled reach with ordinary Americans through his radio broadcasts and other media—and because of the capacity he still wields to create an instant response that will resound in the mahogany-paneled halls of power in the federal government.

"It's because he really used what God gave him not just to proclaim the message of James Dobson and his theology and his plan and his ministry, but rather as a God-given forum to use, educate, drive, motivate— even whip the body sometimes—into a higher state of knowledge and learning," says Alan Sears, president and general counsel of the Alliance Defense Fund. "That's his unique role. And every serious faith community in America that you can think of has a lot to be thankful to him for."

Both within and outside the evangelical culture, Dobson has been increasingly cited as a cultural and political leader. For example, he earned the top honor in the Education and Theology category in a poll in 2000 by iBelieve.com, a leading Christian Web site. Dobson and

Franklin Graham emerged on top in a 2004 poll of the "favorability" of religious leaders conducted among both evangelicals and nonevangelicals by *U.S. News & World Report* and *Religion & Ethics Newsweekly* magazines. Dobson and Graham both scored ratings of about 76 on a scale up to 100, while Robertson scored just 55 and Falwell, 46. Among nonevangelicals, both Dobson and Graham had a mean rating of about 49, while Robertson's was 32 and Falwell's, 26.

"Every other ministry and leader," says Janet Parshall, "is measured by James Dobson." Richard Land, president of the Ethics & Religious Liberty Commission of the Southern Baptist Convention, says that Dobson "is the most influential person in evangelical life in America since Billy Graham, which is a remarkable thing for someone who's not a pastor." Land—who, along with Dobson, was named by *Time* magazine in 2005 as one of America's 25 most influential evangelicals—adds that Dobson "has to be the most influential person in evangelical circles today."[10] One anonymous congressional chief of staff called Dobson "an institution that you have to compare with the National Rifle Association, Rush Limbaugh, the Chamber of Commerce, and the National Right to Life Committee."

Another valuable perspective on Dobson's status comes from Michael Medved, a sharp cultural analyst who cut his teeth on movie criticism and is a close observer of evangelicalism as well as an ally of conservative Christians on many issues. While he concedes that Dobson dusts it up from time to time with evangelical allies, Medved has noticed that Dobson "doesn't really have many critics or enemies within the conservative community. It's tough to think of anyone else who has taken comparably vigorous cultural and political positions without alienating big chunks of the base. But he's never done that. Among people who would range from moderate to very conservative, Dr. Dobson is as close to a universally admired figure as this culture possesses."

Even—or especially—Dobson's enemies recognize with whom they're dealing. "Probably more than any other religious Right person at the moment," says Carol Keys, director of research for People for the American Way, "he has the ability to get people to do what he wants done."

Her boss, Ralph Neas, president of People for the American Way, echoes Keys' assessment. "There is no question," Neas told the *New York Times* in May 2004, "that James Dobson is the most powerful and most influential voice on the religious Right."[11]

CHAPTER TWENTY-FIVE

SLOUCHING TOWARDS GOMORRAH

Me and you and a guy named Lou . . .

Paul Shankin, on the Rush Limbaugh
Show, *December 2003, spoofing the seventies
song, "Me and You and a Dog Named Boo"*

B y his own standards at least, James Dobson spent the summer of
2003 almost languidly, including several weeks in London to
write in isolation, followed by a couple of weeks of sightseeing
around Europe with Shirley and their friends, Herb and Dona Fisher.

But just as he was beginning to enjoy the summer, Dobson's long-
held fears about a final offensive by the homosexual-activist community began coming true in North America. In June, the U.S. Supreme
Court overturned a state sodomy law in *Lawrence v. Texas,* and Ontario's
highest court sanctioned homosexual unions. Once he returned to
Colorado Springs in mid-August, Dobson's slight sense of hiatus came
to an abrupt end as he began to push back against the post-*Lawrence* media offensive by homosexual-marriage advocates.

Renewed aggressiveness by gay and lesbian activists in the wake of
the decisions was willingly facilitated by their allies in the national news
media. Among other manifestations of this, the *Washington Post,* the *New
York Times,* and the *Boston Globe* each failed to cover—according to an
analysis in the *National Review*—Senate debate in September of the
Federal Marriage Amendment, which had become a rallying point for
conservative forces opposed to homosexual nuptials.[1] Andrew
Sullivan, a senior editor of *The New Republic* and a *Time* columnist,
opined in a piece on the *Wall Street Journal* editorial page that American

conservatives should welcome homosexuals' embrace of marriage as constructive for the broader society.[2]

The knee-jerk tendency to sanction "gay marriage" also acquired some momentum from the growing libertarian strain that had developed among Americans toward marriage (in part an echo of the attitude that prevailed about abortion through most of the last three decades). According to a 2001 Gallup Poll, 80 percent of men and women aged twenty to twenty-nine agreed that marriage was nobody's business but that of the two people involved, and 45 percent said that the government shouldn't be involved in licensing marriages.

There was even a continuing tendency by some Christian leaders to characterize the threat as more of a zephyr than a hurricane.

It took Dobson until September to hit his stride on the issue, when he used his monthly newsletter to lay out his case. He was characteristically explicit about his fervent opposition to what was happening—and chillingly alarmist about its potential consequences. "They're talking not about gay marriage," he said on a *Larry King Live* appearance on September 5, "but about destroying this institution and then remaking it without commitment."[3]

From that point on, Dobson remained at the front barricades defending the traditional family in the controversy, fully joined in what promised to be the battle of his life—or, as the *Wall Street Journal* editorial page termed it, "Roe, the Sequel."[4]

In *Bringing Up Boys*, Dobson provided the most complete explanation yet for his views on the origins of homosexuality and on why its apparent surge is problematic for Christians and for the culture at large. In an eighteen-page section of the book, which was published in 2001, Dobson plainly stated his position on the key issue that underlies the political, psychological, and religious debate over homosexuality: How does one become so inclined? Dobson posited that homosexuality typically isn't "chosen" and said that he didn't blame homosexuals "for being irritated by that assumption."[5]

But at the same time, Dobson said, "there is no evidence to indicate that homosexuality is inherited, despite everything you may have heard or read to the contrary. There are no respected geneticists in the world today who claim to have found a so-called 'gay gene.' Or other indicators of genetic transmission." He cited arguments including the fact that when one identical twin is homosexual, the probability is only 50 percent that the other has the same condition, even though their genetic material is identical. And Dobson said that homosexuality has been shown to be preventable or changeable, as has happened in more than a thousand cases.

He specifically mentioned that of John Paulk, then head of Focus's Love Won Out ministry to gays and lesbians, who was heavily involved in the gay community until "he found forgiveness and healing in a personal relationship with Jesus Christ" in 1987 and married a former lesbian; they had two children and appeared on the cover of *Newsweek*. Despite the fact that Paulk had a highly publicized setback when he was discovered inside a gay bar in Washington, D.C., in September 2000, Dobson said, "John did not return to his former life nor did he have a homosexual encounter."

Even if it could be demonstrated beyond a shadow of a doubt that the disorder is genetic, Dobson said, "We would still want to know, 'So what?'" Men naturally lust after women before and during marriage, he noted, and genetics in part controls vulnerabilities to behaviors including alcohol addiction—but "being genetically inclined to do immoral things does not make them right," he said. "Promiscuity for unmarried heterosexuals is the moral equivalent of promiscuity for homosexuals."[6]

Yet, Dobson noted, such has been the media drumbeat over the last several years that, according to a Harris Poll in February 2000, 35 percent of Americans believed that homosexuality was genetic.[7] "Gay and lesbian organizations and the media have convinced the public that being homosexual is as predetermined as one's race and that nothing can be done about it," Dobson said.[8]

What actually happens, Dobson said, citing work by clinical psychologist Joseph Nicolosi, is that some young children start out with "gender-identity disorder" that is typified by markers such as cross-dressing and a strong preference for playmates of the opposite sex. If left untreated, Nicolosi had concluded, studies show that "pre-homosexual" boys have a 75 percent chance of becoming homosexual or bisexual. The key determinant seemed to be the effectiveness of a boy's relationship with his father. "In fifteen years, I have spoken with hundreds of homosexual men," said Nicolosi, as excerpted by Dobson. "I have never met one who said he had a loving, respectful relationship with his father."[9] In addition, Dobson said, studies indicate that as many as 30 percent of homosexuals said they were exploited sexually as a child, many of them repeatedly.¹⁰

"The bottom line," Dobson continued, "is that homosexuality is not primarily about sex. It is about everything else, including loneliness, rejection, affirmation, intimacy, identity, relationships, parenting, self-hatred, gender confusion, and a search for belonging. This explains why the homosexual experience is so intense—and why there is such anger expressed against those who are perceived as disrespecting gays and lesbians or making their experience more painful."¹¹

At the same time, however, Dobson only had so much sympathy for the pain of homosexuals. Where he drew the line was activism by gay and lesbian groups not only to knock down existing social strictures against homosexual relationships, but also to expand their foothold in the culture by infiltrating and promoting their "lifestyle" in schools, in the Girl Scouts and Boy Scouts, and in other institutions teeming with impressionable youth. Particularly vile, Dobson said, were efforts by pedophilic homosexuals to lower the age of consent across the Western world and to normalize "man-boy love."¹²

"The gay rights movement has said, in effect: 'We don't merely want your tolerance, we demand your *acceptance* and *affirmation*—forcibly, if necessary,'" Dobson was quoted as saying in David Limbaugh's 2003 title, *Persecution: How Liberals Are Waging War against Christianity*. "We will change the laws in order to thrust our lifestyle upon you. But we will not tolerate the views of those who oppose us. We will label anyone who disagrees with our agenda as hateful, bigoted, and homophobic, and on that basis we will endeavor to eradicate all opposing viewpoints from the public square."¹³

Dobson's views on homosexuality aren't completely shared by all his allies. Some are concerned that Dobson's position on homosexuality has polarized Christians and Christian psychologists. Steve Reinemund faults his friend's "rigidity" in dealing with the influence of homosexuals within charitable organizations including the Salvation Army, of which Reinemund was U.S. chairman a few years ago. "Sometimes things aren't as black-and-white as he interprets them," Reinemund says.

Yet others defend the view that Dobson and Focus essentially share on this issue. "They're a lot better than most church groups I'm connected to," says Dr. Jeffrey Satinover, the former Yale University psychiatrist who wrote *Homosexuality and the Politics of Truth*. "In much of the Christian community, there long was a naive point of view that picking homosexuality was like sitting down at a smorgasbord and making a choice. And they believed that you could drop it at will or simply pray it away. But he and Focus understand that it's a very difficult condition—that, while it's treatable, it has to be approached in a certain way."

And on this issue, Dobson is unmoved by praise or criticism anyway, even from close quarters. He was an early articulator of the peril of the advance of homosexual rights, dating back to Focus's support of Amendment 2 in Colorado in the early nineties. A few years later Dobson urged pastors in Colorado Springs to stress the importance of the issue to their congregations, even as gay and lesbian demonstrators held an anti-Focus vigil on the ministry's very campus.

"He was taking all the fire," recalls David Schultheis, Dobson's friend, neighbor, and state representative. "Only a very few pastors took up his call, and some of them began to meet and pray regularly with him." Yet Schultheis was so infuriated at the lack of open support for Dobson on this issue that he wrote a letter and sent it to 120 local pastors of conservative Christian congregations, saying that "it's time we stood with Dr. Dobson and showed our stance against this, or we could lose the battle." Schultheis received only a single reply, from a pastor who explained that "we have enough issues in our own church."

Some are more optimistic about the issue, however. "Increasingly . . . I see that the recent push toward gay marriage is turning the attitudes of many of my colleagues around because of the threat it poses to the very core of the institution of marriage," says long-time Dobson ally Arch Hart. "No longer is this just Dobson's battle. Many . . . are now rallying to defend the rights of family and marriage, and not just in the United States, but around the world."

After thoroughly laying out his rationale in *Bringing Up Boys,* Dobson stepped up efforts to apply it. In March 2002, on a *Focus* broadcast, Dobson urged a boycott of public schools that facilitated the agenda of homosexual activists by sanctioning on-campus support groups and the like, opining that Christians shouldn't "sacrifice our kids" on the altar of educators' liberal propaganda in the hope that the youngsters could resist indoctrination and instead be salt and light to their peers.[14] Focus urged United Way donors nationwide in early 2003 to withhold contributions to Big Brothers Big Sisters of America and its five hundred local affiliates because the group allowed gays and lesbians to mentor young people.[15]

Dobson also used his growing cable-TV presence as an effective platform on the issue of homosexual political and social agendas. Among other things, he described the nightmare scenario he believed would unfold if homosexual activists ever gained the legal leverage afforded by the legitimizing of gay marriage.

"Homosexuals want to, first of all, change the definition of marriage, which is a major problem for us," he said on *Larry King Live* in March 2002, warming quickly to mount a rhetorical defense of his lifelong passion: the traditional nuclear family. "The family was designed for a purpose. And if you go to tampering with it, the whole thing crumbles. See, if two men can be married or two women, where do you stop that? Two men and three women? Four men and one woman? You open the polygamy debate again . . . Let's put it this way. If the family means everything, the family means nothing. If it does not mean one man and one woman . . . you just begin to include a circle of love. Some people would like the family just to be a circle of love. Well, what happens when somebody falls out of the circle of love? Well, then they're not in the family anymore. And it just creates chaos."[16]

Dobson also castigated entertainment media for its increasingly warm and even admiring depictions of the homosexual orientation in TV and movies. On *Larry King Live* in September 2003, Dobson pointed to the danger "[in] this continuing effort to desensitize people to homosexuality, and to set them up for changes in the law and eventually changes in the family." He cited as examples "the kiss" on the *MTV Video Music Awards* earlier in the year between Madonna and Britney Spears, as well as the then-raging popularity of the Bravo! TV series, *Queer Eye for the Straight Guy* (which, by the end of the year, had also begun appearing in reruns on NBC). "You've got [five] homosexual men and one fool that they're working on," Dobson said.[17]

He tried to disabuse King and his viewers of the notion that what homosexual couples desire is only the same basic legal blessing that husbands and wives enjoy: to simply lead lives of devotion to each other. "I don't think they want to be married, most of them," he said. "If you're looking at the literature now, after this success that is being achieved in Canada and the Netherlands and other places . . . and when it is beginning to look like they might achieve gay marriage—now the goal line has moved. Many, many homosexuals are not committed for life," Dobson continued. "The research shows that they have as many as three hundred to one thousand partners in a lifetime. Why would they want to commit themselves to a binding relationship that prevents that?"[18]

In the January 2005 Focus on the Family Action newsletter, Dobson points out that seventeen of seventeen states have voted to approve a constitutional amendment in support of traditional marriage. However, Dobson's pointed dissection of homosexual relationships stemmed from his grave and growing fear that the advance of the radical homosexual agenda could fatally corrode American society from within. Noting in *Boys* that epidemic homosexuality helped bring down Sodom and Gomorrah and the ancient Greek and Roman empires, Dobson warned that, "as the institution of the family continues to unravel, we are laying the foundation for another epidemic like those that have occurred historically."[19]

CHAPTER TWENTY-SIX

MONTGOMERY AND BEYOND

Put it back!

PROTESTERS CHANTING FOR THE RETURN
OF THE TEN COMMANDMENTS TO THE
ALABAMA STATE JUDICIAL BUILDING,
AUGUST 26, 2003

N ever more effective nor busier in his ministry, James Dobson also never came closer to death than during the last week of October 2003. Yet he believed that the Lord preserved his life once again because he still had important work to do on behalf of the family.

In fact, as 2003 waned, a healthy Dobson was convinced that the stakes involved in how he spent his days had never been bigger. And perhaps most crucially, he sometimes felt that he was practically the lone giant standing in the gap.

By the fall of 2003, just a few months after he had passed the position of chief executive officer of Focus on the Family to Don Hodel, the outlines of Dobson's new role were solidifying quickly. While trying to squeeze in time to revise and update *The Strong-Willed Child,* Dobson's self-adopted primary role became rallying national opinion behind him on a number of crucial issues that kept springing up like mushrooms beneath his feet. The more he exhorted and chastised, the more matters arose, it seemed, that demanded exhortation and chastisement.

Some of these concerns were broad and long-term, including the fight against "judicial tyranny" that was spawning outrages such as decisions friendly to gay "marriage" and the closeting of Judge Roy Moore's Ten Commandments monument in Alabama. Other demands required an immediate and intense burst of activity by Dobson: leading the boy-cott against Abercrombie & Fitch; preserving the life of Terri Schiavo, the Florida woman whose husband wanted to remove the feeding tube that was sustaining her; and defending Lt. Gen. William Boykin against persecution by the *Los Angeles Times* and others for speaking openly about how his Christian faith informed his view of the war against terrorism that he was helping direct.

And Dobson was taking on the weight of it all. Among other things, during the second half of 2003, he preempted the *Focus* schedule six-teen times to substitute urgent discussions of breaking political or so-cial issues—the most of any six-month period in recent years. For all of 2003, *Focus* substituted extemporaneous discussions for scheduled shows a total of twenty-eight times, the most since three years in the midnineties when preemptions averaged thirty-seven annually.[1] Begin-ning in late 2003, Dobson also appeared ever more frequently on a lengthening roster of national radio and television programs. All of that activity was only beginning to hint, of course, at the huge role that Dobson would take on for the 2004 campaign season.

"We're involved in an absolutely critical cultural war, and there are very few people who have a commitment to a deeply felt Christian, conservative perspective, and have an activist constituency, who will address these issues as they come up," he explained. "So I get a full schedule of things that I have to do, and then here comes yet another is-sue that I either have to address immediately, I'm told, or it will be lost.

"I'm just so burdened by this," he continued. "I believe that things are in the balance right now. The country is split fifty-fifty, and the me-dia is hammering daily to take it to the left, and very few people are out there fighting daily to defend things. The needs to defend righteousness are so ubiquitous that I'm reminded of the bird dogs that they use for hunting in South Dakota. There are so many pheasants that the dogs go crazy; everywhere they turn their heads, there's a bird, so they use flushing dogs to help them out.

"Sometimes I feel like a bird dog: Every day I have to decide what I can do to make a difference and what I can't do. I don't want to sound like Elijah saying he's the only [righteous] one left, but I do internalize it. I've got to figure out how to live with that."

But Dobson almost hadn't lived at all—with or without his pro-phetic mantle. On October 24, 2003, a time bomb that had been tick-ing in one of his major abdominal arteries for more than a year finally went off, bringing Dobson to a closer brush with death than when he'd had his heart attack, stroke, or prostate cancer. Apparently, a laser used to treat Dobson's prostate in the spring and summer of 2002 had inadvertently created an ulcer the size of a fingernail that contained a tiny artery in his colon. The weak point had gone undetected.

On that Friday evening, Ryan was in town to speak to a crisis pregnancy center in Colorado Springs, and appropriately enough, his father was on hand to introduce him as the speaker. After Ryan finished his talk, Dobson's artery literally exploded.

"It was a really scary thing; it came out of nowhere," he said. Others in the bathroom called 9-1-1, and though Dobson was losing a lot of blood, he remained conscious. Arriving quickly, the emergency medical team had trouble initially both staunching the flow of blood as well as transfusing new blood through an intravenous tube. At one point, Dobson said, his blood pressure was so low that the cuff used to measure it didn't register at all.

Finally a gastroenterologist inserted an IV into Dobson's jugular vein, and pumped in four pints of blood—replenishing the near 50 percent of Dobson's own blood that he had already lost. At the hospital surgeons cauterized the artery; Dobson remained hospitalized through the weekend. One of his biggest regrets was missing his exercise routine on Saturday, which brought to five the total number of days he had missed in the past ten years.

Even more remarkably, by Monday morning Dobson was back home and wading through his stack of paperwork. He was still feeling the aftereffects of the weekend's frightening episode, but Dobson nevertheless was able to take a call from an aide to Secretary of Defense Donald Rumsfeld at 8:30 a.m. about the Boykin case. "And I might be on *Larry King Live* this week to refute Michael Schiavo," he said at midday. "And I'm doing the daily radio broadcast. And Focus has had seven events recently, and I've spoken at two of them. My workload is just very, very heavy, and I have to figure out how to handle it.

"But I've had four major health crises, and the Lord has returned me to the front lines every single time. I appear to be entirely healthy today, so he still must have things for me to do."

∽∾⌒∾∾

Just as he was gearing up to push back against the post-*Lawrence* media offensive by homosexual-marriage advocates, Dobson was confronted by another egregious and urgent example of judicial overreach. A federal judge was trying to remove Judge Roy Moore's monument in Montgomery, Alabama, from public view, but a growing protest by Christians sought to prevent that from happening. In a highly unusual move, a convicted Dobson not only encouraged Focus listeners to make the trek to Alabama, he also made the trip himself.

Over the previous several years, Moore had become known as "the Ten Commandments judge" because he posted the commandments in his courtroom. After being elected Alabama chief justice in 2000 by a vote of more than 70 percent, Moore fulfilled an election pledge to use leftover campaign funds to pay for a monument depicting the commandments and to place it in the rotunda of the court building in Montgomery in 2001. But the next year, Federal District Judge Myron Thompson in Montgomery ruled that the 5,280-pound Ten Commandments monument was a violation of a First Amendment ban on state endorsement of religion.

Thompson stayed his ruling while Moore appealed to a higher court, where Moore argued that his duty to defend the Alabama and U.S. constitutions—which "acknowledge God"—required him to keep the monument in place. On July 1, 2003, a panel of the Atlanta-based Eleventh U.S. Circuit Court of Appeals ruled unanimously to uphold Thompson's judgment. On August 5 Thompson ordered Moore, under threat of "substantial fines," to remove the four-foot-high granite sculpture by August 20. Moore stood his ground, and a variety of Christian leaders, local and national, began urging people to come to Montgomery to gather around the monument and, if necessary, to use passive resistance including civil disobedience to prevent or discourage its removal. Protesters streamed to the judicial center from throughout the South and beyond, with more than a thousand gathering for nightly rallies. They blocked entrances to the doors and garage of the courthouse, and one hundred spent the night on the courthouse grounds.[2]

That's when Dobson entered the picture. Already indignant because he saw the Moore case and the decisions on homosexuality as closely related facets of judicial activism run amok, Dobson wanted more of a response from Focus listeners than simply a deluge of phone calls to Washington or even to Montgomery. Preempting scheduled Focus programming on August 25, he discussed the issue with Moore, Don Hodel, and Alan Keyes on the air. "We're at a turning point, a pivotal turning point in the history of this country," Dobson said. "This is just not another issue. . . . There are times when you have to respond to a higher law." And then Dobson made his request: Get up and go to Montgomery, he urged his audience.[3]

The exhortation was unusual for Dobson. Rarely during the previous twenty-five years of *Focus* programs—even during the height of antiabortion protests across the country in the early nineties—had he urged civil disobedience, and he had never pleaded with listeners to man the barricades at abortion clinics. As the events in Montgomery intensified, however, Dobson's own intensity kept pace.

The other eight members of the Alabama high court overruled Moore and asked the building manager to remove the sculpture. So on the morning of August 27, hundreds of protesters at the court building stood back as a work crew used a hydraulic jack to lift the monument and pull it into a nearby storage closet; then officials locked the door.[4]

Dobson's next actions were unusual for him too. John Giles, the president of Alabama's Christian Coalition, called and asked Dobson to fly there quickly and participate in a rally on the evening of August 27 that promised to be the largest yet, as protesters reacted to the closeting of the sculpture. Dobson agreed to come as long as organizers could move the rally to the next afternoon. The decision to participate surprised some on his staff because in addressing hundreds or thousands of pumped-up activists, Dobson would be in a far different rhetorical venue than those that he had mastered over the years. Radio monologues, banquet speeches, even hours-long seminars that he had presented to arenas and stadiums full of people—none required the sort of stump-speech mentality and extemporaneous fire that he would need for this.

"He doesn't do that sort of thing often at all," concedes Tom Minnery, *Focus*'s head of public policy. "The only big crowd previously that he had spoken to in a venue like that was in the late eighties when he spoke during a huge pro-life demonstration on the lawn of the Washington Monument." More than 400,000 people were in attendance.

But Dobson was undeterred, and he threw himself into the effort even though it required a monumental bout of concentration, an expenditure of many hours, and the exertion of extraordinary energy in the midst of a jammed schedule that wouldn't seem to have accommodated any of those. On the night of Wednesday, August 27, the Dobsons' forty-third wedding anniversary, Dobson was in Washington, D.C. on *Hannity & Colmes*. After dinner with Minnery and others, Dobson retired to his hotel room, where he worked on his Montgomery speech until 2:30 a.m. He arose at 6 a.m. on Thursday and flew out of Ronald Reagan National Airport with Alan Keyes and Tony Perkins, who was on his first day on the job as the new president of the Family Research Council. The Focus entourage also included Tom Minnery and Paul Hetrick. "It was the highlight of the year for me," Dobson said later, "just because of the excitement and appreciation of my being there, and the issue that I feel so strongly about, and of the need to articulate it."

Dobson arrived at the judicial center on one of the hottest days of the year wearing a medium brown suit to speak to a crowd that had naturally donned shorts and T-shirts. The temperature was around 100 degrees, with humidity in the 90s. "It was an amazing, electric moment when Dr. Dobson got out of the car and went up the steps to the courthouse," Tom Minnery recalls. "The crowd, [about two] thousand people, spotted him, and he got a tremendous ovation. People were reaching out, groping, trying to shake his hand."

He tried to get the permission of Alabama Attorney General William Pryor to visit the monument in its storage compartment. "But it's my understanding that the Attorney General refused to let me see it, so all I could do is stand in front of the closed door," Dobson said later. After the speakers settled on a makeshift dais and the crowd found places on the steps and portico of the building, many with umbrellas that they used as parasols to block the heat, Keyes told listeners that the noontime sun wasn't as hot as the political climate in Alabama would become "for those who cooperated with this federal judge." He said: "We have just begun to fight."[5] Perkins also spoke briefly. Then Reverend Pat Mahoney, one of the local organizers, introduced Dobson.

When Dobson stepped behind the tiny wooden podium in Montgomery—forty years to the day after Martin Luther King Jr.'s march on Washington—he had the clear support of his audience. But in the wider arena, he was stepping into anything but a consensus of support among his allies and other Christian conservatives for Moore's actions. While agreeing that the Ten Commandments display was constitutional, Pat Robertson, for example, commented on a daily radio show hosted by Jay Sekulow that Moore should have obeyed the federal court order. Sekulow, head of the American Center for Law & Justice, a Christian counterpart to the American Civil Liberties Union, agreed with Robertson, as did Richard Land, president of The Ethics & Religious Liberty Commission of the Southern Baptist Convention.[6] Cal

Thomas, perhaps not surprisingly, couldn't resist ripping Dobson at least by inference: "The street theater in Alabama was really less about the commandments than about fund-raising and the continued public visibility of certain organizations."[7] Even one of Dobson's biggest boosters on Capitol Hill, Senator Sam Brownback, said that he would have advised him to rally help for Moore prior to the federal judge's ruling instead of afterward.

Yet in his speech, televised live in its entirety on Fox News that day, Dobson's finely honed rationale shone forth as brilliantly as the dog-day Southern sun. His vigorous support of Moore's brazen defiance of the courts stemmed not just from his conviction that Moore was following God's law over man's law but that other men's interpretations of the Constitution in this regard were mortally flawed. To Dobson, it wasn't just the offense of seeing a granite depiction of the Ten Commandments literally put behind lock and key; his far greater concern was the "judicial tyranny" that the move represented. He noted the irony of the drama's unfolding in Montgomery, where Rosa Parks famously had refused to give up her seat on the bus in 1955. "This great monument has now been put in the back of the bus," Dobson said.[8]

"The liberal elite and the judges at the highest level and some members of the media are determined to remove every evidence of God from this culture," he continued. Dobson listed references to the commandments and to God in inscriptions throughout the nation's capital. "If the ACLU and if the People for the American Way and if Americans United for the Separation of Church and State and all the other liberal organizations are going to accomplish their goal, they're going to have to sandblast half the buildings in Washington."[9]

Finding his rhetorical stride, which was suffused with energy though still in typical Dobsonian measure, he began to ask for responses from the crowd to questions like, "Where did the blessings of liberty come from?" Answer: "God." He gave a short history lesson on how modern mediators had twisted the establishment clause of the Constitution, perverting what even his fourth-grade teacher had been able to make clear to Dobson and his young classmates about the nation's sacred separation of federal powers. Dobson accused Congress of abdicating its responsibility to check the federal judiciary, which has led the latter, including the U.S. Supreme Court, to take more and more advantage of its power—to the point of tyranny.

"It's not about the Ten Commandments," Dobson began, rising

toward his climax. "It's about everything else. It is mostly about the unelected, unaccountable, arrogant, imperious judiciary appointed for life that is determined to make all of us dance to their music. That is not the way a democracy is supposed to function. We need to go to the Congress and demand—absolutely demand—that they rein in this runaway court." He began with *Roe v. Wade* and listed a number of recent examples of judicial tyranny right up to that week, including *Lawrence*. Dobson warned that "the majority on the [Supreme] Court appears to be headed straight as an arrow for the sanction and supposed constitutionality of same-sex marriage." So, he told those assembled near the end of the hour-long rally, "Use your influence. You can't sit this one out, because the time is very short.

"There was a time when I was younger," he continued, "when it stung me to be called a 'right-winger.' There was a time when I didn't want to take that heat. There was a time when I wanted to say what I needed to say, but then I tried to keep my head down. I've got to tell you: Those days are over."

Finally, shifting into a gear that those close to him had never seen him use before, Dobson sucked the crowd further into his oratory so that they could usher him toward his conclusive crescendo. He began asking a series of eight questions, each eliciting an increasingly vocal "Yes," from the listeners, starting with "Do you think it's time to limit the power of the oligarchy?" and ending with "Are you ready to say, 'Enough is enough'?" "Yes!"

Dobson ended by referring to Winston Churchill's leadership during Britain's darkest hour and paraphrasing his hero's famous quote, "'We will never, never, never, never, never give up.' God bless you all."[10]

Though his voice wasn't yet spent even after finishing his oration, Dobson was a mess. He was drenched in sweat. He hadn't gotten all of the makeup off of his face and neck from the *Hannity & Colmes* show the night before, so some rubbed off onto the collar of his white shirt. The handwritten notes for his speech and even his file folder were soggy with perspiration. Red Tic Tac mints that he had stowed in his shirt pocket and forgotten about had completely melted, creating a huge red stain on his breast. "It looked like I'd been shot," Dobson says.

When Dobson's group stopped at a McDonald's on the way to the airport, Tom Minnery reports, "The lady behind the counter was taken aback. She didn't know who he was, but *nobody* wears suits in Montgomery in August. He was quite a sight. He put everything into it that he had."

Despite the clear triumph of the Montgomery speech, questions about the aftermath nagged at some of Dobson's staffers and supporters through the days before, during, and after. Could James Dobson—or any of his allies for that matter—actually fashion "judicial tyranny" into an issue that resonated with the American people, that could truly compel even the most educated and motivated of them to some sort of understanding and even action? Could anyone, even someone as intellectually and rhetorically nimble as Dobson, possibly package such a miscellany of components—including the outrage of *Roe v. Wade* and partial-birth abortion, the ideologically motivated perversion of the First Amendment, and liberals' decades of overreach by judicial fiat— into a concept so coherent, a call so piercing, that it could actually stymie or begin to roll back the abhorrence that Dobson so clearly had proscribed and identified in his own mind?

The final answers would be some months and perhaps years in the making, only hinted at by the resounding success of the 2004 elections. But Dobson's initial, determined responses to those questions were yes and yes. And he had at least three factors going for him. The first was that, almost as if on cue, activist courts across the land continued to supply fresh examples of excess during the weeks immediately after Montgomery. And in almost all cases, they disdainfully trashed a status quo that had been arrived at by the long, arduous—and democratic— process of legislation.

The U.S. Supreme Court agreed in October to rule on the 2002 ban of the words "under God" from the Pledge of Allegiance by the Ninth U.S. Circuit Court of Appeals, which governs nine western states and Guam.

The Massachusetts Supreme Court handed down the *Goodridge* decision in early November, striking down the state's ban on same-sex marriage as "unconstitutional" and giving lawmakers six months to craft a way for homosexuals to wed.

On November 5, within hours after President Bush signed into law (with Dobson in attendance) the federal ban on partial-birth abortions, two federal judges in different parts of the country slapped injunctions on it; to Dobson, this was by far the season's most vexing abuse of judicial authority.

And as the year closed, a federal judge in New Hampshire declared

unconstitutional a state law that required at least one parent to be noti-
fied forty-eight hours before his or her minor daughter had an abortion.

Second, Dobson was encouraged because the chorus of outrage
over the issue was growing; it wasn't just Dobson spouting off about judicial tyranny anymore. "*Goodridge* is a decision untethered to the state
or federal constitution and flatly contrary to the explicit desires of the
electorate," said Robert H. Bork, President Reagan's infamously
abused Supreme Court nominee and author of *Slouching Towards Gomorrah: Modern Liberalism and American Decline,* which was published in
2002. "It justifies the phrase 'judicial tyranny.'"[11]

The third favorable factor—and probably the most significant—
was Dobson's willingness to put his own shoulder into the fight. "I don't
think any issue," Tom Minnery says, "ever has motivated him more."

Dobson also devoted considerable resources in the fall of 2003 to battling another manifestation of the decadence that continued to wash
over American culture: Abercrombie & Fitch's pornographic quarterly
Christmas catalog. The 280-page *Christmas Field Guide* was put out by
the clothier that had been making a more and more fevered pitch to the
youth market over the last several years, evolving from its origins as a
sort of rugged Banana Republic. The sumptuously produced new
"magalog" showed teenaged-looking young men and women in various
stages of partial nudity, and it discussed and encouraged orgies, oral
sex, and group masturbation.

"I'm about as burned up as I can be," Dobson fulminated on
Scarborough Country on November 13. "I cannot believe that parents are
going to hold still for this. It's pure exploitation for profit. . . . Do not
buy anything from this wretched company." Joe Scarborough asked
him: "Are you calling for a boycott of Abercrombie & Fitch?" Replied
Dobson: "You bet I am. If you've ever listened to me on anything," he
said, addressing the many thousands of supporters who doubtless were
among the MSNBC audience, "listen to me on this."[12]

The next day, on a *Focus* broadcast that preempted scheduled programming so that he could discuss the boycott and other issues, Don
Hodel said to Dobson: "I don't know that I've ever seen you that irritated on a national TV show." Replied Dobson: "That really does get my
goat." Giving out the name of Michael S. Jeffries, the chief executive officer of New Albany, Ohio–based Abercrombie & Fitch, as well as his

phone and fax numbers, Dobson continued, "I hope his phone smokes."[13] Focus also launched a national advertising campaign against the chain.

Like his fight against homosexual activism, Dobson's differences with Abercrombie & Fitch were not an entirely new battle: Dobson had complained about the company's increasingly racy catalogs and other marketing materials over the previous few years. In 1998, for instance, the chain launched a binge-drinking promotion (which Mothers Against Drunk Driving got the company to ditch), and in 2002 Abercrombie & Fitch offered young girls thong underwear with phrases such as "Eye Candy" printed on them. But Dobson hadn't gone so far as to launch a boycott before. It wasn't that he was afraid or unwilling to take on corporate America: Fairly regularly, Dobson complained about sexually exploitive or other kinds of materials.

Dobson preferred other means. In 2000, for instance, he got Procter & Gamble to drop advertisements on MTV's *The Tom Green Show* and *Undressed,* which featured sexual references, including a nonexplicit lesbian love scene; and an episode of NBC's *Law & Order* that featured a negative portrayal of evangelicals who tried to convert gays to be straight.[16] Procter & Gamble had scrapped plans in May to advertise on the then-planned television talk show featuring radio host Laura Schlessinger—an ideological sympathizer with Dobson who regularly criticized homosexuality—after gay-rights groups threatened a boycott. Dobson invited executives of the Cincinnati-based consumer goods giant to Colorado Springs. While they agreed that their ads didn't belong on the shows highlighted by Focus, Procter & Gamble executives didn't change their minds about withdrawing support for Schlessinger. Eventually, the broadening controversy scuttled Schlessinger's show shortly after it began airing.

But this time Dobson was so incensed at Abercrombie & Fitch that he wouldn't allow the fear of failure to get in the way. Other national groups, including Citizens for Community Values and the National Coalition for the Protection of Children and Families, called for Christians to stop buying goods at Abercrombie & Fitch and at its Hollister-brand stores, but Focus's megaphone was by far the loudest. And it didn't take long before Jeffries' phone was smoking—and his sales plummeting. The chain's same-store sales for November, the most crucial measuring stick in the retail business, declined by 13 percent; its stock price slid from near thirty dollars a share in early November to less than twenty-five dollars a share for the rest of 2003; and a securities analyst for Merrill Lynch downgraded his recommendation on Abercrombie & Fitch stock.

Over Thanksgiving Abercrombie management suddenly decided to remove the catalog from its stores, dissembling with the explanation that it needed more counter space to sell bottles of perfume. But by December 9 a presumably enlightened cadre of top executives at Abercrombie & Fitch announced that they would retire the catalog; they had decided that it was "time for new thinking," as a company press release put it, promising "an innovative and exciting campaign" in the spring.[15] Dobson urged supporters "to continue to refuse to do business" with the company until they had earned consumers' trust.[16]

Dobson had focused his energy with the devastation of a lightning bolt on the Abercrombie & Fitch outrage. But he still had plenty of voltage in store.

⌗⌗⌗⌗⌗⌗⌗

Besides judicial licentiousness, gay marriage, and pornographic Christmas marketing, Dobson had to deal with other issues in the fall of 2003. For example, he joined director Mel Gibson in promoting *The Passion of the Christ* by hosting a screening of it for evangelical Christian leaders, soliciting their endorsements, and devoting a Focus broadcast to an interview with Gibson.

California alone presented two concerns that Dobson couldn't ignore. First, he felt compelled to take the time as a private citizen to express strong support for state representative Tom McClintock—a conservative who was the favorite of most evangelicals as a gubernatorial candidate—amid the circuslike atmosphere that led up to the October 7 election of Arnold Schwarzenegger as governor of California. And Dobson was outraged by the publication on October 16 of an article in the *Los Angeles Times* criticizing the open evangelicalism of a top U.S. general in the war on Iraq.

"The Pentagon has assigned the task of tracking down and eliminating Osama bin Laden, Saddam Hussein, and other high-profile targets to an Army general who sees the war on terrorism as a clash between Judeo-Christian values and Satan," wrote Washington-based Richard T. Cooper in the *Times* about Lt. Gen. William "Jerry" Boykin, the new deputy undersecretary of defense for intelligence. The reporter cited instances such as when Boykin "appeared in dress uniform and polished jump boots before a religious group in Oregon [to] declare that radical Islamists hated the United States 'because we're a Christian nation, because our foundation and our roots are Judeo-Christian . . . and the enemy is a guy named Satan.' " Cooper concluded early in the article: "Although the Army has seldom if ever taken official action against officers for outspoken expressions of religious opinion, outside experts see remarks such as Boykin's as sending exactly the wrong message to the Arab and Islamic world."[17]

A few weeks after the *Times* article set off anti-Boykin commentary in Washington, Dobson addressed it in an extemporaneously scheduled *Focus* broadcast that covered a number of front-burner issues and featured Don Hodel, Gary Bauer, and Tony Perkins. The media "is trying to have a chilling effect on people in government and the military," Dobson said, then urged listeners to "call the White House comment line and express your support for General Boykin. The *Los Angeles Times* ran Bob Vernon out of town in a similar circumstance," Dobson recalled, referring to the fact that Assistant Police Chief Vernon was denied promotion to Los Angeles Chief of Police in 1989 after the *Times* had painted him as a "religious extremist."

At almost exactly the same time, an urgent worry flashed on Dobson's overloaded radar screen from the East Coast: the case of Terri Schiavo. The thirty-nine-year-old Florida woman had been severely brain damaged since her heart stopped beating briefly one night thirteen years earlier because of a chemical imbalance. She was in what doctors called a "persistent vegetative state" in which they said she couldn't eat or drink on her own and, in fact, had no consciousness. A judge ordered the removal of her feeding tube on October 15 at the insistence of her husband, Michael Schiavo, who said that his wife had indicated long before that she'd never want to be kept alive by artificial means. Over the next weekend, her husband even forbade Terri from being administered last rites by a Roman Catholic priest because it would have involved her ingestion of a Communion wafer.

But her parents, Bob and Mary Schindler, were going on their own offensive. Showing a video that they had secretly taped of their daughter in the Woodside Hospice Center in Pinellas Park, Florida, they pointed out that Terri could say words such as *Mommy* and phrases such as *Help me*, alleged that she could follow objects with her eyes, and observed that she responded to Mary Schindler's touch. The Schindlers pleaded on TV news reports for restoration of the feeding tube to their daughter. They openly speculated that their son-in-law's motives might include the fact that he wanted to marry another woman and that he had basically spent the one-million-dollar malpractice settlement that he had received years earlier in their daughter's case.

The couple also lobbied the state legislature and, largely with the help of Christian talk radio hosts and other activists in Florida, managed to get Republican lawmakers to slap together a bill that would give Governor Jeb Bush the authority to order nourishment for Terri Schiavo. Lawyers reassured the governor that he had the legal standing to do so.

Still, the Schindlers needed the kind of clout that could quickly overwhelm state legislators' misgivings about crossing the courts. So they turned to Dobson. On Monday morning, October 20, Dobson was in the Washington, D.C. area for a meeting with allies to discuss their strategy to promote the Federal Marriage Amendment "when I got a call that they're going to let this woman die if you don't do something," Dobson remembers.

He didn't immediately take up the gaunstlet, however. Exhausted, Dobson's first inclination was to resist getting involved. "I already had a full schedule of things that I had to do, and then here comes another issue that I either have to address, or it's going to be lost. I told Sherry [Hoover, one of his assistants] that I just couldn't fight any more battles at once."

Marge Smith, the lifelong best friend of Dobson's mother, Myrtle Dobson, later suggested that something else—and even more personal—might have been at work amid Dobson's initial reluctance to get involved in the Schiavo case: a remembrance of his mother's last days attached to a feeding tube in a nursing home more than two decades earlier.

But Dobson gently disagrees with his mother's old friend. "If I had it to do over again, I think I probably wouldn't have allowed [Myrtle Dobson] to be put on a feeding tube, because she was in the latter stages of life, and she couldn't relate even the way that Terri Schiavo does—she *was* in a vegetative state," Dobson says. "But I never connected" the two situations.

In any event, on the morning of October 20, Dobson immediately ordered staffers to research the case and to brief him once he landed in Colorado Springs that afternoon. "I came home and understood that this woman was being starved to death," Dobson says, "and I couldn't say no."

Then ensued one of the most intense two-day lobbying blitzes that Dobson had ever launched. He preempted Tuesday's scheduled broadcast to make an appeal to *Focus* listeners on behalf of Schiavo, a program that would continue to air throughout the rest of the day and night as radio stations across the country played the broadcast at its appointed hour, sometimes more than once. Focus's CitizenLink Web site alerted its 66,000 subscribers by e-mail. "I did everything I could do to rain down a hail of opposition on that legislature," Dobson said.

Dobson also personally peppered Florida legislators with calls. He went on Joe Scarborough's MSNBC-TV show in the evening and on Sean Hannity's nationally syndicated radio show late on Monday afternoon, during the latter calling Michael Schiavo's efforts "Nazi-esque," with the potential to "open the door to euthanasia even wider." He urged tens of thousands of people across the country to call on Terri Schiavo's behalf and lasered a public message to Governor Bush: "If Governor Jeb Bush has to call out the militia . . . he must not allow her to die."[18]

Setting aside his long-standing misgivings about granting interviews to national television reporters for prerecorded segments, Dobson even agreed to a five-minute interview with ABC the next day in which a reporter asked him questions via a telephone squawk box that Dobson answered on camera in his satellite-linked TV studio at Focus. Yet just as Dobson had feared, the story on Peter Jennings' broadcast that evening included only a six-second snippet from Dobson: "There is a growing crescendo of concern across the country. People have responded in massive numbers"; only a little more of the interview ran that night on ABC's *Nightline*.[19] Moreover, ABC's producers titled the evening story about the Schiavo case "The Right to Die" when, as Dobson pointed out on a *Focus* broadcast on October 22, "Terri Schiavo wasn't trying to die. It was about the right to live! They were trying to kill her."[20]

Finally, after Terry Schiavo had endured six days without food, Florida's legislators got the message. A key factor included the acquiescence of Senator James E. King Jr., a Republican who was president of the Senate and had been one of the strongest supporters of the right-to-die law that the legislature passed in 1988. In the late afternoon of October 21, both houses approved "Terri's Bill" by big numbers, and Governor Bush quickly ordered the feeding tube reinserted into her starving body.

Others credited Dobson and the overall Focus communications apparatus with turning the tide. "You're the one that can deliver the phone calls like no one else," Janet Folger, a Florida-based talk-show host who had generated much of the earlier support for Terri Schiavo, said to Dobson on the October 22 edition of *Focus*.[21] Dobson didn't shy from the kudos. "There was a tremendous outpouring of support, and part of it—maybe a lot of it—came from [Focus], because we asked for it yesterday," Dobson agreed on the broadcast, which also included Joni Eareckson Tada. "And we got more than we've seen in a long time." CitizenLink subscribers alone sent more than twenty thousand e-mail messages to Florida legislators over a seven-hour period, Focus reported—twenty times higher volume than it had generated on any previous issue. In particular, Senator King "has been hit pretty hard, and he changed his mind," Dobson said.[22]

Terri Schiavo would survive what Tada called "the *Roe v. Wade* of disabilities" cases.[23] Afterward, Dobson said, he got a phone call from "the man in the [Florida] legislature whom I respect more than any other"— and whom he declines to identify—"and he said that if I hadn't done what I did, she'd be dead."

◡◠◠◡

Just a couple of weeks later, Dobson also had the opportunity to savor a moment he'd begun campaigning for twenty-five years earlier. On November 5 in the White House, President Bush spent a half hour with a small handful of pro-life leaders including Dobson, Charles Colson, Don Hodel, and Tony Perkins. And then they got the opportunity to watch over Bush's shoulder as he signed into law a federal ban on partial-birth abortions that had been trying to reach a president's desk for years. Not even the predictable actions of two federal judges just a few hours later to suspend the ban could remove the glow from that moment for Dobson.

"I remember 1998, when Charles Colson and I were standing near the Senate chamber after the attempt failed to override President Clinton's veto of the partial-birth abortion ban then," Dobson said on the *Focus* broadcast two days later. "I was in tears, and he was too." In the meantime nearby, Kate Michelman, who was head of the National Abortion Rights Action League, and others "were high-fiving each other because babies were going to continue to be murdered in this way.

"So President Bush's signing that bill was a high moment of many,

many years," he said. "There are a few highlights in life that you'll remember for a long time," he said. "This was one of them."

౨ూ౷ూౣ౨౼

As 2003 concluded, further events swiftly affirmed the magnitude of the struggle that the push for homosexual marriage would entail. The Episcopal church began a journey down a path toward likely schism by electing an openly gay cleric, Gene Robinson, as bishop of New Hampshire. Several dozen gays and lesbians gathered at the Focus on the Family campus on October 11 for a "Gay Day" that included a tour of the facility and group prayer that Dobson would stop persecuting them. As expected, in November in the case *Goodridge v. Department of Public Health*, the Massachusetts Supreme Court struck down the state's ban on same-sex marriage, calling it unconstitutional, and gave state lawmakers six months to craft a way for homosexual couples to wed.

And in a December 16, prime-time interview with Diane Sawyer on ABC, President Bush finally signaled to his evangelical supporters what they had been urging him all along to declare. "If necessary," he told Sawyer, "I will support a constitutional amendment which will honor marriage between a man and a woman."[24]

As the national debate over homosexual marriage intensified in late 2003 and through 2004, cascading into the performance of hundreds of actual homosexual nuptial rites in Massachusetts and elsewhere, Dobson emerged as a key player. Conservatives' Beltway strategy coalesced around his leadership. News media billboarded Dobson as the spokesman for the Christian Right on the matter.

As evangelical leaders grappled with the best way to present a united front against the political and cultural momentum that was building behind homosexual marriage, they first had to deal with a division among themselves over strategy. Some, notably the Family Research Council, were determined that they should oppose not only homosexual marriage but also the notion of government recognition of "civil unions" between same-gender partners. Recognition of civil unions would force states and companies to recognize these couples as families for purposes of economic arrangements such as health insurance policies, as in Vermont.

But others, including Dobson, insisted that their movement should more pragmatically draw the line at defending only the institution of marriage itself. They gathered their support around a particular codification of their view that had become known as the Federal Marriage Amendment. Written by Matt Daniels, who headed the not-for-profit Alliance for Marriage, the would-be amendment to the U.S. Constitution, introduced on Capitol Hill as House Joint Resolution 56, stated simply: "Marriage in the United States shall consist only of the union of a man and a woman. Neither this Constitution or the constitution of any State, nor state or federal law, shall be construed to require that marital status or the legal incidents thereof be conferred upon unmarried couples or groups."[25]

Once Dobson's side carried the day and evangelicals rallied behind the amendment, many leaders and groups began pounding out the message. Dozens of these allies even formed an ad hoc coalition called the Arlington Group (after Arlington, Virginia, where they first met) to serve as a nexus for their efforts. But they relied heavily on Dobson as a lead communicator. That was underscored after about two dozen bright lights of the Christian Right—including Dobson, Charles Colson, Gary Bauer, and Richard Land of the Southern Baptists—held a strategy meeting in Washington in October. In a cab ride the two shared departing the meeting, Sandy Rios, then president of Concerned Women for America, asked William Bennett who he thought would carry the message about the defense of marriage to the most people.

"We agreed immediately that it would be Jim Dobson, because he's got the biggest audience, and people will do what he asks them to do," Bennett says.

ᔕᑊᐦᣝᣝᐦᔕ

Even awash in victories over Abercrombie & Fitch, Michael Schiavo, and partial-birth abortionists, however, Dobson felt the growing burdens of his unique position and capabilities weighing heavily on him as 2003 closed. And while he was displaying greater drive and effectiveness in his public policy involvements than at any other time in his ministry, James Dobson was also expressing more weariness than ever before.

"I'm not by nature a workaholic," Dobson continues to insist, "because I have many things that I'm interested in. I love being with Shirley and just going to the mall with her. There's nothing I'd rather do than simply just take her out to eat. I love televised sports, especially college football. So why do I do it? The Schiavo case is an example of what I'm talking about. Over and over again, members of Congress and other leaders say to me, 'If you don't help us, we're going to lose it.'"

Compounding his weariness was the need to undergo six weeks of time-consuming hyperbaric-oxygen treatments to ensure the quick and thorough healing of the weak spot in the artery that had burst in his colon on October 24. Just like a deep-sea diver who is isolated in a hypobaric chamber so that he doesn't get the bends after he comes back up, Dobson was isolated for two hours a day, five days a week, for six weeks from early November through mid-December. Most afternoons, he didn't arrive at his office at Focus until about two o'clock. Nevertheless, Dobson still found time to make four trips to Washington, D.C. during those six weeks. Few doubted Bill Maier's prediction that "over the next few years, the American public is going to get to know Dr. Dobson even a lot more still. He is fired up on these issues."

Yet as matter-of-fact as Dobson had always been about not "letting the last check bounce," neither was he seeking to waste himself into an early grave. So his family, friends, coworkers, and allies were relieved to see him taking steps as 2003 closed to ensure that, in his newly won liberation from the demands of day-to-day administration of Focus, Dobson didn't simply step into another even more rigorous kind of grind. One of the most significant was his decision to reprise the streamlining-by-committee that Dobson's schedule had undergone in the midnineties. The "gold-ribbon panel" convened and made general recommendations, but unlike its predecessor group, this panel didn't try to detail how Dobson could make better use of his time.

In fact, following the panel's work, Dobson still did not sound like a man who was scaling back. "My workload is still very, very heavy," he said, repeating yet again a reality that had become a mantra for his life, "and I've got to figure out a way to do everything."

Indeed, instead of a man looking for an exit strategy to a plush retirement, the sixty-seven-year-old James Dobson sounded instead very much like the young James Dobson who had found time to develop his skills as a speech maker even as he was striving to make his mark in two demanding careers. Like the James Dobson who wasn't satisfied with spreading his ideas about discipline only through best-selling books but who also wanted to connect with American families in an unprecedented way on the radio. Like the James Dobson who built one of the world's most effective ministries even as he was earning the title of one of Christendom's most influential leaders. Like the James Dobson who felt compelled to mount every barricade, against an increasingly hostile culture, in defense of the values he held dear.

On the eve of what would rank as the most strenuous episode of his life, the crucial election season of 2004, he was once again talking like the James Dobson who sometimes felt like getting off the train—but who also realized, as always, that he wanted to do God's bidding, not his own.

RIGHTEOUS REVOLUTION

> *"If there were an evangelical*
> *Mt. Rushmore, Dr. Dobson would*
> *have to be on it."*
>
> RICHARD LAND, PRESIDENT,
> THE ETHICS & RELIGIOUS LIBERTY
> COMMISSION OF THE SOUTHERN
> BAPTIST CONVENTION

James Dobson had formed a firm conviction regarding his involvement in the 2004 campaign season. "We really were being asked to determine if we were going to be a people who assaults unborn children and tiny, little, embryonic human life," he said on his November 4 *Focus* broadcast, "whether we were going to redefine marriage; what we were going to do with school curricula in regard to our children across the nation; and the way our beleaguered family was going to be taxed; national security; the role of the United Nations in this nation; control of our military; and, especially, the defining issue of all: the United States Supreme Court. Because every other issue from partial-birth abortion to prayer in schools to the Ten Commandments on the walls [of classrooms and courtrooms] to the Pledge of Allegiance—all of those things have been usurped by the court.

"And what was at stake [on Election Day] was the power to make the appointments to those positions that will either control our lives or will grant us the freedoms as intended by the founding fathers, and many years later [by] Abraham Lincoln, as he said in the Gettysburg Address: It's a government of the people, by the people and for the people."

Against that lofty goal, Dobson had pressed every asset at his disposal: his name, his face, his talents, his ministry, his reputation, and his popularity. He had paid a physical price, delivering twenty-eight speeches during the three months before the election. He frequented cable-TV news hours, hammered his radio listeners about the importance of their votes, and taped secular-radio ads in states where same-sex marriage was on the ballot. Dobson allowed his comments and image to be used for Internet ads for Tom Coburn, the Oklahoma Republican who ultimately prevailed in his U.S. Senate race, and for John Thune in South Dakota. While all of that was going on, Dobson also launched a Focus boycott of Tide and Crest products, because manufacturer Procter & Gamble was tacitly endorsing homosexual marriage in an electoral fight over a "civil rights" ordinance in its headquarters city of Cincinnati.

Dobson's biggest activity during the last several weeks of the campaign season was a schedule that included a half-dozen rallies called Stand for the Family, which Focus Action and the state-level Family Policy Councils were organizing in three states where conservatives could benefit from a boost in their bids for the U.S. Senate. Joined by Tony Perkins, a former congressman from Louisiana; Gary Bauer, whose outfit is called Campaign for Working Families; and Bishop Wellington Boone of Promise Keepers, Dobson opened the schedule on September 6 and 7 with rallies in Charlotte and Raleigh in North Carolina, where Republican Representative Richard Burr was neck and neck in the polls with Democratic candidate Erskine Bowles, a chief of staff for former President Clinton. In late September, Dobson headlined rallies in Shreveport and Baton Rouge in Louisiana, where Republican Representative David Vitter was trying to pick off a Democratic seat in the U.S. Senate that had been held by the retiring John Breaux.

"I really believe that the institution of the family is going to survive, or fail, in the next year—and probably this year," Dobson told a crowd of about six thousand people at Cricket Arena in Charlotte. "It's hanging on the ropes, literally. And so many people of faith, so many good people, have sat around—sometimes myself included—for thirty-five years and let everything we care about erode away. And it is time to say, 'Enough is enough.'"

An emotional high point for Dobson and his entourage came the next evening when more than thirteen thousand people packed the RBC Center on a rainy night in Raleigh. Dobson built the intensity of his remarks and crowd involvement by relying on a series of questions that begged one-word shouted responses from the audience, an oratorical approach that he had used to great effect more than a year earlier in Montgomery.

"I have to ask you some questions about what you believe," Dobson said in Raleigh. "Do you believe it should be legal again to have prayer in the schools?" The crowd's answer, of course: "Yes!" "Do you believe that there should be Bible reading in the schools again? Do you believe that there should be prayer at graduation ceremonies? Do you believe that it's appropriate to have prayer at sporting events? Do you believe that the Ten Commandments should be on the bulletin boards of our schools? Do you believe that the Pledge of Allegiance should be recited by our children in schools? Do you believe there should be a ban on the horrible procedure of partial-birth abortion?"

With each question, the crowd offered up a resounding "Yes!" in response. Dobson recalls that "people were on their feet eight or ten or twelve times during my remarks" that night, "and it made me believe that I was seeing a greater energy and a greater enthusiasm in the church than I'd ever seen."

⋈⌇⌇⌇⌇⋈

Tom Daschle, Pete Coors, and Arlen Specter learned in very personal ways the impact that Dobson could have on the hearts, minds, and votes of citizens and solons alike.

From the moment he stood before the crowd at The Broadmoor in Colorado Springs in August 2003, Dobson never wavered from his fixation on Daschle. The opponent of the diminutive Democrat was John Thune, a native South Dakotan, a longtime Republican politician and a congressman, who had challenged and lost by only 524 votes to Democratic Senator Tim Johnson in 2002. An evangelical Christian and a sometime pheasant-hunting partner of Dobson's, Thune didn't hesitate in turning from his 2002 defeat to a determined but long-shot race to unseat Daschle.

"But he'd already lost to the weaker candidate," notes Bob Fischer, a furniture company owner, an evangelical activist, and an influential Republican in his home state of South Dakota. "Taking on Daschle two years later was like David against Goliath. And Daschle already had been advertising for a little over a year before the election, and much of that time without an opponent."

When he finally threw his hat into the ring, Thune had only

counted on the same level of arm's-length support that he had received from Dobson in 2002. But personally determined to dash Daschle and unencumbered legally under Focus Action to go after him, Dobson had decided to help his friend Thune at an entirely more intense level this time around.

"I not only decided to weigh in on the great moral issues and on candidates, but I targeted Tom Daschle as the man I wanted to see removed," Dobson says. Daschle had "gotten a little arrogant," Dobson told his *Focus* audience in a campaign retrospective. He says that he "wanted the people in South Dakota to understand that there was a difference between the Tom Daschle that they thought they knew and the one we saw in the Senate, with his hostility to anything conservative and his unprecedented filibustering of wonderful judges who ought to have been put on the federal bench. He never even allowed them to get an up or down vote. But he never went back to South Dakota and admitted that to anyone. He presented himself as a conservative who was just like South Dakota, which is a very conservative place."

A number of conservative groups, including Catholic organizations, smelled Daschle's blood in the water and pitched in. Dobson lent his name to a full-page advertisement that ran in many of the state's newspapers and was paid for by Bauer's organization. "An Important Message from Dr. James C. Dobson" was the banner on the ad, which charged that Daschle was "doing the two-step: Saying one thing to South Dakotans and doing the opposite in Washington, D.C.," on issues including abortion and same-sex marriage.

Dobson believed he had the best chance of contributing some momentum against Daschle by appearing at rallies in the state. So Focus handlers scheduled him for a Christian-music festival in Sioux Falls on Labor Day weekend. The festival was held at the fairgrounds, where Dobson had access to more than forty thousand people in each of two speeches. And near the end of Dobson's grand circuit of electioneering, on October 3 and 4, he came back to South Dakota to try to seal the deal against Daschle. Returning to Sioux Falls again after his fall in nearby Sioux City, Iowa, Dobson spoke to about five thousand South Dakotans and—rather than being hindered by his horrific near miss of the night before—managed characteristically to work his stumble into his speech as an anecdote. The next night, in Rapid City, South Dakota, he closed to an enthusiastic audience of about seven thousand supporters.

Focus executives and others figure that, culling duplicate attendees, Dobson may have spoken in person to as many as seventy-five thousand South Dakotans, or about 10 percent of the state's population of approximately 750,000 people. Colson believes that Dobson "helped a lot, particularly in South Dakota. He actually may have been decisive there." Thune's own polls even on Election Day showed him losing narrowly to Daschle, says Bob Fischer, but Dobson "made a big difference in Thune's favor.

"It wouldn't have happened without [Dobson's] coming here," Fischer insists. "There just weren't that many other factors in the election."

In any event, Dobson, who clearly sees the Republican Party as being more in sync than the Democrats with conservative Christianity, says, "What I hope that the Democrats in the Senate are going to think about is that conservative Christians have had enough and that what happened to Tom Daschle can also happen to them."

Tom Daschle at least was cognizant of the threat that Dobson posed as the senator tried to file off the sharp edges of his Beltway liberalism in order to become more palatable to his conservative constituents. But in Colorado, Pete Coors didn't seem to fully grasp Dobson's significance. Some say that lack of insight was a monumental blunder in a state where evangelicals have such a huge influence and where Dobson has more than once made the list—along with Coors—of *Colorado* magazine's most influential Coloradans. And in a significant way, Coors' failure to at least acknowledge Dobson, his ideas, and his huge shadow could very well have contributed to Coors' loss to Democratic candidate Ken Salazar in the U.S. Senate race.

To many observers in Colorado, Coors oozed a sense of entitlement not only to the Republican nomination but also to a general-election victory. The scion of the Golden, Colorado-based brewing empire and very often the company's public face in Coors commercials that featured him with the pristine Rocky Mountains in the background, Pete Coors, in the primary, beat out former U.S. Representative Robert Schaffer, the favorite of Dobson and his allies. "I think the Republican Party in its 'wisdom' passed over Schaffer and didn't support him," Dobson says, "because I think that it often wants to avoid having members of the Senate who are going to be embarrassingly conservative."

Furthermore, while Coors and his company long supported many conservative political causes, the CEO's candidacy was actually disappointing to Colorado conservatives. Coors liked to label himself "pro-family," but one reason he had for making that claim was the fact that his company pays health insurance and other benefits to the gay and lesbian domestic partners of its employees—a policy that is anathema to traditionalists. Neither did Coors gain much currency with "values voters" owing to his company's full slate of risqué television advertisements for its products.

Yet Dobson wanted to be able to help preserve the Republican Senate seat, especially one based in his home state. Dobson met several times with Coors in the spring of 2004 to determine if he could, indeed, recommend him. Dobson quizzed Coors with "very specific questions, and I got disturbing answers," he says. "I asked him how he felt [about the ads]", Dobson says, "and he said, 'Well, we've got to sell beer to the younger drinker.' And I said, 'Does it bother you at all that you're helping to corrupt those younger drinkers?' He said that he didn't see it this way." Coors added to Dobson's disgust in an appearance on *Meet the Press,* when host Tim Russert asked Coors about his company's sponsorship of dubious entities such as a male nude revue. Did he see that as a contradiction of his claim to be a "pro-family" candidate? Russert asked. Coors said no. "That really pushed me over the edge," Dobson says.

Dobson probed for some way for his conscience to accommodate Coors' candidacy. "I said, 'Can you blame this type of advertising on the ad agency? Is there someone at your company other than yourself who's actually responsible for this [approach]?' And he said, 'No, the buck stops here.'" When Dobson switched to the question of the brewer's "diversity" training to raise employees' consciousness about homosexuality, the candidate told the psychologist, as Dobson recalls, "'We don't believe in discriminating.' And I said, 'That's not the question: Do you exempt Christians who work there who are offended by that?' And [Coors] said, 'If they believe in discrimination, they shouldn't work for Coors.'"

Neither did Coors' answer on sanctity-of-life issues assuage Dobson. "I found him very politically naive," Dobson says. "I just didn't believe that he could go to Washington and be a force on the things that we cared about." So Dobson made no endorsement in the Colorado Senate race. And Coors didn't go to Washington.

Arlen Specter is one of a vanishing breed: a proabortion Republican in the U.S. Senate. And if, before his 2004 race, the four-term senator thought his "pro-choice" position wouldn't prove a significant political liability, the seventy-four-year-old Philadelphian might have thought otherwise after Election Day.

Flush with victory, politicians sometimes say ill-advised things. But Specter's comments after his own reelection on November 2 would come back to haunt him. Tradition dictated that Specter, with the highest seniority on the Senate Judiciary Committee, would become its chairman in the 109th Congress, replacing Republican Senator Orrin Hatch. That committee vets the president's judicial nominees, so there was great interest in Specter's views in the wake of an election where issues surrounding the federal judiciary at all levels—and especially the probability that the next president would be selecting one or more Supreme Court justices—had become such an important focus. And on the day after the election, Specter set off a firestorm by letting pro-lifers know that they shouldn't get too hopeful even after Bush's victory.

"When you talk about judges who would change the right of a woman to choose, overturn *Roe v. Wade,* I think that is unlikely," Specter said. And then, as if to warn President Bush and his conservative supporters not to get their hopes up about pro-life nominees, he added: "I would expect the president to be mindful of the considerations I am mentioning."

Reaction by Dobson and other conservatives was swift and blistering. "This has to be one of the most foolish, ill-considered comments ever made in politics," Dobson said on the November 4 *Focus* broadcast. The host also noted that Specter had mentioned Dobson several times in his victory speech on Election Night, among other things disdaining the fact that Dobson (who isn't a pastor) had "left his pulpit in Colorado" to try to defeat Specter.

"We need to contact every Republican senator and express [our] outrage and insist that they not vote . . . to make [Specter] chairman of this powerful committee," Dobson continued on the broadcast. "We've got to stop that, because he stands right in the middle of the road. We've got to derail that." He added: "I can hardly believe, two days after the election, that we have to call people and let our wishes be known. But we're going to win or lose the impact of this election very quickly."

Dobson's outcry was joined by other conservative leaders and, sure enough, by the end of Election Week, the offices of Republican senators, including Specter's, had received thousands of such calls. And Dobson and others were beating up Specter in the news media. Specter "is a problem, and he must be derailed," Dobson told host George Stephanopoulos on ABC's *This Week* on Sunday morning, November 7.

Specter backpedaled fiercely, explaining that he had meant that the reality of the Senate makeup in the next Congress—an expected fifty-five Republicans and forty-five Democrats—would continue to dictate that Democrats could still use filibustering to frustrate Bush's nominations. And he also noted, over and over again, that he had supported all of Bush's previous nominees.

By mid-November, Specter had managed to hang on to the expected chairmanship, but only after some extraordinary concessions that many laid right at the feet of Dobson and his allies. Other Republicans actually required Specter to write and read to a news conference a statement assuring the public that he would give Bush's nominees "quick committee hearings and early committee votes" and that he had "no reason to believe that I'll be unable to support any individual President Bush finds worthy" of the federal bench.

Dobson said he was disappointed that Specter was going to be seated as chairman but also made it clear that he was going to watch the Pennsylvanian closely. "He will assume his new position," Dobson told *USA Today,* "on a very short leash."

∽∽∽∽∽

Dobson's elevated profile during the campaign season, his winning scorecard on Election Day, and his aggressiveness toward Specter during the days afterward splashed him all over the news-media landscape as never before. As a genial child psychologist and occasional tough-talking rabble-rouser, before 2004 Dobson had been a favorite guest on a number of cable TV shows, including *Larry King Live, Hannity & Colmes,* and *Scarborough Country.* But suddenly this election season Dobson seemed to be everywhere, especially in the national media. And people were listening to what he had to say.

David Kirkpatrick of the *New York Times,* newly assigned early in the year to a "conservatism" beat, had discovered Dobson and was regularly featuring him and his comments in preelection stories.[1] Dobson made an appearance on Neil Cavuto's afternoon show on Fox on October 15. On his October 26 show, Rush Limbaugh quoted a "chilling thought" that Dobson had presented the night before on *Hannity & Colmes:* a victorious John Kerry filling any new U.S. Supreme Court vacancies with Bill or Hillary Clinton. In an October 27 opinion-page piece in the *Wall Street Journal,* the authors of a new book on American conservatives mentioned Dobson as part of "a clique of aging culture warriors." And right before the election, even the *New Yorker* magazine's "Talk of the Town" column mentioned "the fatherly chairman [of Focus] gleefully tearing into 'activist judges' and 'imperious courts'" at a rally in early October in Washington, D.C.

In Election Night coverage, it took TV pundits awhile to catch on to the trend toward Bush and the Republicans because early exit polls had hinted at a Kerry victory. But in the wee hours of November 3, as commentators began to grasp what actually had happened, some began to hitch their analysis to the importance of "values voters." Among others, Chris Wallace on Fox News mentioned the influence of Dobson and Focus on the Family in Colorado's voting results.

In the days after the election, Dobson was again in demand as he fomented a movement to block Specter from gaining the judiciary chairmanship. Dobson even appeared on Fox's *At Large with Geraldo Rivera* for several minutes. Clearly, the James Dobson of 1990 or even of 2003 couldn't have imagined a circumstance that would have him calmly fielding questions from the likes of Rivera, whose former TV talk show had featured guests throwing chairs at one another.

Some media personalities who weren't familiar with Dobson got a taste of his feistiness—and even his thin skin—if he didn't like a comment or an inference in an interview. In his November 7 appearance on *This Week,* for instance, George Stephanopoulos referred to a remark Dobson had made during the campaign in which he said Senator Patrick Leahy, a Vermont Democrat on the Senate Judiciary Committee, was a "God's-people hater."

"Now, Dr. Dobson," Stephanopoulos began framing his question, during which time Dobson already was getting up his dander, "that doesn't sound like a particularly Christian thing to say. Do you think you owe Senator Leahy an apology?"

"George," Dobson shot back, "you think you ought to lecture me on what being a Christian is all about? You know, I think I'll stand by the things I have said. Patrick Leahy has been in opposition to most of the things that I believe. . . . No apology."

A few days after the election, Dobson said that it was "really exciting to me that the media—which we often refer to as the left-wing media—is asking questions, legitimate questions, about values and about issues that they [ignored] in the past and now are genuinely trying to figure out." Now, he added, in a new era of evangelical muscularity and the rise of the values voter, the news media "are almost forced to deal with it."

೧౧౩౦౫౧

Having poured so much of himself into the results on election night and having so radically changed his stance toward partisan political involvement, Dobson knew he had done the right thing. But even so, for months before that day of reckoning, Dobson vacillated between doubt and confidence in the election's outcome.

"I felt [God] wanted me this time to pour myself into this, no matter how much pain or stress or physical inconvenience, to try to influence this election," he told Kirkpatrick for a November 1 *Times* story.[2] "God may have chosen a different track. I don't perceive it, but He might." Dobson said that evangelicals were "more energized this time around than I have ever seen in my lifetime." But, he told the *Times* reporter: "I just don't know if it is going to be enough to counter Bruce Springsteen and Michael Moore."

After the election, Dobson confessed to his *Focus* audience that he was "fighting depression" in the days before the election, "because I felt we were going to lose." He explained that he had felt a bit conflicted during that period because "my theological view told me that God is in control and that people by the hundreds of thousands were praying and that nothing could happen to us that wasn't permitted by Him. On the other hand, I was nervous as a cat because everything I cared about was on the line and because the liberal media seemed determined to elect John Kerry."

Several more days removed from Election Day, however, Dobson instead recollected much more confidence on his part in the run-up to the balloting. "I don't want to sound like a prophet here, but we saw this coming," he said in a November 12 appearance on Neil Cavuto's show.

In any event, after the magnitude of the Republican victory became clear, Dobson rushed forward to take credit not for himself specifically but for his constituency. He estimated on his show that "maybe 80 percent to 90 percent of our listeners voted." It would take awhile for statisticians to figure out if the evangelical vote really did turn out in significantly larger numbers than they did in 2000, but exit-polling data and other information suggested that they must have.

Dobson cast the election results in the biggest possible terms. "I think what happened here," he told his *Focus* audience on November 4, "was one of the most significant events ever in the history of our great nation."

Even as conservatives reveled in the afterglow of victory, Dobson believed that the 2004 election results were not the culmination of an era but rather just the beginning of a process that would take them to even greater political influence. Dobson and his allies were painfully aware that the Grand Old Party had borrowed freely from their support and influence over much of the preceding decade, but that social conservatives had little to show for it politically, legislatively, or judicially.

But in the weeks immediately following the 2004 election, Dobson made two things abundantly clear. First, he wasn't going to rest on his laurels. Second, he would make sure that the Republicans he had helped elect weren't going to rest either.

"We're simply expecting the president and the Republicans in the House and Senate to implement the agenda on which they ran," he said. With the election results, he believed, "God has only given us a reprieve, another opportunity to get in and work for spiritual and scriptural principles. What this means politically, for the Republican Party primarily, is that they have four and maybe only two years to get this right."

Soon, it became apparent what Dobson and his allies meant first and foremost: They fully expected Senate Republicans to take advantage of their party's increased majority to vanquish the so-called filibuster rule. Tom Daschle and the Democrats had been able to stall judicial nominees during Bush's first term because Senate procedure allowed them to filibuster with just forty votes. Requiring a full fifty-vote majority to support a filibuster would breach Senate tradition, to be sure. But the Democrats already had blasted away at the body's decorum by preventing nominees who had majority support, for the first time, from getting a vote on the full floor of the Senate.

And conservatives' frustrations over the blocking of constructionist judicial nominees contributed to their conclusion that, in the modern era, the American judiciary had become a thoroughly hostile institution.

Dobson likes to tell how his fourth-grade teacher presented with such clarity the Founding Fathers' strategy for a separation of powers and checks and balances among the three branches of federal government, so that no one of them would become too powerful. Things had begun going wrong, he and others concluded, as far back as the 1963 U.S. Supreme Court decision that banned prayer and Bible reading in public schools, clearly flouting what the American people preferred. Dobson and other critics fixated on *Roe v. Wade*, the 1973 Supreme Court decision that had invented a right to abortion where, again, the public wasn't demanding one. When federal-court decisions in 2003 and 2004 showed that judges also seemed to be discovering a right to gay marriage, it was becoming easier for Dobson and his cohorts to connect the dots for their constituency.

The death of Terri Schiavo in March 2005 kindled the smoldering resentment over "imperious judges" into a full blaze. With attentive care by her parents, the forty-one-year-old woman obtained her nutrition from a feeding tube in the Pinellas Park, Florida, hospice. Dobson had helped thwart Michael Schiavo's efforts in 2003 to have her feeding tube disconnected by lobbying the state legislature to pass a bill initiated by Governor Jeb Bush specifically protecting Terri Schiavo's life.

But by early 2005, Michael again got a Florida judge to order that Terri's feeding tube be pulled, and it was removed on March 18. This time, galvanized by the values-voting surge in the November elections and populated by more religious conservatives than any time in memory, Congress swung into action, passing a bill that allowed for federal judicial review of Terri's case. President Bush hopped on Air Force One on Palm Sunday evening to fly from Crawford, Texas, to Washington just to sign the bill at 1 a.m. on March 21, as Terri Schiavo's life ebbed without water or food. But every higher court, including the U.S. Supreme Court, upheld the lower court's order. Terri finally died on March 31.

Many evangelicals were outraged that judges would try so hard to ensure the death of such an innocent person, and the incident crystallized their understanding of the perils of judicial activism as nothing before had done.

"Terri's killing signifies conclusively that the judicial system in this country is far too powerful and is totally out of control," Dobson wrote in the April newsletter of Focus Action, which he called "one of those commentaries that will have significance years from now."

Thus judicial tyranny—about which Dobson had been warning Americans for more than two years—became even less of a distraction and more of a direct threat to life, liberty, and the pursuit of happiness. Dobson "had been Chicken Little to many people when he first started talking about judicial tyranny," says David Barton, an author and expert on the Constitution who heads an educational organization in Aledo, Texas, called WallBuilders. "But when the sky really did start falling, he wasn't Chicken Little anymore. There was the *Lawrence v. Texas* decision [by the U.S. Supreme Court in 2003, overriding state antisodomy statutes], the *Ten Commandments* [monument] ruling, and others, and people said, 'He's right!'"

Having won the battle to define all these rulings under the general rubric of judicial tyranny, Dobson then raised the stakes as the filibuster battle was joined in the Senate. "This may be the most important issue that will be voted on legislatively for many, many years," he told his *Focus* radio audience of eight million people on May 9. "Maybe decades."

Given such stakes, Dobson reacted strongly to vacillation by the Republicans whom he had helped gain more power, criticizing the handful who were trying to forge a compromise with several Democratic senators. "James Dobson: Who does he think he is, questioning my conservative credentials?" said one of the waverers, Mississippi Senator Trent Lott, to *USA Today* as the Senate neared a vote.

Dobson elaborated on his concerns in an interview. "It's one of the critical moments in American history," he said in a way that made clear he didn't believe he was being hyperbolic. "It's by far the most important thing that's happened in this country since World War II. Our constituency clearly sees it that way, and the other side sees it with the same urgency.

"Everything is on the line with this vote in the Senate. Every great social issue is being decided not by the American people, but by the courts. At stake is the sanctity of life, the very definition of marriage and the welfare of the family, the continued spread of obscenity and the loss of decency in the nation, and the forty-three-year assault on religious liberty by the courts that began in 1962."

The media maelstrom around Dobson grew even more in 2005 as two things became apparent both to his enemies and to Beltway pundits who were trying to call the action: how huge Dobson's role truly was in the 2004 elections, and how determined he was to leverage that further, beginning with victory on the filibuster issue.

Though they'd been used to firing across his bow for years, political opponents stepped up their criticism of a more assertive Dobson. "Mr. Dobson's arrogance knows no bounds," Ralph Neas, president of the stalwart liberal group People for the American Way, said a few weeks after the election, following Dobson's threat to come after a half-dozen incumbent Democratic senators in 2006 if they blocked the president's judicial appointments.

U.S. News & World Report put "James Dobson's Righteous Revolution" on a cover in January, and *Time* included him prominently in its cover piece on America's most influential evangelicals. *Newsweek* dispatched Howard Fineman, its senior political correspondent, to Colorado Springs to interview and write a cover story about Dobson.

The more Dobson showed up in the news, the bigger a target he became. Thus it was little surprise how the entire secular-media apparatus came down on Dobson after David Kirkpatrick, in the *New York Times,* skewed an inaugural-week remark that Dobson had made in Washington at a banquet hosted by the Family Research Council. Dobson said he was concerned about a new video that used famous cartoon characters ranging from SpongeBob SquarePants to Winnie the Pooh to teach homosexual propaganda to children under the guise of encouraging acceptance of "diversity." But as if on cue, commentators on MSNBC and CNN and in the *Los Angeles Times* and elsewhere, condemned Dobson because they incorrectly thought he'd accused SpongeBob of being gay. And the *New York Times* published an editorial entitled "Nautical Nonsense" that referred to him as "the intolerant Dr. Dobson."

Hollywood picked up the thread, too, as Dobson was lampooned on *Saturday Night Live.* Robin Williams wanted to skewer Dobson by delivering a sardonic song on the TV telecast of the Academy Awards on February 27, but ABC censors forced the comic to strip out so many of his offensive remarks that he dropped the whole idea.

The attention on Dobson grew even more intense as the filibuster fight got hotter, and the media carried the play-by-play. "Dobson is, arguably, the most powerful social conservative in the country, central to the battle over federal judges—and a danger to the people who would oppose him," Fineman wrote on MSNBC.com on May 4.

Perhaps Fineman was warning Don Imus. In an on-air conversation with Fineman a few weeks earlier, the radio talk-show host had illustrated pundits' aggressive new tenor toward an increasingly assertive Dobson. Imus called Dobson "half a nut," "a jerk," and "a pinhead" and, in his inimitably irascible way, then challenged Dobson to "a fistfight."

Former Vice President Al Gore said in a speech to MoveOn.org that Dobson and Tony Perkins were part of an "aggressive new strain" and a "virulent faction" of fundamentalists. A United Methodist minister in Colorado referred to Dobson and Focus as "the Gestapo." *Harper's Magazine,* in a piece purporting to explain evangelicals' drive for political power, mislabeled Dobson a pastor, said he "espoused . . . gospels of fear and hate," and alleged that he "apparently endorses political candidates who favor the execution of homosexuals and of doctors who provide abortions."

Dobson also called out Democratic Senator Ken Salazar for breaking a campaign promise that he had made to support up-or-down votes on judicial nominees. Focus Action ran an advertisement in Colorado newspapers urging Salazar to stick to his guns. So Salazar called Dobson "unchristian," accused him of trying to hijack Christianity, and blurted out that Focus is "the antichrist of the world."

"I think they're panic-stricken because they've lost nearly every battle, and the judiciary is the last liberal playground," Dobson says about such attacks. "They're the minority party in Washington; they're disappointed with the new pope [Benedict XVI]; and they're searching around for who to blame for this. I'm one of the available candidates. Four to eight years ago, it was Rush Limbaugh."

But Dobson objects to such vilification. "In thirty years of public life, I've never been subjected to what's happening now, the name-calling," he said on his May 9, 2005, broadcast.

As Dobson moved further into the secular spotlight and as more media gatekeepers sought to understand him, some approached this standard-bearer of the religious right with more curiosity and even civility. Thus in early May, while in Washington for the National Day of Prayer activities headed by Shirley Dobson, he met with the editorial board of ABC News, whose members quizzed Dobson for nearly two hours.

That session followed one of Dobson's more interesting encounters with a secular critic. As guests were seating themselves for the White House correspondents' dinner on April 30, where First Lady Laura Bush would go on to mildly roast her husband, a man approached Dobson and said, "I'm Al Franken." Dobson said, "I know who you are" to the former *Saturday Night Live* satirist and host of a show on the liberal talk-radio network, Air America.

"I want to ask you a question," Franken said, as Dobson recalls the conversation. "What's it like to know everything about everything? To be the only person that has a corner on absolute truth?" Without missing a beat, Dobson played along and said, "Oh, Al—it's a burden. You can't believe what a heavy load it is, to be the only one who has all that information.

"But let me ask you a question," Dobson continued. "Do you know what you believe?" Franken, according to Dobson, said, "Sure, I do."

"And when you tell people what you believe, do they ask the same question of you?" Franken countered that some things are gray, not black-and-white. Dobson then described the procedure for partial-birth abortion and asked his fellow radio host, "What if that even happened only once?"

As Dobson recalls, Franken said, "That would be black."

⌘

In mid-May, seven Republican and seven Democratic senators worked out a compromise that delayed to another day any climactic showdown over filibusters of judicial nominees. Working around the objections of conservatives like Dobson and liberal extremists who wanted to see the Democrats continue to thwart all of Bush's nominees, the conferees came up with a deal that would allow some of the president's long-idled federal judge appointments to come to a full vote of the Senate and avoid any change in current Senate rules on filibustering. But another part of the deal was that Democratic leadership reserved the right to go back to its filibustering ways if it deemed any future nominee "extraordinary."

Dobson railed against the agreement, calling it "a complete bailout and betrayal by a cabal of Republicans and a great victory for united Democrats." Meanwhile, Senate Majority Leader Bill Frist, who was allied with social conservatives on this issue, promised to attempt to blow up the delicate deal and change the Senate rules in the future if necessary, perhaps when it came to a new nominee for the Supreme Court.

Dobson was deeply disappointed that Senate Republicans punted the opportunity to exercise crucial control of the body in the appointment of judges. But just as World War II wasn't lost at Pearl Harbor or the Battle of Britain—nor finally won at D-Day, or the Battle of the Bulge—Dobson expects the issues of presidential appointments to federal courts and to the Supreme Court, liberal judicial activism, proper separation of powers, and the many controversies they affect to be long-term concerns for Americans who are moral, cultural, and constitutional traditionalists. At the same time, however, he isn't willing to pause for a moment to see how things might start to work out.

"I'm convinced that the culture wars, which have raged for twenty years, are coming to a climactic end," he says. "It's not that America will ever be safe from evil or the family entirely secure, but civil wars don't go on forever. Eventually, there is a series of battles that proves decisive."

AFTERWORD

If he's told the trophy story once, he's told it a hundred times.

Actually, Dobson estimates that he has dispensed "The Tale of the Trashed Tennis Trophy" at least a few dozen times over the last twenty years—in conversations, in commencement speeches, in books and magazine articles, on videotape and DVD, to friends, strangers, live audiences, and all the people out there in radio land. Most recently, Dobson chose this real-life parable, one of his all-time favorites, as the centerpiece of a chapter that he wrote for Larry King's book that was released in 2004: *Remember Me When I'm Gone,* an anthology of epitaphs self-written by a huge roster of celebrities ranging from Alan Alda to Tommy Hilfiger, Billie Jean King to Stephen King, and Arnold Schwarzenegger to Ted Turner. Dobson's epitaph didn't make the final cut into King's book, but that only gives him freedom to tell it to wider audiences himself.

When Dobson was bounding around the Pasadena College campus for the first time, he came upon the school's sports trophy case standing in the administration building. Amid the many basketball, baseball, and track awards, Dobson spotted the perpetual tennis trophy rising up from the center of the case—all two feet of it, with a shiny little bronze man on top and the names of all the collegiate tennis champions dating back to 1947 inscribed on a plate on the base. After practically memorizing the list of noble, racket-wielding warriors, Dobson vowed to himself, *Some fine day I'm going to add my name to that list of legends*.

Sure enough, Dobson brought his roundhouse forehand and fiery temperament to the court, lettered in tennis all four years, captained the team as a senior, and won the all-campus tournament that got his name inscribed on the trophy (although as 1956 champion Wil Spaite tells it, Dobson first became the champion in 1957 only because Spaite couldn't play with a neck injury). "I left the college with the satisfaction of knowing that future generations of freshmen would stand at the display case and read my name in admiration," Dobson says. "Someday they might be great like me."[1]

Alas, when the Nazarene college moved to a beautiful outcropping of land in the Pacific Ocean called Point Loma in 1973, the old tennis trophy was thrown in a garbage bin behind the administration building. Spaite's son, who was a student there at the time, happened to see this once-proud piece of hardware gleaming in the trash. "My school didn't retire my number," Dobson says. "It retired my entire memory!"[2]

The young Spaite took the trophy home, cleaned it up, and presented it to his father—whose name, after all, was there on the trophy before Dobson's—and Wil Spaite eventually stuck it in a closet and forgot about it. There it sat for about fifteen years until the elder Spaite, who by then was chairman of the board of the renamed Point Loma Nazarene University, invited his now-famous old friend back to be the commencement speaker. At that occasion, Wil and his wife, Polly, heard Dobson talk generically about how "life will trash your trophies." Bemused almost beyond containment, Polly at that moment told her husband, "You should go home and get that trophy out. He's the one who's supposed to have it." Dobson didn't have any idea that the trophy had ended up at the Spaites' home.

Today the refurbished trophy—with a shiny new man on top and a new engraved plate—indeed stands in a corner of Dobson's office in Colorado Springs, an ironic reminder about the importance of humility rather than an expression of athletic pride. "This brief encounter with fame taught me a valuable lesson about success and achievement," Dobson says in the trophy tale, now an appropriately closed loop because he knows that his trophy really was trashed. "If you live long enough, life will trash your trophies too. I don't care how important something seems at the time, if it is an end in itself, the passage of time will render it old and tarnished."[3]

In the draft for King's book, Dobson goes on to underscore the point that "all of our exhilarating accomplishments are going to fade and burn eventually," so "what will stand the test of time?": a loving family, a consistent investment in the lives of people, and an earnest attempt to serve God. "Nothing else makes much sense."

So, concludes the eminently accomplished psychologist, author, entrepreneur, and media star, he wants to be remembered "only as a man who lived by [this] creed, and then went on to Heaven after doing his best, as a flawed human being, to please his Lord and Savior, Jesus Christ. That is all. That is enough."[4]

Yet there's no doubt that Dobson has tried to take a lot of people with him. One at a time, he has treasured lives, touched lives, and even transformed lives for Christ. "This is a noble and gentle warrior," says Representative Trent Franks, one of those lives. "I know the glorified Christ will look in his eyes and say, 'Well done, good and faithful servant.'

FREE Discussion Guide!

A discussion guide for
Family Man is available at

ChristianBookGuides.com

ENDNOTES

CHAPTER 1: CAMPAIGN MODE

1 David D. Kirkpatrick, "Warily, a Religious Leader Lifts His Voice in Politics," *New York Times* (May 13, 2004).

2 David D. Kirkpatrick, "Evangelicals See Bush as One of Them, But Will They Vote?" *New York Times* (November 1, 2004).

3 Speech at Council for National Policy (September 27, 2003).

4 Letter from James Dobson for Focus on the Family Action (July 2004), 1.

CHAPTER 2: PATERFAMILIAS

1 As recounted by James C. Dobson Jr. in Rolf Zettersten, *Dr. Dobson: Turning Hearts Toward Home,* (Nashville: Word Publishing, 1989), 41.

2 Tim Stafford, "His Father's Son," *Christianity Today* (April 22, 1988): 16.

3 Zettersten, *Dr. Dobson: Turning Hearts Toward Home*, 37.

4 James Dobson, *Dare tio Discipline* (Wheaton, Ill.: Tyndale House Publishers, 1970), 30.

5 Stafford, "His Father's Son," 16.

6 Matthew 25:21.

7 Matthew 7:21–23.

8 Romans 1:20.

CHAPTER 3: STRIVER

1 Rolf Zettersten, *Dr. Dobson: Turning Hearts Toward Home* (Nashville: Word Publishing, 1989), 54.

2 Ibid., 57

3 As quoted directly from ibid, 61.

4 "Love Must Be Tough" *Focus* broadcasts aired on January 21–23 and January 27–30, 1987.

5 Zettersten, *Dr. Dobson*, 57–58.

6 Ibid., 59–60.

7 Ibid., 61–62.

8 "Love Must Be Tough," *Focus* broadcasts.

9 Zettersten, *Dr. Dobson*, 68–69.

10 Ibid., 84.

11 Tim Stafford, "His Father's Son," *Christianity Today* (April 22, 1988): 16.

CHAPTER 4: DARING TO DISCIPLINE

1 Rolf Zettersten, *Dr. Dobson: Turning Hearts Toward Home* (Nashville: Word Publishing, 1989), 89; and Ted Engstrom and James Dobson, *Focus on the Family: Celebrating Twenty-Five Years of God's Faithfulness* (San Diego: Tehabi Books, 2002), 52–53.

2 James Dobson, *The New Strong-Willed Child* (Wheaton, Ill.: Tyndale House Publishers, 2004), 172.

3 Ann Hulbert, *Raising America: Experts, Parents, and a Century of Advice about Children* (New York: Knopf, 2003), 235–237.

4 Ibid., 4.

5 Ibid.

6 Ibid., 6.

7 Ibid., 253.

8 Ibid., 257.

9 Ibid.

10 Christopher Jencks, "Is It All Dr. Spock's Fault?" *New York Times Magazine* (March 3, 1968): 27.

11 "Is Dr. Spock to Blame?" *Newsweek* (September 23, 1968): 68.

12 Hulbert, *Raising America*, 14.

13 Ibid., 90.

14 James Dobson, *Dare to Discipline* (New York: Bantam Books, 1977), 3.

15 Ibid, 28.

16 James Dobson, *The Strong-Willed Child* (Wheaton, Ill.: Tyndale House Publishers, 1978), 46.

17 Ibid., 47.

18 Hulbert, *Raising America*, 331.

19 News release by Children's Institute International (June 3, 1999).

20 Based on an ABC News survey conducted in November 2002 using a random sample of 1,015 adults.

21 James Dobson, *When God Doesn't Make Sense* (Wheaton, Ill.: Tyndale House Publishers, 1993), 92–93.

CHAPTER 5: PACKING THE HOUSE

1 Rolf Zettersten, *Dr. Dobson: Turning Hearts Toward Home,* (Nashville: Word Publishing, 1989), 88.

2 Ibid., 130.

3 Ibid., 96.

4 Exodus 18:23.

5 Zettersten, *Dr. Dobson,* 97.

6 Ibid., 100.

CHAPTER 6: THE VELVET MICROPHONE

1 Gil Alexander-Moegerle, *James Dobson's War on America* (Amherst, NY: Prometheus Books, 1997), 65.

2 All quotes from James Dobson (unless otherwise indicated) were obtained during personal interviews conducted during 2003–2005.

3 David Aikman on *The Bob Dutko Show*, WMUZ-FM (November 21, 2003). Among others, that argument was forwarded by David Aikman, who reported for *Time* from China, in his 2003 book, *Jesus in Beijing.*

CHAPTER 7: DEAL WITH A DEVIL

1 Pamela Ellis-Simons, "New Hero of the New Right: A Rising Voice of a Family Crusader," *U.S. News & World Report* (February 6, 1989): 27.

2 Ann Rule, *The Stranger Beside Me: Ted Bundy The Classic Case of Seduction and Murder* (New York: W.W. Norton, 2000), 429.

3 Interview with James Dobson, "Combatting the Darkness: The Pornography Commission's Final Report," as explained by Dr. James Dobson, 2.

4 Ibid.

5 *Focus on the Family* radio broadcasts "Pornography Kills," and "Update on Ted Bundy" aired on February 2–3 and February 22–23, 1989.

6 Ibid.

[7] Ibid.

[8] Dobson, "Combatting the Darkness," 2.

[9] E-mail from Ann Rule to the author (May 3, 2003).

[10] *Focus on the Family* broadcast with John and Marsha Tanner (May 25–26, 1989).

[11] Ibid.

[12] Rule, *The Stranger Beside Me*, 444.

[13] As cited by Patrick Buchanan in *The Washington Times*, "Bundy's Sendoff and the Porn Link" (February 1, 1989): 3.

[14] Dobson's monthly letter to Focus supporters (April, 1990).

[15] William Wilbanks, "Expert Warns: Don't Swallow Bundy's Line," *Ft. Lauderdale Sun Sentinel* (February 5, 1989).

[16] Rule, *The Stranger Beside Me*, 432.

[17] E-mail from Ann Rule to the author (May 3, 2003).

[18] Goldstein publishes *Screw,* considered hard-core porn within mainstream publishing.

[19] Al Goldstein, "Ted Bundy's Last Lie," *New York Times*, date and page unknown.

[20] "A_ _hole of the Month," *Hustler* (May/June 1989).

[21] Michael McWilliams, "Ted Bundy's Last Crime: Serving Pious Zealots," *Detroit News* (January 26, 1989).

[22] Focus on the Family radio broadcast with John and Marsha Tanner (May 25–26, 1989).

[23] Ibid.

CHAPTER 8: A BORN ENTREPRENEUR

[1] Among others, *Non-profit Times*, *Chronicles of Philanthropy*, and *World* magazine as well as the Evangelical Council for Financial Accountability (ECFA) and WallWatchers have given Focus high ratings for fiscal responsibility.

CHAPTER 9: COLORADO, HERE WE COME!

[1] Tony Wauterlek, the Focus board chairman, hadn't anticipated retaining that many staff members, "particularly quality members," he said.

[2] Eric Gorski, "Ministry's Impact Matter of Opinion," *Colorado Springs Gazette* (July 20, 2002).

[3] Eric Schlosser, *Fast Food Nation: The Dark Side of the All-American Meal* (New York: Perennial Books, 2002), 65.

[4] Eric Gorski, "Cause for Celebration, Concern: Who Will Guide Focus Next a Growing Issue as Ministry Turns 25," *Colorado Springs Gazette* (July 20, 2002).

[5] Ibid.

[6] Ibid.

[7] Bill McKeown, "Dore 'Troubled' before Focus Standoff," *Colorado Springs Gazette* (November 15, 1997).

[8] Marcus Montoya and Dennis Huspeni, "Man's Fury Boils into Fearful Day at Focus," *Colorado Springs Gazette* (May 3, 1996).

[9] Schlosser, *Fast Food Nation,* 65.

[10] Montoya and Huspeni, "Fury Boils into Fearful Day."

[11] As of July 2005 approximations, Focus has 2.5 million households on its active mailing list; the *Focus* broadcast is on 3,000 U.S. radio facilities with 7 to 9 million listeners per week; Dobson's short feature is heard on 332 radio stations and 76 TV stations each week; and Dobson is featured in more than 400 publications with a combined circulation of 6 million reaching 15 million readers.

[12] Transcript of *Larry King Live* (September 18, 2002).

[13] Dale Buss, "The Counter Counterculture," *Folio* (January 2002).

CHAPTER 11: THE POLITICAL ANIMAL

1 *Focus* newsletter (March, 1993).

2 Laura Sessions Stepp, "The Empire Built on Family and Faith," *Washington Post* (August 8, 1990).

3 Marc Fisher, "The GOP, Facing a Dobson's Choice," *Washington Post* (July 2, 1996).

4 *Scarborough Country* (December 10, 2003).

5 Patrick Kampert, "James Dobson the Empire Builder," *Chicago Tribune* (July 14, 2002).

6 James Dobson, *Children at Risk* (Nashville: Word Publishing, 1991), book jacket.

7 Republican Contract with America (1994). Accessed at http://www.house.gov/house/Contract/CONTRACT.html

8 Dale Buss, "Focusing on the Family with James Dobson," *The American Enterprise* (November-December 1995).

9 Transcript of James Dobson's speech to the Council for National Policy (February 7, 1998).

10 Buss, "Focusing on the Family."

11 Open letter from James Dobson to Haley Barbour (May 1, 1995).

12 Transcript of James Dobson's speech to the Council for National Policy (February 7, 1998).

13 Ralph Reed, *Active Faith: How Christians are Changing the Soul of American Politics* (New York: The Free Press, 1996), 240.

14 Ibid.

15 *Day One,* ABC TV (September 21, 1995).

16 Buss, "Focusing on the Family."

17 Speech to the Council for National Policy (February 7, 1998).

18 Ibid.

CHAPTER 12: BRINGING THE HAMMER

1 Transcript of James Dobson's speech to the Council for National Policy (February 7, 1998).

2 Ibid.

3 Ibid.

4 Ibid.

5 Ibid.

6 Ibid.

7 Michael Gerson, "A Righteous Indignation," *U.S. News & World Report* (May 4, 1998): 25.

8 Ibid.

9 Ibid.

10 James Dobson's statement to the news media (March 1, 2003).

11 Phillips also believes that Dobson "could be very credible as a third-party candidate" in 2008 should the Democrats nominate Hillary Clinton and the Republicans nominate a moderate such as John McCain.

12 According to Mark J. Rozell, professor of public policy at George Mason University and co-author of *The Christian Right in American Politics: Marching to the Millennium* (Georgetown University Press, 2003).

13 Commercial Law League of America, "Washington Hot News for November 2002," accessed in 2003 {www.clla.org/newswire/Washington_Hot_News.cfm}

14 Letter from James Dobson to Ronald Reagan (January 23, 1984).

15 Tim Stafford, "His Father's Son," *Christianity Today* (April 22, 1988): 16.

CHAPTER 13: STRESS FRACTURES

1 "A Tribute to Pete Maravich," a *Focus on the Family* broadcast that originally aired January 25–27, 1988.

2 Ibid.

3 Ibid.

[4] Ibid.

[5] Ibid.

[6] Ibid.

[7] Ibid.

[8] *Family News from Dr. James Dobson* (June 2003).

[9] Michele Ames, "Dobson Faces Tough Decisions," *Colorado Springs Gazette* (June 24, 1998).

[10] Ibid.

[11] Ibid.

[12] Ibid.

[13] Susan Warmbrunn, "Dobson's Speech Problem Disappears; Tests Look Good," *Colorado Springs Gazette* (June 20, 1998).

[14] Dobson's monthly newsletter.

[15] According to the National Stroke Association, http://www.stroke.org/HomePage.aspx?P=435435784753465

[16] Ames, "Dobson Faces Tough Decisions."

[17] Ibid.

[18] Ibid.

CHAPTER 14: THE DOBSON DIFFERENCE

[1] Dobson delivered the keynote to the Salt Lake City convention in 1998. He was also invited to deliver the keynote in 2001 in New Orleans but he couldn't make the trip due to a mechanical malfunction in the private plane that was to take him there. So Dobson spoke to the convention by satellite uplink from the Focus on the Family campus.

[2] U.S. Census of Religious Bodies 1936, as cited in Colleen McDannell, "Beyond Dr. Dobson: Women, Girls and Focus on the Family," 7.

[3] Based on a recent Needs Assessment study conducted by the Barna Research Group using random sampling.

[4] James Dobson, *Night Light: A Devotional for Couples* (Sisters, Ore.: Multnomah Publishers, 2000), 56.

[5] McDannell, "Beyond Dr. Dobson," 12.

[6] Ibid., 27.

[7] Transcript of *Larry King Live* (August 9, 2001).

[8] Donna Minkowitz, *Ferocious Romance: What My Encounters with the Right Taught Me about Sex, God, and Fury* (New York: Free Press, 1999), 79, 89, 95, 110–111.

[9] Eileen Kelly, "Save Me! I'm Hooked on Christian Talk!" *New York Observer* (February 3, 2003).

CHAPTER 15: TRANSFORMED LIVES

[1] Anna Kuchment, "Throwback: Online Dating Now Gives the Upper Hand to the Virtual Matchmaker, Not to Either Gender," *Newsweek International* (Issues 2004).

[2] Letters to Focus on the Family.

[3] Letter to Focus on the Family from Terry Goodman (September 24, 2001).

[4] Letter to Focus on the Family from Greg LaRance (February 23, 2001).

[5] Letter to Focus on the Family from Beth Rogers (April 11, 2002).

[6] Transcript of speech by James Dobson to National Religious Broadcasters convention (February 19, 2002).

[7] Ted Engstrom and James Dobson, *Focus on the Family: Celebrating Twenty-Five Years of God's Faithfulness* (San Diego: Tehabi Books, 2002), 103.

[8] Estimated by the National Center for Education Statistics, part of the U.S. Education Department.

CHAPTER 17: A SILVER THREAD

1 As told in *Certain Peace in Uncertain Times: Embracing Prayer in an Anxious Age,* by Shirley Dobson (Sisters, Oregon: Multnomah Publishers, 2002), 53.

2 Ibid, 45-46.

3 See Judges 6:36-40.

4 "DeLay Tries, Without Much Success, to Duck the Media Pack," *Washington Post* (May 5, 2005): A11.

CHAPTER 19: BLACK AND WHITE AND RED AND BLUE

1 Search on LexisNexis service, owned by Reed Elsevier, Inc.

2 People For the American Way, "Right Wing Watch," http://www.pfaw.org/pfaw/general/default.aspx?oid=4257.

3 Wayne Besen formerly was spokesman for the Human Rights Campaign, a gay-and-lesbian advocacy group.

4 Michael Weisskopf, "Energized by Pulpit or Passion, the Public is Calling: 'Gospel Grapevine' Displays Strength in Controversy over Military Gay Ban," *Washington Post* (February 1, 1993).

5 Focus on the Family newsletter (March 1993).

6 James Dobson in broadcast from the National Press Club, Washington, DC (June 25, 2004).

7 Hanna Rosin, "God's Hit Man," *GQ* (January 1999).

8 Margaret Carlson, "Facing a Dobson's Choice," *Time* (May 25, 1998).

9 Frank Rich, "Godzilla of the Right," *New York Times* (May 20, 1998): A23.

10 Ibid.

11 Letter from Mike Wallace to James Dobson (July 9, 1996).

12 *Day One,* ABC TV (September 21, 1995).

13 Excerpted from a Web-based critique of James Dobson by Rick Miesel, head of an Indiana-based outfit called Biblical Discernment Ministries.

14 John Woodbridge, "Culture War Casualties: How Warfare Rhetoric is Hurting the Work of the Church," *Christianity Today* (March 6, 1995).

15 James Dobson, "Why I Use 'Fighting Words': A Response to John Woodbridge's 'Culture War Casualities'," *Christianity Today* (June 19, 1995): 28.

16 Cal Thomas and Ed Dobson, *Blinded by Might: Why the Religious Right Can't Save America* (Grand Rapids, Mich.: Zondervan Publishing, 1999), 121–133.

17 Martha Sawyer Allen,"Religious Broadcaster Focuses on Faith," *Minneapolis Star Tribune* (January 5, 2002).

18 Comments in letter from James Dobson to NRB executive committee (March 1, 2002).

19 Ibid.

20 Letter from Robert Neff to Glenn Plummer (February 21, 2002) as cited in "Dobson Fires Back in NRB Fracas," *WorldNetDaily.com* (March 5, 2002).

21 Ibid.

CHAPTER 21: A WEEK IN THE LIFE

1 Account by CitizenLink.org (February 4, 2003).

2 *Focus on the Family* letter by James Dobson (April 2003).

3 Recounted in James Dobson, *Bringing Up Boys* (Wheaton, Ill.: Tyndale House Publishers, 2001), 103.

4 White House press release (February 6, 2003).

5 According to Paul Hetrick, Focus on the Family vice president of media relations, interviewed in 2003.

CHAPTER 22: MAYBE BRUCE WAS RIGHT

1 Bill Wichterman, aide to Sen. Bill Frist, quoted in Focus on the Family press release (May 16, 2003).

[2] Speech by President George W. Bush (April 29, 2003).

[3] White House transcript of speech by George W. Bush (April 29, 2003).

CHAPTER 24: NO SMALL FEAT

[1] Barbara Dafoe Whitehead and David Popenoe, "The Social Health of Marriage in America," 5th annual edition, published by the National Marriage Project (2003), 7.

[2] Ibid., 8.

[3] Ibid., 9.

[4] Speech transcript, Focus on the Family (August 28, 2003).

[5] "A Century of Children's Health and Well-Being," Child Trends (December 1999), cited in Whitehead and Popenoe, "The Social Health of Marriage."

[6] "Facts at a Glance," Child Trends (September 2002), cited in Whitehead and Popenoe, "The Social Health of Marriage."

[7] Press release by Alan Guttmacher Institute (January 10, 2003).

[8] Zogby International press release (January 2003).

[9] Kevin Belmonte, "William Wilberforce's Legacy: Public Service as a Spiritual Calling," {www.frc.org}

[10] David D. Kirkpatrick, "Warily, a Religious Leader Lifts His Voice in Politics," *New York Times* (May 13, 2004).

[11] Ibid.

CHAPTER 25: SLOUCHING TOWARDS GOMORRAH

[1] "Media Blackout," *National Review Online* (September 8, 2003).

[2] Andrew Sullivan, "The State of Our Unions," *Wall Street Journal* (October 8, 2003).

[3] Transcript of *Larry King Live* (September 5, 2003).

[4] "Roe, the Sequel," *Wall Street Journal* editorial (November 20, 2003).

[5] James Dobson, *Bringing Up Boys* (Wheaton, Ill.: Tyndale House Publishers, 2001), 115.

[6] Ibid., 128–129.

[7] Ibid., 116.

[8] Ibid., 117.

[9] Ibid., 120–122, citing Joseph Nicolosi, *A Parent's Guide to Preventing Homosexuality* (Downer's Grove, Ill.: InterVarsity Press, 2002).

[10] Dobson, *Bringing Up Boys*, 124.

[11] Ibid., 123.

[12] Ibid., 124–125.

[13] David Limbaugh, *Persecution: How Liberals Are Waging War against Christianity* (Washington, D.C.: Regnery Publishing, 2003), 330.

[14] Corrie Cutrer, "'Get Our Kids Out': Dobson Says Pro-Gay Curriculum Has Gone Too Far," *Christianity Today* (August 5, 2002): 15.

[15] Eric Gorski, "Focus Issues Boycott: United Way Donors Urged to Exclude Big Brothers Because It Accepts Gays," *Colorado Springs Gazette* (February 21, 2003).

[16] Transcript of *Larry King Live* (March 7, 2002).

[17] Transcript of *Larry King Live,* (September 5, 2003.)

[18] Ibid.

[19] Dobson, *Bringing Up Boys,* 127.

CHAPTER 26: MONTGOMERY AND BEYOND

[1] Focus on the Family statistics.

[2] Transcript of James Dobson speech, "A Historic Occasion," *Citizen* (November 2003): 24.

[3] *Focus on the Family* radio broadcast (August 25, 2003).

[4] "A Historic Occasion," 24.

[5] Stan Bailey, "Dobson, Keyes Urge Reining in Courts," *Birmingham News* (August 29, 2003).

[6] Michael Foust, "Ten Commandments Controversy Pits Evangelicals on Opposite Sides," Baptist Press (August 29, 2003).

[7] Cal Thomas, "A Moving Experience," on TownHall.com (September 2, 2003).

[8] Transcript of speech by James Dobson (August 28, 2003).

[9] Ibid.

[10] Ibid.

[11] Robert Bork, "Judicial Tyranny," *Forbes* (December 22, 2003).

[12] *Scarborough Country* (November 13, 2003).

[13] *Focus on the Family* (November 14, 2003).

[14] Eric Gorski, "Dobson Has Ear of Corporate Giant: Procter & Gamble Pulls Ads after Meeting," *Colorado Springs Gazette* (July 2, 2000).

[15] Abercrombie & Fitch press release (December 9, 2003).

[16] Focus on the Family press release (December 10, 2003).

[17] Richard Cooper, "General Casts War in Religious Terms," *Los Angeles Times* (October 16, 2003).

[18] James Dobson on *The Sean Hannity Show,* WABC Radio (October 20, 2003).

[19] *ABC Evening News with Peter Jennings* (October 21, 2003).

[20] *Focus on the Family* radio broadcast (October 22, 2003).

[21] Ibid.

[22] Ibid.

[23] Ibid.

[24] President Bush interview with Diane Sawyer on ABC-TV (December 16, 2003).

[25] From the Alliance for Marriage Web site, http://www.allianceformarriage.org.

CHAPTER 27: RIGHTEOUS REVOLUTION

[1] John Micklethwait and Adrian Wooldridge, "'Bushism,'" *Wall Street Journal* (October 27, 2004): A16

[2] David D. Kirkpatrick, "Evangelicals See Bush as One of Them, But Will They Vote?", *New York Times* (November 1, 2004).

AFTERWORD

[1] From James Dobson's submitted text for Larry King, *Remember Me When I'm Gone* (New York: Doubleday/Random House, 2004). Dobson's anecdotes were not included in the book.

[2] Ibid.

[3] Ibid.

[4] Ibid.

INDEX